Econometrics in Theory and Practice

Hans Schneeweiß

Robert Galata, Helmut Küchenhoff (Eds.)

Econometrics in Theory and Practice

Festschrift
for
Hans Schneeweiß

With 61 Figures
and 33 Tables

Physica-Verlag
A Springer-Verlag Company

Prof. Dr. Robert Galata
Department of Economics
Fachhochschule of Munich – University of Applied Sciences
Am Stadtpark 20
D-81243 München, Germany

Prof. Dr. Helmut Küchenhoff
Institute of Statistics
University of Munich
Akademiestr. 1
D-80799 München, Germany

Typesetting and layout: Beate Elfinger and Kurt Watzka

ISBN-13: 978-3-642-47029-5

Library of Congress Cataloging-in-Publication Data
Die Deutsche Bibliothek – CIP-Einheitsaufnahme
Econometrics in theory and practice: Festschrift for Hans Schneeweiß; with 33 tables / Robert Galata; Helmut Küchenhoff (ed.). – Heidelberg; New York: Physica-Verl., 1998
ISBN-13: 978-3-642-47029-5 e-ISBN-13: 978-3-642-47027-1
DOI: 10.1007/978-3-642-47027-1

Softcover reprint of the hardcover 1st edition 1998

SPIN 10678407 88/2202-5 4 3 2 1 0 – Printed on acid-free paper

Preface

Hans Schneeweiß is one of the best-known German econometricians and statisticians. He was born in Glatz, Silesia, on March 13, 1933.

Hans Schneeweiß studied mathematics and physics and received his Ph. D. degree from the Johann-Wolfgang-Goethe University, Frankfurt, in 1960. He was member of the academic staff of the Faculty of Law and Economics of the Saar University between 1959 and 1965. Following his Habilitation in 1964, he was appointed to the chair of Statistics and Econometrics at the same university. As a visiting professor he worked at the Institute for Academic Studies in Vienna in 1967 and at the Department of Statistics of the University of Waterloo, Canada, in 1970/71. He has been a full professor of Econometrics and Statistics at the Ludwig-Maximilians-University in Munich since 1973. His extensive research activities abroad included important projects in Waterloo, Vienna, Dundee (Scotland), Sidney, China, Kiev.

During the more than 40 years of his academic work he has published outstanding, original articles on econometrics and statistics. To give an example, it is his research on decision theory which has marked developments in this field. His book *Entscheidungskriterien bei Risiko*, published in 1967, is an excellent starting for anyone looking for an introduction to the complex issues involved.

Among his more than 60 articles and monographs, his work on errors-in-the-variables deserves special attention. Hans Schneeweiß has crucially stimulated and advanced research in this area. At present, he is director of the research team working on error in variables at DFG special research unit Statistical Analysis of Discrete Structures of the University of Munich. His current research activities have resulted in a number of recent papers, which can be found in the appending list of his publications.

As a reflection of his wide range of interests it should also be mentioned, that he was editor of the Statistical Papers for many years and chairman of the committee for Empirical Research in Economics and Applied Econometrics of the German Society of Statistics. His book on *Ökonometrie*, published in 1971, has become a standard reference work for scientists and students in Germany.

Hans Schneeweiß is not only a prominent figure in his field of research but also an excellent teacher. The articles by his pupils in this volume are proof of this. It is highly impressive to see how he succeeds in explaining complex subjects in a clear, straightforward way without neglecting scientific precision. Those who have had the chance to work with him have always appreciated his extremely efficient work-style, his receptiveness to new ideas and his ability to inspire others; they have also been won over by his friendly, unassuming manner and his serene personality.

This collection of articles by his friends and colleagues covers the manifold research interests of Hans Schneeweiß. It starts with contributions on his current research project, regression models with errors in variables, followed by essays on theoretical and practical aspects of econometrics. The last part consists of articles on statistics and decision theory, his first field of research.

It is a special wish of the authors of this collection to honour Hans Schneeweiß for his scientific achievements and merits. They hope that he will continue his creative work for many years to come.

The editors would like to express their thanks to Kurt Watzka, who had to cope with many difficult manuscripts and who supported them in the production of this collection. They would also like to thank Helgard Geuss for her support and the Physica publishing company for its cooperation.

Munich
13 March 1998

Robert Galata
Helmut Küchenhoff

Table of Contents

Part I

Errors-in-Variables

Errors in Variables in Econometrics

Chi-Lun Cheng and John W. Van Ness

[1] Institute of Statistical Science, Academia Sinica, Taiwan
[2] University of Texas at Dallas, USA

Summary. This article discusses the use of instrumental variables and grouping methods in the linear errors-in-variables or measurement error model. Comparisons are made between these methods, standard measurement error model methods with side conditions, least squares methods, and replicated models. It is demonstrated that there are close relationships between these apparently diverse estimation techniques.

1. Introduction

Much of econometrics is concerned with the estimation of relationships between variables. An important model relating these variables is the regression model with measurement errors in both the "dependent variables" and the "explanatory variables". This model is commonly known as the errors-in-variables or measurement error (ME) model.

The simple linear *classical regression* model is

$$y_i = \beta_0 + \beta_1 x_i + e_i, \tag{1.1}$$

where the x_i are either fixed known constant or random variables which are independent of the random errors, e_i. In many situations, one cannot observed the independent variables x_i directly, and instead, one observes

$$x_i = \xi_i + \delta_i, \qquad \text{and} \qquad y_i = \eta_i + \varepsilon_i = \beta_0 + \beta_1 \xi_i + \varepsilon_i. \tag{1.2}$$

The model (1.2) is the simple linear *measurement error model.* It is assumed that the "errors" satisfy

$$\begin{aligned} &E(\delta_i) = E(\varepsilon_i) = 0, \quad var(\delta_i) = \sigma_\delta^2, \quad var(\varepsilon_i) = \sigma_\varepsilon^2 \qquad \text{for all i,} \\ &cov(\delta_i, \delta_j) = cov(\varepsilon_i, \varepsilon_j) = 0 \qquad \text{for all } i \neq j, \text{ and} \\ &cov(\delta_i, \varepsilon_j) = \sigma_{\delta\varepsilon} \qquad \text{for all i, j.} \end{aligned}$$

If the "true values", ξ_i, are stochastic, then this model is called a *structural* model and the ξ_i are assumed independent of the errors with $var(\xi_i) = \sigma^2$; on the other hand, if the ξ_i are considered unknown fixed parameters, the model is called a *functional* model.

If all the random quantities are assumed normal, then it is well known that the structural model is not identifiable and the functional model, while identifiable, does not have consistent estimates of the key parameter β_1 (Reiersol, (1950) and Wald (1949)). Therefore, one needs some form of additional information, in order to ensure consistent estimates of the parameters. Usually this additional information takes the form of "side conditions" which assume some sort of knowledge about the error variances. Some common side conditions used when $\sigma_{\delta\varepsilon} = 0$ are

(a) the ratio of the error variances, $\lambda \equiv \sigma_\varepsilon^2 / \sigma_\delta^2$, is known;
(b) the reliability ratio, $\kappa_\xi \equiv \sigma^2 / \left(\sigma^2 + \sigma_\delta^2\right)$, is known (structural model);
(c) σ_δ^2 is known;
(d) σ_ε^2 is known; or
(e) both of the error variances, σ_ε^2 and σ_δ^2, are known.

(1.3)

For detailed discussion of the use of side conditions, see Kendall and Stuart (1979, Ch. 29), Schneeweiß and Mittag (1986) and Fuller (1987).

In many applications a second error term, q_i, called the *equation error* is added to the model so that (1.2) is replaced by

$$x_i = \xi_i + \delta_i, \qquad \text{and} \qquad y_i = \eta_i + \varepsilon_i = \beta_0 + \beta_1 \xi_i + q_i + \varepsilon_i, \tag{1.4}$$

where q_i is independent of the measurement errors, δ_i and ε_i, and has mean zero and variance, σ_q^2 (see e.g. Johnston (1972), p. 287). Now the "true variables" have an independent random error in their relationship, $\eta_i = \beta_0 + \beta_1 \xi_i + q_i$. If we write $\varepsilon_i^* = q_i + \varepsilon_i$, then (1.4) is just (1.2) with ε_i replaced by ε_i^*, which makes it appear that there is nothing new in (1.4). The difference is in the way one views q_i. It is assumed that, in practice, one cannot get information about q_i, such as σ_q^2, from other experiments or replications et cetera. Thus, the change from (1.2) to (1.4) has practical ramifications in terms of the types of side conditions which are likely to be available in applications. Assuming that one knows (1.3a) or (1.3d) no longer leads to identifiability of β_0 and β_1. It also does not seem practically reasonable to assume that one knows $\lambda^* \equiv \sigma_{\varepsilon*}^2 / \sigma_\delta^2$ or $\sigma_{\varepsilon*}^2$. This leaves (1.3b) (1.3c) and (1.3e) as the interesting side conditions for the equation error model. For details see, for example, Cheng and Van Ness (1998).

In the following discussion, we will write everything in terms of model (1.2), but the errors, ε_i, may contain equation error, that is they may be of the form, ε_i^*.

Many econometricians prefer not to use the side conditions, (1.3), and, instead, find the use of *instrumental variables* or *grouping variables* a more natural way out of the underidentification problem of errors-in-variables models. In this paper, we review these latter two approaches.

2. Instrumental variables

First consider the simple *classical regression* model (1.1) with random explanatory variable, x, with *cov* $(e_1, \cdots, e_n) = \sigma_e^2 \mathbf{I}^{(\mathbf{n}\times\mathbf{n})}$ and (x_i, y_i) are independent identically distributed. The least squares estimator $\hat{\beta}_{1R} = s_{xy}/s_{xx}$ is consistent if and only if x and e are uncorrelated. Suppose x and e are correlated and that we have a random sample $(z_1, \cdots, z_n)$ from another variable, z, such that

(i) z is uncorrelated with e, and
(ii) z is correlated with x.

The supplementary variable z is called an *instrumental variable*, because it is used merely as an instrument in the estimation. Observe that

$$\frac{1}{n}\sum(z_i-\bar{z})y_i = \frac{1}{n}\sum(z_i-\bar{z})\beta_0 + \frac{1}{n}\sum(z_i-\bar{z})x_i\beta_1 + \frac{1}{n}\sum(z_i-\bar{z})e_i. \quad (2.1)$$

Then the properties of z motivate estimators of β_1 and β_0 of the form

$$\hat{\beta}_{1IV} = \frac{\sum(z_i - \bar{z})y_i}{\sum(z_i - \bar{z})x_i} \quad \text{and} \quad \hat{\beta}_{0IV} = \bar{y} - \hat{\beta}_{1IV}\bar{x}. \quad (2.2)$$

To see this, note that the first term on the right side of (2.1) is zero; then property (i) guarantees that the last term of (2.1) tends to zero whilst property (ii) says that the denominator of β_1 in (2.2) will not go to zero when sample size is large. The estimators (2.2) are called instrumental variable estimators for the simple regression model. Note that one does not need any normality assumption on any variable. The instrumental variable may even be discrete (see the next section on the grouping method). The only assumptions on the instrumental variable are properties (i) and (ii) above.

It can be shown that the instrumental variable estimator (2.2) is consistent and asymptotically normal with variance $\sigma_e^2\sigma_z^2/\sigma_{zx}$, where σ_z^2 is the variance of z and σ_{zx} is the covariance between z and x.

Now we turn to the structural form of the ME model, (1.2), which can be written in the form of (1.1) with $e = \varepsilon - \beta_1\delta$, in which case, the error e is clearly correlated with x. Therefore, if a third variable, z, is available with the properties that

(i') z is uncorrelated with (δ, ε) and
(ii') z is correlated with ξ,

then the instrumental variable estimators of β_0 and β_1 are just (2.2). Again, these estimates are consistent, asymptotically normal with variance

$$\sigma_e^2\sigma_z^2/\sigma_{z\xi}, \quad (2.3)$$

where $\sigma_{z\xi}$ is the covariance between z and ξ and $\sigma_e^2 = \sigma_\delta^2 - 2\beta_1\sigma_{\delta\varepsilon} + \beta_1^2\sigma_\varepsilon^2$. Note that $\sigma_{z\xi} = \sigma_{zx}$ and that one can allow the errors δ and ε to be correlated. Looking at (2.3), one can see that a good instrumental variable, z, is one that is uncorrelated with the error (δ, ε) but is strongly correlated with ξ so that the (asymptotic) variance of the instrumental variable estimator is as small as possible.

One can extend these results to instrumental variables that are fixed and/or to the functional model. This is done by requiring that the instrumental variable z satisfy

(i") $\lim_{n\to\infty} n^{-1}\sum(z_i - \bar{z})(\delta_i, \varepsilon_i) = (0,0)$, and
(ii") $\lim_{n\to\infty} n^{-1}\sum(z_i - \bar{z})\xi_i \neq 0$.

For the no-intercept model (i.e. $\beta_0 = 0$), one drops the term $\bar{z}$ in (i") and (ii"). It is interesting to note that, in the no-intercept model, the instrumental variable $z_i \equiv 1$ is a legitimate instrumental variable provided $\lim_{n\to\infty} n^{-1}\sum \xi_i \neq 0$. In this case, the instrumental variable estimator for β_1 is $\bar{y}/\bar{x}$.

A major difficulty in using instrumental variables for ME models is the practical problem of finding a variable known to be correlated with the unobservable ξ and known not to be correlated with δ and ε. One rarely knows enough about a system to be sure that these conditions are satisfied. Second, the consideration of instrumental variables is based on the consistency arguments only, and this might be insufficient justification in finite sample situations involving large sample variances. Finally, the choice of the instrumental variable seems arbitrary and there is the possibility of very large variations in the resulting estimators as the choice of instrumental variable is varied. A possible remedy is to investigate the efficiency of instrumental variable estimators.

3. Link between using known error variances and using instrumental variables

In the statistical literature, the usual way out of underidentification of normal ME model is to use some form of additional knowledge of the error variances such as listed in (1.3). Suppose, for example, that σ_δ^2 and $\sigma_{\delta\varepsilon}$ are known, then a consistent estimator of β_1 is

$$\hat{\beta}_1 = \frac{s_{xy} - \sigma_{\delta\varepsilon}}{s_{xx} - \sigma_\delta^2},$$

which is the maximum likelihood estimator under the normality assumption in the structural model and can be viewed as method of moments estimator if the distribution is not normal. It is usually believed that the assumption of knowledge of an instrumental variable and the assumption of knowledge of an error variance are quite different assumptions. However, Schneeweiß (1985) made an interesting argument showing that there is a close relation between these two approaches. His argument is as follows. Suppose that the instrumental variables $\{(z_{1i}, \dots, z_{mi}) : i = 1, \cdots, n\}$ are observed with $\{(x_i, y_i) : i = 1, \dots, n\}$. In addition they are linked to the true variable ξ_i by a linear relation (Zellner, 1970)

$$\xi_i = \pi_0 + \sum_{j=1}^{m} \pi_j z_{ji},$$

with unknown parameters π_j for $j = 0, \ldots, m$. Then one can relate x_i and y_i to z_{ji} by

$$x_i = \pi_0 + \sum_{j=1}^{m} \pi_j z_{ji} + \delta_i, \qquad \text{and} \qquad y_i = \rho_0 + \sum_{j=1}^{m} \rho_j z_{ji} + \varepsilon_i, \tag{3.1}$$

with $\rho_j = \beta_1 \pi_j$ for $j = 1, \ldots, m$ and $\rho_0 = \beta_0 + \beta_1 \pi_0$. Note that the equations, (3.1), are just ordinary regression models. One can compute the estimated regression values and residuals

$$\hat{\xi}_i = \hat{\pi}_0 + \sum_{j=1}^{m} \hat{\pi}_j z_{ji}, \qquad \hat{\delta}_i = x_i - \hat{\xi}_i,$$

and

$$\hat{\eta}_i = \hat{\rho}_0 + \sum_{j=1}^{m} \hat{\rho}_j z_{ji}, \qquad \hat{\varepsilon}_i = y_i - \hat{\eta}_i.$$

One can obtain estimates of the elements, σ_δ^2, $\sigma_{\delta\varepsilon}$ and σ_ε^2 of the error covariance matrix, which are $s_{\hat{\delta}\hat{\delta}}$, $s_{\hat{\delta}\hat{\varepsilon}}$ and $s_{\hat{\varepsilon}\hat{\varepsilon}}$, respectively. Therefore, the estimate of β_1 becomes

$$\tilde{\beta}_1 = \frac{s_{xy} - s_{\hat{\delta}\hat{\varepsilon}}}{s_{xx} - s_{\hat{\delta}\hat{\delta}}}.$$

Note that when $m = 1$, that is, when only one instrumental variable is observed, $\tilde{\beta}_1$ coincides with $\hat{\beta}_{1IV}$. In other words, instrumental variables can be used to construct an estimate for error covariance matrix and these estimates in turn can be used to estimate β_1. For more detailed discussion of this approach, see Schneeweiß (1985). Recently, Carroll, Ruppert and Stefanski (1995, p. 107) made a comment, "Thus the assumption that a variable is an instrument is weaker than the assumption it is a replicate measurement". The preceding argument makes this assertion more transparent.

It is well known that for the nonlinear ME model, the usual instrumental variable estimator does not provide a consistent estimator. Schneeweiß' argument deserves more attention because it may be useful in certain nonlinear ME models, such as the polynomial ME model (cf. Cheng and Schneeweiß, 1997).

4. Grouping methods

We have mentioned that the major difficulty in using instrumental variables is finding a random variable known to be correlated with true value of the independent variable, ξ, and known not to be correlated with the errors.

Discrete valued instrumental variables have been proposed with the idea that they might be easier to find in practice. Instrumental variables which can take on only a finite number of possible values have received considerable attention and are generally called *grouping variables*. That is, one classifies the observations according to whether they fall into certain discrete groups, and treats this classification as a discrete-valued instrumental variable. The idea is that there is a better chance in practice of finding grouping variables satisfying the conditions, (i') and (ii') or (i") and (ii"). Note that in order for a grouping variable to satisfy these conditions, the grouping must be based in some way on ξ and independent of the errors, δ and ε.

4.1 Two groups

Suppose that the number of observations, n, is even, and that one somehow divides the data into two equal groups of $m = n/2$ observations each using some method independent of the errors. Let $\bar{x}_1$ be the mean of the first group and $\bar{x}_2$ that for the second group, and similarly define $\bar{y}_1$ and $\bar{y}_2$. The estimate β_1 is obtained by assigning an instrumental variable z with value $+1$ for each observation in the first group and value -1 for each observation in the second group. Then the instrumental variable estimators, (2.2), become

$$\hat{\beta}_{1G} = \frac{\bar{y}_2 - \bar{y}_1}{\bar{x}_2 - \bar{x}_1} \qquad \text{and} \qquad \hat{\beta}_{0G} = \bar{y} - \hat{\beta}_{1G}\bar{x} = \frac{1}{2}\{(\bar{y}_2 + \bar{y}_1) - \hat{\beta}_{1G}(\bar{x}_2 + \bar{x}_1)\},$$

where $\bar{y}$ and $\bar{x}$ are the means of y and x for the entire sample, respectively.

Geometrically, this procedure means that in the (x, y) plane we divide the data points into equal groups according to some criterion, and then determine the center of gravity of each group. The estimator is then obtained as the slope of the line connecting these two centers, namely, $(\bar{x}_1, \bar{y}_1)$ and $(\bar{x}_2, \bar{y}_2)$.

The grouping method was proposed by Wald (1940) and he showed that $\hat{\beta}_{1G}$ is a consistent estimator if the grouping is independent of the errors and if the true values ξ_i satisfy

$$\lim_{n\to\infty} inf\,|\bar{\xi}_2 - \bar{\xi}_1| > 0,$$

which corresponds to (ii') because $cov(z, \xi) = \bar{\xi}_2 - \bar{\xi}_1$. Note that (ii') clearly will not be satisfied if the observations are randomly allocated into two groups since $\lim_{n\to\infty} |\bar{\xi}_2 - \bar{\xi}_1| = 0$. Nor is it satisfactory to allocate the m smallest observed x's to one group and the m largest to the other. Neyman and Scott (1951) showed that in this case the estimator will not be consistent. If the grouping is based on the x's, then, unless one can guarantee that the grouping according to the x's is the same as the corresponding grouping according to the ξ's, the resulting estimator is not consistent.

Estimates of the error variances, confidence intervals, and the like can also be obtained for the grouping method (see, e.g., Kendall and Stuart (1979), Ch. 29). If one violates the assumptions of instrumental variables and groups on x, then these estimates are quite unreliable (see e.g. Cheng and Van Ness (1998), Ch. 4). It is not uncommon, for example, to get negative estimates for the error variance, σ_δ^2.

4.2 Three groups

Nair and Shrivastava (1942) and Bartlett (1949) studied improving the efficiency of the grouping method by increasing the number of groups from two to three. We investigate this in a generally way, adopting the approach of Pakes (1982).

The idea is to group the n observations into three groups, G_1, G_2, and G_3, with G_1 containing np_1 observations, G_2 containing np_2 observations, and G_3 containing np_3 observations; where $0 < p_1, p_2, p_3$ and $p_1 + p_2 + p_3 = 1$. If the grouping is independent of the errors, the instrumental variable is then

$$z_i = \begin{cases} -1 & \text{if } i\text{th observation in the first group} \\ 0 & \text{if } i\text{th observation in the second group} \\ 1 & \text{if } i\text{th observation in the third group} \end{cases} .$$

The estimator of β_1 is defined as the slope of the line connecting $(\bar{x}_1, \bar{y}_1)$ and $(\bar{x}_3, \bar{y}_3)$:

$$\hat{\beta}_{1T} = \frac{\bar{y}_3 - \bar{y}_1}{\bar{x}_3 - \bar{x}_1}, \tag{4.1}$$

where $\bar{x}_3$ and $\bar{y}_3$ are the sample means over G_3 and $\bar{x}_1$ and $\bar{y}_1$ are the sample means over G_1. For example, $\bar{x}_1 = \frac{1}{\|G_1\|}\sum_{G_1} x_i$ where $\|G_1\|$ denotes the number of points in G_1. Thus, in estimating β_1, the data in the second group are ignored. The estimator of the intercept is still $\hat{\beta}_{0T} \equiv \bar{y} - \hat{\beta}_{1T}\,\bar{x}$, where $\bar{y}$ and $\bar{x}$ are the respective means of y and x for the entire sample. These estimators are consistent under the conditions given earlier. Nair and Shrivastava (1942) and Bartlett (1949) studied the case $p_1 = p_2 = p_3 = 1/3$. Cheng and Van Ness (1998), Ch. 4, compare the two group and three group methods on Monte Carlo data. They found, for example, that for their particular Monte Carlo model, there was no obvious improvement in the confidence intervals obtained from the three group method over the confidence intervals from the two group method.

4.3 Three groups based on the x values

Despite the violation of the instrumental variable assumptions, it is common practice to base the grouping on the x variable. We now investigate the effect of this practice. Let $\bar{w}_A$ and $\bar{w}_B$ be the average values of w for $x < A$ and $x > B$, respectively, where $A \le B$, then the estimator $\hat{\beta}_{1T}$ is from (4.1)

$$\hat{\beta}_{1G} = \frac{\bar{y}_B - \bar{y}_A}{\bar{x}_B - \bar{x}_A}.$$

The two group method is the special case when $A = B$.

If we assume that model is structural and ξ, δ, and ε are mutually independent variable with finite variances, then

$$p\lim \bar{y}_A = E[y \mid x - A < 0] = \beta_0 + \beta_1 E[\xi \mid x - A < 0] = \beta_0 + \beta_1 \bar{\xi}_A,$$

$$p\lim \bar{y}_B = E[y \mid x - B > 0] = \beta_0 + \beta_1 E[\xi \mid x - B > 0] = \beta_0 + \beta_1 \bar{\xi}_B,$$

and

$$p\lim \bar{x}_A = \bar{\xi}_A + E[\delta \mid x - A < 0],$$
$$p\lim \bar{x}_B = \bar{\xi}_B + E[\delta \mid x - B > 0].$$

It is clear that the slope of the line joining $(\bar{y}_A, \bar{\xi}_A)$ to $(\bar{y}_B, \bar{\xi}_B)$ is a consistent estimator of β_1, but unfortunately, one cannot observe $\bar{\xi}_A$ and $\bar{\xi}_B$. The problem arises if, values of ξ bigger than A associated with sufficiently large negative values of δ will give values of x less than A, whilst values of ξ smaller than A associated with sufficiently large positive values of δ will give values of x larger than A. If the distance between the ξ's in the domain around A and B is smaller than the range of δ, then there is a positive probability that the grouping on the basis of the observed values x will be different from that on the basis of the true values ξ.

In practice, the cut-off points A and B are often the estimates of p-th quantile of the x variable. For example, in the two-group case, the cut-off point is the median of x.

It is clear that when $(\xi, \delta, \varepsilon)$ is normal, this grouping method does not provide a consistent estimator because Reiersol (1950) showed that β_1 is unidentifiable in this case and, when we group on x, no new information has been added to make consistent estimation possible. However, it is interesting to compare this grouping estimator with the least squares estimator. Pakes (1982) showed that the asymptotic bias of $\hat{\beta}_{1G}$ is precisely the same as that of least squares estimator $\hat{\beta}_{1R}$. This is true regardless of the cut-off point chosen. His argument is as follows. One can write the grouping estimator as

$$\hat{\beta}_{1G} = \beta_1 - \beta_1 (\frac{\bar{\delta}_B - \bar{\delta}_A}{\bar{x}_B - \bar{x}_A}) + (\frac{\bar{\varepsilon}_B - \bar{\varepsilon}_A}{\bar{x}_B - \bar{x}_A}).$$

Since the last term of the equation above is independent of x, and therefore of the selection criterion,

$$p\lim \hat{\beta}_{1G} = \beta_1 - \beta_1 p\lim (\frac{\bar{\delta}_b - \bar{\delta}_A}{\bar{x}_B - \bar{x}_A}).$$

Note that

$$p\lim \bar{\delta}_B = E[\delta \mid x - B > 0] = (1 - \kappa_\xi) E[x \mid x - B > 0],$$
$$p\lim \bar{\delta}_A = E[\delta \mid x - A < 0] = (1 - \kappa_\xi) E[x \mid x - A < 0],$$
$$p\lim \bar{x}_B = E[x \mid x - B > 0], \quad p\lim \bar{x}_A = E[x \mid x - A < 0],$$

where κ_ξ is the reliability ratio defined in (1.3). It follows that

$$p\lim \beta_{1G} = \kappa_\xi \beta_1$$

which equals the limit of least squares estimator. In other words, under the normality assumption, the inconsistency of group estimator based on grouping by x is the same as that of the ordinary least squares estimator.

If one groups according to the values of y, reasoning similar to that given above shows that the resultant estimator has the same limiting behavior as $1/\hat{\beta}_{1I}$, where $\hat{\beta}_{1I}$ is the least squares estimator of x regressed on y in the normal model.

5. Discussion and bibliographic notes

The term "instrumental variable" was coined by Reiersol (1941). However, the instrumental variable estimation method was used in as early as the 1920's, see Goldberger (1972) for a historical review. As we pointed out earlier, instrumental variable estimation can be generally adopted to models other than ME models. Instrumental variable methods suit all kinds of regression (with random regressors) for which explanatory variables are correlated with the errors. The ME model application is just a special case. For example, in the econometrics, instrumental variables are used in two-stage least squares estimation of a single equation in a simultaneous system of equations. For more details on the general treatment of instrumental variables, see, White (1984) and Bowden and Turkington (1984).

Perhaps the greatest difficulty using instrumental variables in the ME model is that there is no obvious procedure for finding instrumental variables and they might not be available. The two requirements on instrumental variables require one to have knowledge which is uncorrelated with the errors but correlated with the true values, ξ, and this seems unlikely in many applications. Leamer (1978) studied maximum likelihood estimation using instrumental variable and showed that instrumental variables can give opposite information about the sign of the slope, β_1, in comparison with that given by the original data (x, y). In our opinion, instrumental variables are just another type of additional knowledge which can lead to consistent estimation and they are not automatically available in practical applications.

Wald's grouping method and instrumental variables are popular in econometrics and are considered to be reasonable ways out of the underidentification problem in ME models. Since the first appearance of the grouping method in Wald's (1940) paper, there have been many discussions on improving efficiency of this method, such as groups of unequal size and more than two groups (see, for example, Dorff and Gurland (1961) and Ware (1972)). In particular, Richardson and Wu (1970) compare the grouping method generally with the least squares estimator. Their overall recommendation is that it is safest to use at least fifteen groups to avoid the possibility of a large increase in mean squared error. It would appear that, in practice, finding a true grouping variable with 15 groups is about as difficult as finding a continuous instrumental variable. As Pakes (1982) pointed out, the real problem with grouping method is the consistency. The two conditions (see Section 4.1) required for the consistency of grouping estimator are rarely satisfied in practice without additional information.

The relation between grouping method and instrumental method is also clarified in Section 3. Unless the allocation into groups does not depend on the error, δ, the grouping method is not really a special case of an instrumental variable. Nevertheless, the grouping method is still important in practice, although perhaps not well understood by some users.

Anderson (1951) and Cox (1976) discussed the replicated model with the observations $\{(x_{ij}, y_{ij});\ i = 1, \cdots, k,\ j = 1, \cdots n_i\}$, where

$$x_{ij} = \xi_{ij} + \delta_{ij}, \qquad \text{and} \qquad y_{ij} = \beta_0 + \beta_1 \xi_{ij} + \varepsilon_{ij}.$$

The true independent variables ξ_{ij} are assumed to have independent normal distributions with means μ_i and a common variance σ^2 while the errors δ_{ij} are independently normally distributed with mean zero and variance σ_δ^2 and the error ε_{ij} are independently normally distributed with mean zero and variance σ_ε^2. Moreover, the errors δ_{ij} and ε_{ij} are assumed to be independent of each other and of the ξ_{ij}. When the replication is taken exactly twice, the maximum likelihood estimate of the slope β_1 (under some restrictions of inequalities) is just the grouping estimate, namely, the slope of the line connected the two group means. This is not surprising because, when $k = 2$, the data given have already allocated into two distinct groups. This has already solved one of the difficulties with the grouping method - the allocation satisfying the required condition that it is not affected by the errors. Second, the distinction of the group means μ_1 and μ_2 fulfills the second condition (ii'). It is interesting to note that this model is related to the change-point ME models. When $k = 2$, this is an ME model with exactly one change-point and the grouping estimator is the maximum likelihood estimator under the normality assumption. Some related topics can be found in Chang and Huang (1997).

References

1. Anderson, T. W. (1951). Estimating linear restrictions on regression coefficients for multivariate normal distributions. *Ann. Math. Statist.* **22**, 327-351.
2. Bartlett, M. S. (1949). Fitting a straight line when both variables are subject to error. *Biometrics* **5**, 207-212.
3. Bowden, R. J. and Turkington, D. A. (1984). *Instrumental Variables.* Cambridge: Cambridge University Press.

4. Carroll, R. J., Ruppert, D. & Stefanski, L. A. (1995). *Measurement Error in Nonlinear Model.* London: Chapman & Hall.
5. Chang, Y. P. and Huang, W. T. (1997). Inferences for the linear errors-in-variables with changepoint models. *J. Am. Statist. Assoc.* **56**, 171-178.
6. Cheng, C-L. and Schneeweiß, H. (1997). Polynomial regression with errors in the variables. *Journal of the Royal Statistical Society Ser. B.* To appear.
7. Cheng, C-L. and Van Ness, J. W. (1998). *Statistical Regression with Measurement Error.* London: Edward Arnold. To appear.
8. Cox, N. R. (1976). The linear structural relation for several groups of data. *Biometrika* **63**, 231-237.
9. Dorff, M. and Gurland, J. (1961). Estimation of the parameters of a linear functional relation. *J. R. Statist. Soc. Ser. B* **23**, 160-170.
10. Fuller, W. A. (1987) *Measurement Error Models.* New York: Wiley.
11. Goldberger, A. S. (1972). Structural equation methods in the social sciences. *Econometrica* **40**, 979-1001.
12. Johnston, J. (1972) *Econometric Methods*, 2nd ed., New York: McGraw-Hill.
13. Kendall, M. G. and Stuart, A. (1979) *The Advanced Theory of Statistics.* Vol. **2**, 4th ed., London: Griffin.
14. Leamer, E. E. (1978). Least square versus instrumental variables estimation in a simple errors in variables model. *Econometrica* **46**, 961-968.
15. Nair, K. R. and Banerjee, K. S. (1942). A note on fitting of straight line if both variables are subject to error. *Sankhya* **6**, 331.
16. Neyman, J. and Scott, E. L. (1951). On certain methods of estimating the linear structural relation. *Ann. Math. Statist.* **22**, 352-361.
17. Pakes, A. (1982). On the asymptotic bias of the Wald-type estimators of a straight line when both variables are subject to error. *Inst. Econ. Rev.* **23**, 491-497.
18. Reiersol, O. (1941). Confluence analysis by means of lag moments and other methods of confluence analysis. *Econometrica* **9**, 1-24.
19. Reiersol, O. (1950). Identifiability of a linear relation between variables which are subject to error. *Econometrica* **18**, 375-389.
20. Richardson, D. H. and Wu, D. M. (1970). Least squares and grouping method estimators in the errors-in-variables model. *J. Am. Statist.. Assoc.* **65**, 724-748.
21. Schneeweiß, H. (1985). Estimating linear relations with errors in the variables; the merging of two approaches. In *Contributions to Econometrics and Statistics Today.* H. Schneeweiß and H. Strecker Eds., Berlin: Springer-Verlag.
22. Schneeweiß, H. and Mittag, H. J. (1986). *Lineare Modelle mit Fehlerbehafteten Daten.* Heidelberg: Physica-Verlag.
23. Wald, A. (1940). Fitting of straight lines if both variables are subject to error. *Ann. Math. Statist.* **11**, 284-300.
24. Wald, A. (1949). Note on the consistency of the maximum likelihood estimate. *Ann. Math. Statist.* **20**, 595.
25. Ware, J. H. (1972). Fitting straight lines when both variables are subject to error and the ranks of the means are known. *J. Am. Statist.. Assoc.* **67**, 891-897.
26. White, H. (1984). *Asymptotic Theory for Econometricians.* New York: Academic Press.
27. Zellner, A. (1970). Estimating of regression relationships containing unobservable variables. *Int. Econ. Rev..* **11**, 441-454.

Estimation for the Nonlinear Errors-in-Variables Model

Wayne A. Fuller

Department of Statistics, Iowa State University, USA

Summary. An estimator for the parameters of the nonlinear errors-in-variables model with smaller bias than that of the functional maximum likelihood estimator is presented. The estimator is a least squares estimator with an internal Monte Carlo adjustment for bias.

1. Introduction

In the errors-in-variables model, the true values are assumed to satisfy a given mathematical relationship. The observations are the sums of true values and measurement errors. We study the model in which the true values are assumed to satisfy

$$y_t^0 = g\left(\mathbf{x}_t^0;\ \beta^0\right), \qquad t = 1,\ 2,\ \ldots,\ n, \tag{1.1}$$

where the $\mathbf{x}_t^0$ are $1 \times (p-1)$ unobservable vectors belonging to a subset of $(p-1)$-dimensional Euclidean space and β^0 is a $1 \times k$ vector of unknown parameters belonging to a subset of k-dimensional Euclidean space. If $g\left(\mathbf{x}_t^0; \beta^0\right)$ is nonlinear in $\mathbf{x}_t^0$ for fixed β^0 or nonlinear in β^0 for fixed $\mathbf{x}_t^0$, we say the model is nonlinear. The observations are $(Y_t,\ \mathbf{X}_t)$, where

$$\begin{aligned} (Y_t, \mathbf{X}_t) &= (y_t, \mathbf{x}_t) + (e_t, \mathbf{u}_t), \\ (e_t, \mathbf{u}_t)' &\sim NI\left(\mathbf{0},\ \mathbf{I}\sigma^2\right). \end{aligned} \tag{1.2}$$

Carroll, Ruppert, and Stefanski (1995) is an extensive treatment of estimation for this model. The authors consider both the functional model in which the $\mathbf{x}_t$ are considered fixed and the structural model in which the $\mathbf{x}_t$ are considered to be random vectors. Fuller (1987) also contains a discussion of estimation for the nonlinear model emphasizing maximum likelihood and the functional model. Consistent estimation of the parameters of the nonlinear functional model typically requires a sequence in which the error variances become small. See Wolter and Fuller (1982b) and Amemiya and Fuller (1988). Consistent estimators have been constructed for some special functions under weaker assumptions. See Wolter and Fuller (1982a).

2. Estimation

Our estimation procedure is based on the following components. It is assumed that we begin with an estimation procedure such as least squares or maximum likelihood. This procedure should be such that the sequence of estimators will converge to some quantity. The point of convergence is not necessarily the true value. The initial estimator is then adjusted by an estimator of the bias. In our implementation of the procedure, we use Monte Carlo methods to estimate the bias. We give a theorem containing conditions under which the procedure is root n consistent.

Theorem 2.1. *Consider a sequence* $(Y_t,\ \mathbf{X_t},\ \mathbf{x_t})$, $t = 1,\ 2,\ \ldots,$ *satisfying*

$$\begin{aligned} Y_t &= g\left(\mathbf{x_t};\ \beta^0\right) + e_t, \\ \mathbf{X_t} &= \mathbf{x_t} + \mathbf{u_t}, \\ (e_t,\ \mathbf{u_t})' &\sim NI\left(0,\ \mathbf{I}\sigma^2\right), \end{aligned} \tag{2.1}$$

where $g\left(\mathbf{x_t};\ \beta\right)$ *is continuous and the first two partial derivatives of* $g\left(\mathbf{x_t};\ \beta\right)$ *with respect to* $\mathbf{x_t}$ *and* β *are continuous for all* $\mathbf{x_t}$ *and* β. *Consider a sequence of samples, where* $\mathbf{Z_t} = (\mathbf{Y_t},\ \mathbf{X_t})$, $\mathbf{t = 1,\ 2,\ \ldots,\ n}$, *is observed. Let* β^0 *and* $\mathbf{x}^0_{(\mathbf{n})} = (\mathbf{x}^0_1, \ldots, \mathbf{x}^0_\mathbf{n})$ *be the true values of* β *and* $\mathbf{x_{(n)}} = (\mathbf{x_1}, \ldots, \mathbf{x_n})$, *respectively. Let* $\hat{\gamma}_\mathbf{n}$ *and* $\ddot{\mathbf{x}}_{(\mathbf{n})} = (\ddot{\mathbf{x}}_1, \ldots, \ddot{\mathbf{x}}_\mathbf{n})$ *be* $1 \times h$ *and* $1 \times n$ *functions of the sample satisfying the following assumptions:*

(a) For each fixed $\mathbf{x_{(n)}}$ *in the parameter space for* $\mathbf{x_{(n)}}$, $\gamma_\mathbf{n}(\beta; \mathbf{x_{(n)}}) = \mathrm{E}\{\hat{\gamma}_\mathbf{n} \,|\, (\beta; \mathbf{x_{(n)}})\}$ *is a one-to-one mapping from* β *to* $\gamma_\mathbf{n}$ *with a continuous first derivative with respect to* β.

(b) $\beta_\mathbf{n}(\hat{\gamma}_\mathbf{n}; \ddot{\mathbf{x}}_{(\mathbf{n})}) - \beta_\mathbf{n}(\hat{\gamma}_\mathbf{n}; \mathbf{x}^0_{(\mathbf{n})}) = \mathbf{O_p}(\mathbf{n}^{-1/2})$, *where* $\beta_\mathbf{n}(\gamma_\mathbf{n}; \mathbf{x_{(n)}})$ *is the inverse function of* $\gamma_\mathbf{n}(\beta; \mathbf{x_{(n)}})$.

(c) $\hat{\gamma}_\mathbf{n} - \gamma_\mathbf{n}(\beta^0; \mathbf{x}^0_{(\mathbf{n})}) = \mathbf{O_p}(\mathbf{n}^{-1/2})$.

(d) $\gamma_\mathbf{n}(\beta^0; \mathbf{x}^0_{(\mathbf{n})}) = \gamma^0 + \mathbf{o}(1)$ *for some* γ^0.

Then,

$$\beta_\mathbf{n}\left(\hat{\gamma}_\mathbf{n}; \ddot{\mathbf{x}}_{(\mathbf{n})}\right) - \beta^0 = \mathbf{O_p}\left(\mathbf{n}^{-1/2}\right).$$

Proof. By (a), $\beta_\mathbf{n}(\gamma; \mathbf{x}^0_{(\mathbf{n})})$ has a continuous first derivative with respect to γ. Thus,

$$\begin{aligned} \beta_\mathbf{n}\left(\hat{\gamma}_\mathbf{n}; \mathbf{x}^0_{(\mathbf{n})}\right) - \beta^0 &= \beta_\mathbf{n}\left(\hat{\gamma}_\mathbf{n}; \mathbf{x}^0_{(\mathbf{n})}\right) - \beta_\mathbf{n}\left(\gamma_\mathbf{n}\left(\beta^0; \mathbf{x}^0_{(\mathbf{n})}\right); \mathbf{x}^0_{(\mathbf{n})}\right) \\ &= \frac{\partial \beta_\mathbf{n}\left[\hat{\gamma}^*_\mathbf{n}\left(\mathbf{x}^0_{(\mathbf{n})}\right); \mathbf{x}^0_{(\mathbf{n})}\right]}{\partial \gamma} \left[\hat{\gamma}_\mathbf{n} - \gamma_\mathbf{n}\left(\beta^0; \mathbf{x}^0_{(\mathbf{n})}\right)\right] \\ &= O_p\left(n^{-1/2}\right), \end{aligned}$$

where $\partial \beta_\mathbf{n}[\mathbf{a}, \mathbf{b}] / \partial \gamma$ is the vector of partial derivatives of $\beta_\mathbf{n}(\gamma; \mathbf{x_{(n)}})$ evaluated at $(\mathbf{a}, \mathbf{b})$, $\hat{\gamma}^*_\mathbf{n}(\mathbf{x}^0_{(\mathbf{n})})$ is on the line segment joining $\gamma_\mathbf{n}(\beta^0; \mathbf{x}^0_{(\mathbf{n})})$ and $\hat{\gamma}_\mathbf{n}$, and assumptions (c) and (d) were used. The result follows from assumption (b).

The assumptions of the theorem are strong in that the set of **x**-values must have distributional behavior similar to that of the unknown true values. This can be accomplished if the unknown true values are random vectors selected from a known distribution. In the general functional situation, it will be possible to estimate the first few moments of the unknown values with an $O_p\left(n^{-1/2}\right)$ error, but this will not always be sufficient to give assumption (b). The theorem's importance is that it defines the types of conditions required to obtain a consistent estimator of β . In practice it will often be difficult to verify condition (b).

3. Monte Carlo Study

To investigate the possibilities of the suggested estimation procedure, a small Monte Carlo study was conducted. In the Monte Carlo study the functions $\hat{\gamma}_{\mathbf{n}}$ and $\ddot{\mathbf{x}}_{(\mathbf{n})}$ are the maximum likelihood estimators of β and $\mathbf{x}_{(\mathbf{n})}$. The function $\gamma_{\mathbf{n}}(\beta;\mathbf{x})$ is evaluated by simulating the distribution of $\hat{\gamma}_{\mathbf{n}}$ for particular values of $(\beta;\mathbf{x})$. The difficult part of the procedure is the identification of a set $\ddot{\mathbf{x}}_{(\mathbf{n})}$ such that assumption (b) holds, or holds in some approximate sense.

In our Monte Carlo study we assume that the distribution of the errors is known. We choose as $\ddot{\mathbf{x}}_{(\mathbf{n})}$ the maximum likelihood estimator of $\mathbf{x}_{(\mathbf{n})}$ adjusted so that the first two moments are equal to the unbiased estimators of the first two moments. The true x-values were a set of values with equal numbers at five distinct points. This set was chosen because it produces a set of maximum likelihood estimated values with an empirical distribution that is much different from the original configuration of values. Thus, it was anticipated that the modified estimator would be biased.

The model for the Monte Carlo study is

$$\begin{aligned} Y_t &= \beta_0 + \beta_1 x_t + \beta_2\left(x_t^2 - 0.55\right) + e_t \\ X_t &= x_t + u_t, \\ (e_t, u_t)' &\sim NI\left(\mathbf{0}, \mathbf{I}\,\sigma^2\right). \end{aligned} \tag{3.1}$$

It is assumed that σ^2 is known. The form of the equation was chosen so that the estimates of $\beta = (\beta_0, \beta_1, \beta_2)'$ are nearly uncorrelated.

The estimation procedure consisted of several steps. First β and $\mathbf{x} = (\mathbf{x_1}, \mathbf{x_2}, ..., \mathbf{x_n})$ were estimated by minimizing

$$\sum_{t=1}^{n}\left[\,(Y_t - \hat{y}_t)^2 + (X_t - \hat{x}_t)^2\,\right], \tag{3.2}$$

where $\hat{y}_t = \hat{\beta}_0 + \hat{\beta}_1\,\hat{x}_t + \hat{\beta}_2\left(\hat{x}_t^2 - 0.55\right)$. This is the method of maximum likelihood applied to model (3.1) under the assumption of fixed $\mathbf{x}$. The estimator of β that minimizes (3.2) is denoted by $\hat{\beta}_{(1)}$ and is the $\hat{\gamma}_{\mathbf{n}}$ of the

Theorem. Then the set of $\hat{x}_t$-values was modified so that the first two moments matched the directly estimated first two estimated moments of x_t. The modified values are

$$\ddot{x}_t = \bar{X} + s_{\hat{x}}^{-1}\, \hat{\sigma}_x \left(\tilde{x}_t - \hat{\mu}_x\right), \tag{3.3}$$

where

$$\begin{aligned}
\tilde{x}_t &= \bar{X} + \left[\hat{\sigma}_x^2 \left(\hat{\sigma}_x^2 + \hat{V}\left\{\hat{x}_t\right\}\right)^{-1}\right]^{1/2} \left(\hat{x}_t - \overset{\triangle}{x}\right) \\
\left(\bar{X}, \overset{\triangle}{x}\right) &= n^{-1} \sum_{t=1}^{n} \left(X_t, \hat{x}_t\right), \\
\hat{\sigma}_x^2 &= (n-1)^{-1} \sum_{t=1}^{n} \left(X_t - \bar{X}\right)^2 - \sigma^2, \\
s_{\hat{x}}^2 &= (n-1)^{-1} \sum_{t=1}^{n} \left(\tilde{x}_t - \hat{\mu}_x\right)^2, \\
\hat{\mu}_x &= n^{-1} \sum_{t=1}^{n} \tilde{x}_t, \\
\hat{V}\left\{\hat{x}_t\right\} &= \left[1 + \left(\hat{\beta}_1 + 2\hat{\beta}_2\, \hat{x}_t\right)^2\right]^{-1} \sigma^2.
\end{aligned}$$

Note that $\bar{X}$ and $\hat{\sigma}_x^2$ are unbiased estimators of the mean and mean of squares of the true x-values, respectively. The error in the estimators is $O_p(n^{-1/2})$.

Using $\hat{\beta}_{(1)}$ and $\ddot{\mathbf{x}} = (\ddot{\mathbf{x}}_1, \ddot{\mathbf{x}}_2, \ldots, \ddot{\mathbf{x}}_n)$, 4,000 samples satisfying model (3.1) with $\beta = \hat{\beta}_{(1)}$ and $\mathbf{x} = \ddot{\mathbf{x}}$ were generated. An estimator of β was calculated for each generated sample and the average of the 4,000 estimates calculated. A new estimator of β is

$$\hat{\beta}_{(2)} = 2\hat{\beta}_{(1)} - \bar{\beta}_{(1)} \tag{3.4}$$

where $\bar{\beta}_{(1)}$ is the mean of the estimates of β for the 4,000 samples. Then $\hat{\beta}_{(2)}$ and $\ddot{\mathbf{x}}$ were used to generate 4,000 samples satisfying model (3.1) with $\beta = \hat{\beta}_{(2)}$ and $\mathbf{x} = \ddot{\mathbf{x}}$. The estimator of β is updated as

$$\hat{\beta}_{(3)} = \hat{\beta}_{(1)} + \left(\hat{\beta}_{(2)} - \bar{\beta}_{(2)}\right).$$

A third set of 4,000 samples was generated with $\hat{\beta} = \hat{\beta}_{(3)}$ and $\mathbf{x} = \ddot{\mathbf{x}}$. The final estimator is $\hat{\beta}_{(4)} = \hat{\beta}_{(1)} + (\hat{\beta}_{(3)} - \bar{\beta}_{(3)})$. This is a numerical approximation to the β-value that would generate a population of estimates with mean value $\hat{\beta}_{(1)}$.

Tables 1, 2, and 3 contain the empirical properties of estimators of β for model (3.1) with

$$\left(\beta_0, \beta_1, \beta_2, \sigma^2\right) = (0, 0, 1, 0.09).$$

The samples of Table 1 contained 60 observations with 12 observations at the five x-values $(-1.0, -0.5, 0.0, 0.5, 1.0)$. Table 2 contains results for samples of size 120 with 24 observations at each of the five points and Table 3 contains results for samples of size 240 with 48 observations at each of the five points. The first estimator in the tables is the ordinary least squares estimator given by the regression of Y_t on $\left[1, X_t, (X_t^2 - 0.55)\right]$. As expected, this procedure produces a very biased estimator for β_2. Because the true value of the linear coefficient, β_1, is zero and because X is nearly uncorrelated with $(X_t - 0.55)^2$, the estimator of β_1 is essentially unbiased and has a small variance. If β_1 were not zero the estimator would be biased.

Table 1. Empirical mean and standard deviation of estimators of quadrate model
(400 samples of size 60)

Procedure	Parameter and Property					
	β_0		β_1		β_2	
	mean	s.d.	mean	s.d.	mean	s.d.
OLS	-0.065	0.047	0.002	0.074	0.506	0.100
ML	-0.024	0.085	0.004	0.139	1.206	0.273
$\hat{\beta}_{(2)}$	0.000	0.078	0.003	0.128	1.012	0.224
$\hat{\beta}_{(4)}$	-0.001	0.078	0.003	0.129	1.036	0.223

Table 2. Empirical mean and standard deviation of coefficients of quadrate model
(200 samples of size 120)

Procedure	Parameter and Property					
	β_0		β_1		β_2	
	mean	s.d.	mean	s.d.	mean	s.d.
OLS	-0.069	0.033	-0.002	0.050	0.486	0.066
ML	-0.032	0.059	-0.003	0.087	1.169	0.193
$\hat{\beta}_{(2)}$	-0.004	0.054	-0.004	0.079	0.991	0.149
$\hat{\beta}_{(4)}$	-0.004	0.055	-0.004	0.079	1.016	0.154

The ordinary least squares estimator of β_0 is slightly biased because there is a slight correlation with the estimator of β_2.

The properties of the maximum likelihood estimator are given on the second line of the tables. The estimator of β_2 has a bias that is about seventeen percent for samples of size 120 and 240. The bias is somewhat larger for samples of size 60. For the reasons given for ordinary least squares, the maximum likelihood estimator of β_1 is essentially unbiased and the maximum likelihood estimator of β_0 has a modest bias.

The estimators with the interior Monte Carlo adjustment for bias have much smaller bias. The two additional rounds of adjustment have a very modest effect on the estimators. In fact, the bias for the first adjusted value is somewhat less than that for the estimator (3.4) constructed with a single adjustment for bias. The final estimator of β_2 has a positive bias for all sample sizes. The bias is about three times the standard error for samples of size 60 and 200. It is presumed that the bias arises from the fact that the $\ddot{x}_t$ are used in place of the true x_t to estimate the bias.

Table 3. Empirical mean and standard deviation of estimators of quadratic model
(200 samples of size 240)

Procedure	Parameter and Property					
	β_0		β_1		β_2	
	mean	s.d.	mean	s.d.	mean	s.d.
OLS	-0.071	0.022	-0.002	0.038	0.481	0.045
ML	-0.036	0.038	-0.004	0.067	1.169	0.114
$\hat{\beta}_{(2)}$	-0.004	0.035	-0.004	0.062	0.995	0.087
$\hat{\beta}_{(4)}$	-0.004	0.035	-0.004	0.062	1.020	0.091

One result that was not anticipated is that the standard deviations of the bias adjusted estimators are less than those of maximum likelihood. In the case of β_2, the adjusted estimator has a variance that is less than seventy percent of that of maximum likelihood. The mean square error of the modified estimator $\hat{\beta}_{2(4)}$ is about forty-four percent, thirty-six percent, and thirty percent of that of maximum likelihood for samples of size 60, 120 and 240 respectively.

The maximum likelihood and modified estimator of β_1 are nearly unbiased, but the modified estimator has a variance that is nearly twenty percent smaller than that of maximum likelihood.

The maximum likelihood estimator of β_0 is only slightly biased in this parameterization but the curve is displaced by a distance of about 0.13 at $x = 0$. As with the estimator of β_1, the variance of the modified estimator is smaller than the variance of the maximum likelihood estimator.

Acknowledgements

This research was partly supported by Cooperative Agreement 43-3AEU-3-080088 with the National Agricultural Statistics Service and the U.S. Bureau of the Census.

I thank Yasuo Amemiya for useful comments. Zugeng Zheng carried out the computations of the Monte Carlo study with the assistance of Cong Chen.

References

1. Amemiya, Y. and Fuller, W. A. (1988). Estimation for the nonlinear functional relationship. *Ann. Statist.*, **16**, 147-160.
2. Carroll, R. J., Ruppert, D. and Stefanski, L. A. (1995). *Measurement Error in Nonlinear Models*, Chapman and Hall, London.
3. Fuller, W. A. (1987). *Measurement Error Models*, Wiley, New York.
4. Wolter, K. M. and Fuller, W. A. (1982a). Estimation of the quadratic errors-in-variables model. *Biometrika*, **69**, 175-182.
5. Wolter, K. M. and Fuller, W. A. (1982b). Estimation of nonlinear errors-in-variables models. *Ann. Statist.*, **10**, 539-548.

Nonparameteric Regression Splines for Generalized Linear Measurement Error Models

Raymond J. Carroll, Jeffrey D. Maca, and Suojin Wang

Department of Statistics, Texas A&M University, USA

Summary. In many regression applications both the independent and dependent variables are measured with error. When this happens, conventional parametric and nonparametric regression techniques are no longer valid. This is further complicated when one instead wants to fit a generalized linear model to the collected data. We consider two different estimation techniques. The first method is the SIMEX (SIMulation EXtrapolation) algorithm which attempts to estimate the bias, and remove it. The second method is a structural approach, where one hypothesizes a distribution for the independent variable which depends on estimable parameters. For both methods, two different knot selection methods are developed.

1. Introduction

We consider the problem of nonparametric regression function estimation in the presence of measurement error in the predictor for the family of *generalized linear models* (GLIM). Suppose that a response Y has a distribution in the exponential family of the form

$$f_Y(y, \theta, \phi) \quad = \quad \exp\left[\{y\theta - b(\theta)\} a(\phi) + c(y, \phi)\right] \tag{1.1}$$

for known functions, $a(\cdot), b(\cdot)$, and $c(\cdot)$. In generalized linear models, we use the data (Y, X) to estimate the conditional expectation of Y. However, instead of observing X, we can only observe W, an error-prone measurement related to X by an additive error model $W = X + U$, where U is a mean-zero normal random variable with variance σ_u^2. Since X is not available, conventional methods for estimating this function cannot be used.

Nonparametric regression in the presence of measurement error has been addressed previously by Fan & Truong (1993) for the nonparametric regression for data with normal errors. Suppose that $E(Y|X) = m(X)$. Their results showed that if we allow $m(\cdot)$ to have up to k derivatives, and if the measurement error was normally distributed, even with known error variance, then based on a sample of size n, no *globally* consistent nonparametric estimator of $m(\cdot)$ converges faster than the rate $\{\log(n)\}^k$. This result might be interpreted to say that consistent nonparametric regression function estimation in the presence of measurement error is impractical.

By changing the interpretation of their result, Carroll, Maca & Ruppert (1997) found more encouraging results. That is, they changed the criteria for *globally* consistent estimators to that of *approximately* consistent estimators. As reviewed by Carroll, Ruppert & Stefanski (1995), much of the enormous progress made in the field of measurement error for nonlinear models for *globally* consistent estimators to that of *approximately* consistent estimators. As reviewed by Carroll, Ruppert & Stefanski (1995), much of the enormous progress made in the field of measurement error for nonlinear models has been through the use of *approximately* consistent estimators, i.e., estimators which correct for most of measurement error induced bias, but not all. The SIMEX (SIMulation EXtrapolation) algorithm is one method for finding an approximately consistent estimator. The SIMEX estimator was developed by Cook & Stefanski (1994), see Carroll, Küchenhoff, Lombard & Stefanski (1996) and Stefanski & Cook (1995) for related theory, and Carroll, Ruppert, and Stefanski (1995) for detailed discussion of implementation.

A second interpretation by Carroll, Maca & Ruppert (1997) is to remember that the Fan & Truong results say nothing about estimators which are consistent for a flexible yet parametric subclass of the nonparametric family. Regression splines are a well-known parametric family with the capability of estimating wide classes of regression functions. Thus, if one is willing to estimate $E(Y|X)$ by a regression spline, then effective semi-parametric estimation of $E(Y|X)$ is possible even in the presence of measurement error.

This paper develops both these ideas of approximately consistent estimators and estimators consistent for a parametric subclass in the context of regression splines for logistic regression in the presence of measurement error. In Section 2 we show how to implement the SIMEX method, while Section 3 develops a structural method in the context of regression splines for generalized linear models using generalized cross–validation (GCV, see Hastie and Tibshirani, 1990). The SIMEX method is a functional method, i.e., one that can be applied without estimation of the distribution of the unobservable X. In Section 3, we take up the structural approach in the context of regression splines, showing that the observed data follow a type of regression spline depending on the conditional distribution of X given W. If W given X is normally distributed, X given W depends on the marginal distribution of X, which we fit flexibly by a mixture of normal distributions with an unknown number of mixtures. This flexible distribution is fit by using Gibbs sampling algorithm of Carroll, Maca & Ruppert (1997) and Wasserman & Roeder (1997). Special emphasis will be put on the specific model of logistic regression, as an approximation for this model can be used. Section 5 gives a number of numerical examples and simulations. Section 6 has concluding remarks.

2. The SIMEX Estimator

We write the regression spline of order p and with ℓ knots $(\xi_1, \ldots, \xi_\ell)$ as

$$m_{p\ell}(x;\boldsymbol{\beta}) = \sum_{j=0}^{p} \beta_j x^j + \sum_{j=1}^{\ell} \beta_{p+j}(x - \xi_j)_+^p, \tag{2.1}$$

where $v_+ = vI(v > 0)$, and $I(\cdot)$ is the indicator function. If the number of knots and the knots themselves are fixed, then fitting (2.1) to error-prone data is simply a parametric problem, to which the SIMEX idea applies. The SIMEX algorithm can then be implemented for generalized linear models in the following manner. Assume at this point that the knot points are fixed and known. Then with data $(\mathbf{W_i}, \mathbf{Y_i})$, initial estimates for the coefficients for $\boldsymbol{\beta}$ can be calculated using least squares. The method of scoring detailed in Section 3.3 can then be used to find the generalized linear models $\boldsymbol{\beta}$ coefficients. This finds the *naive* estimate as this estimate ignores the presence of the measurement error. Next, more measurement error is artificially added to the data, by $W^* = W + \lambda^{1/2}\varepsilon$, where $\varepsilon \sim \text{Normal}(0, \sigma_u^2)$, and λ has values such as (.25,.50,.75,1.00,.1.25,1.50). To reduce simulation variability, for each lambda value, the naive estimate is calculated $B = 50$ times, and the average estimate is recorded. The SIMEX is then calculated by extrapolating linearly to $\lambda = -1$.

3. Structural Approach to Regression Splines

3.1 Structural Estimation in Generalized Linear Models

Structural estimation in measurement error models means that one hypothesizes a distribution for X depending on a parameter Θ. Since W given X is normal with variance σ_u^2, (σ_u, Θ) together produce the conditional distribution of X given W. Thus, if Y given X has mean determined by the spline (2.1), Y given W has the expectation of

$$\begin{aligned} E(Y|W) &= E\{E(Y|W,X)|W\} \\ &= E\{E(Y|X)|W\} \\ &= E\{f(X)|W\}. \end{aligned} \tag{3.1}$$

In simple nonparametric regression, the function $f(\cdot)$, called the link function, is the identity function, and the expectation of Y given the data W is a simple linear function of the expectations of X given the data W, and the β's can be estimated by ordinary least squares, or ridge regression. However, for generalized linear models , the link functions are more complicated functions which does not lead to nice linear functions of the conditional expectations of X given W.

3.2 Logistic Regression

As outlined in Section 3.1, a structural approach can be fit to any generalized linear models using numerical methods. However, for the specific model of logistic regression, an approximation can facilitate the calculations needed to fit the model. With logistic regression, we can make use of *regression calibration*. For further information on regression calibration, see Carroll, Ruppert, and Stefanski (1995). With regression calibration, Equation (3.1) can be approximated by

$$E\{f(X)\,|W\} \;\approx\; f\{E(X|W)\}. \tag{3.2}$$

Equation (3.2) shows that the desired expectation of Y given the data W can be approximated by the linear function of the conditional expectations of X given the data W. These conditional expectations in Equation (3.2) are easily calculated numerically, and the β's can be estimated by ordinary least squares, or the ridge regression approach of Eilers & Marx (1996).

3.3 Model Fitting for Logistic Regression

Using the approximation in Equation (3.2) of Section 3.2, the regression spline for logistic regression will have the form

$$\begin{aligned} E(Y\,|W) &\approx f\{E(X|W)\} \\ &\approx f\left\{\sum_{j=0}^{p} \beta_j E\left(X^j\,|W\right) + \sum_{j=1}^{\ell} \beta_{p+j} E\left(X - \xi_j\right)_+^p |W\right)\right\} \end{aligned} \tag{3.3}$$

Once the conditional expectations are calculated, ordinary logistic regression can be used to compute the estimate of β. However, the final estimates of the regression spline are dependent on the knot points selected. Two methods for knot selection are outlined below.

4. Knot Selection

The first method for knot selection is the GCV method. For this method, we fit the model using ℓ fixed knot points which are equally spaced in the quantiles of X. The adequacy of the model can be determined by calculating deviance, which for logistic regression is calculated by

$$D \;=\; \sum_{i=1}^{n} \left[Y_i\left(X_i\widehat{\beta}\right) - \log\left\{1 - H\left(X_i^t\widehat{\beta}\right)\right\}\right]. \tag{4.1}$$

The model is fit for each number of knot points ℓ in a range such as $1 \leq \ell \leq \ell_{max}$, and the optimal number of knot points is then the number of knot points which minimizes

$$GCV_\ell \;=\; \frac{n^{-1}\sum_{i=1}^{n} D_\ell(Y,\widehat{\beta})}{\{1-(\ell+p+1)/n\}^2}, \tag{4.2}$$

where p is the order of the spline, and n is the sample size.

The second method is the ridge regression smoothing method of Eilers and Marx (1996). For this method, one chooses an arbitrary fixed number of knot points, ℓ, e.g., $10 \leq \ell \leq 20$. The spline is then smoothed using a continuous scalar value, α, a penalty function on the knot point coefficients, and a criterion such as GCV.

5. Simulations

In this section we present a few simulations showing the improved estimating abilities of the structural regression spline using Gibbs sampling and regression calibration. For all simulations the average squared error (ASE) was calculated for each type of spline to facilitate comparisons. The spline coefficients were calculated using the ridge regression method of Eilers & Marx (1996) using a quadratic order spline with 10 equally spaced knot points.

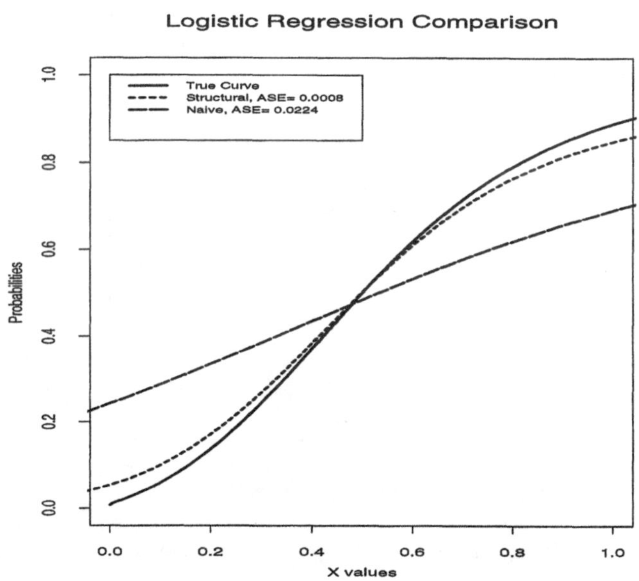

Fig. 5.1. *Comparison of Gibbs spline to naive spline.*

First, we compare the structural spline to the naive spline. For this example, there were 1000 data points, (X), which were generated from an Uniform(0,1) random variable. The true probability curve was then generated as

$$p = H\left\{5(2X)^{1/2} - 1\right\},$$

where $H(\cdot)$ is the logistic distribution function. The Y values where then generated from a Bernoulli random variable with $Pr(Y_i = 1) = p_i$. The measurement error was generated from the Normal(0, .125) distribution. The comparison of the naive spline to the Gibbs spline can be found in Figure 5.1. The Gibbs spline had an ASE value of 0.0008, which compares to the ASE value for the naive spline of 0.0224.

The SIMEX estimator was calculated by the following algorithm. At each point in a grid of equally spaced points over the X range, $m_{p\ell}\{x; \widehat{\beta}(\lambda)\}$ was calculated. This was done for $B = 100$ generated datasets, and the mean was recorded for each level of $\lambda = (0.0, 0.2, 0.4, 0.6, 0.8, 1.0, 1.25)$. The SIMEX estimate for that point was then calculated by linearly extrapolating back to $\lambda = -1$. The SIMEX estimator, which is not pictured into Figure 5.1, had ASE value of 0.0116.

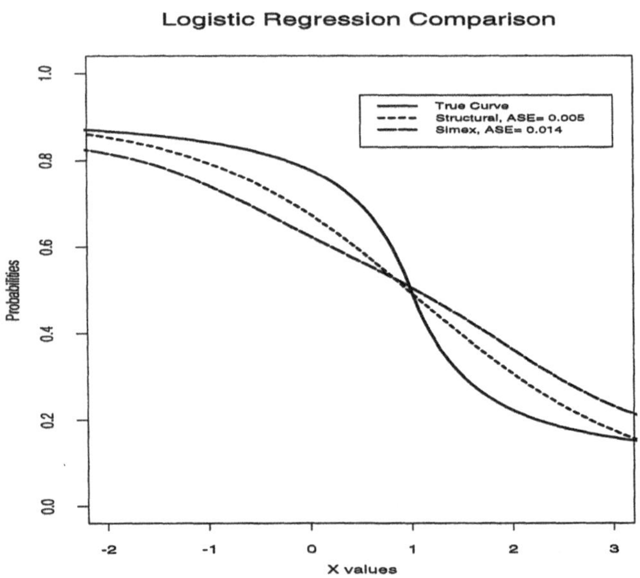

Fig. 5.2. *Comparison of Gibbs spline to SIMEX spline.*

The second example compares the structural method using Gibbs sampling to the SIMEX method. For this example, there were 1000 data points, X, generated from a Normal$(1, 1.5^2)$ random variable. The true probability curve was then generated as

$$p = H\left\{\left(\frac{5 - X}{2X} - 2\right) I(X > 1) + \left(\frac{13 - 9X}{4 - 2X} - 2\right) I(X \leq 1)\right\}.$$

The Y values where then generated from a Bernoulli random variable with $Pr(Y_i = 1) = p_i$. The measurement error was generated from the

Normal(0, 2) distribution. The comparison of the naive spline to the Gibbs spline can be found in Figure 5.2. The Gibbs spline had an ASE value of 0.0029, which compares to the ASE value for the SIMEX spline of 0.0074. For reference, the naive spline had an ASE value of 0.0165, although is not shown in Figure 5.2.

6. Discussion and Generalizations

The generalized linear model primarily focus on in this paper is the logistic model. However, there are many other models, such as the Gamma model or Poisson model which often arise. The SIMEX algorithm can easily be extended using the method described in the paper using both knot selection methods. However, the structural method would take additional modification as described in Section 3.1, as numerical methods for obtaining the conditional expectations would be needed.

Acknowledgment

This research was supported by a grant from the National Cancer Institute (CA–57030).

References

1. Carroll, R. J., Küchenhoff, H., Lombard, F., & Stefanski, L. A. (1996). Asymptotics for the SIMEX estimator in structural measurement error models. *Journal of the American Statistical Association*, 91, 242–250.
2. Carroll, R. J., Maca, J. D., and Ruppert, D. (1997). Nonparametric kernel and regression spline estimation in the presence of measurement error. Preprint.
3. Carroll, R. J., Ruppert, D. and Stefanski, L. A. (1995), *Measurement Error in Nonlinear Models*. London: Chapman and Hall.
4. Cook, J. R. & Stefanski L. A. (1994). Simulation–extrapolation estimation in parametric measurement error models. *Journal of the American Statistical Association*, 89, 1314-1328.
5. Eilers, P. H. C. & Marx, B. D. (1996). Flexible smoothing with B–splines and penalties. *Statistical Science*, 11, 89–121.
6. Fan, J. & Truong, Y. K. (1993). Nonparametric regression with errors in variables. *Annals of Statistics*, 21, 1900–1925.
7. Hastie, T. & Tibshirani, R. (1990). *Generalized Additive Models*, Chapman and Hall, New York.
8. Stefanski, L. A., & Cook, J. R. (1995). Simulation–Extrapolation: The measurement error jackknife. *Journal of the American Statistical Association*, 90, 1247–1256.
9. Wasserman, L. & Roeder, K. (1997). Bayesian density estimation Using mixtures of normals. *Journal of the American Statistical Association*, to appear.

Different Nonlinear Regression Models with Incorrectly Observed Covariates

Markus Thamerus

Department of Statistics, Ludwig-Maximilians-Universität München, Germany

Summary. We present quasi-likelihood models for different regression problems when one of the explanatory variables is measured with heteroscedastic error. In order to derive models for the observed data the conditional mean and variance functions of the regression models are only expressed through functions of the observable covariates. The latent covariable is treated as a random variable that follows a normal distribution. Furthermore it is assumed that enough additional information is provided to estimate the individual measurement error variances, e.g. through replicated measurements of the fallible predictor variable. The discussion includes the polynomial regression model as well as the probit and logit model for binary data, the Poisson model for count data and ordinal regression models.

1. Introduction

It is a familiar situation for practical researchers that some of the predictors of a regression model cannot be observed correctly and instead are only measured with error. One of the first monographs on that topic is Schneeweiß and Mittag (1986), which contains a comprehensive summary of the different methods to treat measurement errors in the linear model. If the occurrence of measurement errors is not taken into account in the analysis the estimators of the model parameters will be biased. This was shown by Stefanski (1985) in general for all regression models where the parameters of interest are estimated by an *M*-estimator, which is consistent in the absence of measurement error.

For all discussed models in this paper the response variables Y_i are related to the explanatory variables $Z_i = (Z_{i1}, \dots, Z_{ik})'$ and X_i by a nonlinear regression function. The continuous regressors X_i can only be observed by their incorrect measurements W_i. We assume that the true predictors X_i are related to the observed covariates W_i through $W_i = X_i + U_i$, where the measurement errors U_i are independent stochastic variables with expectations zero and we do not restrict the error variances to be constant but allow for heteroscedasticity.

We will consider the structural case of errors-in-variables models and treat the latent regressors X_i as independent and identically distributed random variables. The structural approach to regression models with covariate error consists of three main components:

a) the unobservable true regression model, that relates the response variables Y_i and the true regressors Z_i and X_i,
b) the error model, that characterizes the relationship between the latent regressors X_i and their measurements W_i and
c) the assumed marginal distribution of the X_i's.

For the main part of nonlinear regression models likelihood analysis depending on the associated distributions of all three parts a)–c) remains computationally difficult, since it requires numerical optimization routines to evaluate an integral in the likelihood function of the observed data. Carroll, Ruppert and Stefanski (1995) give an excellent overview of methods for treating measurement error in nonlinear regression models including likelihood models as well. For more details on the maximization of likelihood functions in errors-in-variables models see e.g. Crouch and Spiegelman (1990) or Liu and Pierce (1994). An indirect method to obtain maximum likelihood estimates of the regression parameters is to use an EM algorithm as it is proposed by Schafer (1993) for a probit regression model or by Schafer and Purdy (1996) for the linear regression model. Due to all the computational difficulties associated with likelihood analysis in the errors-in-variables problem we prefer an alternative method, that directly allows to model heteroscedastic measurement errors as well.

We will use quasi-likelihood models, see e.g. McCullagh (1991) for an introduction, that solely base on the first and second conditional moments of the response Y_i given the known explanatory variables Z_i and the observed measurements W_i. If the mean and variance function of the model in the observable variables can be specified estimation is carried out by the usual iteratively reweighted least square algorithm for such models which is easier to implement than the numerical integration methods for the likelihood analysis. The unbiasedness of the quasi-score function guarantees the consistency and asymptotic normality of the parameter estimates. One of the first to use quasi-likelihood methods to analyse errors-in-variables models is Armstrong (1985). The subject is also considered by Liang and Liu (1991).

In this article we will discuss the quasi-likelihood approach for different nonlinear regression models with incorrectly observed covariates under the assumption of heteroscedastic measurement errors. We will state a structural approach for the polynomial regression model and the Poisson regression model. The use of quasi-likelihood methods for binary regression models in the case of nonconstant measurement error variances is discussed and the idea is extended to the multicategorial case when ordinal response variables are observed. In the next section we discuss quasi-likelihood models for the errors-in-variables problem in general and state a heteroscedastic error model. Section three reviews the use of quasi-likelihood methods for the different nonlinear regression models with heteroscedastic measurement errors in one of the covariates and it is shown how a model in the observable variables is derived when the latent regressors follow a normal distribution.

2. Model of the Observed Data

The fundamental idea of using quasi-likelihood methods to analyse regression models with incorrectly observed covariates is to make a transition from the unobservable model, formulated in terms of the latent variables, to a model of the observable data. The unobservable model of interest is given by a nonlinear regression model, where the vector of the regression parameters β is estimated by solving an unbiased estimating equation. In the case of no measurement error estimation is based on the mean and variance function of the observed data, i.e., the conditional mean and variance of Y_i as a function of Z_i and X_i. These are given by

$$\begin{aligned} \mu(Z_i, X_i; \beta) &= \mathrm{E}(Y_i \mid Z_i, X_i) \quad \text{for the mean and} & (2.1) \\ \sigma^2(Z_i, X_i; \beta, \nu) &= \mathrm{V}(Y_i \mid Z_i, X_i) \quad \text{for the variance function,} & (2.2) \end{aligned}$$

where ν denotes an additional (optional) variance parameter. This includes the class of generalized linear models where the conditional distribution of Y_i given Z_i and X_i belongs to the exponential family and the mean function (2.1) is given by

$$\mu(Z_i, X_i; \beta) = g(\beta_0 + Z_i'\beta_Z + \beta_X X_i) \quad \text{with} \quad \beta = (\beta_0, \beta_Z', \beta_X)$$

and where $g^{-1}(\cdot)$ is the link function of the model. To derive a model in the observable variables we denote the first two moments of the conditional distribution of Y_i given Z_i and W_i with

$$\begin{aligned} m_Q(Z_i, W_i; \beta) &= \mathrm{E}(Y_i \mid Z_i, W_i) \quad \text{for the mean and} \\ v_Q(Z_i, W_i; \beta, \nu) &= \mathrm{V}(Y_i \mid Z_i, W_i) \quad \text{for the variance function.} \end{aligned}$$

If those two functions can be specified, the estimation of β can be carried out by the usual IRLS algorithm for quasi-likelihood models (see e.g. McCullagh, 1991). The quasi-score function

$$\mathrm{s}(\beta) = \sum_{i=1}^{n} \frac{\partial m_Q(Z_i, W_i; \beta)}{\partial \beta} v_Q^{-1}(Z_i, W_i; \beta, \nu)(Y_i - m_Q(Z_i, W_i; \beta)) = \sum_{i=1}^{n} \mathrm{s}_i(\beta)$$

provides an unbiased estimating equation for β and the quasi-likelihood estimator $\hat{\beta}_{ql}$ is found as the root of the equation $s(\beta) = 0$. This provides the asymptotic properties of $\hat{\beta}_{ql}$ and it holds that $\hat{\beta}_{ql}$ is a consistent estimator of β with

$$\hat{\beta}_{ql} \overset{a}{\sim} N(\beta, n^{-1}F^{-1}(\beta)V(\beta)F^{-1}(\beta)).$$

The covariance matrix of $\hat{\beta}_{ql}$ is of the 'sandwich' form and its parts are the inverse of the expected quasi-information matrix and the covariance matrix of the score function. It is estimated empirically by

$$\widehat{\mathrm{Cov}}(\hat{\beta}_{ql}) = n^{-1}\hat{F}^{-1}(\hat{\beta}_{ql})\hat{V}(\hat{\beta}_{ql})\hat{F}^{-1}(\hat{\beta}_{ql})$$

with its components given through

$$\hat{F}(\hat{\beta}_{ql}) = \frac{1}{n}\left(\sum_{i=1}^{n} -\frac{\partial\, s_i(\beta)}{\partial\, \beta'}\bigg|_{\beta=\hat{\beta}_{ql}}\right)$$

and

$$\text{and} \quad \hat{V}(\hat{\beta}_{ql}) = \frac{1}{n}\left(\sum_{i=1}^{n} s_i(\beta)\ (s_i(\beta))'\bigg|_{\beta=\hat{\beta}_{ql}}\right).$$

It is supposed that the measurement errors are nondifferential, which is defined as the conditional independence of Y_i and W_i given X_i and Z_i. For most measurement problems this assumption is reasonable since it implies that no additional information about the response Y_i is provided by the measurement W_i if the true explanatory variables Z_i and X_i are observed. In the case of nondifferential measurement error the fallible predictor W_i is called a surrogate. With this assumption the construction principle for the functions m_Q and v_Q can be demonstrated. For all models in the next section we have to compute the expectations

$$\begin{aligned} m_Q\,(Z_i, W_i; \beta) &= \mathrm{E}\,(\mathrm{E}\,(Y_i \mid Z_i, X_i, W_i) \mid Z_i, W_i) \\ &= \mathrm{E}\,(\mathrm{E}\,(Y_i \mid Z_i, X_i) \mid Z_i, W_i) \\ &= \mathrm{E}\,(\mu\,(Z_i, X_i; \beta) \mid Z_i, W_i) \end{aligned} \tag{2.3}$$

and

$$\begin{aligned} v_Q\,(Z_i, W_i; \beta, \nu) &= \mathrm{V}(\mathrm{E}\,(Y_i \mid Z_i, X_i, W_i) \mid Z_i, W_i) \\ &\quad + \mathrm{E}\,(\mathrm{V}(Y_i \mid Z_i, X_i, W_i) \mid Z_i, W_i) \\ &= \mathrm{V}(\mathrm{E}\,(Y_i \mid Z_i, X_i) \mid Z_i, W_i) \\ &\quad + \mathrm{E}\,(\mathrm{V}(Y_i \mid Z_i, X_i) \mid Z_i, W_i) \\ &= \mathrm{V}(\mu\,(Z_i, X_i; \beta) \mid Z_i, W_i) \\ &\quad + \mathrm{E}\,(\sigma^2\,(Z_i, X_i; \beta, \nu) \mid Z_i, W_i)\,. \end{aligned} \tag{2.4}$$

After we have set up the framework to estimate regression models with surrogate predictors we now regard the relationship between the latent regressors X_i and their measurements W_i. For all discussed models in section three we assume an additive heteroscedastic measurement error model:

For $i = 1, \ldots, n$ it holds that $W_i = X_i + U_i$ with $U_i \sim N(0, \sigma_i^2)$
where $\mathrm{Cov}\,(U_i, U_j) = 0$ for $i \neq j$, $j = 1, \ldots, n$ and
the errors U_i are independent from the variables Y_i, X_i and Z_i. (2.5)

This implies that the measurement errors are nondifferential. For some applications the assumption of a heteroscedastic measurement error model is more reasonable than to assume constant error variances. Thamerus (1997) describes an example where the true regional concentration of radon X_i is approximated by the average of n_i single measurements W_{ij} of X_i within one region. For those individual measurements of X_i, $i = 1, \ldots, n$ the error model

$$W_{ij} = X_i + \varepsilon_{ij} \qquad \text{with } \mathrm{E}(\varepsilon_{ij}) = 0 \text{ and } \mathrm{Var}(\varepsilon_{ij}) = \sigma^2_{\varepsilon_i} \text{ for } j = 1, \ldots, n_i$$
$$\text{and } \mathrm{Cov}(\varepsilon_{ij}, \varepsilon_{il}) = 0 \text{ for } j \neq l,\ l = 1, \ldots, n_i$$

was assumed. The observed averages $W_i = n_i^{-1} \sum_{j=1}^{n_i} W_{ij}$ therefore follow the additive heteroscedastic error model

$$W_i = X_i + U_i \text{ with } U_i \sim N(0, \sigma_i^2) \text{ for } i = 1, \ldots, n.$$

The heteroscedastic error variances $\sigma_i^2 = {n_i}^{-1} \sigma^2_{\varepsilon_i}$ can be estimated with the help of the sample variances $s^2_{W_i}$ of the measurements within each region by $\hat{\sigma}_i^2 = {n_i}^{-1} s^2_{W_i}$. In general the analysis of errors-in-variables models is non-practical without additional information on the measurement error process. For our discussion we will assume that the heteroscedastic error variances σ_i^2 are known or that enough information e.g. replicated measurements of the fallible predictor variable as in the example above is provided so that the individual variances σ_i^2 at least can be estimated consistently.

In a structural errors-in-variables model the latent regressors X_i are treated as independently and identically distributed random variables and an assumption has to be made about the distribution of the true covariates X_i. This in fact is a crucial point of the analysis and requires careful examination of what is known about this distribution through the observed sample of the W_i's. The normal distribution is often used in the literature. If the distribution of the true covariates is skewed one choice is to assume that the true covariates X_i are lognormally distributed and often the transformation $\log(X_i)$ along with a multiplicative error model is used in the analysis. For more details on transformations of the X-variables see the recent paper of Eckert, Carroll and Wang (1997). More complex situations lead to the assumption of a mixture of normal distributions, see e.g. Küchenhoff and Carroll (1997), which is computationally more demanding but yields similar convenient properties as the assumption of a normal distribution. Thamerus (1997) used a normal mixture distribution together with an heteroscedastic measurement error model in a Poisson regression model. For all discussed models in section three we assume that the true variables X_i are independently and identically distributed normal variables with expectation μ_X and variance σ_X^2. Under the assumption of an additive heteroscedastic measurement error model unbiased estimators of these parameters are given by $\hat{\mu}_X = \bar{w}$ and $\hat{\sigma}_X^2 = s_W^2 - \frac{n-1}{n^2} \sum_{i=1}^n \sigma_i^2$ where $\bar{w}$ is the sample mean and s_W^2 is the sample variance of the observed measurements W_i, $i = 1, \ldots, n$.

In order to state the mean and variance functions of the different quasi-likelihood models it is necessary to specify the conditional distributions of W_i given the true covariates Z_i and X_i. If we furthermore assume that X_i is independent of the other correctly observed covariates Z_i we find for the conditional distributions of X_i given the surrogate W_i for $i = 1, \ldots, n$:

$$\begin{aligned} X_i \mid Z_i, W_i \sim X_i \mid W_i &\sim N(\mu_i, \tau_i^2) \text{ with} \\ \mu_i &= \mu_X + \sigma_X^2(\sigma_X^2 + \sigma_i^2)^{-1}(W_i - \mu_X) \text{ and} \\ \tau_i^2 &= \sigma_X^2\left(1 - \sigma_X^2(\sigma_X^2 + \sigma_i^2)^{-1}\right). \end{aligned} \tag{2.6}$$

Note, that the variances τ_i^2 of this conditional distributions differ between individuals as a consequence of the heteroscedastic error variances σ_i^2. At the end of this section we summarize all the assumptions under which the functions m_Q and v_Q, given in (2.3) and (2.4), for the different models in the next section will be derived.

Assumptions

(A1) The variables X_i and W_i, $i = 1, \ldots, n$ are related by an additive heteroscedastic measurement error model as defined in (2.5).

(A2) For the latent variables it holds: $X_i \overset{i.i.d}{\sim} N(\mu_X, \sigma_X^2)$, $i = 1, \ldots, n$.

(A3) The variables X_i and Z_i, $i = 1, \ldots, n$ are independent.

3. Application to Different Regression Models

3.1 Polynomial regression models

In a forthcoming paper Cheng and Schneeweiß (1998) develop a functional errors-in-variables model for the polynomial regression model by correcting the scorefunction of the model to adjust for measurement error in the observed covariates. Moon and Gunst (1995) give a summary of the work on polynomial regression models with covariate errors. In contrast to these two papers and the work cited therein we allow for heteroscedastic measurement error and show how under the assumptions (A1)–(A3) a structural model is accomplished.

In the notation of (2.1) and (2.2) the polynomial regression model without additional variables Z_i is given by

$$\mu(X_i; \beta) = \beta_0 + \beta_1 X_i + \beta_2 X_i^2 + \ldots + \beta_k X_i^k \quad \text{and} \quad \sigma^2(X_i; \beta, \nu) = \sigma_\varepsilon^2 \tag{3.1}$$

with $\beta = (\beta_0, \ldots, \beta_k)'$ and $\nu = \sigma_\varepsilon^2$. The model of the observable data depends on higher moments of the conditional distributions of W_i given X_i. The k-th moment of that distribution will be denoted by

$$\mu'_{k,i} = \mathrm{E}(X_i^k \mid W_i) \quad \text{for} \quad k = 1, 2, \ldots \quad \text{with} \quad \mu'_{0,i} = 1.$$

If the two functions of the unobservable model (3.1) are inserted into the general formulas (2.3) and (2.4) for the mean and variance function m_Q and v_Q we find

$$\begin{aligned}
&m_Q(W_i;\beta)\\
&\quad= \mathrm{E}\left(\mu\left(X_i;\beta\right) \mid W_i\right)\\
&\quad= \beta_0+\beta_1\mathrm{E}\left(X_i \mid W_i\right)+\beta_2\mathrm{E}\left(X_i^2 \mid W_i\right)+\ldots+\beta_k\mathrm{E}\left(X_i^k \mid W_i\right)\\
&\quad= \beta_0+\beta_1\mu'_{1,i}+\beta_2\mu'_{2,i}+\ldots+\beta_k\mu'_{k,i} \quad \text{and}\\
&v_Q(W_i;\beta,\nu)\\
&\quad= \mathrm{E}\left(\sigma^2\left(X_i;\beta,\nu\right) \mid W_i\right)+\mathrm{V}\left(\mu\left(X_i;\beta\right) \mid W_i\right)\\
&\quad= \sigma_\varepsilon^2+\mathrm{V}\left(\beta_0+\beta_1X_i+\beta_2X_i^2+\ldots+\beta_kX^k \mid W_i\right)\\
&\quad= \sigma_\varepsilon^2+\sum_{j=1}^{k}\beta_j^2\,\mathrm{V}(X_i^j \mid W_i)+2\sum_{l=1}^{k-1}\sum_{m=l+1}^{k}\beta_l\beta_m\,\mathrm{Cov}\left(X_i^l,X_i^m \mid W_i\right)\\
&\quad= \sigma_\varepsilon^2+\sum_{j=1}^{k}\beta_j^2\left(\mathrm{E}\left(X_i^{2j} \mid W_i\right)-\left(\mathrm{E}\left(X_i^j \mid W_i\right)\right)^2\right)\\
&\qquad+2\sum_{l=1}^{k-1}\sum_{m=l+1}^{k}\beta_l\beta_m\left(\mathrm{E}\left(X_i^{l+m} \mid W_i\right)-\mathrm{E}\left(X_i^l \mid W_i\right)\mathrm{E}\left(X_i^m \mid W_i\right)\right)\\
&\quad= \sigma_\varepsilon^2+\sum_{j=1}^{k}\beta_j^2\left(\mu'_{2j,i}-(\mu'_{j,i})^2\right)+2\sum_{l=1}^{k-1}\sum_{m=l+1}^{k}\beta_l\beta_m\left(\mu'_{l+m,i}-\mu'_{l,i}\mu'_{m,i}\right).
\end{aligned}$$

The mean function m_Q of the quasi-likelihood model is a linear function of the first k moments of the conditional distributions of W_i given X_i. The variance function m_Q uses moments up to the order $2k$. All those moments can be computed under the normal assumption (A2) for the latent variables X_i since the conditional distributions for X_i given W_i, defined in (2.6), are normal as well with parameters μ_i and τ_i^2. The k-th central moments of that distributions will be denoted by

$$\mu_{k,i}=\mathrm{E}\left(\left(X_i-\mu'_{1,i}\right)^k \mid W_i\right), \quad \text{for} \quad k=1,2,\ldots \quad \text{with} \quad \mu_{0,i}=1.$$

Normality yields the calculation of the moments $\mu_{k,i}$ in dependence of the variances τ_i^2. For $r=0,1,2,\ldots$ it holds that

$$\mu_{k,i}=\begin{cases} 0 & \text{for} \quad k=2r+1,\\ \tau_i^k(k-1)(k-3)\cdot\ldots\cdot3\cdot1 & \text{for} \quad k=2r. \end{cases} \tag{3.2}$$

The different moments are connected by the Binomial theorem. In general we have

$$\mu'_{k,i}=\sum_{j=0}^{k}\binom{k}{j}\mu_{k-j,i}(\mu'_{1,i})^j \quad \text{for} \quad k=1,2,\ldots. \tag{3.3}$$

With the help of the results (3.2) and (3.3) all necessary moments to compute the functions m_Q and v_Q can be determined under the knowledge of the means $\mu'_{1,i}=\mu_i$ and variances $\mu_{2,i}=\tau_i^2$. We will demonstrate this for the quadratic regression model ($k=2$) that is given by

$$\mu(X_i;\beta) = \beta_0 + \beta_1 X_i + \beta_2 X_i^2 \quad \text{and} \quad \sigma^2(X_i;\beta,\nu) = \sigma_\varepsilon^2.$$

Mean and variance function of the model of the observed data are found as

$$\begin{aligned} & m_B(W_i;\beta) \\ &\quad = \beta_0 + \beta_1 \mu'_{1,i} + \beta_2 \mu'_{2,i} \\ &\quad = \beta_0 + \beta_1 \mu_i + \beta_2(\tau_i^2 + \mu_i^2) \text{ and} \end{aligned} \tag{3.4}$$

$$\begin{aligned} & v_B(W_i;\beta,\nu) \\ &\quad = \sigma_\varepsilon^2 + \beta_1^2\left(\mu'_{2,i} - (\mu'_{1,i})^2\right) + \beta_2^2\left(\mu'_{4,i} - (\mu'_{2,i})^2\right) \\ &\qquad + 2\,\beta_1\beta_2\left(\mu'_{3,i} - \mu'_{1,i}\mu'_{2,i}\right) \\ &\quad = \sigma_\varepsilon^2 + \beta_1^2\left(\tau_i^2 + \mu_i^2 - \mu_i^2\right) \\ &\qquad + \beta_2^2\left(3\tau_i^4 + 6\tau_i^2\mu_i^2 + \mu_i^4 - \tau_i^4 - 2\tau_i^2\mu_i^2 - \mu_i^4\right) \\ &\qquad + 2\,\beta_1\beta_2\left(3\tau_i^2\mu_i + \mu_i^3 - \mu_i\tau_i^2 - \mu_i^3\right) \\ &\quad = \sigma_\varepsilon^2 + \beta_1^2\tau_i^2 + 2\beta_2^2\left(\tau_i^4 + 2\tau_i^2\mu_i^2\right) + 4\beta_1\beta_2\tau_i^2\mu_i. \end{aligned} \tag{3.5}$$

A particular property of the polynomial regression model with incorrectly observed covariates is that the measurement error itself is raised to the power of k. The regressors of the naive approach $W_i^j = (X_i + U_i)^j$, $j = 1, \ldots, k$ are replaced in the quasi-likelihood model by the moments $\mu'_{j,i}$, $j = 1, \ldots, k$ and additionally the different variance structure of the model that is caused by the measurement errors is taken into account. This can already be seen in the example of the quadratic regression model. The variance σ_ε^2 that occurs in the variance function v_Q has to be updated in every iteration step of the estimation procedure. This can be done by the residual variance which in the $r+1$-th step can be computed with the help of the estimator $\hat{\beta}_1^{(r)}$ from the previous step as

$$(\hat{\sigma}_\varepsilon^2)^{(r+1)} = (n-k-1)^{-1} \sum_{i=1}^{n} \left(y_i - (\hat{\beta}_0^{(r)} + \hat{\beta}_1^{(r)}\mu'_{1,i} + \ldots + \hat{\beta}_k^{(r)}\mu'_{k,i})\right)^2.$$

3.2 Poisson regression model

Quasi-likelihood methods in Poisson regression models were mostly used to account for overdispersion, see e.g. Breslow (1990). Additional variation in the data can also be caused by measurement error in the covariates. Armstrong (1985) derives a model in the observable variables for the Poisson regression model when the erroneous predictor variables follow a normal distribution. This approach was adopted by Thamerus (1997) and modified for a mixture of normal distributions combined with a heteroscedastic measurement error model. We will demonstrate how a model under the assumptions (A1)–(A3) can be derived.

The mean and variance function (2.1) and (2.2) of the unobservable Poisson regression model are identical and given by

$$\mu(Z_i, X_i; \beta) = \sigma^2(Z_i, X_i; \beta) = \exp(\beta_0 + Z_i'\beta_Z + \beta_X X_i). \tag{3.6}$$

To derive the model of the observable data we insert the mean and variance function given in (3.6) into the equations (2.3) and (2.4). Under the assumptions (A1) and (A3) we at first obtain for the mean and variance function m_Q and v_Q the expressions

$$\begin{aligned} m_Q(Z_i, W_i; \beta) &= \mathrm{E}(\exp(\beta_0 + Z_i'\beta_Z + \beta_X X_i) \mid Z_i, W_i) \\ &= \exp(\beta_0 + Z_i'\beta_Z)\,\mathrm{E}(\exp(\beta_X X_i) \mid W_i) \quad \text{and} \qquad (3.7) \\ v_Q(Z_i, W_i; \beta) &= \mathrm{V}(\exp(\beta_0 + Z_i'\beta_Z + \beta_X X_i) \mid Z_i, W_i) \\ &\quad + \mathrm{E}(\exp(\beta_0 + Z_i'\beta_Z + \beta_X X_i) \mid Z_i, W_i) \\ &= \exp(2\beta_0 + 2Z_i'\beta_Z)\,\mathrm{E}(\exp(2\beta_X X_i) \mid W_i) \\ &\quad - \left(\exp(\beta_0 + Z_i'\beta_Z)\,\mathrm{E}(\exp(\beta_X X_i) \mid W_i)\right)^2 \\ &\quad + \exp(\beta_0 + Z_i'\beta_Z)\,\mathrm{E}(\exp(\beta_X X_i) \mid W_i). \qquad (3.8) \end{aligned}$$

As can be seen from (3.7) and (3.8) the essential task is to compute expectations of the form $\mathrm{E}(\exp(c X_i) \mid W_i)$, where the constant factor c has to be replaced by β_X or $2\beta_X$. As a result of the further assumption (A2) the conditional distributions of X_i given W_i are normal with the associated parameters μ_i and τ_i^2, see (2.6), and hence all expectations can be expressed as

$$\mathrm{E}(\exp(c X_i) \mid W_i) = \exp\left(c\,\mu_i + \frac{c^2\,\tau_i^2}{2}\right).$$

With this result all expectations in (3.7) and (3.8) can be calculated and we finally get the mean and variance function of the observable model as

$$\begin{aligned} m_Q(Z_i, W_i; \beta) &= \exp\left(\beta_0 + Z_i'\beta_Z + \beta_X \mu_i + \frac{\beta_X^2 \tau_i^2}{2}\right) \quad \text{and} \\ v_Q(Z_i, W_i; \beta) &= \exp\left(2\beta_0 + 2Z_i'\beta_Z + 2\beta_X \mu_i + 2\beta_X^2 \tau_i^2\right) \\ &\quad - \left(\exp\left(\beta_0 + Z_i'\beta_Z + \beta_X \mu_i + \frac{\beta_X^2 \tau_i^2}{2}\right)\right)^2 \\ &\quad + \exp\left(\beta_0 + Z_i'\beta_Z + \beta_X \mu_i + \frac{\beta_X^2 \tau_i^2}{2}\right) \\ &= \exp\left(2\beta_0 + 2Z_i'\beta_Z + 2\beta_X \mu_i + 2\beta_X^2 \tau_i^2\right) \\ &\quad - (m_Q(Z_i, W_i; \beta))^2 + m_Q(Z_i, W_i; \beta). \end{aligned}$$

3.3 Binary regression models

The most popular method to treat covariate measurement error in a logistic regression model is the regression calibration approach. It was initiated by Rosner, Willett an Spiegelman (1989) and generalized for any regression model by Carroll and Stefanski (1990). Carroll et al. (1995) give a detailed description of the different approaches, structural and functional, to model measurement errors in binary regression models. Quasi-likelihood methods for such models have also been studied by Liang and Liu (1991) assuming homoscedastic measurement errors.

We will extend this idea to the heteroscedastic case and consider the probit and logit model for binary responses. For the conditional distribution of the response variables given the true covariates it holds that $Y_i \mid Z_i, X_i \sim B\,(1, \pi_i(\beta))$.

3.3.1 Probit regression. Mean and variance function (2.1) and (2.2) of the unobserved probit regression model are given by

$$\begin{aligned} \mu\,(Z_i, X_i; \beta) &= \Phi(\beta_0 + Z_i'\beta_Z + \beta_X X_i) = \pi_i(\beta) \quad \text{and} && (3.9) \\ \sigma^2\,(Z_i, X_i; \beta) &= \pi_i(\beta)(1 - \pi_i(\beta)). && (3.10) \end{aligned}$$

With $\phi(\cdot)$ and $\Phi(\cdot)$ we denote the density and distribution function of the standard normal distribution. For establishing the quasilikelihood model under the assumptions (A1)–(A3) we make use of a probit integral argument, see e.g. Tosteson, Schafer and Stefanski (1989): For the fixed quantities $s > 0$ and m it holds in general that

$$\int_{-\infty}^{+\infty} s^{-1}\Phi(a + bx)\phi\,(\frac{x-m}{s})\,dx = \Phi\left(\frac{a + bm}{(1 + b^2 s^2)^{\frac{1}{2}}}\right). \qquad (3.11)$$

If we insert the functions (3.9) and (3.10) into the general equations (2.3) and (2.4) of the quasi-likelihood model, the relation (3.11) enables us to determine the functions m_Q and v_Q. For the mean function m_Q of the observable data we find

$$\begin{aligned} m_Q\,(Z_i, W_i; \beta) &= \mathrm{E}\,(\Phi(\beta_0 + Z_i'\beta_Z + \beta_X X_i) \mid Z_i, W_i) \\ &= \int_{-\infty}^{+\infty} \Phi(\beta_0 + Z_i'\beta_Z + \beta_X x_i)\, f_{X_i|W_i}(x_i)\, dx_i \\ &= \int_{-\infty}^{+\infty} \frac{1}{\tau_i}\Phi(\beta_0 + Z_i'\beta_Z + \beta_X x_i)\, \phi\left(\frac{x_i - \mu_i}{\tau_i}\right) dx_i \\ &= \Phi\left(\frac{\beta_0 + Z_i'\beta_Z + \beta_X \mu_i}{(1 + \beta_X^2 \tau_i^2)^{\frac{1}{2}}}\right) = \pi_i^*(\beta). && (3.12) \end{aligned}$$

The variance function of that model simply results in

$$v_Q\,(Z_i, W_i; \beta) = \pi_i^*(\beta)(1 - \pi_i^*(\beta)).$$

Hence we find for the conditional distribution of Y_i given the observable regressors Z_i and W_i under the assumptions of (A1)–(A3) that $Y_i \mid Z_i, W_i \sim B\,(1, \pi_i^*(\beta))$ with the probabilities $\pi_i^*(\beta)$ given in (3.12). The functions m_Q

and v_Q therefore provide a likelihood model for the probit regression with heteroscedastic measurement error. As a consequence of the individual factors $(1+\beta_X^2\tau_i^2)^{\frac{1}{2}}$ in the denominator of the argument of $\pi_i^*(\beta) = \Phi(\ldots)$ the model in the observable data differs from a probit regression model.

3.3.2 Logistic regression. In order to state the logistic regression model we will denote the logistic distribution function with $H(t) = (1+\exp(-t))^{-1}$ and therefore can write the mean function (2.1) of the true model in this case as

$$\mu(Z_i, X_i; \beta) = H(\beta_0 + Z_i'\beta_Z + \beta_X X_i) = \pi_i(\beta). \tag{3.13}$$

To derive the mean function m_Q under the assumptions (A1)–(A3) we insert (3.13) into (2.3) and with the conditional distribution given in (2.6) we end up with the integral

$$\begin{aligned} m_Q(Z_i, W_i; \beta) &= \mathrm{E}\left(H(\beta_0 + Z_i'\beta_Z + \beta_X X_i) \mid Z_i, W_i\right) \\ &= \int_{-\infty}^{+\infty} \frac{1}{\tau_i} H(\beta_0 + Z_i'\beta_Z + \beta_X x_i)\phi\left(\frac{x_i - \mu_i}{\tau_i}\right) dx_i \end{aligned}$$

which can not be expressed in closed form. Alternatively to numerical integration methods the function m_Q can be sufficiently approximated by exploiting the relation $H(t) \approx \Phi(\frac{t}{c})$ with $c = \frac{15\pi}{16\sqrt{3}}$, see Johnson and Kotz (1970, Ch. 22). With the help of the relation (3.11) this leads to an approximation of the mean function m_Q for the logistic model by a 'scaled' probit model

$$\begin{aligned} m_Q(Z_i, W_i; \beta) &\approx \int_{-\infty}^{+\infty} \frac{1}{\tau_i} \Phi\left(\frac{1}{c}(\beta_0 + Z_i'\beta_Z + \beta_X x_i)\right) \phi\left(\frac{x_i - \mu_i}{\tau_i}\right) dx_i \\ &= \Phi\left(\frac{1}{c}\left(\frac{\beta_0 + Z_i'\beta_Z + \beta_X \mu_i}{(1 + c^{-2}\beta_X^2\tau_i^2)^{\frac{1}{2}}}\right)\right) =: \pi_i^a. \end{aligned}$$

The variance function v_Q of the observed model is thus approximated by $v_Q(Z_i, W_i; \beta) \approx \pi_i^a(\beta)(1 - \pi_i^a(\beta))$. Just like in the probit case but merely approximately we find for the conditional distribution

$$Y_i \mid Z_i, W_i \overset{a}{\sim} B\left(1, \pi_i^a(\beta)\right)$$

3.4 Ordinal regression models

Ordinal regression models with measurement error in the covariates were examined by Tosteson et al. (1989) who supposed to estimate the model parameters by adjusting the estimator that is obtained if the regression calibration method is used. We will restrict our discussion on the cumulative probit model for ordinal data and show that the results of the probit model for binary data under the assumptions (A1)–(A3) can easily be transferred to the multicategorial case.

With $Y_i^* \in \{1, \ldots, p\}$ we will denote the observed ordinal response variables that are modeled by the vector of dummy variables $Y_i = (Y_{i1}, \ldots, Y_{iq})'$ and it holds that $Y_{ir} = 1 \Leftrightarrow Y_i^* = r$ for $r = 1, \ldots, q = p-1$. The observed variables Y_i^* are categorized versions of the latent response variables ξ_i where

$$Y_i^* = r \Leftrightarrow \vartheta_{r-1} < \xi_i \leq \vartheta_r, \; r = 1, \ldots, p \; \text{ with } \; -\infty = \vartheta_0 < \ldots < \vartheta_p = \infty.$$

The latent response variables ξ_i are related to the true covariates Z_i and X_i by

$$\xi_i = -\left(Z_i'\beta_Z + \beta_X X_i\right) + \varepsilon_i \; \text{ with } \; \varepsilon_i \sim N(0,1). \tag{3.14}$$

The vectors Y_i given the true covariates Z_i and X_i are multinominal distributed with $Y_i \mid Z_i, X_i \sim M(1, \Pi_i(\vartheta, \beta))$. The q-dimensional mean function (2.1) of the cumulative probit model is given by

$$\begin{aligned} &\mu\left(Z_i, X_i; \vartheta, \beta\right) = \Pi_i(\vartheta, \beta) = \left(\pi_{i1}(\vartheta_1, \vartheta_0, \beta), \ldots, \pi_{iq}(\vartheta_q, \vartheta_{q-1}, \beta)\right)' \\ &\text{with the elements } \pi_{ir}(\vartheta_r, \vartheta_{r-1}, \beta) \text{ for } r = 1, \ldots, q \text{ given by} \\ &\pi_{ir}(\vartheta_r, \vartheta_{r-1}, \beta) = \Phi(\vartheta_r + Z_i'\beta_Z + \beta_X X_i) - \Phi(\vartheta_{r-1} + Z_i'\beta_Z + \beta_X X_i). \end{aligned} \tag{3.15}$$

The model parameters are denoted by $\vartheta = (\vartheta_1, \ldots, \vartheta_q)'$ and $\beta = (\beta_Z', \beta_X)'$. The variance function (2.2) of the unobserved regression model is given by

$$\sigma^2\left(Z_i, X_i; \vartheta, \beta\right) = \operatorname{diag} \Pi_i(\vartheta, \beta) - \Pi_i(\vartheta, \beta)(\Pi_i(\vartheta, \beta))'.$$

To derive a model in the observable variables under the assumptions (A1)–(A3) we have to compute the conditional expectation (2.3) of the mean function (3.15), that is

$$m_Q\left(Z_i, W_i; \vartheta, \beta\right) = \mathrm{E}\left(\Pi_i(\vartheta, \beta) \mid Z_i, W_i\right).$$

The same arguments that were used to find the mean function (3.12) in the univariate case can be applied to every element of the vector m_Q. This leads to the result

$$\begin{aligned} &m_Q\left(Z_i, W_i; \vartheta, \beta\right) = \Pi_i^*(\vartheta, \beta) = \left(\pi_{i1}^*(\vartheta_1, \vartheta_0, \beta), \ldots, \pi_{iq}^*(\vartheta_q, \vartheta_{q-1}, \beta)\right)' \\ &\text{with the elements } \pi_{ir}^*(\vartheta_r, \vartheta_{r-1}, \beta) \text{ for } r = 1, \ldots, q \text{ given by} \\ &\pi_{ir}^*(\vartheta_r, \vartheta_{r-1}, \beta) = \Phi\left(\frac{\vartheta_r + Z_i'\beta_Z + \beta_X \mu_i}{(1 + \beta_X^2 \tau_i^2)^{\frac{1}{2}}}\right) - \Phi\left(\frac{\vartheta_{r-1} + Z_i'\beta_Z + \beta_X \mu_i}{(1 + \beta_X^2 \tau_i^2)^{\frac{1}{2}}}\right). \end{aligned} \tag{3.16}$$

The variance function (2.4) of that model is just given by

$$v_Q\left(Z_i, W_i; \vartheta, \beta\right) \;\; = \;\; \operatorname{diag} \Pi_i^*(\vartheta, \beta) - \Pi_i^*(\vartheta, \beta)(\Pi_i^*(\vartheta, \beta))'.$$

The vectors Y_i given Z_i and W_i follow a multinomial distribution and it holds that $Y_i \mid Z_i, W_i \sim M(1, \Pi_i^*(\vartheta, \beta))$ with the probability vector $\Pi_i^*(\vartheta, \beta)$ given in (3.16).

4. Conclusion

Quasi-likelihood models offer an useful method to analyze nonlinear regression models with measurement error in the covariates. Provided additional information on the error process is given an heteroscedastic variance structure of the measurement errors can be embedded into the models as well. In this approach the latent regressor variables are treated as stochastic variables following a normal distribution. Even if mandatory this assumption may not be fulfilled for some applications and one way to consider this would be a straightforward extension to the case of a mixture of normal distributions.

References

1. Armstrong, B. (1985). Measurement error in the generalized linear model. *Communications in Statistics.* **14**, 529-544.
2. Breslow, N. (1990). Tests of hypotheses in overdispersed Poisson regression and other quasi-likelihood models. *Journal of the American Statistical Association.* **85**, 565-571.
3. Carroll, R.J., Ruppert, D. and Stefanski, L.A. (1995). *Measurement Error in Nonlinear Models.* Chapman and Hall, London.
4. Carroll, R.J. and Stefanski, L.A. (1990). Approximate quasilikelihood estimation in models with surrogate predictors. *Journal of the American Statistical Association.* **85**, 652-663.
5. Cheng, C.L. and Schneeweiß, H. (1998). Polynomial regression with errors in the variables. To appear in *Journal of the Royal Statistical Society B.*
6. Crouch, E.A.C. and Spiegelman, D. (1990). The evaluation of integrals of the form $\int_{-\infty}^{+\infty} f(t)exp(-t^2)dt$: application to logistic-normal models. *Journal of the American Statistical Association.* **85**, 464-469.
7. Eckert, R.S., Carroll, R.J. and Wang, N. (1997). Transformations to additivity in measurement error models. *Biometrics.* **53**, 262-272.
8. Johnson, N.L. and Kotz, S. (1970). *Continuous univariate distributions - 2.* John Wiley, New York.
9. Küchenhoff, H. and Carroll, R. J. (1997). Segmented regression with errors in predictors: semi-parametric and parametric methods. *Statistics in Medicine.* **16**, 169-188.
10. Liang, K. Y. and Liu, X. (1991). Estimating equations in generalized linear models with measurement error. In *Estimating Functions.* V.P. Godambe (ed.). Oxford University Press, New York.
11. Liu, Q. and Pierce D.A. (1994). A note on Gauss-Hermite quadrature. *Biometrika.* **81**, 624-629.
12. McCullagh, P. (1991). Quasi-likelihood and estimating functions. in *Statistical Theory and Modelling,* D.V. Hinkley, N. Reid and E.J. Snell (eds.). Chapman and Hall, London.
13. Moon, M.S. and Gunst, R.F. (1995) Polynomial measurement error modelling. *Computational Statistics & Data Analysis.* **19**, 1-21.
14. Rosner, B., Willett, W.C. and Spiegelman, D. (1989). Correction of logistic regression relative risk estimates and confidence intervals for systematic within-person measurement error. *Statistics in Medicine.* **8**, 1051-1069.

15. Schafer, D.W. (1993). Likelihood analysis for probit regression with measurement error. *Biometrika.* **80**, 899-904.
16. Schafer, D.W. and Purdy, K.G. (1996). Likelihood analysis for errors-in-variable regression with replicate measurements.
17. Schneeweiß, H. and Mittag, H.J. (1986). *Lineare Modelle mit fehlerbehafteten Daten.* Physica–Verlag, Heidelberg.
18. Stefanski, L.A. (1985). The effect of measurement error on parameter estimation. *Biometrika.* **72**, 583-592.
19. Thamerus, M. (1997). Modelling Count Data with Heteroscedastic Measurement Error in the Covariates. *Discussion Paper 58, SFB 386.* Ludwig-Maximilians-Universität München.
20. Tosteson, T.D., Stefanski, L.A. and Schafer, D.W. (1989). A measurement error model for binary and ordinal regression. *Statistics in Medicine.* **8**, 1139-1147.

ML Estimation from Binomial Data with Misclassifications

A Comparison: Internal Validation versus Repeated Measurements

Gerhard Schuster

Department of Statistics, Ludwig-Maximilians-Universität München, Germany

Summary. Tenenbein (1970) presented a double sampling scheme to estimate the proportion parameter of binomial data in presence of misclassification. In the context of measurement error models this strategy is known as the internal validation method. A second broad strategy is the use of repeated measurements. We show how to apply this strategy for the estimation of a binomial proportion parameter and try to answer the question which method should be preferred by comparing the asymptotic variances of the estimators.

1. Introduction

Our objective is to estimate a binomial proportion parameter. If the sample units can be measured without misclassification the well-known binomial model, which we will call the simple model (SM), can be used.

Table 1.1. Notation for the SM

	classification		
	$+$	$-$	$\sum$
cell probabilities	p	q	1
cell counts	s_1	s_2	n_S

The ML estimate $\hat{p}_S$ of p is given by the relative frequency of the corresponding cell; i.e.: $\hat{p}_S = s_1/n_S$.

If a measurement can misclassify units, there are two kinds of misclassification that have to be distinguished. Firstly a unit which in reality belongs to the negative category can be misclassified as belonging to the positive category. Let a denote this misclassification probability; i.e.: $a = \mathbb{P}(''+''|-)$. The second kind of misclassification is that a unit which in reality belongs to the positive category can be misclassified. The probability for this is denoted with b; i.e.: $b = \mathbb{P}(''-''|+)$.
Bross (1954) has shown, that under misclassification the sample proportion

is a biased estimate of the parameter p and the bias may be substantial.

Suppose we have an exact and a fallible measurement. The exact measurement is an expensive procedure which is subject to no misclassification, whereas the fallible measurement is a relatively inexpensive procedure which tends to misclassify units. If an exact measurement is available, we can ignore the fallible measurement and use the SM to estimate p. But if the exact measurement is very expensive and/or the misclassification probabilities of the fallible measurement are small, Tenenbein (1970) suggested to use a double sampling scheme which we will call the internal validation model (VM).

Table 1.2. Notation for the VM

	classification by one exact and one fallible measurement					classification by one fallible measurement		
	+"+"	+"−"	−"+"	−"−"	Σ	"+"	"−"	Σ
cell probabilities	$p(1-b)$	pb	qa	$q(1-a)$	1	π	$\bar{\pi}$	1
cell counts	v_1	v_2	v_3	v_4	n_{V1}	v_5	v_6	n_{V2}

$$\text{with} \quad \pi = p(1-b) + qa$$
$$\bar{\pi} = pb + q(1-a)$$

First a random sample of $n_{V1} + n_{V2}$ units is drawn from the population of interest. Then a random subsample of n_{V1} units is drawn from the main sample. Each of these n_{V1} units are classified by the exact as well as by the fallible measurement. The remaining n_{V2} units are classified only by the fallible measurement. In Section 2 we present formulas for the ML estimate $\hat{p}_V$ of p and its asymptotic variance which have been derived by Tenenbein (1970).

As an alternative to the VM we will consider replications of the fallible measurement. This leads us to the repeated measurements model (RM).

As in the VM, in a first step a random sample of $n_{R1} + n_{R2}$ units is drawn from the population of interest. In a second step a random subsample of n_{R1} units is drawn from the main sample. Now each of these n_{R1} units are measured three times by the fallible classifier.[1] The remaining n_{R2} units are again classified by using the fallible measurement once. We have to require

[1] At least three fallible measurements are necessary to make the model identifiable.

Table 1.3. Notation for the RM

	classification by three fallible measurements					classification by one fallible measurement		
	three times "+"	twice "+" and once "−"	twice "−" and once "+"	three times "−"	Σ	"+"	"−"	Σ
cell probabilities	ϖ_1	ϖ_2	ϖ_3	ϖ_4	1	π	$\bar{\pi}$	1
cell counts	r_1	r_2	r_3	r_4	n_{R1}	r_5	r_6	n_{R2}

$$\text{with} \quad \begin{aligned} \varpi_1 &= p(1-b)^3 + qa^3 \\ \varpi_2 &= 3pb(1-b)^2 + 3qa^2(1-a) \\ \varpi_3 &= 3pb^2(1-b) + 3qa(1-a)^2 \\ \varpi_4 &= pb^3 + q(1-a)^3 \end{aligned}$$

one basic assumption:

$$\begin{aligned} \mathbb{P}(\Diamond, \triangle, \nabla | \Box) &= \mathbb{P}(\Diamond|\Box)\, \mathbb{P}(\triangle|\Box)\, \mathbb{P}(\nabla|\Box) \\ & \Diamond, \triangle, \nabla \in \{"+", "-"\}, \quad \Box \in \{+,-\} \end{aligned} \tag{1.1}$$

which means that the fallible measurements are conditionally independent given the true status.
Here is one example of how to calculate the cell probabilities. The probability of the first cell is given by

$$\begin{aligned} \mathbb{P}("+","+","+") &= \mathbb{P}("+","+","+"|+)\mathbb{P}(+) \\ &\quad + \mathbb{P}("+","+","+"|-)\mathbb{P}(-) \\ &\overset{(1)}{=} \left(\mathbb{P}("+"|+)\right)^3 \mathbb{P}(+) \;+\; \left(\mathbb{P}("+"|-)\right)^3 \mathbb{P}(-) \\ &= p(1-b)^3 + qa^3 = \varpi_1 \end{aligned}$$

In Section 3 we show how the *EM* algorithm can be applied to obtain the ML estimate $\hat{p}_R$ of p for the RM and we derive a formula for its asymptotic variance.
In Section 4 we compare the (asymptotic) variances of the three models under the assumption that the sampling costs for each model are the same.

2. Internal Validation Method

Tenenbein (1970) has shown that for the VM the ML estimates of p, a and b are given by

$$\hat{p}_V = \frac{v_2}{v_2+v_4}\cdot\frac{v_2+v_4+v_6}{n_{V1}+n_{V2}} + \frac{v_1}{v_1+v_3}\cdot\frac{v_1+v_3+v_5}{n_{V1}+n_{V2}}$$

$$\hat{a}_V = \frac{v_3}{v_1+v_3}\cdot\frac{v_1+v_3+v_5}{n_{V1}+n_{V2}}\cdot\frac{1}{1-\hat{p}_V}$$

$$\hat{b}_V = \frac{v_2}{v_2+v_4}\cdot\frac{v_2+v_4+v_6}{n_{V1}+n_{V2}}\cdot\frac{1}{\hat{p}_V} \quad .$$

The asymptotic variance of $\hat{p}_V$ is given by

$$\sigma_V^2 \doteq \frac{pq(1-K)}{n_{V1}} + \frac{pqK}{n_{V1}+n_{V2}} \quad \text{with} \quad K = \frac{pq(1-a-b)^2}{\pi\bar{\pi}} \tag{2.1}$$

Note that the estimates are not defined for $v_1+v_3=0$ or $v_2+v_4=0$, see Tenenbein (1970).

3. Repeated Measurements Method

Table 3.1. Notation for the unobservable data and the cell probabilities for the RM with an exact measurement

	classification by three fallible measurements and one exact measurement				
	three times "+" and		twice "+", once "−" and		
	+	−	+	−	
cell probabilities	$p(1-b)^3$	qa^3	$3pb(1-b)^2$	$3qa^2(1-a)$	
cell counts	e_1	$\bar{e}_1$	e_2	$\bar{e}_2$	
	twice "−", once "+" and		three times "−" and		$\sum$
	+	−	+	−	
cell probabilities	$3pb^2(1-b)$	$3qa(1-a)^2$	pb^3	$q(1-a)^3$	1
cell counts	e_3	$\bar{e}_3$	e_4	$\bar{e}_4$	n_{R1}
	classification by one fallible measurement and one exact measurement				
	+ "+"	− "+"	+ "−"	− "−"	$\sum$
cell probabilities	$p(1-b)$	qa	pb	$q(1-a)$	1
cell counts	e_5	$\bar{e}_5$	e_6	$\bar{e}_6$	n_{R2}

In addition to (1.1) we introduce the identifiability assumption

$$1 - a - b > 0 \quad . \tag{3.1}$$

Otherwise we would obtain the same π, $\bar{\pi}$ and ϖ_i ($i = 1, \ldots, 4$) for p, a, b as well as for q, $1 - b$, $1 - a$. Assumption (3.1) is plausible, because the fallible measurement would not be of much practical interest, if $1 - a - b \leq 0$.

To obtain the ML estimates $\hat{p}_R$, $\hat{a}_R$ and $\hat{b}_R$ of p, a and b we apply the *EM* algorithm (see Dempster, Laird, and Rubin (1977)). In order to apply the *EM* algorithm, we imagine that in addition to the fallible measurements all the sample units are classified by an exact measurement (see Table 3.1).

These "e"-data in Table 3.1 is unobservable. We can only observe the "r"-data from Table 1.3. Between the "e"-data and the "r"-data we have the relation

$$e_i + \bar{e}_i = r_i \qquad (i = 1, \ldots, 6) \quad .$$

In the E step the *EM* algorithm computes the expectations of the conditional distributions of the "e"-data given the "r"-data:

$$\begin{aligned}
\mathbb{E}(e_1) &= \frac{r_1 p(1-b)^3}{\varpi_1} \\
\mathbb{E}(e_2) &= \frac{3r_2 pb(1-b)^2}{\varpi_2} \\
\mathbb{E}(e_3) &= \frac{3r_3 pb^2(1-b)}{\varpi_3} \\
\mathbb{E}(e_4) &= \frac{r_4 pb^3}{\varpi_4} \\
\mathbb{E}(e_5) &= \frac{r_5 p(1-b)}{\pi} \\
\mathbb{E}(e_6) &= \frac{r_6 pb}{\bar{\pi}} \\
\mathbb{E}(\bar{e}_i) &= r_i - \mathbb{E}(e_i) \qquad (i = 1, \ldots, 6)
\end{aligned}$$

For the unknown parameters, we have to put in the estimates which are computed in the M step. The estimates of p, a and b in the M step are the ML estimates based on the "e"-data:

$$\begin{aligned}
\hat{p}_e &= \frac{\sum_{i=1}^{6} e_i}{n_{R1} + n_{R2}} \\
\hat{a}_e &= \frac{3\bar{e}_1 + 2\bar{e}_2 + \bar{e}_3 + \bar{e}_5}{3\sum_{i=1}^{4} \bar{e}_i + \bar{e}_5 + \bar{e}_6} \\
\hat{b}_e &= \frac{3e_4 + 2e_3 + e_2 + e_6}{3\sum_{i=1}^{4} e_i + e_5 + e_6}
\end{aligned}$$

For the unknown "e"-data we put in the results of the E step. The algorithm starts with the M step by using the following starting values:

$$\begin{aligned} \mathbb{E}(e_i) &= \frac{(4-i)r_i}{3} \qquad (i=1,\ldots,4) \\ \mathbb{E}(e_5) &= r_5 \\ \mathbb{E}(e_6) &= 0 \\ \mathbb{E}(\bar{e}_i) &= r_i - \mathbb{E}(e_i) \qquad (i=1,\ldots,6) \end{aligned}$$

Both steps are iterated until convergence. Finally we have to check condition (3). Let $\hat{p}_e$, $\hat{a}_e$ and $\hat{b}_e$ be now the results of the last iteration. If we obtain $1-\hat{a}_e-\hat{b}_e > 0$ the ML estimates are $\hat{p}_R = \hat{p}_e$, $\hat{a}_R = \hat{a}_e$ and $\hat{b}_R = \hat{b}_e$, otherwise they are $\hat{p}_R = 1-\hat{p}_e$, $\hat{a}_R = 1-\hat{b}_e$ and $\hat{b}_R = 1-\hat{a}_e$.

Let us have a look what will happen, if we use the *EM* algorithm in the special case of no misclassification $a=b=0$. Then of course we will obtain $r_2 = r_3 = 0$. In the first iteration the *M* step will yield:

$$\hat{p}_e = \frac{r_1 + r_5}{n_{R1} + n_{R2}} \quad \text{and} \quad \hat{a}_e = \hat{b}_e = 0$$

and the following *E* step yields:

$$\mathbb{E}(e_1) = r_1, \ \ \mathbb{E}(e_5) = r_5 \ \text{ and } \ \mathbb{E}(e_2) = \mathbb{E}(e_3) = \mathbb{E}(e_4) = \mathbb{E}(e_6) = 0$$

and we already have convergence. We would also obtain

$$\hat{p}_R = \frac{r_1 + r_5}{n_{R1} + n_{R2}} \quad ,$$

if we have classified $n_{R1} + n_{R2}$ units with one measurement subject to no misclassification. It is obvious that a second and a third measurement are in this special case clearly unnecessary.

The asymptotic variance σ_R^2 of $\hat{p}_R$ is given by the following theorem. The proof is given in the appendix.

Theorem 3.1. *In the RM the asymptotic variance of the estimate $\hat{p}_R$ is given by:*

$$\sigma_R^2 = \frac{1}{n_{R1}} \cdot \left(pq + z - \frac{3n_{R2}p^2q^2(1-a-b)^2}{(3n_{R1}+n_{R2})\pi\bar{\pi} + 2n_{R2}pq(1-a-b)^2} \right)$$

with

$$z = \frac{3(1-a-b)^2\left(pb^2(1-b)^2 + qa^2(1-a)^2\right) + 4\left(pb^3(1-b)^3 + qa^3(1-a)^3\right)}{(1-a-b)^6}$$

In the special case of $a=b=0$ we have seen that $\hat{p}_R$ is equivalent to $\hat{p}_S$, if $n_S = n_{R1} + n_{R2}$. Therefore we must obtain

$$\sigma_R^2 = \frac{pq}{n_{R1} + n_{R2}}$$

for this special case, which, in fact, we get after some calculation.

4. Comparison

Let us assume that the cost for one exact measurement is c_e. For one fallible measurement let the cost be c_f. We define the relative cost $c = c_e/c_f > 1$. We further assume that we have money for n fallible measurements. Therefore we have the following restrictions on the subsample sizes:

$$\begin{aligned} c \cdot n_S &= n && \text{for the SM} \\ (c+1)n_{V1} + n_{V2} &= n && \text{for the VM} \\ 3n_{R1} + n_{R2} &= n && \text{for the RM} \end{aligned}$$

Under these restrictions and $n_{V1}, n_{V2}, n_{R1}, n_{R2} \geq 0$ we will now choose optimal subsample sizes in each model separately in order to obtain minimal variances.

For the VM this has been done by Tenenbein (1970) The optimal subsample sizes are

$$\tilde{n}_{V1} = n \cdot \frac{t_V}{ct_V + 1} \qquad \text{and} \qquad \tilde{n}_{V2} = n - \tilde{n}_{V1}(c+1)$$

$$\text{with} \qquad t_V = \min\left\{\sqrt{(1-K)/(cK)}, 1\right\} \qquad \text{and } K \text{ as in (2.1)}$$

Theorem 4.1. *The optimal subsample sizes $\tilde{n}_{R1}$ and $\tilde{n}_{R2}$ for the RM are given by*

$$\tilde{n}_{R1} = \frac{n - \tilde{n}_{R2}}{3} \qquad \textit{and} \qquad \tilde{n}_{R2} = n \cdot t_R \tag{4.1}$$

$$\textit{with} \qquad t_R = \left\{ \begin{array}{lll} \max\{u_1, 0\} & \textit{if} & 2z - pq = 0 \\ \max\{u_2, 0\} & \textit{if} & 2z - pq \neq 0 \end{array} \right\} \qquad \textit{and}$$

$$\begin{aligned} u_1 &= \frac{1}{4} - \frac{pb(1-b) + qa(1-a)}{4pq(1-a-b)^2} \\ u_2 &= -\frac{2\pi\bar{\pi}(pq+z)}{2pq(1-a-b)^2(2z-pq)} \\ &\quad + \frac{\sqrt{6\pi\bar{\pi}pq\left[3pq(1-a-b)^2 z + (pb(1-b) + qa(1-a))(pq+z)\right]}}{2pq(1-a-b)^2(2z-pq)} \end{aligned}$$

The proof of theorem 4.1 is given in the appendix.

The question is now how to optimize the subsample sizes without knowing the parameters. In the VM the optimal sizes depend only on K. Tenenbein (1971) suggests to take a pilot sample in order to estimate K. For the RM we suggest (except one expects that $a+b$ is very small) to take a sample of at least $n/4$ units and measure every unit three times. Then we get estimates for p, a and b with the *EM* algorithm. By putting these estimates into (4.1) we obtain $\hat{\hat{n}}_{R1}$ and $\hat{\hat{n}}_{R2}$. In a second step we take $\hat{\hat{n}}_{R1} - n/4$ (hopefully $\hat{\hat{n}}_{R1} - n/4$ is not negative) additional units to measure them three times. $\hat{\hat{n}}_{R2}$ units will be measured once.

Putting the corresponding optimal subsample sizes into σ_R^2, σ_V^2 and σ_S^2 (σ_S^2 is the variance of $\hat{p}_S$) we obtain the minimal variances

$$\begin{aligned}
\tilde{\sigma}_S^2 &= \frac{pqc}{n} \\
\tilde{\sigma}_V^2 &= \frac{pq(ct_V + 1)(1 - K + t_V K)}{nt_V} \\
\tilde{\sigma}_R^2 &= \frac{3}{n(1 - t_R)} \left(pq + z - \frac{3t_R p^2 q^2 (1 - a - b)^2}{\pi\bar{\pi} + 2t_R pq(1 - a - b)^2} \right) .
\end{aligned}$$

Note that comparison of the variances does not depend on n.

Let us have a look at the case $a = b = 0$: We obtain $\tilde{n}_{V2} = \tilde{n}_{R2} = n$ and $\tilde{n}_{V1} = \tilde{n}_{R1} = 0$. This means that in both models all the units are measured once with the inexpensive measurement. This is reasonable, because in this case the inexpensive measurement is exact. The RM and the VM are of equal quality. For the variances we obtain $\tilde{\sigma}_R^2 = \tilde{\sigma}_V^2 = pq/n$.

Note that for $\tilde{\sigma}_S^2$, $\tilde{\sigma}_V^2$ and $\tilde{\sigma}_R^2$ we have the following kind of symmetry: Taking p, a, b instead of q, b, a will yield the same formulas. Therefore it is sufficient to consider the case $p \leq 0.5$.

Figure 4.1 and Figure 4.2 show the results of the comparison of the SM, VM and RM for $p = 0.2$ and $p = 0.4$. Each Figure consists of two pictures. The lower picture results from the upper picture by a turn through 180°. Therefore the two lower pictures do not contain new information. The four bright areas in each figure are just a help for the orientation. They locate the areas where $c = 5, 10, 25, 50$.

The two dark figures in each picture are of particular interest. For all a, b and c resulting in points which are right from the two dark figures in the two upper pictures, we have $\tilde{\sigma}_R^2 < \min\{\tilde{\sigma}_V^2, \tilde{\sigma}_S^2\}$. This means that repeated measurements should be preferred. The area which is left from the two dark figures in the two upper pictures consists of all points with the coordinates a, b and c for which $\tilde{\sigma}_S^2 < \min\{\tilde{\sigma}_V^2, \tilde{\sigma}_R^2\}$. SM should be preferred. Only for a, b and c resulting in points which are between the two dark figures the VM should be used. Specially for small c the space between the two dark figures is very small.

The VM is almost always dominated. For not too high misclassification probabilities or not too small c the RM and otherwise the SM is the best model.

Fig. 4.1. Comparison of the methods for $p = 0.2$

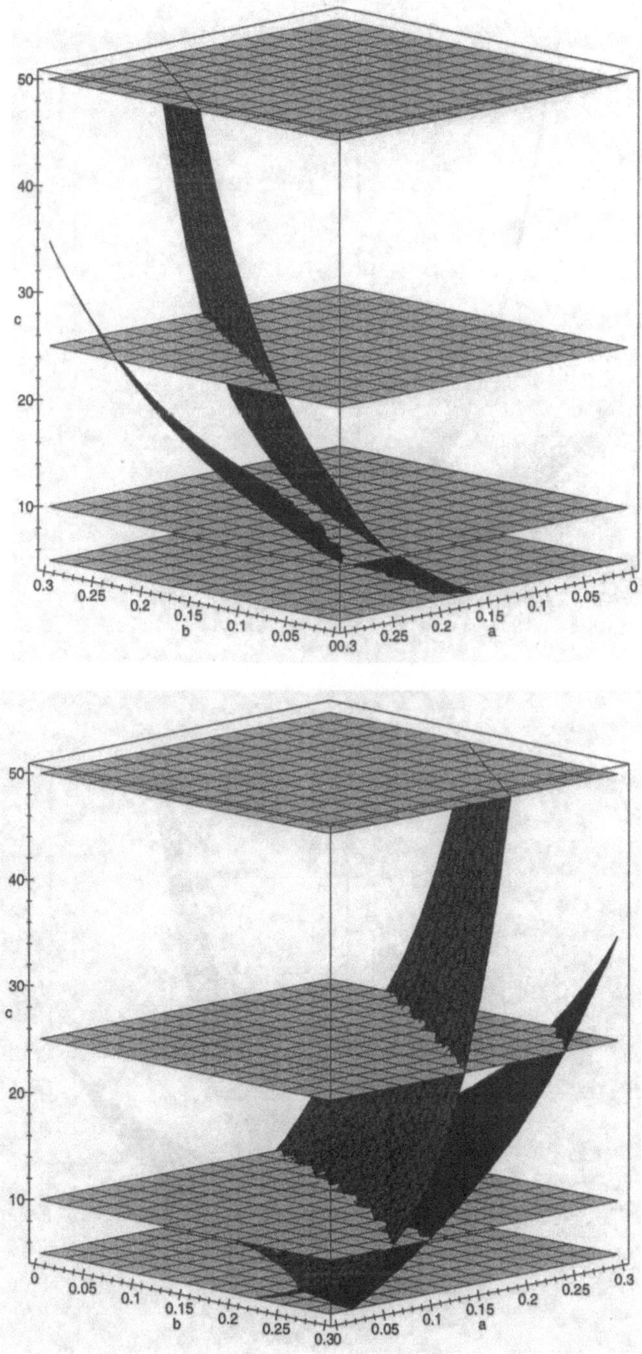

Fig. 4.2. Comparison of the methods for $p = 0.4$

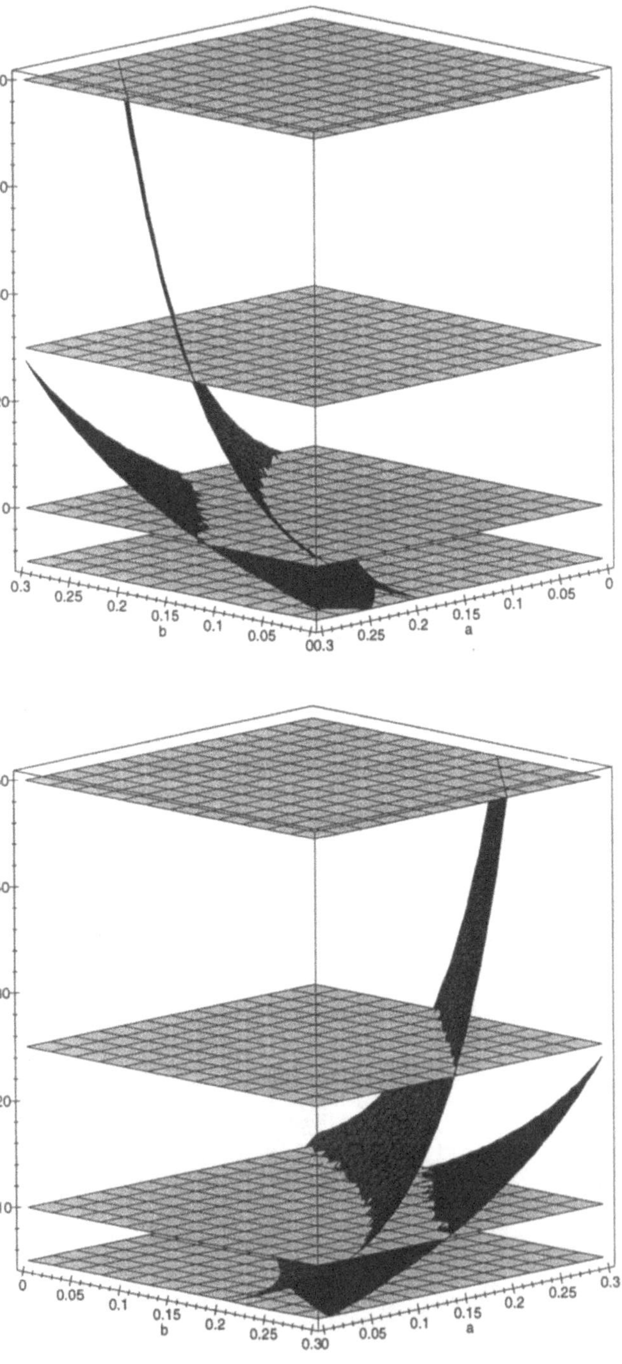

Appendix

Proof of Theorem 3.1

We have two independent distributions: a multinomial distribution,

$$(r_1, r_2, r_3, r_4) \sim M(n_{R1}; \varpi_1, \varpi_2, \varpi_3, \varpi_4)$$

and a binomial distribution,

$$r_5 \sim B(n_{R2}; \pi) \quad .$$

Therefore the logarithm of the likelihood function L is given by

$$L = \gamma + \sum_{i=1}^{4} r_i \ln \varpi_i + r_5 \ln \pi + r_6 \ln \bar{\pi} \quad ,$$

where γ is a constant, which is independent of p, a and b.

In a first step we calculate the Fisher Information matrix $\mathcal{I} = (\iota_{jl})_{1 \le j,l \le 3}$. The elements of $\mathcal{I}$ are given by

$$\iota_{11} = \mathbb{E}\left(-\frac{\partial^2 L}{\partial^2 p}\right) \qquad \iota_{22} = \mathbb{E}\left(-\frac{\partial^2 L}{\partial^2 a}\right) \qquad \iota_{33} = \mathbb{E}\left(-\frac{\partial^2 L}{\partial^2 b}\right)$$

$$\iota_{12} = \mathbb{E}\left(-\frac{\partial^2 L}{\partial p \partial a}\right) \qquad \iota_{13} = \mathbb{E}\left(-\frac{\partial^2 L}{\partial p \partial b}\right) \qquad \iota_{23} = \mathbb{E}\left(-\frac{\partial^2 L}{\partial a \partial b}\right) \quad .$$

Straightforward calculation of $\mathcal{I}$ yields

$$\mathcal{I} = \mathcal{I}_R + \frac{n_{R2}}{\pi\bar{\pi}} y y' \quad \text{with} \quad \begin{array}{rcl} y' & = & (1-a-b, q, -p) \\ \mathcal{I}_R & = & (\kappa_{jl})_{1 \le j,l \le 3} \end{array} \quad \text{and}$$

$$\begin{aligned}
\kappa_{11} &= n_{R1} \left(\frac{(b^3 - (1-a)^3)^2}{\varpi_4} + \frac{(3(1-b)b^2 - 3a(1-a)^2)^2}{\varpi_3} \right. \\
&\quad \left. + \frac{(3(1-b)^2 b - 3a^2(1-a))^2}{\varpi_2} + \frac{((1-b)^3 - a^3)^2}{\varpi_1} \right) \\
\kappa_{22} &= 3^2 q^2 n_{R1} \left(\frac{(1-a)^4}{\varpi_4} + \frac{(1-4a+3a^2)^2}{\varpi_3} + \frac{(2a-3a^2)^2}{\varpi_2} + \frac{a^4}{\varpi_1} \right) \\
\kappa_{33} &= 3^2 p^2 n_{R1} \left(\frac{b^4}{\varpi_4} + \frac{(2b-3b^2)^2}{\varpi_3} + \frac{(1-4b+3b^2)^2}{\varpi_2} + \frac{(1-b)^4}{\varpi_1} \right) \\
\kappa_{12} &= 3q n_{R1} \left(-\frac{(1-a)^2(b^3 - (1-a)^3)}{\varpi_4} \right. \\
&\quad + \frac{3(1-4a+3a^2)((1-b)b^2 - a(1-a)^2)}{\varpi_3}
\end{aligned}$$

$$+\frac{3(2a-3a^2)((1-b)^2b-a^2(1-a))}{\varpi_2}+\frac{a^2((1-b)^3-a^3)}{\varpi_1}\Bigg)$$

$$\begin{aligned}\kappa_{13} &= 3pn_{R1}\left(\frac{b^2(b^3-(1-a)^3)}{\varpi_4}+\frac{3(2b-3b^2)((1-b)b^2-a(1-a)^2)}{\varpi_3}\right.\\ &\quad+\frac{3(1-4b+3b^2)((1-b)^2b-a^2(1-a))}{\varpi_2}\\ &\quad\left.-\frac{(1-b)^2((1-b)^3-a^3)}{\varpi_1}\right)\\ \kappa_{23} &= 3^2pqn_{R1}\left(-\frac{(1-a)^2b^2}{\varpi_4}+\frac{(1-4a+3a^2)(2b-3b^2)}{\varpi_3}\right.\\ &\quad\left.+\frac{(2a-3a^2)(1-4b+3b^2)}{\varpi_2}-\frac{a^2(1-b)^2}{\varpi_1}\right)\end{aligned}$$

Note that $\mathcal{I}_R$ is, as well as $\mathcal{I}$, a symmetric matrix. In order to find the inverse of $\mathcal{I}$ (which is the asymptotic variance-covariance matrix of $(\hat{p}_R, \hat{a}_R, \hat{b}_R)$) we apply the identity (see Henderson and Searle (1981))

$$\left(\mathcal{I}_R+\frac{n_{R2}}{\pi\bar{\pi}}yy'\right)^{-1}=\mathcal{I}_R^{-1}-\frac{\frac{n_{R2}}{\pi\bar{\pi}}}{1+\frac{n_{R2}}{\pi\bar{\pi}}y'\mathcal{I}_R^{-1}y}\mathcal{I}_R^{-1}yy'\mathcal{I}_R^{-1} \tag{4.2}$$

First we have to find $\mathcal{I}_R^{-1}$. Let $\Lambda=(\lambda_{jl})_{1\le j,l\le 3}$ be a symmetric matrix with elements

$$\begin{aligned}\lambda_{11} &= \frac{3(1-a-b)^2\left(pb^2(1-b)^2+qa^2(1-a)^2\right)}{n_{R1}(1-a-b)^6}\\ &\quad+\frac{4\left(pb^3(1-b)^3+qa^3(1-a)^3\right)}{n_{R1}(1-a-b)^6}+\frac{pq}{n_{R1}}\\ \lambda_{22} &= \frac{(1-a-b)^2\left(pb^2(1-b)^2+4qa^2(1-a)^2\right)}{3n_{R1}q^2(1-a-b)^4}\\ &\quad+\frac{3\left(pb^3(1-b)^3+qa^3(1-a)^3\right)}{3n_{R1}q^2(1-a-b)^4}+\frac{a(1-a)}{3n_{R1}q}\\ \lambda_{33} &= \frac{(1-a-b)^2\left(4pb^2(1-b)^2+qa^2(1-a)^2\right)}{3n_{R1}p^2(1-a-b)^4}\\ &\quad+\frac{3\left(pb^3(1-b)^3+qa^3(1-a)^3\right)}{3n_{R1}p^2(1-a-b)^4}+\frac{b(1-b)}{3n_{R1}p}\\ \lambda_{12} &= -\frac{(1-a-b)^2\left(pb^2(1-b)^2+2qa^2(1-a)^2\right)}{n_{R1}q(1-a-b)^5}\\ &\quad-\frac{2\left(pb^3(1-b)^3+qa^3(1-a)^3\right)}{n_{R1}q(1-a-b)^5}\\ \lambda_{13} &= \frac{(1-a-b)^2\left(2pb^2(1-b)^2+qa^2(1-a)^2\right)}{n_{R1}p(1-a-b)^5}\end{aligned}$$

$$+\frac{2\left(pb^3(1-b)^3+qa^3(1-a)^3\right)}{n_{R1}p(1-a-b)^5}$$

$$\lambda_{23} = -\frac{2(1-a-b)^2\left(pb^2(1-b)^2+qa^2(1-a)^2\right)}{3n_{R1}pq(1-a-b)^4} - \frac{3\left(pb^3(1-b)^3+qa^3(1-a)^3\right)}{3n_{R1}pq(1-a-b)^4}$$

We obtain $\mathcal{I}_R \cdot \Lambda = \begin{pmatrix} 1 & 0 & 0 \\ 0 & 1 & 0 \\ 0 & 0 & 1 \end{pmatrix}$ which means $\Lambda = \mathcal{I}_R^{-1}$.
It follows from (4.2) that

$$\mathcal{I}^{-1} = \left(\mathcal{I}_R + \frac{n_{R2}}{\pi\bar{\pi}}yy'\right)^{-1}$$

$$= \frac{1}{n_{R1}}\left(n_{R1}\Lambda - \frac{3n_{R2}}{(3n_{R1}+n_{R2})\pi\bar{\pi}+2n_{R2}pq(1-a-b)^2}xx'\right)$$

$$\text{with} \quad x' = n_{R1}y'\Lambda = \left(pq(1-a-b), \frac{1}{3}a(1-a), -\frac{1}{3}b(1-b)\right)$$

The element in the first row and first column of $\mathcal{I}^{-1}$ is σ_R^2. It is obvious that $z = n_{R1}\lambda_{11} - pq$. This finishes the proof.

Proof of Theorem 4.1

We have to minimize σ_R^2 subject to the restriction $3n_{R1} + n_{R2} = n$, or equivalently $n_{R1} = (n - n_{R2})/3$. Putting the expression into σ_R^2 and setting $\partial\sigma_R^2/\partial n_{R2} = 0$ yields

$$2n_{R2}^2p^2q^2(1-a-b)^4(2z-pq) + 4n_{R2}n\pi\bar{\pi}pq(1-a-b)^2(pq+z)$$
$$+n^2\pi\bar{\pi}\left(\pi\bar{\pi}(pq+z) - 3p^2q^2(1-a-b)^2\right) = 0$$

For the case $2z - pq = 0$ we obtain:

$$n_{R2} = \frac{n}{4}\left(1 - \frac{pb(1-b)+qa(1-a)}{pq(1-a-b)^2}\right)$$

Because of $n_{R2} \geq 0$ we have to choose $\tilde{n}_{R2} = n \cdot \max\{u_1, 0\}$.

For the case $2z - pq \neq 0$ we solve the quadratic equation. Take now into account that $0 \leq n_{R2} \leq n$. Therefore we obtain: $\tilde{n}_{R2} = n \cdot \max\{u_2, 0\}$.

References

1. Bross I. (1954). Misclassification in 2×2 Tables, *Biometrics*, **10**, 478-486

2. Dempster A. P., Laird N. M. and Rubin D. B. (1977): Maximum Likelihood from Incomplete Data via the EM Algorithm, *Journal of the Royal Statistical Society B*, **39**, 1-38
3. Henderson H. V. and Searle S. R. (1981). On deriving the Inverse of a Sum of Matrices, *SIAM Review*, **23**, No. 1, 53-60
4. Tenenbein A. (1970). A Double Sampling Scheme for Estimating from Binomial Data with Misclassifications, *Journal of the American Statistical Association*, **65**, 1350-1361
5. Tenenbein A. (1971). A Double Sampling Scheme for Estimating from Binomial Data with Misclassifications: Sample Size Determination, *Biometrics*, **27**, 935-944

The Indeterminacy of Latent Variable Models

David J. Bartholomew

London School of Economics and Political Science, U. K.

1. The background

It is well-known that the standard normal factor model is indeterminate in the sense that linear rotations in the factor space leave the covariance matrix unchanged. Thus if the model is written

$$\mathbf{x} = \mu + \Lambda\mathbf{y} + \mathbf{e} \tag{1.1}$$

where $\mathbf{y} \frown N_q(\mathbf{0}, \mathbf{I})$, $\mathbf{e} \frown N_p(\mathbf{0}, \Psi)$ where Ψ is diagonal and $\mathbf{E}(\mathbf{e}\ \mathbf{y}') = \mathbf{0}$ then this model is indistinguishable from one with factors $\mathbf{z} = \mathbf{My}$ and loading matrix $\Lambda^* = \Lambda\mathbf{M}$ where $\mathbf{M}$ is a non-singular orthogonal matrix with $\mathbf{MM}' = \mathbf{I}$. In both cases the covariance matrix is $\Sigma = \Lambda\Lambda' + \Psi$.

It appears to be less well-known that this indeterminacy is common to a much wider class of latent variable model and that it is also a special case of a broader kind of indeterminacy. To illustrate this point at a very elementary level, suppose we make a non-linear transformation to new latent variables

$$z_i = e^{y_i} \qquad (i = 1, 2, \ldots, q). \tag{1.2}$$

The model may now be written

$$\mathbf{x} = \mu + \Lambda \log \mathbf{z} + \mathbf{e} \tag{1.3}$$

where $\log \mathbf{z}$ means $(\log z_1, \log z_2, \ldots, \log z_q)$ and each z now has a lognormal distribution. The vector $\mathbf{x}$ has the same covariance matrix as before but is now expressed in terms of lognormal latent variables. This seemingly trivial change actually has far-reaching implications which only become apparent when we view the problem in a broader context.

2. Indeterminacy in general

A latent variable model is simply a statistical model in which some of the random variables are unobservable — either in principle or in practice. Let us suppose that there are p observable (or manifest) variables denoted by $\mathbf{x}$ and q latent variables (or factors) denoted by $\mathbf{y}$. A latent variable model will therefore be a complete or partial specification of the joint probability distribution $f(\mathbf{x}, \mathbf{y})$. (This may be interpreted as a density or probability mass function according as the variables are continuous or categorical. We shall treat them as continuous without losing any generality.) Since only $\mathbf{x}$ can be observed, all inferences must be via the marginal distribution

$$\begin{aligned} f(\mathbf{x}) &= \int f(\mathbf{x},\mathbf{y})\,\mathrm{d}\mathbf{y} \\ &= \int f(\mathbf{y})\mathrm{f}(\mathbf{x} \mid \mathbf{y})\,\mathrm{d}\mathbf{y}. \end{aligned} \tag{2.1}$$

A latent variable model involves the specification of $f(\mathbf{y})$, the prior distribution, and the conditional distribution, $f(\mathbf{x}|\mathbf{y})$. The latter is simplified by introducing the postulate of conditional (or local) independence. This arises from the fact that if the dependencies among the x's arise wholly from the y's then if the y's are held constant the dependencies will be removed. Since the number of latent variables necessary to achieve this will usually be unknown, we merely require that the factorization

$$f(\mathbf{x} \mid \mathbf{y}) = \prod_{\mathrm{i}=1}^{\mathrm{p}} \mathrm{f_i}(\mathrm{x_i} \mid \mathbf{y}) \tag{2.2}$$

be possible for some $q < p$. For any latent variable model we therefore have that

$$f(\mathbf{x}) = \int \mathrm{f}(\mathbf{y}) \prod_{\mathrm{i}=1}^{\mathrm{p}} \mathrm{f_i}(\mathrm{x_i} \mid \mathbf{y})\,\mathrm{d}\mathbf{y} \tag{2.3}$$

for some q.

The normal linear model introduced in (1.1) is a special case as can easily be seen from the fact that it assigns standard normal distributions to the y's and has

$$\mathbf{x} \mid \mathbf{y} \frown \mathrm{N_p}(\mu + \Lambda\mathbf{y},\, \Psi). \tag{2.4}$$

We have already seen that this model is not unique because by transforming $\mathbf{y}$ we arrived at a second model with the same covariance matrix.

Within this general framework we now note that two models are empirically indistinguishable if and only if they lead to the same $f(\mathbf{x})$. The fit of any model is to be judged by how close the observed distribution of $\mathbf{x}$ is to $f(\mathbf{x})$. All models with the same $f(\mathbf{x})$ will thus fit equally well.

The general form of indeterminacy to which we referred in Section 1 arises from the fact that any transformation $\mathbf{y} \to \mathbf{z}$ in (2.1) leaves $f(\mathbf{x})$ unchanged since, mathematically speaking, it is merely a change of variable in the integral. Yet, substantively, each such transformation leads to a different prior distribution and a different form for the regression of $\mathbf{x}$ on $\mathbf{y}$. It would therefore appear that there can be no empirical justification for any inference which is not invariant under arbitrary transformations. It is clear then, that if some models are to have a preferred status,the selection will have to be made them on substantive or structural grounds.

3. Rotation indeterminacy

One particular type of transformation has figured prominently in the literature of factor analysis and this goes under the name of orthogonal rotation. This arises when the transformation is a linear orthogonal transformation. We illustrated this for the normal linear factor model in Section 1, remarking that it left the covariance matrix unchanged. In fact we can make the stronger statement that it leaves the joint distribution of **x** unchanged because if **y** $\frown N_q(\mathbf{0}, \mathbf{I})$ then $\mathbf{z} \frown N_q(\mathbf{0}, \mathbf{I})$ and we know that the multivariate normal distribution of **x** depends on the parameters only through the covariance matrix. All models generated by such transformations are therefore equivalent in the sense that they lead to the same joint distribution of observables . The practice of rotation in factor analysis has been to select rotations which lead to easily interpretable factors.

The next thing to notice is that rotational indeterminacy is not confined to the linear factor model. If we consider the wider class of models in which the conditional distribution of x_i |**y** belongs to the exponential family with distribution

$$f_i(x_i \mid \mathbf{y}) = \mathrm{F_i(x_i)G_i}(\theta_\mathrm{i})\, \mathrm{e}^{\theta_\mathrm{i} \mathrm{u_i(x_i)}} \qquad (\mathrm{i} = 1, 2, \ldots .\mathrm{p}) \tag{3.1}$$

where

$$\theta_i = \alpha_{i0} + \alpha_{i1} y_1 + \ldots + \alpha_{iq} y_q$$

a similar result follows. Any linear transformation of **y** leaves the joint prior distribution of **y** the same and preserves the linearity of θ_i. The normal model is, of course, included here because the normal distribution is a member of the exponential family.

The reasons for using this family were given in Bartholomew (1984, 1987) and, more recently in Bartholomew (1997). For our present purpose we need to know that for models of this class the posterior distribution of **y** given **x** depends on **x** only through the q functions

$$\mathbf{X} = \mathbf{A}\mathbf{u} \tag{3.2}$$

where $\mathbf{A} = \{\alpha_{ij}\}$ and $\mathbf{u}' = (u_1(x_1), u_2(x_2), \ldots, u_p(x_p))$. The X's, therefore, contain all the information in the x's about the y's. These have been called *components* because, for purposes of interpretation, they function in much the same way as principal components. In the case of the normal distribution $u_i(x_i) = x_i/\sigma_i$ so the components may then be written, using the notation of Section 1, as

$$\mathbf{X} = \Lambda' \Psi^{-\frac{1}{2}} \mathbf{x}. \tag{3.3}$$

Another important case is when all of the x's are binary. We may then suppose the conditional distribution of x_i given **y** to be a Bernoulli random variable with

$$\Pr\{x_i = 1 \mid \mathrm{y}\} = \pi_\mathrm{i}(\mathrm{y}), \ \Pr\{\mathrm{x_i} = 0 \mid \mathrm{y}\} = 1 - \pi_\mathrm{i}(\mathrm{y}). \tag{3.4}$$

The Bernoulli distribution is also a member of the exponential family and the linear model then takes the form

$$\mathrm{logit}\pi_i(y) = \alpha_{i0} + \alpha_{i1}y_1 + \ldots + \alpha_{iq}y_q \quad (i = 1, 2, \ldots, p). \tag{3.5}$$

This is called the logit/probit model. The components in this case are

$$\mathbf{X} = \mathbf{A}'\mathbf{x} \tag{3.6}$$

where $\mathbf{A} = \{\alpha_{ij}\}$.

All of the models in this class are subject to the same rotational indeterminacy and the question to which we now turn is whether, among the infinite set of rotations, there is one which can claim any special status. Another way of putting the question is to ask; "What constraints might it be reasonable to impose in order to render the model unique?"

4. Orthogonality constraints

There are a number of approaches which all lead to what we shall call an orthogonality constraint. We shall motivate these by considering first the normal model. In this case, the method of maximum likelihood used for estimating the parameters provides the unique solution for which $\Lambda'\Psi^{-1}\Lambda$ is diagonal. This constraint arises naturally out of the mathematics of the maximization but it also possesses two further properties of wider relevance. First, it ensures that when $\mathbf{x}$ is given, the y's are independent (see Bartholomew (1987)). This means that measures of precision (or reliability) based on such things as $\mathrm{var}(y_i \,|\mathbf{x})$ can be used independently. Secondly, the components of (3.3) are uncorrelated. The sufficiency property implies that the components are proxies for the underlying latent variables and are therefore easier to interpret if they are uncorrelated.

The constraint that $\Lambda'\Psi^{-1}\Lambda$ be diagonal is an example of what we shall call an orthogonality constraint.

Orthogonality constraints are also linked with what is known as simple structure. This term is used for the situation where each factor loads on a subset of the manifest variables and where the subsets are non-overlapping. In the extreme case the loading matrix will have a form like that illustrated in (4.1) below.

$$\Lambda = \begin{bmatrix} + & 0 & 0 \\ + & 0 & 0 \\ 0 & + & 0 \\ 0 & + & 0 \\ 0 & + & 0 \\ 0 & 0 & + \end{bmatrix} \tag{4.1}$$

where + denotes a non-zero loading. We note that for such a matrix $\Lambda'\mathbf{D}\Lambda$ is diagonal when $\mathbf{D}$ is diagonal. The converse does not hold because an orthogonality condition does not ensure simple structure but the association of simple structure with an orthogonality condition does give such solutions particular interest.

5. Obtaining a rotation to satisfy a given orthogonality constraint

Suppose that we have a $p \times q$ matrix $\mathbf{A}$ and wish to find an orthogonal transformation $\mathbf{A}^* = \mathbf{AM}$ such that $(\mathbf{A}^*)'\mathbf{A}^*$ is diagonal. This may be done as follows. The singular value decomposition (SVD) of $\mathbf{A}$ is

$$\mathbf{A} = \mathbf{UDV}' \tag{5.1}$$

where $\mathbf{D}$ is a diagonal matrix of singular values, $\mathbf{U}$ is a $p \times q$ matrix of eigen vectors of $\mathbf{AA}'$ corresponding to the q non-zero eigen values and $\mathbf{V}$ is an orthogonal matrix of eigen vectors of $\mathbf{AA}'$. The required matrix is then

$$\mathbf{A}^* = \mathbf{UD}. \tag{5.2}$$

This is an orthogonal rotation of $\mathbf{A}$ because $\mathbf{V}$ is an orthogonal matrix and it satisfies the diagonality requirement because

$$(\mathbf{A}^*)'\mathbf{A}^* = \mathbf{DU}'\mathbf{UD} = \mathbf{D}^2 \tag{5.3}$$

the last step being a consequence of the orthogonality of $\mathbf{U}$. We note also that

$$\mathbf{A}^*(\mathbf{A}^*)' = \mathbf{UD}^2\mathbf{U}' \tag{5.4}$$

implying that the singular values are the (positive) square roots of the eigen values of $\mathbf{A}^*\mathbf{A}^{*\prime} = \mathbf{AA}'$. This, in turn, means that $\mathbf{A}^*$ is *rotation-invariant* in the sense that its elements depend only on the matrices $\mathbf{AA}'$ and $\mathbf{A}'\mathbf{A}$ which are invariant under orthogonal rotation.

This result can now be applied to obtain rotations satisfying a given orthogonality requirement. For example, if we had an arbitrary solution Λ for a normal model and wished to rotate it so that $\Lambda'\Psi^{-1}\Lambda$ was diagonal we would choose $\mathbf{A} = \Psi^{-\frac{1}{2}}\Lambda$. The transformed loadings would then be

$$\mathbf{A}^* = \Psi^{-\frac{1}{2}}\Lambda^* = \mathbf{UD} \quad \text{or} \quad \Lambda^* = \Psi^{\frac{1}{2}}\mathbf{UD} \tag{5.5}$$

where $\mathbf{U}$ and $\mathbf{D}$ are obtained from the singular value decomposition of $\Psi^{-\frac{1}{2}}\Lambda$.

In the case of the logit/probit model the existing program, called TWOMISS, for estimating the loading imposes no constraints and hence the solution reaches an arbitrary maximum. The constraints required to make the y's independent *a posteriori* or to make the components uncorrelated could be used, but these are complicated. A much simpler constraint, which is almost equivalent and often yields something close to simple structure, is $\mathbf{A}'\mathbf{A}$ diagonal where, here, $\mathbf{A} = \{\alpha_{ij}\}$.

We illustrate the use of our result numerically using an example from Bartholomew and de Menezes (1996). Fitting a logit/probit model to a set of 4 items by maximum likelihood yielded the matrix of loadings

$$\mathbf{A} = \begin{bmatrix} -0.23 & 0.96 \\ -5.51 & 5.55 \\ 5.24 & 10.00 \\ -1.59 & -1.85 \end{bmatrix} \tag{5.6}$$

To find a transformation satisfying $\mathbf{A}'\mathbf{A}$ diagonal we need the matrices $\mathbf{U}$ and $\mathbf{D}$ of the SVD. These were obtained using S-Plus as follows.

$$\mathbf{U} = \begin{bmatrix} -0.07 & -0.07 & 0.73 & -0.68 \\ -0.31 & -0.94 & -0.11 & 0.01 \\ -0.93 & 0.30 & 0.11 & 0.19 \\ 0.19 & -0.14 & 0.66 & 0.71 \end{bmatrix} \tag{5.7}$$

and

$$\mathbf{D} = \begin{bmatrix} 11.94 & 0 \\ 0 & 7.28 \end{bmatrix} \tag{5.8}$$

from which

$$\mathbf{A}^* = \begin{bmatrix} -0.85 & -0.49 \\ -3.74 & -6.87 \\ -11.08 & 2.16 \\ 2.20 & -0.99 \end{bmatrix} \tag{5.9}$$

Apart from the changes of sign, which are arbitrary, the rotated solution is quite close to the original except that the order of the two columns has changed. Unlike the original solution this satisfies the orthogonality condition precisely.

A particularly useful feature of this analysis is that it not only provides a unique solution but it also facilitates the calculation of standard errors by Monte Carlo methods. This is only possible if the maximum likelihood estimator is unique.

References

1. Bartholomew, D. J. (1984). The foundations of factor analysis. *Biometrika*, **71**, 221-232.
2. Bartholomew, D. J. (1987). Latent Variable Models and Factor Analysis, Griffin: London and Oxford University Press: New York.
3. Bartholomew, D. J. (1997). Latent variable modeling. In *Encyclopedia of Statistical Sciences* Update Volume I. Wiley-Interscience: New York, 354-360.
4. Bartholomew D. J. and de Menezes, L. M. (1996). New developments in latent structure analysis applied to social attitudes. *J.R.Statist.Soc.*, A, **159**, 213-224.

Part II

Theoretical Econometrics

An Introduction to the Economic Study of Knowledge

Martin J. Beckmann

Department of Economics, Brown University, USA

Philosophy is expected to give answers to three basic questions: What can we know? What may we hope? What shall we do? The theory of knowledge or epistemology deals with the first of these.

But does philosophy exhaust knowledge as a subject of human inquiry? Apparently not, for other disciplines such as sociology and history have felt free to look at knowledge as well. In fact, apart from a "general sociology of knowledge" (Simmel, Mannheim) there is a more specific sociology of science (Merton, Barber, Zuckermann).

Students of intellectual history, and notably the history of science (de Solla Price, Kuhn) have closely examined how knowledge, in particular scientific knowledge, has fared historically.

Economists do not need much encouragement to take up anything as a possible subject of inquiry. Public choice, political activity, crime, marriage, fertility have all become topics in recent economics. In fact, there has been a vast expansion of subjects of interest which economists have studied (Machlup, Becker). There is, of course, no guarantee that just anything taken on for economic analysis will also yield worthwhile results. In the end the reader must decide if an "economics of knowledge" is worth the candle.

From the outset, attempts at an economics of knowledge are baffled by the vagueness of the subject. How are we even to define knowledge in economically unassailable terms? Should we make this the starting point of our inquiry in the face of dire warnings from Walter Eucken about the dangers of "Begriffsnationalökonomie" (Eucken).

A pragmatic procedure appears more promising: we shall envelope the elusive concept of knowledge by looking (casting a cold eye) at the economic activities and institutions that concern knowledge, taking the broadest possible view of what might constitute knowledge, using as a working hypothesis that

$$\text{knowledge} = \text{sets of ideas and pertinent facts}$$

admitting even idiosyncratic and erroneous ideas. For it is not the business of the economist to decide what is true or false in other fields or sciences. As the sociologist W. I. Thomas has observed in a similar context "if people believe something to be true, then for sociological purposes it is true." At the same time we should be aware of the economic consequences of falsehood and error. In the long run, economic activities based on wrong ideas should fail the market test. In fact, economic advantage is one of the main springs of the search for new knowledge.

This essay will thus comprise mainly questions an economist may ask concerning knowledge, sometimes naively. Occasional answers that are thrown in should be regarded as tentative.

If the subject of economics need be defined, we reiterate the neoclassical formula: the allocation of scarce resources towards satisfying human wants.

Among the economic activities and institutions concerning knowledge are:

1. Discovery or knowledge: *production*. This may be a chance event, a free gift of the Gods. But more often and typically it is the result of a deliberate economic activity set up to find new knowledge. This activity, research, is an obvious target for economic analysis, involving such matters as output, inputs, technology and organizations. There exist, in fact, a considerable economic literature on "R&D" e.g., (Mansfield).
2. Knowledge *processing*. This includes labeling and classification of knowledge to enable the integration of new knowledge into the body of existing knowledge, thus making knowledge cumulative. Knowledge becomes thereby a stock and not just a flow variable, capable of accumulation, that is, growth.
3. Further processing assumes the form of *criticism* and verification/falsification. The digesting and criticism of knowledge is an economic activity on the way towards its use or utilization. The nature of knowledge processing varies greatly among disciplines. It may be merely classificatory, as in some sciences like botany, zoology and chemistry, and almost automatic, or it may be intellectually challenging, determining what is important among the flood of the new matter, as in literary criticism.
4. Knowledge *distribution* through writing, selling and speaking. This is the last stage before.
5. Knowledge *consumption*, or rather knowledge use as a consumption good, (since knowledge is not used up in the consumption process) satisfying a human want "to know." For this, knowledge must enter the consumer's mind. The process of distribution involves as further activities the organization of teaching.

Knowledge distribution and even knowledge production require the embodiment of knowledge, i.e., publication in documents such as books and periodicals or in computer programs or an embodiment of as yet unpublished knowledge in persons who then act as instructors and/or researchers. In the event the reception of knowledge by the user as consumer requires also effort or labor on the part of the recipient. In the light of the cost of embodiments and of labor required by its user, the consumer must decide what is worth knowing. In this he/she may seek the advice of teachers, tutors, gurus or friends in their role as knowledge consultants. "What one should know" is in principle a difficult decision problem under uncertainty, comparable to exploration in mining and oil drilling.

While knowledge as a consumption good is valuable, notably as a contribution to our cultural life and heritage, the economically most significant uses of knowledge occur in production, not consumption. It is the application of knowledge to production technology. All efforts in applied science are ultimately directed towards the creation of new goods to satisfy human wants or towards improved methods of production for goods already known. This economic activity of knowledge production falls under the heading of research and development and assumes an ever increasing role in all modern economies. It has been an object of much economic study and will not be considered here in extenso.

The scientist, in the business of expanding knowledge and cultivating a specialty, will always want to know more. Existing knowledge serves to point out open questions in a more or less compelling way. Still, landmark discoveries will come as total surprises, lending excitement to the game of scientific discovery. As well as hunches or instinct, scientific intuition formed by experience is needed to discover results worth more than the cost. For scientific research is basically a search process which leads up many a blind alley. The able researcher is one good at avoiding (or escaping) from dead-end paths.

What should be taught to the general public, viz. school-children, from the body of known knowledge, is a decision problem handled by government bodies, (departments of education, for example) in which economic considerations appear subordinate. But surely, how much schooling is "needed" or more properly is "socially desirable" might also be looked at from a cost/benefit perspective. Is there a technically defined absolute minimum, say reading and writing, but no longer arithmetic since cheap pocket calculators are now available? How much beyond that should a rich society choose to teach us? Should hygiene, genetics, chemistry, biochemistry, sexual behavior, economic principles, be taught to all? We merely raise this question in passing.

A problem closer to the economics of science is this: How much of each specialty making up the body of a scientific discipline, like mathematics or economics, should be taught to potential scientists, i.e., to graduate students? Since there is specialization, can one safely leave out some specialties altogether which are not currently in vogue? In fact, what determines which subjects are "en courant" or not? That is a subject one may want to look at in the context of the "dynamics of knowledge specialties."

Another aspect of knowledge consumption is making new knowledge available to an interested public, not as material for school instruction but as a pure consumption good, sold through lecturing and popular writing. Scientists often take a condescending attitude to popularizers (among them journalists) while at the same time taking for granted that ample support for scientific research, especially basic research, should be forthcoming from willing taxpayers. A more rational, i.e., economically sound view would be to understand popular presentation of science as an instrument of marketing. Economic analysis should then ask to what extent or under what conditions basic scientific knowledge can thus be turned into a consumption good and hence a product of market value. For it is axiomatic that pure basic research produces nothing of much value. Basic knowledge is thus a prime example of a free public good.

In the case of applied research and development, the economic situation is entirely different. Here knowledge is not a consumption good but a factor of production or intermediate good produced for use in economic production processes. Once again, "use" does not mean being used up but keeping its stock intact. This permits the use of an item of knowledge by several economic agents simultaneously. Such common use is, in general, socially beneficial. But its exclusive use may create a private economic advantage. Paradoxically, this private benefit in the face of the social cost of excluding others, through private ownership of knowledge, has served as an important device for the development of practically useful knowledge. We have here another established subject area of economic inquiry, the economics of the patent system and of knowledge ownership in general (Edelman, Foltz).

In the case of "useless" knowledge, ownership by a private person may have intellectual snob appeal or bestow an advantage in social intercourse ("What is new?" or "Let me tell you something?") but this seems to have no great economic import.

What drives the process(es) of knowledge accumulation? In the aggregate production of pure knowledge is, of course, limited by the resources (essentially labor) that society makes available for basic research, while research and development, responding to business financing, experiences the ups and downs of the business cycle. At the level of individual branches of knowledge, disciplines, it is a question of their internal dynamics. Special fields expand and contract, old subjects are abandoned and new topics of interest are discovered and more or less aggressively cultivated, depending to some extent on "scientific entrepreneurship."

Knowledge production is driven not only by the availability of manpower and other economic resources but by the effort and engagement of the scientists as producers. This economic activity relies largely on individual choice of the levels of effort and engagement. Thus motivation is all important. Unlike other economic production activities monetary rewards are not immediate motivating forces. The mode of exchange in knowledge production is one of knowledge for prestige, that is, recognition of "priority in knowledge discovery."

The possibilities and opportunities for using prestige as a means towards further ends such as: research support and tangible monetary rewards is another subject vital to an economic understanding of knowledge.

The growth of a discipline itself can be understood only as the result of processes at the level of fields or specialties centering around topical questions. The direction that basic science takes is thus largely self-determined, while that of applied science and development responds to market forces set in motion by expected demand and costs.

The fact that applied research can have a larger immediate impact on human welfare than basic research is neatly highlighted by a remark attributed to Brillat-Savarin: "He who invents a new recipe does more for mankind's happiness than one who discovers a new star."

Return to teaching, whether of useless or of practically useful knowledge. A technical question, capable of economic analysis, concerns the organization of teaching, whether as a private activity between one tutor and one disciple, or a public or even compulsory activity. What are the advantages of class instruction and what should be a reasonable or optimal class size? Should each school offer a variety of subjects or just one in order to gain maximum advantage from specialization?

Should students be tested for success in acquiring knowledge and to what extent? Should they be tested before admission to class instruction or should admission be open to all? Testing for admission beforehand is known to have a "signaling" effect (Spence) even in the absence of subsequent testing for successful completion of a course of study. The economic value of a college education, which has been variously estimated (Stigler), may in some cases be nothing more than this "signal."

One would hope, of course, for more. That knowledge can serve as the foundation of further knowledge and in fact can create a demand for it, being addictive as a drug, is one of its intriguing economic properties. In teaching students, the educational establishment also builds a market for additional products of "higher education" and "continuing education."

Turn to another part of knowledge distribution, publishing. An efficient publishing industry is essential to scientific activity and progress (Borchard). What should be published? In principle, all pieces of new knowledge, that have passed scientific tests of validity. The decision whether some report constitutes valid new scientific knowledge that should be published as an article is made by the scientific community through peer review in the form of refereeing for recognized scientific journals. This voluntary, and usually unpaid service works well only when referees have no motives to block publication by others in order to promote their own scientific prestige and access to resources. This is a sore point in those fields where an infusion of money has threatened to commercialize scientific work. What is left of the ethos of science as an activity free from motives of envy and self-promotion while competition takes place within the rules of the game: to give credit to whom it is due, is alas, somewhat of a moot question.

We touch here on a wider problem concerning scientific prestige, its role, its acquisition and its relationship to economic rewards. While prestige may be thought of as a subject for sociologists (Goode, Hertz) it is, or should be, a scarce commodity and thus falls squarely into the realm of economic analysis. There is, essentially, a fixed total of prestige around in any particular discipline. Its allocation thus becomes a constant sum game. Any scientist's prestige is therefore subject to erosion through the appearance of newcomers to the field. Hence, unless augmented by further effort, any person's prestige suffers decline over time. Published research in book form as monographs requires either a subsidy to be secured by the author from other agencies or from own resources, or a favorable judgment by a commercial publisher concerning its profitability. While articles aim to report specialized "latest results" books aim at the presentation of a broader area of knowledge, which by the time of its appearance may be "hot off the press" but not "hot stuff" any more. The complaint that too many books are published goes back to the middle ages. In fact, there may also be too many journals publishing too many articles, for "who can read all this?". The incentive system of scientists which bases scientific prestige on publication, makes writing to publish a rewarding activity for researchers without any regard to potential readers. An economic analysis of the prestige system should take this aspect of benefit and cost to readers into account as well as look into the mechanism of starting new journals.

Citation indexes (or indices?) open a way to look at the uses of scientific products. What inferences can be drawn from these about the value or "scientific worth" of published research? Since citation may result also from the detection of a serious error, citation does not by itself measure usefulness. How important this effect is will depend on the discipline. In certain of the social sciences, what is error to some may be but a different perspective to others.

Another question to be examined concerns the expected life of articles. It has been estimated from the "Citation index" to be quite short, from about seven years for chemistry to fifteen years or so in some areas of physics (de Solla Price).

The life of scientific books on the market is often shortened by commercial considerations and many an author has found his/her works "remaindered" at a price of a dollar or less. In this way an author may acquire a substantial library consisting of multiple copies of his/her own works.

Whether scientific publications should be subsidized, or perhaps taxed, is part of the larger question concerning the financial support of scientific research in general, notably that of pure basic research, which, as noted, is a "public good." But not all public goods are also in demand.

Now the market test, whether the price that interested users are willing to pay for a book will cover its cost, comes close to the Lindahl criterion for justifying a public good, provided this test is not distorted by an expectation of the free use of the book in a library.

To encourage rapid dissemination of scientific discoveries, access to articles and books should be as cheap as possible. While authors of articles have long learned to forgo any honoraria, and are now even charged submission fees, publishers have felt free to practice monopoly pricing, driving the private possessions of scientific journals and monographs almost out of existence. This has also led to serious rationing of subscriptions by the libraries concerned.

Scientific libraries currently do not impose charges per item borrowed, but may impose flat fees over certain periods, a pricing policy that does not conflict with welfare optimization for its users.

Knowledge distribution plays an important part in the internal operation of scientific research long before knowledge sees the light of publication. In fact, interaction and exchange of ideas are essential to the creative process (Pelz and Andrews). These economies of interaction are the economic reason for the emergence of modern research institutions such as university departments and government or industrial research laboratories or institutes. For the exchange among isolated individuals by correspondence or lectures in academies is a model of the past, of the 17th and 18th century in fact, superseded by the institutions of modern knowledge production and distribution, today's "research establishment."

The accumulated products of publishing, even when technically obsolete, are preserved in libraries, another institution of the knowledge industry. By their nature libraries are faced with an ever rising demand for storage space. Libraries face two important decisions: What to acquire, (and keep) and how to provide access. The later is also a location problem. Which part of the collection of a university library should be decentralized for current use in university departments, and which should be kept centrally in the main library? Also to what extent should duplicates be held? Occasionally libraries will also sell or otherwise dispose of holdings deemed to be demanded no more. the patterns of circulation have been studied and revealed as a Markov process: the probability of a book being checked out depends on its having been demanded recently (Morse).

Turn to another institution in knowledge distribution: Congresses, conventions and symposis. These are periodic markets in the manner of trade fairs, first held in connection with feast days during the middle ages. Generally speaking, periodic fairs survive in activities which do not justify trading on a daily basis. Timing depends on demand. Once a year for big national meetings seems to be the rule nowadays, with international congresses meeting at longer intervals, while workshops and symposia on current hot topics may be called in more often.

Location is important to conventions, accessibility should be combined with attractiveness and ambiance: Why meet in Dullesville when one could go to Las Vegas? Incidentally, the meeting place most accessible to members of the American Economic Association (requiring minimum air mileage) has been calculated to be Pittsburgh, Pa. (Siegfried). Workshops for a small number of invited participants should not be sensitive to transportation cost but rather require an isolated but attractive setting, attractive to draw the participants and isolated to keep them there.

The economic value to an author of presenting or publishing a paper can only be understood in the context of markets for scientists. A scientists "quality" is identified with his/her scientific reputation and this in turn is based on previous achievement as measured by scientific publications. Of course, it is not past work as such but the promise of more to come that defines the economic value of a scientist in terms of his/her "scientific reputation."

The physicist R. Reif has said "A scientist's reputation is all he has" (Reif). A scientist's career from doctorate to research director or senior professor follows the rise of his/her record of publications and/or patents. Actually great differences exist in the organization of the science establishment between different countries. An economic question of some import is to examine, how the reward system operates to stimulate scientific productivity. Tying economic rewards too closely to scientific success is liable to upset their delicate balance: an unhurried, patient, and persistent pursuit of problem solving that constitutes scientific research at its best.

While in some ways "ignorance is bliss," science and all economic activities involving knowledge rest on the contrary position that knowledge is a good: the more of it, the better.

References

1. Barber, B. (1952). *Sciences and the Social Order.* Glencoe: Free Press.
2. Becker, Gary S. (1976). *The Economic Approach to Human Behavior.* Chicago: University of Chicago Press.
3. Brillat-Savin (1975). *Physiologist der groot.* Paris: Herman.
4. Edelman, P. E. (1915). *Inventions and Patents.* New York for Van Nostrand Co.
5. Eucken, W. (1951). *The Foundations of Economics Translation by T.W. Hutchison.* Chicago: University of Chicago Press.
6. Foltz, R. D. (1988). *Protecting Scientific Ideas and Inventories.* Boca Raton: CRC Press.
7. Goode, W. J. (1978). *The Celebration of Heroes: Prestige as a Social Control System.* Berkeley: University of California.
8. Hertz, R. (1955). *Studying Elites Using Quantitative Methods.* Thousand Oaks: Sage Publishing.
9. Kuhn, T. S. (1970). *The Structure of Scientific Revolutions.* Chicago: University of Chicago Press.
10. Machlup, F. (1980-84). *Knowledge its Creation, Distribution and Economic Significance, Vol. 1-3.* Princeton: Princeton University Press.
11. Mannheim, K. (1962). *Essays on the Sociology of Knowledge.* Edited by P. Kei-Ckeuch, New York: Oxford University Press.
12. Mansfield, E. (1968). *Individual Research and Technology Innovation.* New York: Norton.
13. Merton, R. K. (1965). *On the Shoulder of Giants.* New York: Free Press.
14. Morse, Philip (1968). *Library Effectiveness: A Systems Approach.* Cambridge: MIT Press.
15. Simmel, G. (1950) *The Sociology of George Simmel.* Edited by K. H. Wolff, Glencoe: Free Press.
16. de Solla Price, D. (1963). *Little Science Big Science.* New York: Columbia University Press.

17. de Solla Price, D. (1961). *Science since Babylon*. New Haven: Yale University Press.
18. Spence, A. Michael (1974). *Market Signaling*. Cambridge: Harvard University Press.
19. Stigler, G. (1984), *The Intellectual at the Market Place*. Cambridge: Harvard Press.
20. Stigler, G. (1957). *The Demand and Supply of his Personnel*. New York: National Business of Economic Research.
21. Thomas, W. I. (1966). *Approaches to Social Theory*. S. Lindenberg, J.S. Coleman, S. Novak, eds., New York: Russell Sage Foundation, 1966.
22. Reif, R. (1960). *"The Competitive World of the Pure Scientist."* Science, AAAS Washington.
23. Pelz, Donald Campbell and Frank M. Andrews (1976). *Scientists in Organizations: Productive Climates for Research*. Ann Arbor: University of Michigan.
24. Zuckerman, H. (1977). *Scientific Elite: Nobel Laureates in the U.S.*. New York: Free Press.

Potentials and Limitations of Econometric Forecast and Simulation Models

Gerd Ronning *

Universität Tübingen, Germany

1. Introductory Remarks

Formal methods and models have become an integrated part of social sciences and in particular of economics. The availability of empirical data and the data processing capacity of computers have indeed created demand for quantitative analysis which in former times had been done mostly in a qualitative manner. In this paper I give an overview about different approaches to modelling and empirically analysing economies starting from early approaches of the Cowles type which were first discussed in the 50's. I also treat large scale models which have been developped in the 60's and 70's and which were and still are used mainly for forecasting. However during the last two decades two types of quantitative models have become important which are drastically differerent in their approaches compared to econometric models: One is the "Real Business Cycle" (RBC) approach which is based mainly on macroeconomic theory and the other is the "Computational General Equilibrium (CGE) approach which starts from microeconomics. I shortly describe some recent developments in economics which were at least partly responsible for these two new classes of models which could be characterized as *empirical models without data*[1] since there is no longer need for a large sample, i.e. a long time series. For economies which have undergone a radical change such as most Eastern-European countries this is the only way to anlyse formally the new structure of the economy and to forecast the future development although equilibrium models in particular may be not the most adequate way of describing the present structure of these economies. An effort should therefore be made to adapt for the still ongoing structural change.

The exposition of this paper is rather informal and disregards the technicalities of the different approaches. The main aim of the paper is to point

---

* Critical comments by a referee on an earlier version were very helpful and are gratefully acknowledged. The paper has been presented at the conference "Sustainability Analysis of Social Systems - The Use of Forecasting and Simulation Models" at Ljubljana, March 1995.

[1] In an earlier version of this paper I used the term "econometric models without data" to indicate that I consider these two types to belong to a (very broadly defined) family of econometric models which however does not use statistical estimation or hypothesis testing. See also the discussion about 'econometrics' in RBC and CGE models by Kydland and Prescott (1995 p. 188-191)

out that econometricians should no longer disregard these new approaches which are not econometrics in the classical sense.

2. Classical Econometric Models

2.1 Early Approaches (Cowles Type)

The first econometric models that have been developped by the members of the Cowles commission.[2] It was Haavelmoo (Haavelmoo 1944) who brought the 'probability approach' into the econometric analysis. Although they were important for the later models, they were all too restrictive to be considered as "models of an economy". They were confined to linear specifications whereas a typical economic relation would be nonlinear. Moreover the emphasis was on statistical methodology of estimation and hypothesis testing. No special considerations with regard to forecasts were made.

2.2 Large Scale Econometric Forecast Models

The first econometric analyses considered a single equation like a demand function or a two-equation system of demand and supply which by assumption of market clearance could be again reduced to a single equation model. The cobweb theorem which considers cyclical demand and supply in specific markets is a nice early example which was empirically tested also by the famous German econometrician Hanau as early as 1930 (Hanau 1930). Economists learned that expectations and plans of consumers and producers had to be considered which lead to more complex and at the same time more realistic models. Keynes was the first who proposed a system of equation by which to describe an economy and to analyse impacts of policy measures. Such models were transformed to "operational" econometric models by using just those variables which are observable or using proxies for those variables which are unobserved (like quality of a good).

The wish of describing the economy in more detail and – more importantly – to make forecasts for special segments of the economy let the models grow to sizes which were only manageable by main-frame computers which entered the market at that time. Many models had equations for different industries and different markets (goods, labour). Some of these models contained more than 500 equations. The upcoming of monetarism also initiated special models. The following list contains a few which became particularly well-known:

- Wharton, St. Louis, Brookings, Fair (all for the US)[3],

---

[2] The book by Christ (1966) nicely summarizes this class of econometric models.
[3] See Klein and Burmeister (1976) for their 'model performance'.

- RWI model, econometric model of the German Bundesbank[4]
- LINK (a world model linking country models together)[5]

The main features of these "large scale" econometric models were (i) the use of nonlinear and dynamic specifications, (ii) the recognition of expectations , (iii) the possibility of making forecasts and simulating the consequences of different scenarios, and (iv) the rather sloppy use of estimation techniques including "fine tuning" which means setting some parameters intentionally to plausible values.

There was a strong debate about the question whether pure time series models (ARIMA- Models) as developped by Box and Jenkins (1970) had a better performance in forecasts than these large scale econometric models.[6] Clearly each econometric model has to set (or forecast) the future values of the exogenous values first and only then can predict the time path of the endogenous variables, but only conditional on the setting of exogenous variables. On the contrary the ARIMA models do not impose any economic structure on the variables and exploit the common correlation structure of the full set of variables considered. Therefore forecasts from this approach are unconditional. From an economic point of view it seems reasonable first to use unstructured time series analysis as an initial step in building a model and then exploit the economic structure in forecasting since then the conditionality of the forecasts may even be an advantage in modifying forecasts when the economic conditions change.

2.3 New Developments

Christopher Sims (Sims 1980) has been one of the propagators of unstructured time series analysis which by now is known as the approach of 'vector autoregressive' (VAR) processes. In these specifications all variables of the system are treated symmetrically: They are linked to all other variables for the same and some lagged periods. Many important findings ("stylized facts") have been found from this kind of analysis which abstains from economic theory when looking at the data.

Another important finding related to the name of Granger (Granger 1966) is that most economic variables are nonstationary whereas most econometric methods rely on the assumption of stationarity. Box and Jenkins (Box and Jenkins 1970) tried to bring together assumptions and data by differencing. However by now it is clear that the phenomenon of "cointegration" cannot adequately be treated by this simple procedure. During the last decade there has been a formidable step towards the adequate treatment of nonstationary

---

[4] Schober and Plötzeneder (1978) provide a good insight into the early days of these models.

[5] For a short description see, for example, Intriligator, Bodkin and Hsiao (1996, p. 454).

[6] See, for example, Intriligator, Bodkin and Hsiao (1996 chapter 15.6).

time series in econometric models. See, for example, Lütkepohl (1993) or Hamilton (1994) for the present state of the art.

By far the most important point with regard to the validity of econometric models was made by Lucas (1976) who pointed out that if economic agents behave rationally and know the structure of the economy ("rational expectations hypothesis" (REH)), then by each policy measure of the government the coefficients of the economic structure will be altered (because the agents behave differently) making any econometric forecast useless.[7] Modern econometric models have learned to integrate the REH hypothesis at least approximately which however lead to very involved estimation procedures since future expectations have to be taken into account. The "generalized method of moments" (GMM) which by now is a standard procedure in econometric analysis has been developped in connection with the estimation of econometric models under the REH.

3. Two Modern Approaches to Economic Modelling

3.1 Introductory Remarks

The analysis of econometric models has always been based on the provision that data hopefully were available for a longer time span. Therefore econometric analysis following the traditional approach of inference statistics and in particular hypothesis testing has always tried to identify the "true model". However the mostly poor quality of data and the high probability of structural changes which ist usually not incorporated into the estimation approach makes it almost unbelievable that the estimated model is near to or even "the" true model.

Additionally the fact that no experimental design[8] is possible in applied economic research, makes it hard to identify different causes of the observed phenomena. For example, the quantity of a good may rise because prices fall (and therefore demand increases) or because producers supply more at a higher price.

The nonexperimental situation in economics is characterised by the fact that it is not known which hypothesis is true and that no "second try" is possible to get more information. Another example is the tax incidence problem: It is not conceivable that different income tax structures are tried in different

[7] The survey by Ericson and Irons (1995) reviews the recent literature with respect to confirmation of the Lucas Critique. They conclude that there is no empirical evidence in favour of this critique. In particular "agents' formation of of expectations is simply not model-based." (Ericson and Irons , 1995, p. 301).

[8] Experimental design is possible if certain explanatory variables can be varied in a 'controlled' fashion holding all other explanatory variables fixed. In econometric studies we have to use the 'design points' as offered by reality. Modern experimental economics try to overcome this difficulty.

parts of a country in order to get a comparison of the effects of these differing tax schemes. However the "Negative Income Tax Experiments" in the United States can be seen as one of the starting points of 'Experimental Economics' which try to overcome these identification problems.

On the other hand each economist feels the need for analysing the effects of different policy measures or , more generally, of alternative scenarios with respect to the effect of realignment of exchange rates, slowdown of exports or wage increases in the "Neue Bundesländer" to mention only a few. Therefore economic models have been used more and more for simulation purposes almost completely disregarding the estimation step. Rather the parameter of the model are fixed at some plausible values. It is quite common to choose these values in such a way that the model fits exactly to some "base period" which then is called "calibration" to differentiate it from the econometric approach of estimation.

Almost independently of each other two lines of building such simulation models have been chosen:

- "real business cycle (RBC) models" to analyse macroeconomic behaviour of the aggregate economy[9] and
- "computable general equilibrium (CGE) models" to describe microeconomic behaviour of representative agents of the economy.[10]

3.2 Real Business Cycle (RBC) Models

The RBC type of model has been initiated partly by the aim to model technology induced supply shocks in contrast with foregoing models which concentrated on the effects of demand shocks.[11] These models considered markets of goods and labour sometimes also taking care of government behaviour. Foreign trade has been included in some of these models. Household behaviour and firm behaviour is described by a set of relations. In particular the investment behaviour of firms is modelled in detail since it is the transfer from technological innovations to production and employment.

A characteristic feature of these models is the modelling of dynamic behaviour taking an infinite planning horizon into account. The resulting highly nonlinear dynamic model is difficult to estimate. Rather the parameters of the model are fixed by calibration. Even the solution for the jointly endogenous variables (i.e. the reduced form) is only possible by using approximation methods. However simulation of the model on the basis of certain scenarios can be done without much difficulty. The real difficulty is to summarize the findings from such simulation experiments. A common approach is to compare statistical measures such as "moments" from the simulations with those

[9] See, for example, Kydland and Precott (1982), Long and Plosser (1983) and King, Plosser and Rebello (1988).

[10] See, for example, Dixon and Parmenter (1996).

[11] See, for example, Kugler (1996). 372-374.

which are observed under the calibrated version of the model and which are taken as "reality".

In recent years researchers have taken account of the critique of earlier approaches. Kugler (1996) mentions the approach by Blanchard and Quah (1989) which allows for testing for the persistence of supply shocks as maintained by the RBC models. Semmler and Gong (1997) point out that more recent RBC analysis has used the GMM approach in order to *estimate* the model instead of just calibrating it. They also propose an dynamic programming algorithm to incorporate the decision rules of the economic agents. A simulation estimation approach has been proposed by Lee and Ingram (1991) which has been used in applied work by Roeger (1996).

Although RBC models have not been used in forecasting so far[12], the dynamic structure of this approach could be used for predicting the time path of the aggregate economy. However it will become clear from the description of the other type of model in the next section that short-term oriented RBC models are less adequate for the analysis of long-tern planning problems such as, for example, restructuring or building up of the social security system in Eastern-European Countries.

3.3 Computational General Equilibrium (CGE) Models

The starting point of CGE models are rather formal specifications used in the 50's to describe the (microeconomic) behaviour of firms and households.[13] In this approach the individual behaviour of economic agents has been of interest. This type of model is typically a static one facing only a one-period optimisation problem.

CGE models have been used as simulation models by Shoven and Whalley (1984) to test various tax schemes and their incidence effects. This question has remained one of the predominant problems in the use of CGE models. See, for example, the model of the World Bank (1992) which was constructed in order to analyse the tax system of the Ivory Coast. Other recent studies are mentioned in Dixon and Parmenter (1996 p. 8/9). Parameters in these models have always been calibrated on the basis of some base period within the observation interval. Sometimes the observations interval consists of only a few observations making proper estimation impossible. For example, Slowenia's economic structure has changed radically just recently so that observations from earlier periods are useless. Here calibration is the only meaningful approach to obtaining plausible values for the parameters.

In these simulations a social accounting matrix (SAM) is used as the data base. This data base is an extension of the classical input-output matrix. Therefore the model uses data of aggregate economy when running the model. Here aggregate consumption, for example, is viewed as consumption of the

[12] This was pointed out by the referee.

[13] Quirk and Saposnik (1968) is an early reference to this approach.

representative consumer so that in effect the aggregate economy is simulated instead of individual behaviour. It should be added that since the SAM can be disaggregated to various sectors and goods, the simulation results can be broken down to this level of disaggregation.

The lack of dynamic relations in earlier studies made this type of model rather useless for real forecasts.[14] A typical forecast in this type of model consisted of a scenario fixing the exogenous variables and then looking at the resulting values of the jointly endogenous variables. More recent approaches have indeed expanded the one-period to a multi-period specification. See, for example, Pereira and Shoven (1988), Keuschnigg and Kohler (1991) or Dixon and Parmenter (1996, section 2.3) . An especially interesting approach is given by the dynamic general equilibrium model of Auerbach and Kotlikoff (1987). These authors point out that the often employed assumption of steady state (= constant growth rates) does not recognise the feedbacks of expectations on behaviour and therefore will give misleading results.

It seems that this type of model will join other modern applied approaches in bringing together more closely economic theory and applied economics. Dixon and Parmenter (1996 section 4) point out that the main success of the CGE approach was to link different parts of the economy. Moreover they consider the analysis of welfare effects within these models as an advantage. Last but not least the potential for obtaining *disaggregated* forecasts seems particularly promising.

During the last years there is also an tendency to combine ideas from RBC and CGE. See, for example, Kydland and Prescott (1995) who also discuss the 'econometrics' of such an approach. To mention a second example, the newly published journal 'Review of Economic Dynamics' announces for its inaugural issue , among others, an article by James Heckman entitled "Dynamic General Equilibrium Models to Evaluate Tax and Training Policies to Promote Skill Formation".

4. Concluding Remarks

Readers who have been familiar to the literature regarding RBC and CGE models might not at all be satisfied by the very general remarks made in this paper. The author has to apologize to them. The main aim of the paper is to point out that econometricians should no longer disregard these new approaches which are to some extent no longer econometrics in the classical sense.

[14] See also the more general critique by Chipman (1991).

References

1. Auerbach, A.L., ,and L.J. Kotlikoff (1987). *Dynamic Fiscal Policy.* Cambridge University Press: Cambridge (MA).
2. Blanchard, O.J., and D. Quah (1989). The Dynamic Effects of Aggregate Supply and Demand Disturbances. *American Economic Review 79*, 65-77.
3. Box, G.E.P, and G.W. Jenkins (1970). *Time Series Analysis. Forecasting and Control.* Holden Day: San Francisco.
4. Chipman, J.S. (1991). Empirical Methods in Computable-General-Equilibrium Modelling. Introductory Statement at the Round-Table "The Payoff of Investment in CGE-Modelling". Workshop on *Issues in International Economics: Questions to and Answers from Computable General Equilibrium Analysis*, 9 July 1991, University of Konstanz. Discussion Paper No. 156 SFB 178, 1991, 1-14.
5. Christ, C.F. (1966). *Econometric Models and Methods.* Wiley: New York.
6. Dixon, P.B., and B.R. Parmenter (1996). Computable General Equilibrium Modelling For Policy Analysis and Forecasting. In: H.M. Ammann, D.A. Kendrick and J. Rust (editors): *Handbook of Computational Economics. Volume I.* Elsevier: Amsterdam, 3-85.
7. Ericson, N.R., and J.S. Irons (1995). The Lucas Critique in Practice: Theory Without Measurement. In: K.D. Hoover (editor). *Macroeconometrics: Developments, Tensions, and Prospects.* Kluwer: Boston, 263-312.
8. Granger, C.W.J. (1966). The Typical Spectral Shape of an Economic Variable. *Econometrica 34*, 150-161.
9. Hamilton, James D.: *Time Series Analysis.* Princeton Unversity Press: Princeton, 1994.
10. Hanau, Arthur (1930). *Die Prognose der Schweinepreise.* Vierteljahreshefte zur Konjunkturforschung . Sonderheft 18.
11. Haavelmoo, T. (1944). The Probability Approach in Econometrics. *Econometrica 12*, Supplement (July), 118 pp.
12. Intriligator, M.D. , R.G. Bodkin and C. Hsiao (1996). *Econometric Models, Techniques, and Applications.* North-Holland: Amsterdam, second edition.
13. Keuschnigg, C. and W. Kohler (1991). An Intertemporal CGE Model for Austria. SFB 178 Diskussionspapier No. 152 (Oktober 1991).
14. Klein, L., and E. Burmeister (1976): *Econometric Model Performance. Comparative Simulation Studies of the U.S. Economy.* University of Pennsylvania Press, Philadelphia.
15. King, R.G., C.I. Plosser and S.T. Rebelo (1988). Production Growth and Business Cycles: 1. The Basic Neoclassical Model. *Journal of Monetary Economics 21*, 195-232.
16. Kugler, P. (1996). Empirische Makroökonomik. In: J. von Hagen u.a. (editors): *Handbuch der Volkswirtschaftslehre. Band I: Grundlagen*, Springer: Berlin, 347-386.
17. Kydland , F.E. and E.C. Prescott (1982). Time to Build and Aggregate Fluctuations. *Econometrica 50*, 1345-1370.
18. Kydland , F.E. and E.C. Prescott (1995). The Econometrics of the General Equilibrium Approach to Business Cycles. In: K.D. Hoover (editor). *Macroeconometrics: Developments, Tensions, and Prospects.* Kluwer: Boston, 181-198.
19. Lee, B.S., und B.F. Ingram (1991). Simulation Estimation of Time Series Models. *Journal of Econometrics 47*, 197-205.
20. Long, J.B., and C.I. Plosser (1983). Real Business Cycles. *Journal of Political Economy 91*, 39-69.

21. Lucas, R.E. (1976). Econometric Policy Evaluation: A Critique. In: K. Brunner and A.H. Meltzer (editors): *The Phillips Curve and Labor Markets. Carnegie Rochester Conference Series in Public Policy. Vol. 1, Journal of Monetary Economics.* supplementary issue, 19-46.
22. Lütkepohl, H. (1993). *Introduction to Multople Time Series.* Springer: Berlin, second edition.
23. Pereira, A.M., and J.B. Shoven (1988). Survey of Dynamic Computational General Equilibrium Models for Tax Policy Evaluations. *Journal of Policy Modeling 10*, 401-436.
24. Quirk, J. and R. Saposnik (1968). *Introduction to General Equilibrium Theory and Welfare Economics.* McGraw Hill: New York.
25. Roeger, W. (1996). *International Equilibrium Business Cycle Modelling. Theory, Estimation and Testing.* Unpublished Manuscript.
26. Schober, F., and H.D. Plötzeneder (editors) (1978): *Ökonometrische Modelle und Systeme.* Oldenbourg: Munich.
27. Semmler, W., and G.Gong (1997). A Numerical Procedure to Estimate Real Business Cycle Models Using Simulated Annealing. In: H. Ammann, B. Rustem and A. Whinston (editors): *Computational Approaches to Economic Problems.* Kluwer: Dordrecht, 327 - 343.
28. Shoven, J.B. and J. Whalley (1984). Applied General-Equilibrium Models of Taxation and International Trade: An Introduction and Survey. *Journal of Economic Literature XXII*, 1007-1051.
29. Sims, C. (1980). Macroeconomics and Reality. *Econometrica 48*, 1-48.
30. World Bank (editor) (1992) *Social Policy Models for the Ivory Coast.* Washington.

Consistent Estimation of the Number of Cointegration Relations in a Vector Autoregressive Model

Helmut Lütkepohl[1] and Don S. Poskitt[2]

[1] Department of Statistics and Econometrics, Humboldt–Universität Berlin, Germany
[2] Department of Statistics, Australian National University, Canberra, Australia

Summary. A class of criteria is developed which estimate the cointegration rank of a vector autoregressive (VAR) model consistently. It turns out that the usual consistent criteria for lag length selection can be adapted for the present purpose. However, alternative criteria may be advantageous. The small sample relevance of the asymptotic results is demonstrated by a small simulation study.

1. Introduction

In econometric analyses of systems of time series variables the cointegration relations or, alternatively, the common trends are usually of primary interest because they can often be interpreted in some economic way. Therefore determining the number of cointegration relations or common trends is an important part of an empirical analysis of a system of economic time series. A number of statistical tests have been proposed for this purpose. Well-known examples are Johansen's trace and maximum eigenvalue tests (Johansen (1988, 1991)), a modification due to Reinsel & Ahn (1988) as well as the tests suggested by Stock & Watson (1988), Phillips & Ouliaris (1994), and Bierens (1997). These tests are derived under differing sets of assumptions. A unifying theme is, however, that they are applicable if the true DGP is a finite order VAR (vector autoregressive) process which is the most popular model in practice.

Unfortunately, it was found in a small sample investigation by Reimers (1992) that none of the tests does very well in detecting the true number of cointegration relations for a range of different processes which may be met in applied work. The tests have, in fact, problems in achieving the nominal Type I error and in addition may not be very powerful. Therefore, in this paper we will consider the possibility of determining the cointegration rank of a finite order VAR process by appropriate model selection criteria. In particular we will give conditions for consistency of such criteria.

The idea of using model selection criteria in this context is not new. Reimers (1992) also includes some of the standard model selection procedures in his small sample comparison and finds that they also did not perform very well in some situations. Therefore we propose modifications which may be helpful in small samples. This is confirmed in a small simulation study.

The plan of the paper is as follows. In the next section the consistency result is given and the asymptotic properties of some standard criteria are discussed. Moreover, modified criteria are proposed which are hoped to result in small sample improvements. A small sample comparison of different criteria and tests based on Monte Carlo simulations is reported in Section 3. Concluding remarks are given in the last section.

2. Consistent Criteria for Specifying the Cointegration Rank

We consider a finite order, K-dimensional VAR process

$$y_t = \nu + A_1 y_{t-1} + \cdots + A_p y_{t-p} + u_t \tag{2.1}$$

where $y_t = (y_{1t}, \ldots, y_{Kt})'$ consists of K component variables, $\nu = (\nu_1, \ldots, \nu_K)'$ is a K-dimensional vector of constants, the A_i are $(K \times K)$ coefficient matrices and u_t is K-dimensional white noise with zero mean and nonsingular covariance matrix Σ_u. All components of y_t are assumed to be at most $I(1)$ (integrated of order 1), that is, they can be made stationary by differencing them once. Some or all of the variables may be stationary. Although excluding higher order integration is somewhat restrictive, in econometric practice $I(d)$ variables with $d > 1$ seem to be rare. The components of y_t may be cointegrated, that is, certain linear combinations of them may be stationary. To accomodate this situation in the process (2.1) we assume that

$$\det(I_K - A_1 z - \cdots - A_p z^p) \neq 0 \quad \text{for} \quad |z| \leq 1, \, z \neq 1,$$

that is, the determinant has all roots outside the complex unit circle except that there may be roots for $z = 1$. Here I_K denotes the $(K \times K)$ identity matrix. This is the standard framework usually used in analyzing systems of integrated variables.

Subtracting y_{t-1} on both sides of (2.1) and rearranging terms leads to the error correction (EC) form

$$\Delta y_t = \nu - \Pi y_{t-1} + \Gamma_1 \Delta y_{t-1} + \cdots + \Gamma_{p-1} \Delta y_{t-p+1} + u_t \tag{2.2}$$

where Δ is the differencing operator, i.e., $\Delta y_t = y_t - y_{t-1}$,

$$\Pi = I_K - A_1 - \cdots - A_p$$

and

$$\Gamma_i = -(A_{i+1} + \cdots + A_p), \quad i = 1, \ldots, p-1.$$

The rank of Π is the cointegration rank of the system. It is the quantity of interest in the following and will be denoted by r_0. For the moment we will assume that the VAR order p is known although this is unrealistic in practice. At the end of this section we will comment on how to choose p.

Assuming a Gaussian error process u_t, Johansen (1988, 1991) derives the LR (likelihood ratio) statistic for testing

$$H_0 : r_0 = r \quad \text{against} \quad H_1 : r_0 > r\,, \quad r = 0, \ldots, K-1. \tag{2.3}$$

For a sample of size T and p presample vectors we define

$$\Delta Y = [\Delta y_1, \ldots, \Delta y_T],\ \Delta X_t = \begin{bmatrix} 1 \\ \Delta y_t \\ \vdots \\ \Delta y_{t-p-2} \end{bmatrix},\ \Delta X = [\Delta X_0, \ldots, \Delta X_{T-1}],$$

$$Y_{-1} = [y_0, \ldots, y_{T-1}], \qquad M = I - \Delta X'(\Delta X \Delta X')^{-1},$$

$$R_0 = \Delta Y M, \quad R_1 = Y_{-1} M$$

$$S_{ij} = R_i R_j' / T, \quad i = 0, 1.$$

Let G be a Choleski component of S_{11} such that $G S_{11} G' = I_K$ and let $\lambda_1 \geq \cdots \geq \lambda_K$ be the eigenvalues of $G S_{10} S_{00}^{-1} S_{01} G'$. Then the LR statistic for testing (2.3) turns out to be

$$Q_T(r) = -T \sum_{i=r+1}^{K} \ln(1 - \lambda_i) \tag{2.4}$$

(see also Lütkepohl (1991, Chapter 11) or other textbooks dealing with cointegration).

From results in Johansen (1995, Chapters 10-13) it follows that

$$\operatorname{plim} Q_T(r)/T > 0 \quad \text{for} \quad r < r_0 \tag{2.5a}$$

and

$$Q_T(r) = O_p(1) \quad \text{if} \quad r \geq r_0, \tag{2.5b}$$

where $O_p(\cdot)$ is the usual symbol for boundedness in probability. These results hold regardless of the value and treatment of ν. In other words, it also holds if ν is assumed to be zero and is hence omitted in the estimation or if ν can be absorbed into the cointegration relations. In fact, in the latter case it is not even necessary that the true VAR order is finite (see Saikkonen & Luukkonen (1997)). This generality is important because (2.5) is the crucial condition for proving consistency of a class of criteria for choosing the cointegration rank.

The general form of the criteria is

$$CIR_T(r) = Q_T(r) + \varphi(r) c_T, \quad r = 0, \ldots, K, \tag{2.6}$$

where $Q_T(K)$ is defined to be zero, $\varphi(r)$ is any strictly monotonically increasing function of r and c_T is a sequence of numbers indexed by the sample size T. CIR stands for cointegration rank. The estimator $\hat{r}$ of r_0 is chosen such that $CIR_T(r)$ is minimized over $r = 0, \ldots, K$. For a suitable choice of the sequence c_T the estimator $\hat{r}$ is consistent. The following theorem contains the details.

Theorem 1:*Suppose the process y_t is such that (2.5) holds and let $c_T \to \infty$ as $T \to \infty$ such that $c_T = o(T)$, then plim $\hat{r} = r_0$, that is, CIR is (weakly) consistent.*

Proof: Suppose $r < r_0$. Then for $T \to \infty$,

$$Pr\left[CIR_T(r) > CIR_T(r_0)\right] = Pr\left[\frac{Q_T(r)}{c_T} - \frac{Q_T(r_0)}{c_T} > \varphi(r_0) - \varphi(r)\right]$$

$$= Pr\left[\frac{Q_T(r)}{T} > \frac{c_T}{T}\left(\frac{Q_T(r_0)}{c_T} + \varphi(r_0) - \varphi(r)\right)\right] \longrightarrow 1$$

because plim $Q_T(r)/T > 0$ by (2.5a). Hence, $Pr\left[\hat{r} < r_0\right] \to 0$.

Alternatively, if $r > r_0$,

$$Pr\left[CIR_T(r) > CIR_T(r_0)\right] = Pr\left[\varphi(r) - \varphi(r_0) > (Q_T(r_0) - Q_T(r))/c_T\right] \to 1$$

since $\varphi(r) - \varphi(r_0)$ is a positive constant plim $Q_T(r)/c_T = 0$ for $r \geq r_0$ by (2.5*b*). Hence, $Pr\left[\hat{r} > r_0\right] \to 0$. Thus, we have in summary, $Pr\left[\hat{r} = r_0\right] \to 1$. □

The theorem is in a way too general to be of direct practical use because it leaves open the choice of the function $\varphi(\cdot)$ and also it does not specify the term c_T explicitly. Of course, at the extreme end one could choose the borderline sequence $c_T = T$ for every finite sample size and pretend that c_T gets smaller than T eventually for large samples. The simplest choice for $\varphi(\cdot)$ is the identity function, $\varphi(r) = r$. Another choice that has been used in this context is $\varphi(r) = r(2K - r)$, that is, $\varphi(r)$ represents the number of freely varying parameters in the $(K \times K)$ matrix Π when its rank is r. Obviously $\varphi(r)$ is strictly monotonically increasing and thereby qualifies here. With this choice we get, for instance, the standard model selection criteria

$$AIC(r) = Q_T(r) + 2r(2K - r), \tag{2.7}$$

where $c_T = 2$,

$$HQ(r) = Q_T(r) + 2r(2K - r)\ln\ln T, \tag{2.8}$$

where $c_T = 2\ln\ln T$, and

$$SC(r) = Q_T(r) + r(2K - r)\ln T, \tag{2.9}$$

where $c_T = \ln T$ (see e.g., Lütkepohl (1991, Chapter 4) for a discussion of these criteria in a time series context). Note that instead of $Q_T(r)$ usually the more common $T \ln \det \tilde{\Sigma}_u(r)$ is used, where $\tilde{\Sigma}_u(r)$ is the Gaussian ML (maximum likelihood) estimator of the residual covariance matrix Σ_u for cointegration rank r. Since $Q_T(r)$ and $T \ln \det \tilde{\Sigma}_u(r)$ differ only by a constant which is independent of r (see Lütkepohl (1991, Chapter 11)), replacing the latter term by the former results in equivalent criteria. Using $Q_T(r)$ in the present context is more convenient from a computational point of view.

Clearly, Theorem 1 implies that HQ and SC are both consistent criteria whereas AIC may not be consistent. On the other hand, even for the SC criterion which has the largest penalty term, the sequence c_T is still much smaller than the upper bound obtained from Theorem 1. Hence, from this point of view even much more parsimonious criteria could be justified. In fact, in the simulation study by Reimers (1992) the criteria did overall quite poorly. Even SC, the most parsimonious criterion, frequently overestimated the cointegration rank which suggests that more parsimonious criteria may be justified not only on the basis of asymptotic theory but also by small sample evidence.

To get an indication of useful specifications of $\varphi(\cdot)$ and c_T in the criterion in (2.6), it may be helpful to view the result in Theorem 1 from a hypothesis testing angle. The property (2.5a) of the test statistic $Q_T(r)$ shows that a test based on this statistic is consistent. Thereby we achieve that the criterion does not underestimate the cointegration rank in large samples. To guarantee that it does not overestimate r_0 with some positive probability, we have to let the significance level go to zero at an appropriate rate. The penalty term $\varphi(r)c_T$ corresponds to the associated sequence of critical values, that is, the upper quantiles of the distributions of the $Q_T(r)$ for $T \to \infty$. Hence, to choose c_T properly it may be helpful to consider the upper quantiles of the distributions of the test statistics. For that purpose the following proposition is helpful which relates convergence in distribution to the law of the iterated logarithm via the tail behaviour of the limiting distribution.

Proposition 1 *Let x_T be a sequence of random variables which converges in distribution to a random variable x. Moreover, let N_T be a sequence of positive constants such that $N_T \to \infty$ as $T \to \infty$. If there exists a constant $c > 1$ and $k(c) > 0$ is such that*

$$Pr\left[|x| \geq k(c)(N_T \ln \ln N_T)^{1/2}\right] = O(\exp(-c \ln \ln N_T))$$

as $T \to \infty$, then

$$\limsup_{T \to \infty} |x_T| / (N_T \ln \ln N_T)^{1/2} \leq k(c) \quad a.s.$$

The proof is given in the Appendix. Now choose some $c > 1$ and $0 < c' < 1$ and let $\alpha_T(c)$ be such that $-\ln \alpha_T(c) = c \ln \ln T - \ln c'$. Then

$$-\ln \alpha_T(c) / (T \ln \ln T)^{1/2} = O(1)$$

and therefore it follows from Theorem 5.8 of Pötscher (1983) that for the $(1-\alpha_T(c))-$ quantile $\chi^2(r)_{\alpha_T(c)}$ of a χ^2-distribution with r degrees of freedom we have

$$\frac{\chi^2(r)_{\alpha_T(c)}}{(T\ln\ln T)^{1/2}} \longrightarrow 0 \quad \text{as} \quad T \to \infty.$$

Hence, the proposition is applicable for a sequence of random variables z_T converging in distribution to a $\chi^2(r)$ random variable. Assuming that the upper tail of the limiting distribution of $Q_T(r)$ behaves in a similar way as that of a $\chi^2(r)$ distribution (i.e., $Q(r)_{\alpha_T(c)}/\chi^2(r)_{\alpha_T(c)} = O(1)$), c_T in the criterion (2.6) should be chosen such that

$$\liminf_{T\to\infty} \frac{c_T}{(T\ln\ln T)^{1/2}} > 1. \tag{2.10}$$

For instance, $c_T = T^{1/2}\ln\ln T$ would be a possible choice. In practice it may also be reasonable to choose the lower bound $c_T = (T\ln\ln T)^{1/2}$. We have used both of these possibilities in the Monte Carlo study reported in the next section. In addition we have used two alternative specifications of $\varphi(\cdot)$, namely, $\varphi(r) = r$ and $\varphi(r) = r(2K-r)$. The latter $\varphi(\cdot)$ function resulted in criteria which drastically underestimated the true cointegration rank. The results are therefore not reported. Hence, we have the two alternative criteria

$$CIR1(r) = Q_T(r) + rT^{1/2}\ln\ln T \tag{2.11}$$

$$CIR2(r) = Q_T(r) + r(T\ln\ln T)^{1/2} \tag{2.12}$$

which will be compared among themselves and with other criteria in the simulations. It may be worth pointing out here already that both criteria choose the cointegration rank at most as large as the SC criterion for large samples and processes of moderate dimension K. This follows straightforwardly from Lemma 4.1 of Lütkepohl (1991, p. 133) and the fact that $Q_T(r)$ is a nonincreasing function of r. Also $CIR1$ is more parsimonious than $CIR2$.

In practice, the VAR order is usually also unknown. One possible strategy would be to specify that order by one of the usual consistent criteria first. These criteria maintain their consistency properties even for cointegrated processes (see Paulsen (1984)). In a second step the cointegration rank can then be chosen by one of the criteria presented for this purpose.

3. Monte Carlo Comparison of Criteria and Tests

We have used a number of different VAR processes and sample sizes to investigate the performance of different criteria for estimating the cointegrating rank in small samples and compare them to testing procedures. Some of the processes have been used earlier in the related literature. In particular,

Reimers (1992) uses a three–dimensional VAR(1) process consisting of three independent Gaussian random walks, i.e.,

$$y_t = A_1 y_{t-1} + u_t \tag{3.1}$$

with $A_1 = I_3$ and $u_t \sim N(0, I_3)$. This process has cointegration rank 0 and hence favours parsimonious criteria. Therefore we also consider processes with cointegration ranks 1, 2, and 3 by choosing

$$A_1 = \begin{bmatrix} .7 & 0 & 0 \\ 0 & 1 & 0 \\ 0 & 0 & 1 \end{bmatrix}, \quad A_1 = \begin{bmatrix} .7 & 0 & 0 \\ 0 & .7 & 0 \\ 0 & 0 & 1 \end{bmatrix}, \quad \text{and} \quad A_1 = .7 I_3.$$

Thus the three components are still independent processes. Hence, there is no cointegration in the classical understanding of the concept. It may be preferable to think of the processes as having $K - r$, $r = 0, \dots, 3$, stochastic trends which should be picked up by the criteria and tests compared in the following.

We consider three sample sizes, $T = 50$, 100 and 200 and in each case we have generated 10 presample values starting with zero initial values. T is the net sample size so that some of the presample values are also used in the estimation. Although there are no intercepts in the generation processes a constant term is included in the computation of the test statistics. Also we use orders different from 1 in some cases to determine the impact of overestimating the VAR order which may also give some information on the performance of the tests for higher order processes. Instead of using the Johansen statistic $Q_T(r)$ in the testing procedure we apply the modified statistic

$$Q_T^*(r) = -(T - Kp) \sum_{i=r+1}^{K} \ln(1 - \lambda_i)$$

due to Reinsel & Ahn (1988) which performed better than $Q_T(r)$ in Reimers' Monte Carlo study. The tests are carried out sequentially testing from the smallest to the largest rank, that is, the following sequence of null hypotheses is considered:

$$H_0 : r_0 = 0,\ H_0 : r_0 = 1, \dots,\ H_0 : r_0 = K - 1.$$

The procedure terminates when the null hypothesis cannot be rejected for the first time. The nominal significance level is 5% in each individual test.

In Tables 3.1 and 3.2 results for $T = 100$ and 200, respectively, obtained from 1000 replications of the experiment are given. Obviously there is no clear winner. While AIC and HQ are clearly too generous and overestimate the true rank quite often when it is small, SC is too parsimonious when the rank is large and is not focussed very well on the true rank. Although the new criteria are somewhat better in some situations they are clearly not satisfactory for all processes, for instance, when the cointegrating rank is 3.

Also the modified Johansen tests are hardly satisfactory. The fact that they tend to deteriorate with growing order of the process was also observed by Reimers (1992). The results for $T = 50$ are not given in order to save space. For that sample size the ability of the tests and criteria to locate the correct rank tends to deteriorate relative to the behaviour observed for $T = 100$.

Another set of simulations is based on bivariate processes corresponding to those used by Gonzalo (1994) which are similar to the ones used by other researchers as well:

$$\begin{aligned} y_{1t} &= y_{2t} + \rho(y_{1,t-1} - \beta y_{2,t-1}) + u_{1t} \\ \Delta y_{2t} &= u_{2t} \end{aligned}$$

where

$$u_t = \begin{bmatrix} u_{1t} \\ u_{2t} \end{bmatrix} \sim N\left(0, \begin{bmatrix} 1 & \theta \\ \theta & 1 \end{bmatrix}\right),$$

$\theta = -.5, .5$, $\beta = 1$ and $\rho = .5, .9$. The latter parameter is chosen so that the relative importance of the cointegration relation $y_{1t} = \beta y_{2t}$ varies. Of course, all these processes contain one genuine cointegration relation. Having one cointegration relation in a bivariate process allows for possible over- as well as underestimation of the true rank. Some results are given in Tables 3.3 and 3.4. Again a similar picture emerges as in the previous example. None of the tests and criteria dominates the others for all processes in terms of finding the correct cointegration rank. Generally they all behave unsatisfactorily. The results for $\theta = -.5$ are very similar to those for $\theta = .5$. Therefore they are not shown here.

4. Conclusions

In this study we have derived a class of criteria for choosing the cointegration rank of a finite order VAR process. The criteria are shown to be consistent. In a simulation study the small sample properties of some representatives of this class are explored. While they perform well for some data generation processes they have poor properties in other cases.

Acknowledgements

Part of this research was conducted while the first author was visiting the Australian National University and the University of California, San Diego, and the second author was visiting the Institute of Statistics and Econometrics, Humboldt University, Berlin. Both authors gratefully acknowledge financial support by the DFG, Sonderforschungsbereich 373. We thank Dirk Büttner for carrying out the simulations and we regret that we learnt only after finishing this paper that the result in Theorem 1 was also obtained by Gonzalo & Pitarakis (1995).

Table 3.1. Monte Carlo Results for Three–dimensional VAR(1)s, $T = 100$

A_1	VAR order p	coint. rank r	proportions of ranks selected: mod. Johansen test	criterion: AIC	HQ	SC	CIR1	CIR2
I_3 ($r_0 = 0$)	1	0	0.946	0.185	0.666	0.967	0.685	0.423
		1	0.050	0.313	0.243	0.032	0.315	0.559
		2	0.004	0.275	0.050	0.000	0.000	0.018
		3	0.000	0.227	0.041	0.001	0.000	0.000
	3	0	0.956	0.145	0.622	0.940	0.638	0.381
		1	0.042	0.307	0.266	0.057	0.356	0.600
		2	0.002	0.292	0.061	0.003	0.006	0.019
		3	0.000	0.256	0.051	0.000	0.000	0.000
diag(0.7,1,1) ($r_0 = 1$)	1	0	0.466	0.000	0.037	0.490	0.048	0.007
		1	0.497	0.265	0.615	0.459	0.920	0.878
		2	0.035	0.365	0.209	0.035	0.032	0.115
		3	0.002	0.370	0.139	0.016	0.000	0.000
	3	0	0.732	0.006	0.153	0.691	0.171	0.043
		1	0.249	0.245	0.493	0.274	0.808	0.855
		2	0.018	0.369	0.223	0.025	0.021	0.102
		3	0.001	0.380	0.131	0.010	0.000	0.000
diag(0.7,0.7,1) ($r_0 = 2$)	1	0	0.026	0.000	0.000	0.148	0.004	0.000
		1	0.348	0.000	0.002	0.095	0.330	0.093
		2	0.581	0.429	0.581	0.561	0.666	0.905
		3	0.045	0.571	0.417	0.196	0.000	0.002
	3	0	0.288	0.000	0.024	0.466	0.064	0.004
		1	0.489	0.001	0.061	0.180	0.661	0.384
		2	0.198	0.439	0.531	0.232	0.274	0.610
		3	0.025	0.560	0.384	0.122	0.001	0.002
$0.7 \cdot I_3$ ($r_0 = 3$)	1	0	0.000	0.000	0.000	0.002	0.000	0.000
		1	0.001	0.000	0.000	0.001	0.083	0.005
		2	0.028	0.000	0.000	0.000	0.695	0.384
		3	0.971	1.000	1.000	0.997	0.222	0.611
	3	0	0.024	0.000	0.003	0.163	0.024	0.002
		1	0.117	0.000	0.000	0.025	0.488	0.165
		2	0.302	0.001	0.002	0.005	0.474	0.708
		3	0.557	0.999	0.995	0.807	0.014	0.125

Table 3.2. Monte Carlo Results for Three–dimensional VAR(1)s, $T = 200$

			proportions of ranks selected					
	VAR order	coint. rank	mod. Johansen	criterion				
A_1	p	r	test	AIC	HQ	SC	CIR1	CIR2
I_3 ($r_0 = 0$)	1	0	0.949	0.194	0.783	0.988	0.972	0.860
		1	0.046	0.323	0.171	0.010	0.028	0.138
		2	0.005	0.280	0.031	0.002	0.000	0.002
		3	0.000	0.203	0.015	0.000	0.000	0.000
	3	0	0.948	0.172	0.743	0.983	0.961	0.847
		1	0.046	0.318	0.193	0.013	0.039	0.152
		2	0.006	0.290	0.042	0.004	0.000	0.001
		3	0.000	0.220	0.022	0.000	0.000	0.000
diag(0.7,1,1) ($r_0 = 1$)	1	0	0.003	0.000	0.000	0.016	0.003	0.000
		1	0.941	0.281	0.687	0.940	0.992	0.981
		2	0.052	0.396	0.219	0.035	0.005	0.019
		3	0.004	0.323	0.094	0.009	0.000	0.000
	3	0	0.125	0.000	0.001	0.231	0.097	0.005
		1	0.826	0.260	0.666	0.726	0.898	0.973
		2	0.047	0.394	0.235	0.035	0.005	0.022
		3	0.002	0.346	0.098	0.008	0.000	0.000
diag(0.7,0.7,1) ($r_0 = 2$)	1	0	0.000	0.000	0.000	0.000	0.000	0.000
		1	0.009	0.000	0.000	0.000	0.038	0.000
		2	0.948	0.409	0.614	0.833	0.962	1.000
		3	0.052	0.591	0.386	0.167	0.000	0.000
	3	0	0.000	0.000	0.000	0.015	0.010	0.000
		1	0.041	0.000	0.000	0.013	0.480	0.087
		2	0.924	0.424	0.622	0.808	0.510	0.913
		3	0.035	0.576	0.378	0.164	0.000	0.000
$0.7 \cdot I_3$ ($r_0 = 3$)	1	0	0.000	0.000	0.000	0.000	0.000	0.000
		1	0.000	0.000	0.000	0.000	0.001	0.000
		2	0.000	0.000	0.000	0.000	0.187	0.007
		3	1.000	1.000	1.000	1.000	0.812	0.993
	3	0	0.000	0.000	0.000	0.000	0.001	0.000
		1	0.000	0.000	0.000	0.000	0.200	0.008
		2	0.000	0.000	0.000	0.000	0.662	0.341
		3	1.000	1.000	1.000	1.000	0.137	0.651

Table 3.3. Monte Carlo Results for Bivariate Processes with $\rho = .5$, $\beta = 1$, $\theta = .5$, $r_0 = 1$

sample size T	VAR order p	coint. rank r	proportions of ranks selected: mod. Johansen test	criterion: AIC	HQ	SC	CIR1	CIR2
50	1	0	0.152	0.000	0.000	0.014	0.002	0.000
		1	0.803	0.390	0.517	0.686	0.973	0.953
		2	0.045	0.610	0.483	0.300	0.025	0.047
	3	0	0.657	0.004	0.039	0.212	0.102	0.052
		1	0.312	0.387	0.481	0.506	0.876	0.901
		2	0.031	0.609	0.480	0.282	0.022	0.047
100	1	0	0.000	0.000	0.000	0.000	0.000	0.000
		1	0.945	0.424	0.596	0.754	0.997	0.993
		2	0.055	0.576	0.404	0.246	0.003	0.007
	3	0	0.075	0.000	0.000	0.013	0.034	0.008
		1	0.877	0.421	0.604	0.754	0.963	0.982
		2	0.048	0.579	0.396	0.233	0.003	0.010
200	1	0	0.000	0.000	0.000	0.000	0.000	0.000
		1	0.939	0.421	0.645	0.831	0.999	0.999
		2	0.061	0.579	0.355	0.169	0.001	0.001
	3	0	0.000	0.000	0.000	0.000	0.001	0.000
		1	0.945	0.418	0.647	0.828	0.998	0.999
		2	0.055	0.582	0.353	0.172	0.001	0.001

Table 3.4. Monte Carlo Results for Bivariate Processes with $\rho = .9$, $\beta = 1$, $\theta = .5$, $r_0 = 1$

sample size T	VAR order p	coint. rank r	proportions of ranks selected: mod. Johansen test	criterion: AIC	HQ	SC	CIR1	CIR2
50	1	0	0.926	0.151	0.397	0.731	0.583	0.441
		1	0.069	0.335	0.300	0.169	0.417	0.553
		2	0.005	0.514	0.303	0.100	0.000	0.006
	3	0	0.938	0.145	0.355	0.689	0.539	0.401
		1	0.058	0.379	0.340	0.197	0.457	0.589
		2	0.004	0.476	0.305	0.114	0.004	0.010
100	1	0	0.787	0.046	0.282	0.714	0.832	0.633
		1	0.186	0.394	0.379	0.195	0.168	0.367
		2	0.027	0.560	0.339	0.091	0.000	0.000
	3	0	0.845	0.065	0.308	0.733	0.841	0.668
		1	0.129	0.385	0.374	0.181	0.159	0.331
		2	0.026	0.550	0.318	0.086	0.000	0.001
200	1	0	0.404	0.000	0.039	0.433	0.908	0.644
		1	0.553	0.422	0.582	0.446	0.092	0.356
		2	0.043	0.578	0.379	0.121	0.000	0.000
	3	0	0.542	0.002	0.067	0.547	0.930	0.739
		1	0.417	0.417	0.575	0.357	0.070	0.261
		2	0.041	0.581	0.358	0.096	0.000	0.000

Appendix. Proof of Proposition 1

From Skorohod's construction, Billingsley (1986, Theorem 25.6), we know that there exist random variables z_T and z on the same probability space as x_T and x, possessing the same probability measures, such that $z_T \to z$ with probability one. Let $T_n, n = 1, 2, \ldots$ denote a subsequence such that the event $\{|z_{T_n} - z| < \delta_n, \forall T \geq T_n\}$ occurs with probability arbitrarily close to one. If M_n with $T_n \leq M_n < T_{n+1}$ is chosen so that

$$|z_{M_n}| = \max_{T_n \leq j < T_{n+1}} |z_j|$$

then the triangle inequality $|z_j - z_{M_n}| \leq |z_j - z| + |z_{M_n} - z|$ implies that

$$\max_{T_n \leq j < T_{n+1}} |z_j - z_{M_n}| < 2\delta_n$$

with arbitrarily large probability and it follows that

$$|z - z_{M_n}| \leq \max_{T_n \leq j < T_{n+1}} \{|z - z_j| + |z_j - z_{M_n}|\} \leq 3\delta_n$$

will occur with probability arbitrarily close to one. Now suppose that δ_n is selected such that $|Pr(z_{T_n} < k_{T_n}) - Pr(z < k_{T_n})| < \delta_n < 2^{-n}$ where $k_T = k(c)(N_T \ln \ln N_T)^{1/2}$. Then

$$\begin{aligned} Pr\{|z_{M_n}| > k_{M_n}\} &< Pr(|z| > k_{T_n}) + 2\delta_n \\ &\leq O(1/(\ln N_{T_n})^c) + 2^{-(n+1)} \end{aligned}$$

The proposition now follows from the Borel-Cantelli Lemma and the fact that z_T and x_T share the same probability distribution.

References

1. Bierens, H.J. (1997). Nonparametric cointegration analysis, *Journal of Econometrics*, 77, 379 - 404.
2. Billingsley, P. (1986). *Probability and Measure, 2nd Ed.*, New York: Wiley.
3. Gonzalo, J. (1994). Five Alternative Methods of Estimating Long-Run Equilibrium Relationships, *Journal of Econometrics*, 60, 203 - 234.
4. Gonzalo, J. & J.-Y. Pitarakis (1995). Comovements in Large Systems, mimeo.
5. Johansen, S. (1988). Statistical Analysis of Cointegration Vectors, *Journal of Economic Dynamics and Control*, 12, 231 - 254.
6. Johansen, S. (1991). Estimation and Hypothesis Testing of Cointegration Vectors in Gaussian Vector Autoregressive Models, *Econometrica*, 59, 1551 - 1580.
7. Johansen, S. (1995). *Likelihood Based Inference on Cointegration in the Vector Autoregressive Model*, Oxford: Oxford University Press.
8. Lütkepohl, H. (1991). *Introduction to Multiple Time Series Analysis*, Berlin: Springer-Verlag.

9. Paulsen, J. (1984). Order Determination of Multivariate Autoregressive Time Series With Unit Roots, *Journal of Time Series Analysis*, 5, 115 - 127.
10. Phillips, P.C.B. & S. Ouliaris (1988). Testing for Cointegration using Principle Components Methods, *Journal of Economic Dynamics and Control*, 12, 205 - 230.
11. Pötscher, B.M. (1983). Order Estimation in ARMA-Models by Lagrangian Multiplier Tests, *Annals of Statistics*, 11, 872 - 885.
12. Reimers, H.-E. (1992). Comparison of Tests for Multivariate Cointegration, *Statistical Papers*, 33, 335 - 359.
13. Reinsel, G.C. & S.K. Ahn (1988). Asymptotic Distribution of the Likelihood Ratio Test for Cointegration in the Nonstationary Vector AR Model, Technical Report, *University of Wisconsin, Madison, Department of Statistics.*
14. Saikkonen, P. & R. Luukkonen (1997). Testing for Cointegration in Infinite Order VAR Processes, *Journal of Econometrics,* forthcoming.
15. Stock, J.H. & M.W. Watson (1988). Testing for Common Trends, *Journal of the American Statistical Association*, 83, 1097 - 1107.

Locally Weighted Autoregression

Yuanhua Feng and Siegfried Heiler

University of Konstanz, Germany

Summary. Estimation of mean and volatility functions for nonlinear time series models of the ARCH type is discussed. The mean function is estimated with local linear autoregression. The volatility function is estimated with a kernel estimator based on the squared residuals of the mean function. Asymptotic bias and variance of these estimators are investigated. The proposals are applied to daily exchange rates of DEM/USD.

Keywords. Locally weighted autoregression; Asymptotics; Volatility

1. Introduction

Nonlinear time series analysis has become an active research area (Priestley, 1988; Tong, 1990). The ARCH (Autoregressive Conditional Heteroskedastic) models (Engle, 1982) are well known in this context. In this paper we are concerned with the estimation of the conditional mean and volatility functions of general nonlinear systems of the ARCH type using nonparametric techniques. The method used here is locally weighted regression. Local regression using a uniform kernel has a long tradition in time series analysis. Kernel based locally weighted regression was first introduced into statistical literature by Stone (1977) and Cleveland (1979). For the studies on this topic we refer to Fan and Gijbels (1992, 1996), Ruppert and Wand (1994) and the references therein.

Nonparametric time series analysis based on kernel estimators as introduced by Nadaraya (1964) and Watson (1964) is studied by many authors (e.g. Robinson, 1983; Collomb, 1983; Auestad and Tjøstheim, 1990; Masry and Tjøstheim, 1995). Kernel estimators have the advantage of simplicity. However, these estimators are affected by bias and boundary problems. Locally weighted regression estimators share the simplicity of the kernel estimators but overcome the main problems of them. Nonparametric time series analysis using local regression was recently proposed by Härdle and Tsybakov (1997) for local polynomial fitting and Härdle, Tsybakov and Yang (1997) for vector autoregression. See the paper of Härdle, Lütkepohl and Chen (1997) for a most recent review on nonparametric time series analysis. The present paper focuses on multivariate locally linear autoregression.

Let $\{Y_i\}$, $i = 1, ..., n$, be a univariate time series. A general model that contains many of the nonlinear time series classes discussed in the literature is

$$Y_i = m\left(Y_{i-1}, \ldots, Y_{i-p}\right) + v^{1/2}\left(Y_{i-1}, \ldots, Y_{i-p}\right) \xi_i\,, \tag{1.1}$$

where $\{Y_i\}$ is assumed to be strictly stationary, ξ_i is an i.i.d. sequence of random variables with means zero and variance $\sigma^2 = 1$. Conditions leading to strict stationarity and strong mixing of $\{Y_i\}$ will be given in section 3 in conjunction with Lemma 3.1. Model (1.1) is called an ARCH-related system (Masry and Tjøstheim, 1995). It is the scalar case of the so-called vector CHARN (Conditional Heteroskedastic Autoregressive Nonlinear) Model (Härdle, Tsybakov and Yang, 1997).

It is easy to see that

$$E[Y_i|Y_{i-1} = y_{i-1}, ..., Y_{i-p} = y_{i-p}] = m(y_{i-1}, ..., y_{i-p}) \tag{1.2}$$

and

$$\text{var}[Y_i|Y_{i-1} = y_{i-1}, ..., Y_{i-p} = y_{i-p}] = v(y_{i-1}, ..., y_{i-p}), \tag{1.3}$$

where $v(y_{i-1}, ..., y_{i-p})$ is the volatility function. Our purpose is to estimate the conditional mean and volatility functions with locally weighted autoregression.

The proposed estimators are defined in section 2. Section 3 contains the main results. In section 4 the proposals are applied to financial market and environmental data. Some open questions are briefly discussed in section 5, while the proofs of theorems are given in the appendix.

2. Locally Weighted Autoregression

Let the process be started with the initial value $X_p = (Y_0, Y_1, ..., Y_{p-1})^T$ which is a random vector independent of $\{\xi_i\}$. We study the problem of estimating the mean function m and the volatility function v, given a time series $Y_0, ..., Y_n$. Let $X_i = (Y_{i-p}, ..., Y_{i-1})^T$ with $i = p, ..., n+1$. Let $f(\cdot)$ be the joint density of X_i with respect to Lebesgue measure, which is assumed to exist. Finally, let $X_{i,j}$ denote the jth entry of X_i, i.e. $X_{i,j} = Y_{i-p+j-1}$, $j = 1, ..., p$. If all second-order derivatives of m are continuous, we may obtain an estimate of $m(\cdot)$ at a point x using local linear autoregression, which is just a solution $\hat{\alpha}$ of the following local least squares problem

$$\sum_{i=p}^{n} \{Y_i - \alpha - \beta^T(X_i - x)\}^2 \frac{1}{nh^p} \prod_{j=1}^{p} K_j\left(\frac{X_{i,j} - x_j}{h}\right) \Rightarrow \min, \tag{2.1}$$

where $\beta = (\beta_1, ..., \beta_p)^T$, the K_j's are symmetrical nonnegative kernels and h is the bandwidth. If (2.1) does not have a solution, we define $\hat{m} := 0$. The weighting function, $K(\mathbf{u}) := \prod_{j=1}^{p} K_j(u_j)$ with $\mathbf{u} = (u_1, ..., u_p)^T$, is a p-dimensional product kernel. For simplicity we use the same bandwidth in all directions. This choice is justified by the assumption that the underlying process be stationary. However, this choice is not necessary. A general bandwidth matrix is proposed by Ruppert and Wand (1994). The use of a product kernel is also not essential (see assumption A5 in section 3).

Let

$$\mathbf{X}_x = \begin{bmatrix} 1 & (X_p - x)^{\mathrm{T}}/h \\ \vdots & \vdots \\ 1 & (X_n - x)^{\mathrm{T}}/h \end{bmatrix} \tag{2.2}$$

and $\mathbf{K}_x = diag(k_i)$ with $k_i = \frac{1}{nh^p}\prod_{j=1}^p K_j\left(\frac{X_{i,j}-x_j}{h}\right)$. Then we arrive at the solution

$$\begin{aligned} \hat{m}(x) &= \mathbf{e}_1^{\mathrm{T}}(\mathbf{X}_x^{\mathrm{T}}\mathbf{K}_x\mathbf{X}_x)^{-1}\mathbf{X}_x^{\mathrm{T}}\mathbf{K}_x\mathbf{Y} \\ &=: \sum_{i=p}^n W_{xi}Y_i \end{aligned} \tag{2.3}$$

of (2.1), where $\{W_{xi}\} = \mathbf{e}_1^{\mathrm{T}}(\mathbf{X}_x^{\mathrm{T}}\mathbf{K}_x\mathbf{X}_x)^{-1}\mathbf{X}_x^{\mathrm{T}}\mathbf{K}_x$, $\mathbf{Y} = (Y_p, ..., Y_n)^{\mathrm{T}}$ and $\mathbf{e}_1 = (1, 0, ..., 0)^{\mathrm{T}}$. The local linear estimator given in (2.3) is a weighted sum of the observations, but it is not a linear smoother in this context, because the weights depend on the observations. In an area spanned by the regressor vectors the weight system defined in (2.3) has the property that

$$\sum_{i=p}^n W_{xi} = 1 \qquad \text{and} \qquad \sum_{i=p}^n W_{xi}(X_i - x) = 0\,. \tag{2.4}$$

Property (2.4) makes $\hat{m}$ conditionally unbiased for linear functions.

Local polynomial estimators with a general degree $q > 1$ can be defined in a similar way. A kernel estimator is a local polynomial estimator of degree zero, i.e. a local constant estimator.

As far as we know, all nonparametric estimators of the volatility function proposed in the literature are of the form $\hat{v}(x) = \hat{g}(x) - \{\hat{m}(x)\}^2$, where $\hat{g}$ is defined as in (2.3) but with Y_i replaced by Y_i^2. These considerations are based on the fact that $\mathrm{var}(Y|X = x) = E[Y^2|X = x] - (E[Y|X = x])^2$. However, in local linear or vector autoregression such an estimator may sometimes be negative (see Härdle, Tsybakov and Yang, 1997), since now some of the weights are negative. In all practical applications we have tried so far this happend to be the case from time to time. Hence we propose a residual based estimator of v, which is defined by

$$\hat{v}(x) = \frac{\sum_{i=p}^n \prod_{j=1}^p K_j\left(\frac{X_{i,j}-x_j}{h}\right) r_i^2}{\sum_{i=p}^n \prod_{j=1}^p K_j\left(\frac{X_{i,j}-x_j}{h}\right)} =: \sum_{i=p}^n W_{xi,v} r_i^2\,, \qquad \frac{0}{0} =: 0\,, \tag{2.5}$$

where $r_i = Y_i - \hat{m}(X_i)$ are the residuals. The estimator $\hat{v}$ is similar to the one proposed by Fan and Gijbels (1995) and it is trivially always non-negative. The main idea behind $\hat{v}$ is that for a consistent estimator $\hat{m}$ r_i is a good approximation for $v^{1/2}(X_i)\xi_i =: \epsilon_i(X_i)$, at least for large n, i.e. $r_i = Y_i - m(X_i) + \mathrm{o}(1) = \epsilon_i(X_i) + \mathrm{o}(1)$. $\hat{v}(x)$ is a kernel estimator of $v(x)$ with the r_i instead of the unobservable ϵ_i. Hence $\hat{v}$ has similar asymptotic properties as a general kernel estimator. Properties of residual based nonparametric variance estimators in nonparametric regression with i.i.d. errors are studied by Hall and Marron (1990) for kernel estimators and by Ruppert, Sheather and Wand (1995) and Heiler and Feng (1997) for local polynomial fitting. Of course, v might also be estimated by a local linear fit (but not necessarily non-negative) with respect to the residuals r_i, as in (2.1) for the function m.

3. Results

In this section we discuss the asymptotic bias and variance of $\hat{m}$ and $\hat{v}$. Besides standard assumptions for nonparametric estimators strictly stationarity and mixing condition on the process $\{Y_i\}$ are required. A survey of basic properties of different strong mixing conditions can be found in Bradley (1986). For our results $\{X_i\}$ is required to be strong mixing with a geometric convergence rate as given in Lemma 5.1 of Härdle, Tsybakov and Yang (1997). Note that $\{X_i\}$ is a p-dimensional Markov process. This result holds if there exists an invariant probability measure π as defined in (7) of Auestad and Tjøstheim (1990), the initial vector X_p is distributed with π and is geometrically ergodic (Pham, 1986), i.e. $\{X_i\}$ is ϕ-irreducible (Nummelin, 1984, p. 11) and

$$\lim_{n\to\infty} \rho^{-n}||P^n(\cdot,x)-\pi||_{\mathrm{TV}}=0$$

for some positive number ρ with $0<\rho<1$. Here

$$P^n(A|x)=P\{X_n\in B|X_p=x\},$$

for a Borel subset $B\in\mathbb{R}^p$, and $||\cdot||_{\mathrm{TV}}$ denotes the total variation norm (Nummelin, 1984, p. 108). Conditions leading to geometric ergodicity of $\{X_i\}$ are (Masry and Tjøstheim, 1995):

A1: The i.i.d. random variables $\{\xi_i\}$ have a probability density that is positive over $\mathbb{R}$.

A2: The functions m and v are nonperiodic and bounded on compact sets, and $v(x)>0$ for all $x\in\mathbb{R}^p$.

A3: There exist vectors $\underline{a}$, $\underline{d}\in\mathbb{R}^p$ (which both may be zero) with $d_j\geq 0$, $j=1,\dots,p$, such that as $||x||\to\infty$,

$$m(x)=x\underline{a}+o(||x||) \qquad \text{and} \qquad v(x)=\sum_{j=1}^{p} d_j x_j^2+o(||x||^2)\,.$$

A4: The p-dimensional square matrix A defined by 0, if $\underline{a}=0$, and by

$$A=\begin{bmatrix} 0 & 0 & \cdots & 0 & a_1\\ 1 & 0 & \cdots & 0 & a_2\\ \vdots & \vdots & \ddots & \vdots & \vdots\\ 0 & 0 & \cdots & 1 & a_p \end{bmatrix},$$

otherwise, satisfies $\rho(AA^{\mathrm{T}}) + \max(d_j) < 1$ if $\underline{d} \neq 0$ and satisfies $\rho(A) < 1$ if $\underline{d} = 0$. Here ρ denotes the spectral radius (Tong, 1990, p. 134).

Assumptions A3 may almost look like imposing linearity. It should be carefully noted that we only require that the growth at infinity should be dominated by a stable linear model. This is not a severe restriction. For example, any functions m and s that are bounded or with growth at infinity given by $\|x\|^q$ with $q < 1$ will be feasible. Note that functions with growth everywhere *faster* than a stable linear model will be nonstationary (Tjøstheim, 1990). We also assume that the process is started with the invariant probability measure π. This condition together with the existence of π ensure that $\{X_i\}$ is stationary.

Lemma 3.1. (Masry and Tjøstheim, 1995) *Under the assumptions* A1–A4, *the nonlinear model* (1.1) *is strongly mixing with mixing coefficients* $\alpha(k) \sim e^{-\beta k}$ *for some* $\beta > 0$.

It is clear that the mixing coefficients satisfy $\alpha(k) \leq \alpha_0 \rho_0^k$, for some $\alpha_0 > 0$, $0 < \rho_0 < 1$. Other conditions that also lead to geometric ergodicity of $\{X_i\}$ can be found in Härdle and Tsybkov (1997) and Yang and Härdle (1997), where exact stationarity is not required.

Now we state conditions necessary to derive asymptotic bias and variance of $\hat{m}$ and $\hat{v}$ at a fixed point $x \in \mathbb{R}^p$.

A5: The kernel K is a compactly supported bounded density such that $\int uu^{\mathrm{T}} K(u)du = \mu_2(K)I$, where $\mu_2(K) > 0$, I is th $p \times p$ identity matrix. In addition, all odd-order moments of K vanish, that is $\int u_1^{l_1} ... u_p^{l_p} K(u)du = 0$ for all nonnegative integers $l_1, ..., l_p$ such that their sum is odd.

A6: The functions m and v are twice continuously differentiable at the the point $x \in \mathbb{R}^p$.

A7: The density $f(x)$ of the invariant probability measure π exists, is bounded, continuously differentiable and strictly positive in a neighborhood of the point x.

A8: The bandwidth h satisfies $h \to 0$, $nh^p \to \infty$, as $n \to \infty$.

These assumptions are standard in nonparametric regression. They are conditions on the kernel, smoothness condition on the density and the functions to be estimated, and conditions on the bandwidth. A5 is satisfied by spherically symmetric kernels and product kernels based on symmetric univariate kernels. Condition A7 is necessary to compute asymptotic bias and variance at x. Condition A8 ensures that both the bias and variance vanish asymptotically. An optimal rate of the bandwidth will be given later.

Let $R(K) = \int K(u)^2 du$. For an at least twice differentiable p-variate function g let $\nabla_g(x)$ and $\mathcal{H}_g(x)$ denote the $p \times 1$ vector of the gradient and the $p \times p$ Hessian matrix of g at x respectively. We have the following results.

Theorem 1 *Under the assumptions* A1–A8,

$$B[\hat{m}(x)] = \frac{1}{2}\mu_2(K)h^2 \mathrm{tr}\{\mathcal{H}_m(x)\} + o_p(h^2) \tag{3.1}$$

and

$$\mathrm{var}[\hat{m}(x)] = (nh^p f(x))^{-1} R(K) v(x) \{1 + o_p(1)\}\,, \tag{3.2}$$

where $B[\hat{m}]$ denotes the bias of $\hat{m}$.

From (3.1) and (3.2) we obtain that the asymptotic mean squared error (AMSE) of $\hat{m}$

$$\mathrm{AMSE}[\hat{m}(x)] = (nh^p f(x))^{-1} R(K) v(x) + \frac{1}{4}\mu_2^2(K) h^4 \left(\mathrm{tr}\{\mathcal{H}_m(x)\}\right)^2 . \tag{3.3}$$

The optimal bandwidth which minimizes the AMSE is

$$h_{o,m} = c_0 \left(\frac{p}{n}\right)^{\frac{1}{p+4}}, \tag{3.4}$$

with
$$c_0 = \left(\frac{v(x) f^{-1}(x) R(K)}{\mu_2^2(K) \left(\mathrm{tr}\{\mathcal{H}_m(x)\}\right)^2}\right)^{\frac{1}{(p+4)}} .$$

This says that the optimal bandwidth is of order $n^{-1/(p+4)}$ and the optimal MSE is of order $n^{-4/(p+4)}$. The rate of convergence of $\hat{m}$ decreases as p increases.

Theorem 2 *Under the assumptions* A1–A8,

$$B[\hat{v}(x)] = \frac{1}{2}\mu_2(K) h^2 \mathrm{tr}\{\mathcal{H}_v(x) + 2 \nabla_f (x) \nabla_v (x)^{\mathrm{T}} / f(x)\} + o_p(h^2) \tag{3.5}$$

and
$$\mathrm{var}[\hat{v}(x)] = (nh^p f(x))^{-1} R(K) v(x)^2 \mathrm{var}(\xi^2) \{1 + o_p(1)\} . \tag{3.6}$$

The bias of $\hat{v}$ involves the density $f(x)$ and its derivative, since it is asymptotically equivalent to a local constant estimator. One can obtain similar formulas as (3.3) and (3.4). The optimal bandwidth for $\hat{v}$ is of the same order as that for $\hat{m}$, but the constants are different.

4. Application

In this section the proposed estimators are applied to the time series of the daily exchange rates of DEM/USD (Deutsche Mark/US Dollar) from January 2, 1986 to April 30, 1993, a total of 1829 observations (Fig. 4.1). The mean and the volatility functions for the original data were estimated with $p = 1$ and $p = 2$, respectively. The estimators are also applied to the returns of this time series. The bisquare kernel and the two-dimensional product kernel based on it are used as weighting functions. Although for bandwidth selection a data-driven procedure as e.g. described in Heiler and Feng (1997, 1998) is recommended, in the presented application the choice about bandwidths was made according to practical experience.

The DEM/USD data has maximum 247.67 and minimum 138.70 with the range $d = 108.97$. Hence all estimations are evaluated for $Y_{i-1} \in [138, 248]$ except for the case $\hat{m}$ with $p = 1$, for which $\hat{m}$ was calculated for $Y_{i-1} \in$

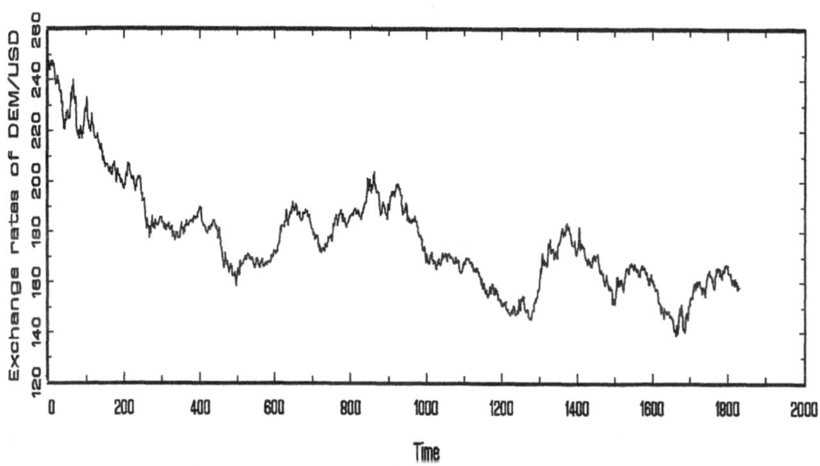

Fig. 4.1. The daily exchange rates of DEM/USD from Jan. 2, 1986 to Apr. 30, 1993

[128, 258]. Figure 4.2 shows the estimated mean function (left) and volatility function (right) for the DEM/USD data with $p = 1$. We used the bandwidth $h = 15$ for $\hat{m}$ and $h = 20$ for $\hat{v}$. Using $h = 15$ allows us to show the boundary effect in $\hat{m}$ outside the interval [138, 248] (compare with $\hat{m}$ for $p = 2$). For this data $\hat{m}$ with $p = 1$ does not have any boundary effect for an actually observed Y_{i-1}. On the interval [138, 248] $\hat{m}$ is almost the identity function.

The estimated volatility function shown on the right hand side of Fig. 4.2 has a U-shaped structure, also called a "smiling face". It says that risks of the exchange rates are much higher for very large or very small values taken on the past day. There is a clear boundary effect on the right edge of the interval where the estimated volatility function decreases. This is due to the fact that there are only a few observations asymmetrically distributed around Y_{i-1} at this end. (In contrast to that there are more observations at the left hand side of the scale.) Specific boundary kernels, which were not used here, might lead to different results at the boundaries. The form of the estimated volatility function is very similar to that obtained by Härdle and Tsybakov (1997) for the DEM/USD data from October 1, 1992 to September 30, 1993 in 20 minutes intervals (see Fig. 2.2 therein).

In Fig. 4.3 the estimated mean and volatility functions with $p = 2$ and $h = 25$ are exhibited. The estimates are calculated for $Y_{i-1} \in [138, 248]$ and $Y_{i-2} \in [Y_{i-1} - 8, Y_{i-1} + 8]$, which include all actual observations (The maximal value of $|Y_i - Y_{i-1}|$ for this data is 7.25). Figure 4.3 shows that the lag 2 variable is not very important. We can also see that for $p = 1$ the boundary effect in $\hat{v}$ is much larger than that in $\hat{m}$, but for $p = 2$ the boundary effects in

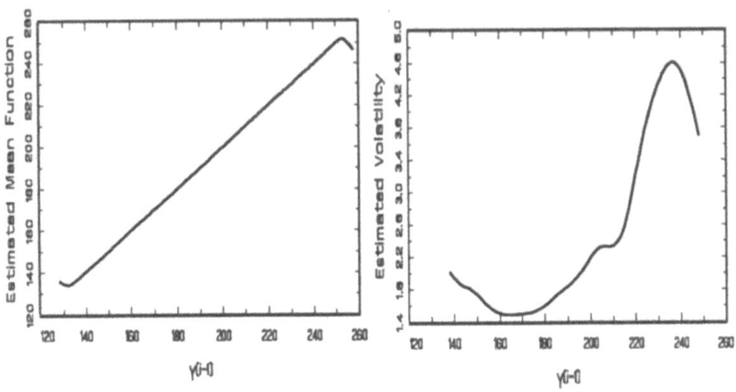

Fig. 4.2. Estimated conditional mean and volatility functions from the DEM/USD data with $p = 1$, $h = 15$ for the mean and $h = 20$ for the volatility function.

both $\hat{v}$ and $\hat{m}$ are similar. Based on the residuals a confidence interval could be calculated with a quantile regression as proposed in Abberger (1997).

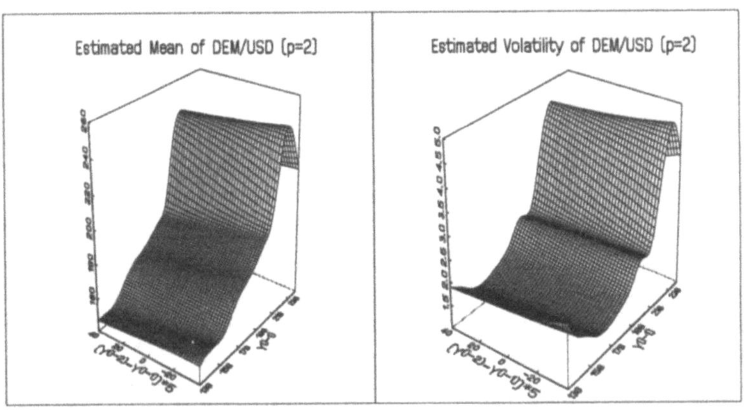

Fig. 4.3. Estimated conditional mean and volatility functions from the DEM/USD data with $p = 2$, $h = 25$.

The time series shown in Fig. 4.1 reveals a downward trend in the observation period, which might be interpreted as non-stationarity. Hence the proposed estimators were also applied to the returns of this time series, defined as $X_i = (Y_i - Y_{i-1})/Y_{i-1}$, $i = 2, ..., n$. The observed returns x_i of the DEM/USD data are shown in the upper part of Fig. 4.4 The lower part of Fig. 4.4 exhibits an estimated conditional mean, which will be described later.

The returns of DEM/USD have maximum 0.0414 and minimum -0.0302. However, most of them are closely scattered around zero and over 98% of

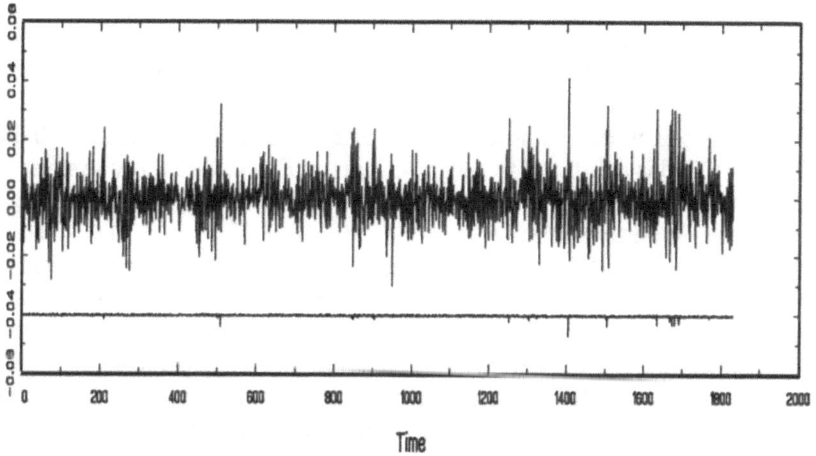

Fig. 4.4. The returns of DEM/USD (up), and an estimated conditional mean $(\hat{x}_i - 0.04)$ (below) given the return of the last day.

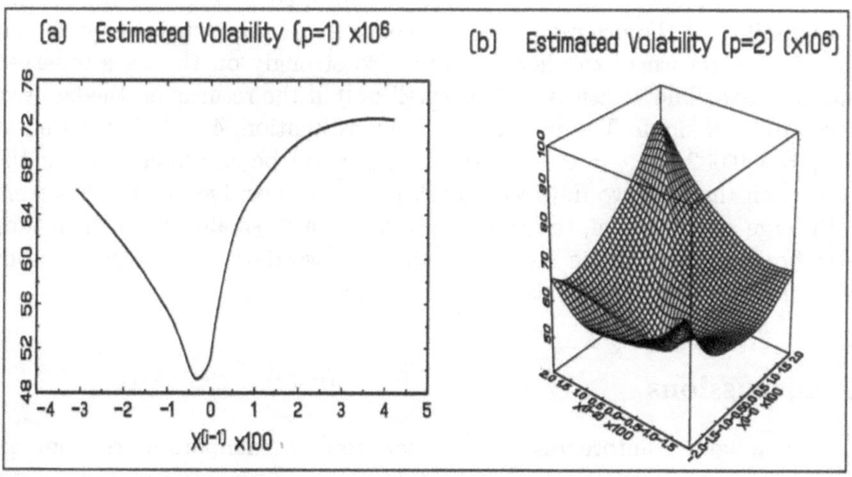

Fig. 4.5. Estimated conditional volatility functions with $p = 1$ (a), $p = 2$ (b) and bandwidths described in the text.

them lie in the interval [-0.02, 0.02]. This suggests using a variable bandwidth. For $p = 1$, to estimate the conditional mean and volatility functions at $X_{i-1} \in [-a, b]$, $a > 0, b > 0$, a variable bandwidth of the form $h = h_{\min} + (h_{\max} - h_{\min})|X_{i-1}|/\max(a, b)$ was used, where $h_{\min}$ is the minimal bandwidth used at $X_{i-1} = 0$ and $h_{\max}$ is the maximal bandwidth used when $|X_{i-1}| = \max(a, b)$. The larger $|X_{i-1}|$, the larger the bandwidth will be.

The estimated mean given the return of the last day with $h_{\min} = 0.005$ and $h_{\max} = 0.036$ is exhibited in the lower part of Fig. 4.4 with the same scale but the zero at -0.04, i.e. it is mostly equal to zero. Figure 4.5 (a) shows the estimated conditional volatility function given $X_{i-1} \in [-0.032, 0.042]$ with residuals obtained from this estimated mean and the same bandwidth. We see that the conditional volatility function has a minimum 4.92e-5 at $X_{i-1} = -0.003$ and it increases as $|X_{i-1} + 0.003|$ increases. The volatility function shows an asymmetric form. The volatility for a positive return on the last day is larger than that for a negative one at the same level. The estimated volatility function is smooth at both boundaries due to the use of a larger bandwidth.

A second-order autoregression was carried out for the mean function with $h_{\min} = 0.0065$ and $h_{\max} = 0.05$ in order to obtain residuals needed for estimating the conditional volatility. Now the bandwidth was determined with $|X_{i-1}|$ replaced by $\max(|X_{i-1}|, |X_{i-2}|)$ in the formula given above. To show the main structure of the conditional volatility function with $p = 2$ only couples $(X_{i-1}, X_{i-2}) \in [-0.02, 0.02]^2$ were considered, which covers about 97% of the observed couples. The estimated conditional volatility function with $h_{\min} = 0.0065$ and $h_{\max} = 0.02$ is exhibited in Fig. 4.5 (b). Unlike the volatility of the original data, the volatility of the returns depends not only on the return of the last day but also strongly on the ones observed two days ago. The volatility will be small only if the returns on the last two days are both small. The minimum of this estimation, 4.590e-5, occured at $X_{i-1} = -0.002, X_{i-2} = 0.002$. The volatility will be extremely large if the returns on the last two days were both large and positive. When they were both large and negative, the volatility will be much smaller than when they were both positive. If the returns on the last two days were both large but with different signs the volatility will be even smaller.

5. Discussions

Locally weighted autoregression is a new topic in nonparametric time series analysis. Related works in this context have been done by Härdle and coauthors. There are still many open questions in the practical use of locally weighted autoregression. Two of them are the determination of the significant lags and the selection of the bandwidth. Determination of the significant lags of the autoregressive models is discussed by Auestad and Tjøstheim (1990),

Tjøstheim and Auestad (1994b). A final prediction error (FPE) is used to select the lags and the order. A connected problem is the "curse of dimensionality", i.e., if p is large, there are only a few points in a neighborhood of a point $x \in \mathbb{R}^p$ (in practice this happens to be the case already for $p \geq 3$). Let $0 \leq i_1 < i_2 < ... < i_p < i_{p+1}$ be integers. Tjøstheim and Auestad (1994a) proposed the use of only the significant lags $0 \leq i_1 < i_2 < ... < i_p$ to estimate $Y_{i_{p+1}}$. Here i_p could be large, but p remains small. The authors also proposed the tool of projections to solve the "curse of dimensionality" problem (see also Yang and Härdle, 1997).

Bandwidth selection for nonparametric autoregression using the cross-validation (CV) criterion was discussed by Härdle and Vieu (1992). It is well known that bandwidths selected following the CV or similar criteria converge very slowly to their optimum. Many fast bandwidth selectors are proposed in the context of nonparametric regression (e.g. Gasser, Kneip and Köhler, 1991; Ruppert, Sheather and Wand, 1994; Fan and Gijdels, 1995; Heiler and Feng, 1997, 1998). The key problem is how these proposals can be adapted to the time series context? As shown in the last section, sometimes a fixed bandwidth does not work well. In this case a variable bandwidth $h(x)$ adapted to $m(x)$, $v(x)$ and $f(x)$ is more preferable. The "curse of dimensionality" can also be partly removed by the use of a variable bandwidth.

Furthermore, strict stationarity is assumed for the theoretical results. In practice many time series have trends and are therefore nonstationary. These trends may be estimated and removed with nonparametric techniques, e.g. using a local polynomial fit with the time t as regressor. A brief survey in this context can be found in Härdle, Lütkepohl and Chen (1997).

6. Appendix: Proofs

Theorem 1 is well known in local linear regression with independent observations. Theorem 2 is similar to the results in kernel regression. The strict stationarity with geometric ergodicity of X_i guarantee that these results also hold. A basic lemma in this context is Lemma 5.2 of Härdle, Tsybakov and Yang (1997) (called HTY hereafter). See also Lemma 5.3 of Härdle and Tsybakov (1997). Under the assumptions of Theorem 1 the Lemmas 5.2–5.4 of HTY hold, which are adaptated into the present context and given in Lemmas A.1–A.3. At a given point x let $u_i = (X_i - x)/h$.

Lemma A.1 *Under the assumptions of Theorem 1 we have*

$$(nh^p)^{-1} \sum_{i=p}^{n} \varphi_1(X_i)\varphi_2(u_i)K(u_i) \xrightarrow{p} f(x)\varphi_1(x) \int \varphi_2(u)K(u) \tag{6.1}$$

$$(nh^p)^{-1} \sum_{i=p}^{n} E\left\{\varphi_1(X_i)\varphi_2(u_i)K(u_i)\right\} \longrightarrow f(x)\varphi_1(x) \int \varphi_2(u)K(u),$$

as $n \to \infty$, provided $\varphi_1(\cdot)$ is a bounded continuous function in a neighborhood of x and $\varphi_2(\cdot)$ is a bounded measurable function.

Proof: See Härdle and Tsybakov (1997) Lemma 5.3. Under the assumption that X_p is distributed with π the process is stationary. Hence only the first part of their proof is needed. ⋈

Lemma A.2 *As $n \to \infty$,*

$$(X_x^{\mathrm{T}} K_x X_x)^{-1} = \frac{1}{f(x)} \begin{bmatrix} 1 & \mathbf{0} \\ \mathbf{0} & \mu_2(K) I_p \end{bmatrix} \{1 + o_p(1)\} \tag{6.2}$$

uniformly on a compact neighborhood of x.

Proof: See HTY Lemma 5.3. ⋈

Lemma A.3 *Let $g : \mathbb{R}^p \to \mathbb{R}^1$ be a twice continuously differentiable function. Then, under the assumptions of Theorem 1,*

$$\frac{1}{nf(x)} \sum_{i=p}^{n} K_h(X_i - x)[g(X_i) - g(x) - (X_i - x)^{\mathrm{T}} \nabla_g (x)]$$
$$= h^2 \frac{\mu_2(K)}{2} \mathrm{tr}\{\mathcal{H}_g(x)\} + o_p(h^2) \tag{6.3}$$

and

$$\frac{1}{nf(x)} \sum_{i=p}^{n} K_h(X_i - x)[g(X_i) - g(x)]$$
$$= h^2 \frac{\mu_2(K)}{2} \mathrm{tr}\{\mathcal{H}_g(x) + 2 \nabla_f (x) \nabla_g^{\mathrm{T}} (x)/f(x)\} + o_p(h^2), \tag{6.4}$$

where $K_h(X_i - x) = \frac{1}{h^p} \prod_{j=1}^{p} K_j(\frac{X_{i,j} - x_j}{h})$.

Proof: (6.3) is the result of Lemma 5.3 in HTY. Note that

$$(\mathrm{A.4}) = (\mathrm{A.3}) + \frac{1}{nf(x)} \sum_{i=p}^{n} K_h(X_i - x)[(X_i - x)^{\mathrm{T}} \nabla_g (x)].$$

Following the first equation of (5.18) in Härdle and Tsybakov (1997)

$$\frac{1}{n} \sum_{i=p}^{n} K_h(X_i - x)[(X_i - x)^{\mathrm{T}} \nabla_g (x)] \xrightarrow{P}$$
$$\frac{1}{h^p} \int K\left(\frac{y-x}{h}\right) f(y)(y-x)^{\mathrm{T}} \nabla_g (x)]dy$$
$$= \int K(u)[hf(y) \nabla_g^{\mathrm{T}} (x)u]du$$
$$= h \int K(u)[(f(x) + hu^{\mathrm{T}} \nabla_f (x) + R) \nabla_g^{\mathrm{T}} (x)u]du,$$

where R is a vector of Taylor series remainder terms. The integral involving R is negligible because of $R = o\{hu^{\mathrm{T}} \nabla_f (x)\}$. The part corresponding to the term

$$\int K(u)[f(x) \nabla_g^{\mathrm{T}} (x)u]du$$

is also negligible, since $\int K(u)udu = 0$. By Lemma A.1 one has, as $n \to \infty$

$$\int K(u)[u^{\mathrm{T}} \nabla_f (x) \cdot \nabla_g^{\mathrm{T}} (x)u]du$$
$$= \int tr[K(u)uu^{\mathrm{T}} \nabla_f (x) \nabla_g^{\mathrm{T}} (x)]du$$
$$= tr\left[\int K(u)uu^{\mathrm{T}} \nabla_f (x) \nabla_g^{\mathrm{T}} (x)du\right]$$
$$= \mu_2(K)tr[\nabla_f(x)\nabla_g^{\mathrm{T}}] .$$

Combining this and (A.3) we obtain (A.4). ⋈

Proof of Theorem 1:

Using (2.4) one has

$$\hat{m}(x) - m(x) = \sum_{i=p}^{n} W_{xi}[Y_i - m(x) - (X_i - x)^{\mathrm{T}} \nabla_m (x)]$$
$$= \sum_{i=p}^{n} W_{xi}[m(X_i) - m(x) - (X_i - x)^{\mathrm{T}} \nabla_m (x)] + \sum_{i=p}^{n} W_{xi}v^{1/2}(X_i)\xi_i$$
$$= \frac{1}{nf(x)}\{1 + o_p(1)\} \sum_{i=p}^{n} K_h(X_i - x)[m(X_i) - m(x) - (X_i - x)^{\mathrm{T}} \nabla_m (x)]$$
$$+ \frac{1}{nf(x)}\{1 + o_p(1)\} \sum_{i=p}^{n} K_h(X_i - x)v^{1/2}(X_i)\xi_i . \tag{6.5}$$

The last equality of (6.5) is due to Lemma A.2. The first term of the last equation of (6.5) dominates the bias of $\hat{m}(x)$, while the second term dominates its variance. Putting $g(x) = m(x)$ in (A.3), one obtains

$$\frac{1}{nf(x)} \sum_{i=p}^{n} K_h(X_i - x)[m(X_i) - m(x) - (X_i - x)^{\mathrm{T}} \nabla_m (x)]$$
$$= h^2 \frac{\mu_2(K)}{2} \mathrm{tr}\{\mathcal{H}_m(x)\} + o_p(h^2) \tag{6.6}$$

as $n \to \infty$. HTY showed that the asymptotic variance of

$$\frac{1}{nf(x)}\{1 + o_p(1)\} \sum_{i=p}^{n} K_h(X_i - x)v^{1/2}(X_i)\xi_i$$

is given by

$$\begin{aligned} G &= \sum_{i=p}^{n} E\left[\left(\frac{1}{nf(x)}K_h(X_i - x)v^{1/2}(X_i)\xi_i\right)^2\right] \\ &= \frac{1}{nh^p f(x)}\{1 + o_p(1)\}\int K^2(u)v(x)du \\ &= \frac{1}{nh^p f(x)}R(K)v(x)\{1 + o_p(1)\}\,. \end{aligned} \tag{6.7}$$

This finishes the proof of Theorem 1. ⋈

Proof of Theorem 2:

We have $\hat{v}(x) = \sum_{i=p}^{n} W_{xi,v}r_i^2$. Again, the weights have the form

$$W_{xi,v} = \frac{1}{nf(x)}\{1 + o_p(1)\}K_h(X_i - x)\,.$$

But now the second part of (2.4) does not hold. This is the main difference between the local linear and the kernel estimators. Note that $r_i = Y_i - \hat{m}(X_i)$. We have

$$\begin{aligned} \hat{v}(x) - v(x) &= \frac{1}{nf(x)}\{1 + o_p(1)\}\sum_{i=p}^{n} K_h(X_i - x)[r_i^2 - v(x)] \\ &= \frac{1}{nf(x)}\{1 + o_p(1)\}\sum_{i=p}^{n} K_h(X_i - x)\{[Y_i - \hat{m}(X_i)]^2 - v(x)\} \\ &= \frac{1}{nf(x)}\{1 + o_p(1)\}\sum_{i=p}^{n} K_h(X_i - x)\{v(X_i)\xi_i^2 \\ &\quad +2v^{1/2}(X_i)\xi_i[m(X_i) - \hat{m}(X_i)] + [m(X_i) - \hat{m}(X_i)]^2 - v(x)\} \\ &= \{1 + o_p(1)\}\sum_{j=1}^{4} T_j\,, \end{aligned} \tag{6.8}$$

where

$$T_1 = \frac{1}{nf(x)}\sum_{i=p}^{n} K_h(X_i - x)[v(X_i)\xi_i^2 - v(X_i)]\,,$$

$$T_2 = \frac{2}{nf(x)}\sum_{i=p}^{n} K_h(X_i - x)v^{1/2}(X_i)\xi_i[m(X_i) - \hat{m}(X_i)]\,,$$

$$T_3 = \frac{1}{nf(x)}\sum_{i=p}^{n} K_h(X_i - x)[m(X_i) - \hat{m}(X_i)]^2\,,$$

and

$$T_4 = \frac{1}{nf(x)} \sum_{i=p}^{n} K_h(X_i - x)[v(X_i) - v(x)] .$$

The term T_3 is obviously negligible, since $[m(X_i) - \hat{m}(X_i)]^2 = O(h^4)$. Analogously to the analysis of T_6 in HTY we obtain

$$E(T_2^2) = O_p\left(\frac{h^4}{nh^p}\right) .$$

The bias of $\hat{v}$ is dominated by T_4. Putting $g(x) = v(x)$ in (A.4) we have

$$E[T_4] = h^2 \frac{\mu_2(K)}{2} \mathrm{tr}\{\mathcal{H}_v(x) + 2 \nabla_f (x) \nabla_v^{\mathrm{T}} (x)/f(x)\} + o_p(h^2) . \quad (6.9)$$

T_1 has the equivalent representation

$$T_1 = \frac{1}{nf(x)} \sum_{i=p}^{n} K_h(X_i - x)[v^{1/2}(X_i)(\xi_i^2 - 1)v^{1/2}(X_i)] . \quad (6.10)$$

This is just the scalar case of T_5 in HTY with lag p. Its asymptotic variance is given by

$$\begin{aligned} G_1 &= \frac{1}{n^2 f(x)^2} \sum_{i=p}^{n} E\left[\left(K_h(X_i - x)v^{1/2}(X_i)(\xi_i^2 - 1)v^{1/2}(X_i)\right)^2\right] \\ &= \frac{1}{nh^p f(x)} R(K)v(x)^2 \mathrm{var}(\xi^2)\{1 + o_p(1)\} . \quad (6.11) \end{aligned}$$

Hence theorem 2 is proved. ⋈

References

1. Abberger, K.(1997). Quantile Smoothing in Financial Time Series. *Statistical Papers* **38** 125–148.
2. Auestad, B.H. and Tjøstheim, D. (1990). Identification of nonlinear time series: First order characterization and order determination. *Biometrika* **77** (1990) 669–687.
3. Bradley, R.C.(1986). Basic properties of strong mixing conditions. In: Dependence in Probability and Statistics. A survey of recent results. Ed. E. Eberlin and M.S. Taqqu. Birkhäuser, Boston 165–192.
4. Cleveland, W.S. (1979). Robust locally weighted regression and smoothing scatterplots. J. Amer. Statist. Assoc. **74** 829–836.
5. Collomb, G. (1983). Non-parametric time series analysis and prediction: Uniform almost sure convergence of the window and k-NN autoregression estimates. Statistics **16** 297–307.
6. Eberlin, E. and Taqqu, M.S. (1986). Dependence in Probability and Statistics. A survey of recent results. Birkhäuser, Boston 165–192.

7. Engle, R. (1982). Autoregressive conditional heteroscedasticity with estimates of the variance of United Kingdom inflation. *Econometrica* **50** 978–1007.
8. Fan, J. and Gijbels, I. (1992). Variable bundwidth and local linear regression smoothers. *Annals of Statistics* **20** 2008–2036.
9. Fan, J. and Gijbels, I. (1995). Data-driven bandwidth selection in local polynomial fitting: Variable bandwidth and spatial adaptation. *J. Roy. Statist. Soc. Ser. B* **57** 371–394.
10. Fan,J. and Gijbels, I. (1996). Local Polynomial Modeling and its Applications. Chapman & Hall, London .
11. Gasser, T., Kneip, A. and Köhler, W. (1991): A flexible and fast method for automatic smoothing. *J. Amer. Statist. Assoc.* **86** 643–652.
12. Härdle, W., Lütkepohl, H. and Chen, R. (1997). A review of nonparametric time series analysis. *International Statistical Review* **65** (1997) 49–72.
13. Härdle, W. and Tsybakov, A.B. (1997) Local polynomial estimators of the volatility function in nonparametric autoregression. To appear in Journal of Econometrics (1997).
14. Härdle, W., Tsybakov, A.B. and Yang, L. (1997). Nonparametric vector autoregression. To appear in Journal of Statistical Planning and Inference.
15. Härdle, W. and Vieu, P.(1992). Kernel regression smoothing of time series. *J. Time Series Analysis* **13** (1992) 209–232.
16. Hall, P. and Marron, J.S. (1990). On variance estimation in nonparametric regression. *Biometrika* **77** (1990) 415–419.
17. Heiler, S. and Feng, Y. (1997). A bootstrap bandwidth selector for local polynomial fitting. Discussionpaper, SFB178 **II–344,** University of Konstanz (1997).
18. Heiler, S. and Feng, Y. (1998). A simple root n bandwidth selector for nonparametric regression. To appear in J. Nonpar. Statist.
19. Masry, E. and Tjøstheim, D. (1995). Nonparametric estimation and identification of nonlinear ARCH time series. *Econometric Theory* **11** 258–289.
20. Michels, P. (1992). Nichtparametrische Analyse und Prognose von Zeitreihen. Physica-Verlag, Heidelberg.
21. Nadaraya, E.A. (1964). On estimating regression. *Theory Probab. Appl.* **9** 141–142.
22. Nummelin, E.: General Irreducible Markov Chains and Non-negative Operators. Cambridge University Press, Cambridge.
23. Pham, D.T.(1986). The mixing property of bilinear and generalized random coefficiet autoregressive models. Stochastic Processes and Their Applications **23** 291–300.
24. Priestley, M.B.(1988). Nonlinear and Non-stationary Time Series Analysis. Academic Press, London.
25. Robinson, P.(1983). Nonparametric estimators for time series. *J. Time Series Analysis* **4** 185–207.
26. Ruppert, D. Sheather, S.J. and Wand, M.P.(1995). An effective bandwidth selector for local least squares regression. *J. Amer. Statist. Assoc.* **90** 1257–1270.
27. Ruppert, D. and Wand, M.P.(1994). Multivariate locally weighted least squares regression. *Annals of Statistics* **22** 1346–1370.
28. Scott, D.W. (1992). Multivariate Density Estimation: Theory, Practice and Visualization. John Wiley, New York.
29. Stone, C.J.(1977). Consistent nonparametric regression (with discussion). *Annals of Statistics* **5** 595–620.
30. Tjøstheim, D.(1990). Non-linear time series and Markov chains. Advances in Applied Probability **22** (1990) 587–611.

31. Tjøstheim, D. and Auestad, B.H.(1994a). Nonparametric identification of nonlinear time series: Projections. *J. Amer. Statist. Assoc.* **89** 1398–1409.
32. Tjøstheim, D. and Auestad, B.H.(1994b). Nonparametric identification of nonlinear time series: Selection of significant lags. *J. Amer. Statist. Assoc.* **89** 1410–1419.
33. Tong, H.(1990). Non-linear Time Series: A Dynamical System Approach. Oxford University Press, Oxford.
34. Watson, G.S.(1964). Smooth regression analysis. *Sankhyā Ser. A* **26** 359–372.
35. Yang, L. and Härdle, W. (1997). Nonparametric autoregression with multiplicative volatility and additive mean. Submitted to Journal of Time Series Analysis.

Locally Weighted Least Squares in Categorical Varying-Coefficient Models

Gerhard Tutz and Göran Kauermann

Department of Statistics, Ludwig-Maximilians-Universität München, Germany

Summary. In varying-coefficient models the number of coefficients that have to be estimated is usually very high. Consequently local likelihood estimates which are based on an iterative procedure are rather time-consuming. In the present paper an alternative local estimation procedure is proposed. It is based on the weighted least squares estimate applied locally for fixed effect modifier but additionally observations in the neighbourhood are used in a weighted form. Asymptotic behaviour of the locally weighted least squares estimator is shown to be equivalent to the local likelihood estimate. The performance of the estimator is illustrated by a small simulation study and an application to ordinal regression.

1. Introduction

In varying-coefficient models it is assumed that the coefficients vary with the value of another variable, the so-called effect modifier (Hastie & Tibshirani, 1993). Thus the effect of predictors depends on the effect modifier. Often the effect modifier is time and the models are referred to as dynamic models. Alternatively, the varying coefficients approach may be considered as a way of modelling interaction between variables. The basic model considered here is an extension of the multivariate generalized linear model for multinomial response $y \in \{1,\dots,k\}$. It has the form

$$\pi(x,u) = h(Z(x)\beta(u))$$

where $\pi(x,u)' = (P(y=1|x,u),\dots,P(y=q|x,u))$ denotes the response vector with $q = k-1$ components, $Z(x)$ stands for a design matrix built from the predictor x and $\beta(u)$ is the vector of coefficients which depends on the effect modifier u. The response function (the inverse of the link function) $h : \mathbb{R}^q \to \mathbb{R}^q$ links the response vector and the linear predictor $\eta = Z(x)\beta(u)$. For examples of categorical response models see McCullagh & Nelder, 1989, or in the multivariate case ($k > 2$) Fahrmeir & Tutz, 1994. For the principles of varying-coefficient modelling and many examples see Hastie & Tibshirani, 1993.

Hastie & Tibshirani, 1993 used a penalized least squares procedure for the estimation of the varying coefficients. Kauermann & Tutz, 1995, Tutz & Kauermann, 1997 considered a local likelihood estimation procedure and showed consistency and asymptotic normal distribution under mild regularity conditions. In the present paper an alternative approach based on the weighted least squares estimator is introduced. Weighted least squares estimates for categorical data have been made popular by Grizzle, Starmer

& Koch (1969) and have been considered e.g. by Koch et.al. (1977), Imrey et.al. (1981). For a comparison with the maximum likelihood estimate see also Agresti, 1990 (p 458ff). With the increasing availability of computer software ML analyses have become the prefered procedure. However, the advantage of weighted least squares approaches, namely the simplicity of computation, becomes crucial if many parameters — as in the case of varying-coefficient models — have to be estimated.

2. Locally weighted least squares

Let the observations be given by $(p_{ti}, x_{ti}, u_t), t = 1, \ldots, T,\ i = 1, \ldots, m_t$, where $p_{ti} = (p_{ti1}, \ldots, p_{tiq})$ is the vector of relative frequencies computed from n_{ti} observations taken at (x_{ti}, u_t) with x_{ti} being a vector of categorical covariates and u_t denoting the value of the discrete effect modifier. Thus for fixed value u_t (e.g. at time u_t) $x_{ti},\ i = 1, \ldots, m_t$, represent the different values the predictor can take. The consequence of the discrete effect modifier is asymptotic behaviour that is different from asymptotics in the continuous case. The reason is that in the continuous case observations become more dense with increasing sample size whereas in the discrete case observations are collected on a fixed grid. The model has the form

$$\pi_{ti} = h(Z_{ti}\beta_t), \qquad t = 1, \ldots, T,\ i = 1, \ldots, m_t, \tag{2.1}$$

with $\pi'_{ti} = (P(y = 1|x_{ti}, u_t), \ldots, P(y = q|x_{ti}, u_t))$, the design matrix $Z_{ti} = Z(x_{ti})$ and $\beta_t = \beta(u_t)$. With the link function $g = h^{-1}$ model (2.1) is given by

$$g(\pi_{ti}) = Z_{ti}\beta_t, \qquad t = 1, \ldots, T,\ i = 1, \ldots, m_t. \tag{2.2}$$

Probabilities and design matrices for the fixed value u_t may be collected in the vector $\pi'_t = (\pi'_{t1}, \ldots, \pi'_{tm_t})$ and the design matrix $Z'_t = (Z'_{t1}, \ldots, Z'_{tm_t})$. Then (2.1) and (2.2) have the form

$$\pi_t = \bar{h}(Z_t\beta_t) \quad \text{or} \quad \bar{g}(\pi_t) = Z_t\beta_t$$

where $\bar{h} = (h, \ldots, h) : \mathbb{R}^{q \times m_t} \to \mathbb{R}^{q \times m_t}$ is the total response function composed of the q dimensional function h, and $\bar{g} = \bar{h}^{-1}$. The usual weighted least squares estimator of β_t minimizes

$$(\bar{g}(p_t) - Z_t\beta_t)' C_t^{-1} (\bar{g}(p_t) - Z_t\beta_t) \tag{2.3}$$

where the relative frequencies $p'_t = (p_{t1}, \ldots, p_{tm_t})$ are substituted for π_t and $C_t = \text{Diag}\{C_{ti}\}$ is the block diagonal matrix composed of the blocks $C_{ti} = \partial g(\pi_{ti})/\partial \pi' (\text{Diag}(\pi_{ti}) - \pi_{ti}\pi'_{ti})(\partial g(\pi_{ti})/\partial \pi)/n_{ti}$ which are a linear approximation for $\text{cov}\, g(p_{ti})$.

Even if the weighted least squares estimate of β_t exists, the resulting curve will be quite jagged since only observations taken at the measurement point

u_t are used. The alternative estimate of β_t which is considered here is based on the locally weighted least squares criterion

$$\sum_{s=1}^{T} w(u_t, u_s)(\bar{g}(p_s) - Z_s\beta_t)'C_s^{-1}(\bar{g}(p_s) - Z_s\beta_t)$$
$$= \sum_{s=1}^{T} w(u_t, u_s) \sum_{i=1}^{m_s}(g(p_{si}) - Z_{si}\beta_t)'C_{si}^{-1}(g(p_{si}) - Z_{si}\beta_t) \to \min, \quad (2.4)$$

where $w(u_t, u_s)$ is a weight function. In the following, kernel based weights of the Nadaraya-Watson type given by

$$w(u_t, u_s) = K\left(\frac{u_t - u_s}{\gamma}\right)/K(0)$$

are used with K being a unimodal, symmetric kernel function. By using these weights in (2.4), observations close to the 'target point' u_t are taken more serious than observations far away from u_t. For $u_s = u_t$ one obtains $\omega(u_t, u_s) = 1$ and if $u_s \neq u_t$ one has $\omega(u_t, u_s) < 1$.

Straightforward derivation yields the locally weighted least squares estimate (LWLS-) estimate

$$\hat{\beta}_t = \left\{\sum_{s=1}^{T}\sum_{i=1}^{m_s} w(u_t, u_s)Z_{si}'C_{si}^{-1}Z_{si}\right\}^{-1} \sum_{s=1}^{T}\sum_{i=1}^{m_s} w(u_t, u_s)Z_{si}'C_{si}^{-1}g(p_{si}). \quad (2.5)$$

It is easily seen that for $\gamma \to 0$ the weight

$$w(u_t, u_s) = \begin{cases} 1 & u_t = u_s \\ 0 & \text{otherwise} \end{cases}$$

yields

$$\begin{aligned} \hat{\beta}_t &= \left(\sum_{i=1}^{m_t} Z_{ti}'C_{ti}^{-1}Z_{ti}\right)^{-1} \sum_{i=1}^{m_t} Z_{ti}'C_{ti}^{-1}g(p_{ti}) \quad (2.6) \\ &= (Z_t'C_t^{-1}Z_t)^{-1}Z_t'C_t^{-1}\bar{g}(p_t) \end{aligned}$$

which is the usual least squares estimate minimizing (2.3). For $\gamma \to \infty$ the weight becomes $w(u_t, u_s) = 1$ for all u_s and the ultra smooth estimate $\hat{\beta}_1 = \ldots = \hat{\beta}_T$ follows.

3. Asymptotic behaviour

Fixed cell asymptotics in the context of varying-coefficient models assumes $n_{ti}/n_t \to \lambda_{ti} \in (0,1)$, $n_t/n \to \lambda_t \in (0,1)$ for $n \to \infty$ where $n_t = \sum_i n_{ti}$ is the total sum of observations taken at u_t and $n = \sum_t n_t$ is the total sample size. In order to obtain useful estimates it is sensible to assume $w(u_t, u_s) \to 0$ for $u_t \neq u_s$ for increasing sample size $n = \sum_t n_t$.

In the following let the asymptotic behaviour of the weights be controlled by

$$w(u_t, u_s) = O\left(n^{-\alpha}\right) \qquad \text{for } u_t \neq u_s.$$

The bias of the locally weighted least squares estimate

With $\tilde{C}_{si} = n_{si} C_{si}$, the estimator (2.5) may be written as

$$\begin{aligned} \hat{\beta}_t &= \left(\textstyle\sum_{s=1}^T \frac{n_s}{n_t} w(u_t, u_s) \sum_{i=1}^{m_s} \frac{n_{si}}{n_s} Z_{si}' \tilde{C}_{si}^{-1} Z_{si}\right)^{-1} \\ &\quad \left(\textstyle\sum_{s=1}^T \frac{n_s}{n_t} w(u_t, u_s) \sum_{i=1}^{m_s} \frac{n_{si}}{n_s} Z_{si}' \tilde{C}_{si}^{-1} g(p_{si})\right). \end{aligned}$$

The observations taken at the target value u_t are separated from the smoothing terms by defining

$$\begin{aligned} A_t &= \sum_{i=1}^{m_t} w(u_t, u_t) \frac{n_{ti}}{n_t} Z_{ti}' \tilde{C}_{ti}^{-1} Z_{ti}, \\ \bar{A}_t &= \sum_{s \neq t} w(u_t, u_s) \frac{n_s}{n_t} \sum_{i=1}^{m_s} \frac{n_{si}}{n_s} Z_{si}' C_{si}^{-1} Z_{si}, \\ B_t &= \sum_{i=1}^{m_t} w(u_t, u_t) \frac{n_{ti}}{n_t} Z_{ti}' \tilde{C}_{ti}^{-1} g(p_{ti}) \\ \bar{B}_t &= \sum_{s \neq t} \frac{n_s}{n_t} w(u_t, u_s) \sum_{i=1}^{m_s} \frac{n_{si}}{n_s} Z_{si}' \tilde{C}_{si}^{-1} g(p_{si}). \end{aligned}$$

Thus one obtains

$$\hat{\beta}_t = (A_t + \bar{A}_t)^{-1}(B_t + \bar{B}_t). \tag{3.1}$$

It should be noted that in $A_t, \bar{A}_t, B_t, \bar{B}_t$ the sample sizes occur only in the form n_s/n_t and n_{si}/n_s which converge to λ_s and λ_{si} respectively.

Expanding the expectation of (3.1) in a Taylor series about A_t yields

$$E\hat{\beta}_t = A_t^{-1}(EB_t + E\bar{B}_t) - A_t^{-1}\bar{A}_t A_t^{-1}(EB_t + E\bar{B}_t) + O(||A_t^{-3}\bar{A}_t^2||)(EB_t + E\bar{B}_t).$$

Since $A_t^{-1}B_t$ is the usual weighted least squares estimate at u_t,given in (2.6) the expectation is given by $A_t^{-1}EB_t = \beta_t + O(n_t^{-1})$.

With

$$\begin{aligned} B_t(\pi) &= \sum_i \frac{n_{ti}}{n_t} w(u_t, u_t) Z_{ti} \tilde{C}_{ti}^{-1} g(\pi_{ti}) \\ \bar{B}_t(\pi) &= \sum_{s \neq i} \frac{n_s}{n_t} \sum_i \frac{n_{si}}{n_s} w(u_t, u_s) Z_{si} \tilde{C}_{si}^{-1} g(\pi_{si}) \end{aligned}$$

one obtains from simple derivation

$$\begin{aligned} EB_t &= B_t(\pi) + O(n_t^{-1}) \\ E\bar{B}_t &= \bar{B}_t(\pi) + O(n^{-1-\alpha}) = O(n^{-\alpha}) + O(n^{-1-\alpha}) \\ \bar{A}_t &= O(n^{-\alpha}) \\ A_t^{-1} \bar{A}_t A_t^{-1} &= O(n^{-\alpha}) \\ O(||A_t^{-3} \bar{A}_t^{-2}||) &= O(n^{-2\alpha}). \end{aligned}$$

Thus the bias reduces to

$$E\hat{\beta}_t - \beta_t = A_t^{-1} \bar{B}_t(\pi) - A_t^{-1} \bar{A}_t A_t^{-1} B_t(\pi) + O(n^{-2\alpha}) + O(n^{-1}) \tag{3.2}$$

where the leading term has the order $O(n^{-\alpha})$. Therefore we have the following result.

Proposition 1: *The bias of the locally least squares estimator has the order*

$$E(\hat{\beta}_t - \beta_t) = O(n^{-\alpha}) + O(n^{-1}).$$

The smoothing over neighbourhood observations adds a bias of the order $O(n^{-\alpha})$.

Consistency and asymtotic normality

For the covariance of $B_t + \bar{B}_t$ one obtains

$$\text{cov}\,(B_t + \bar{B}_t) = \sum_s \frac{n_s}{n_t} w(u_t, u_s) \sum_i \frac{n_{si}}{n_s} Z'_{si} \tilde{C}_{si}^{-1} \text{cov}\, g(p_{si}) \tilde{C}_{si}^{-1} Z_{si}.$$

Since $\text{cov}\, g(p_{si}) = \tilde{C}_{si}/n_{si} + O(n^{-3/2})$ the covariance reduces to

$$\text{cov}\,(B_t + \bar{B}_t) = \frac{1}{n_t} \sum_s w(u_t, u_s) \sum_i Z'_{si} \tilde{C}_{si}^{-1} Z_{si} + O(n^{-3/2}).$$

The covariance of $\hat{\beta}_t$ is given by

$$\begin{aligned} &\text{cov}\,(\hat{\beta}_t) \\ &= (A_t + \bar{A}_t)^{-1} \text{cov}\,(B_t + \bar{B}_t)(A_t + \bar{A}_t)^{-1} \\ &= A_t^{-1} \left[\frac{1}{n_t} \sum_s w(u_t, u_s) \sum_i Z'_{si} \tilde{C}_{si}^{-1} Z_{si} \right] A_t^{-1} + O(n^{-1-\alpha}) + O(n^{-3/2}). \end{aligned}$$

By extracting terms of order $O(n^{-1-\alpha})$ from the leading term one obtains the simpler form

$$\begin{aligned}\operatorname{cov}(\hat{\beta}_t) &= \tfrac{1}{n_t}\textstyle\sum_i A_t^{-1} Z_{ti}' \tilde{C}_{ti}^{-1} Z_{ti} A_t^{-1} + O(n^{-1-\alpha}) + O(n^{-3/2}) \\ &= \tfrac{1}{n_{ti}} A_t^{-1} A_t A_t^{-1} + O(n^{-1-\alpha}) + O(n^{-3/2}) \\ &= \tfrac{1}{n_{ti}} A_t^{-1} + O(n^{-1-\alpha}) + O(n^{-3/2}).\end{aligned}$$

Thus consistency holds for any $\alpha > 0$.

Proposition 2: *The mean squared error has the order*

$$MSE = O(n^{-2\alpha}) + O(n^{-1}).$$

For $\alpha = 1/2$ the mean squared error has the same order as the usual weighted least squares estimate (2.6).

The usual asymptotics $\sqrt{n_t}(\hat{\beta}_t - \beta_t)$ which works for the weighted least squares estimate (2.6) will fail in the smoothed case, since $E[\sqrt{n_t}(\hat{\beta}_t - \beta_t)] = O(n^{1/2-\alpha})$ and therefore for $\alpha \le 1/2$ the bias does not vanish. For $\alpha > 1/2$ the asymptotic normal distribution follows from the asymptotic normal distribution of $\sqrt{n_{si}}(g(p_{si}) - g(\pi_{ti})) \to N(0, \tilde{C}_{si})$.

In closed form $\hat{\beta}_t$ may be written by

$$\hat{\beta}_t = (Z' W_t^{1/2} C^{-1} W_t^{1/2} Z)^{-1} Z' W_t^{1/2} C^{-1} W_t^{1/2} \bar{g}(p)$$

where

$$\begin{aligned} Z' &= (Z_1', \ldots, Z_T') \\ W_t &= \operatorname{Diag}(w(u_t, u_1) I_{m_1 \times m_1}, \ldots, w(u_t, u_T) I_{m_T \times m_T}) \\ C &= \operatorname{Diag}(C_1, \ldots, C_T) \\ \bar{g}(p)' &= (\bar{g}(p_1)', \ldots, \bar{g}(p_T)'), \quad p_t' = (p_{t1}, \ldots, p_{tm_t}) \end{aligned}$$

and $I_{m_t \times m_t}$ is the $(m_t \times m_t)$ unit matrix.

From $\operatorname{cov} \bar{g}(p) = C + O(n^{-3/2})$ it follows

$$\begin{aligned}\operatorname{cov} \hat{\beta}_t &= (Z' W_t^{1/2} C^{-1} W_t^{1/2} Z)^{-1} Z' W_t^{1/2} C^{-1} W_t^{1/2} C W_t^{1/2} C^{-1} W_t^{1/2} Z \\ &\quad \times (Z' W_t^{1/2} C^{-1} W_t^{1/2} Z)^{-1} + O(n^{-3/2}).\end{aligned}$$

For $n \to \infty$ one obtains

$$\begin{aligned}\operatorname{cov}(\sqrt{n}\hat{\beta}_t) &\to n(w(u_t, u_t) Z_t' C_t^{-1} Z_t)^{-1} (w(u_t, u_t)^2 Z_t' C_t^{-1} C_t C_t^{-1} Z_t) \\ &\quad \times (w(u_t, u_t) Z_t' C_t^{-1} Z_t)^{-1} \\ &= n(Z_t' C_t^{-1} Z_t)^{-1} = (Z_t' \operatorname{Diag}(\frac{n_{ti}}{n} \tilde{C}_{ti}^{-1}) Z_t)^{-1}\end{aligned}$$

and therefore

$$\operatorname{cov} \sqrt{n}\hat{\beta}_t \to \left(Z_t' \operatorname{Diag}\left(\frac{\lambda_{ti}}{\lambda_t} \tilde{C}_{ti}^{-1} \right) Z_t \right)^{-1} = \left(\sum_i \frac{\lambda_{ti}}{\lambda_t} Z_{ti}' \tilde{C}_{ti}^{-1} Z_{ti} \right)^{-1} \tag{3.3}$$

Proposition 3:
For $\alpha > 1/2$ and $n \to \infty$, $n_{ti}/n_t \to \lambda_{ti}$, $n_t/n \to \lambda_t$ one has asymptotically

$$\sqrt{n}(\hat{\beta}_t - \beta) \sim N\left(0, \left(\sum_i \frac{\lambda_{ti}}{\lambda_t} Z'_{ti} \tilde{C}_{ti}^{-1} Z_{ti}\right)^{-1}\right)$$

and

$$\sqrt{n_t}(\hat{\beta}_t - \beta) \sim N\left(0, \left(\sum_i \lambda_{ti} Z'_{ti} \tilde{C}_{ti}^{-1} Z_{ti}\right)^{-1}\right).$$

Therefore for $\alpha > 1/2$ the asymptotic behaviour is the same as for the unsmoothed weighted least squares estimate which is a BAN estimate.

In applications of the least squares estimator,

$$\tilde{C}_{si} = (\partial g(\pi_{si})/\partial \pi')[\text{Diag}\,(\pi_{si}) - \pi_{si}\pi'_{si}]$$

$(\partial g(\pi_{si})/\partial \pi)$ has to be replaced by

$$\tilde{C}_{si}(p_{si}) = (\partial g(p_{si})/\partial \pi')[\text{Diag}\,(p_{si}) - p_{si}p'_{si})](\partial g(p_{si})/\partial \pi).$$

However, since $E\tilde{C}_{si}(p_{si}) = \tilde{C}_{si} + O(n^{-1})$ and $\tilde{C}_{si}(p_{si}) = \tilde{C}_{si} + O_p(n^{-1/2})$ hold, the asymptotic behaviour is unaltered.

4. Bias correction

According to Proposition 1, smoothing adds a bias of the estimate of order $O(n^{-\alpha})$ to the estimate. For small α the bias will not be neglectable. Equation (3.2) shows a way to reduce the bias. Let A_t and $\bar{A}_t$ be replaced by the empirical versions

$$A_t(p) = \frac{n_{t_i}}{n_t} \sum_i \omega(u_t, u_t) Z'_{ti} \tilde{C}_{ti}(p_{ti})^{-1} Z_{ti}$$

$$\bar{A}_t(p) = \sum_{s \neq t} \omega(u_t, u_s) \frac{n_s}{n_t} \sum_i \frac{n_{s_i}}{n_s} Z'_{si} \tilde{C}_{si}(p_{si})^{-1} Z_{si}.$$

Then, the bias may be estimated by

$$\hat{b}_{t,1} = A_t(p)^{-1}\bar{B}_t(p) - A_t(p)^{-1}\bar{A}_t(p)A_t(p)^{-1}B_t(p) \tag{4.1}$$

yielding the bias corrected estimate

$$\hat{\beta}^c_{t,1} = \hat{\beta}_t - \hat{b}_{t,1}.$$

An alternative bias correction may be derived from

$$E\hat{\beta}_t = (A_t + \bar{A}_t)^{-1}(B_t(\pi) + \bar{B}_t(\pi)) + O(n^{-1}).$$

A simple plug-in estimate of the bias term is not feasible since we have $\hat{\beta}_t = (A_t(p) + \bar{A}_t(p))^{-1}(B_t(p) + \bar{B}_t(p))$. However, in $B_t(\pi)$ and $\bar{B}_t(\pi)$ an essential term is $g(\pi_{si})$. The main source of the bias is the use of neighbourhood observations where one has $g(\pi_{si}) = Z_{si}\beta_s$ instead of $g(\pi_{si}) = Z_{si}\beta_t$. Therefore by approximating the expectation $Eg(p_{si})$ by $Z_{si}\beta_s$ one obtains

$$E\hat{\beta}_t = (A_t + \bar{A}_t)^{-1} \sum_{s=1}^{T} \sum_{i=1}^{m_s} \omega(u_t, u_s) Z'_{si} \tilde{C}_{si}^{-1} Z_{si} \beta_s.$$

By substituting $\hat{\beta}_s$ for β_s one gets the bias approximation

$$\begin{aligned} \hat{b}_{t,2} &= (A_t(p) + \bar{A}_t(p))^{-1} \sum_{s=1}^{T} \sum_{i=1}^{m_s} \omega(u_t, u_s) Z_{si} \tilde{C}_{si}^{-1} Z_{si} \hat{\beta}_s - \hat{\beta}_t \\ &= (A_t(p) + \bar{A}_t(p))^{-1} \sum_{s=1}^{T} \sum_{i=1}^{m_s} \omega(u_t, u_s) Z'_{si} \tilde{C}_{si}^{-1} (Z_{si} \hat{\beta}_s - g(p_{si})) \quad (4.2) \end{aligned}$$

The corresponding corrected estimate is given by

$$\hat{\beta}_{t,2}^c = \hat{\beta}_t - \hat{b}_{t,2}.$$

5. Simulation and application

5.1 A simulation study

In a small simulation study the underlying model has dichotomous response and follows the logistic model

$$p_t = \frac{\exp(\beta(t))}{1 + \exp(\beta(t))}$$

with $\beta(t)$ given by

$$\beta(t) = 2\sin(2\pi(t - 1/20)),\ t = 1, \ldots, 21.$$

At each measurement point t, $n_t = 10$ observations were drawn. The estimation is based on the normal kernel with a smoothing parameter which is optimal for local likelihood estimates under quadratic risk. We deliberately did not choose a smoothing parameter which is optimal for the lwls estimate since in practice it is not known. The graphs show the mean over 100 simulations together with empirical pointwise 0.95 confidence intervals. Throughout the applications in the case of zero cell counts we used the usual correction which adds 0.5 in the numerator and the denominator to obtain empirical logits (e.g. Agresti, 1990, p.87). In Figure 5.1 the uncorrected lwls estimate is given. It is seen that smoothing yields strongly biased estimates. Figure 5.2 shows the bias corrected estimate based on 4.1. Now the bias is strongly reduced. Of course as a side effect the variance is slightly increased.

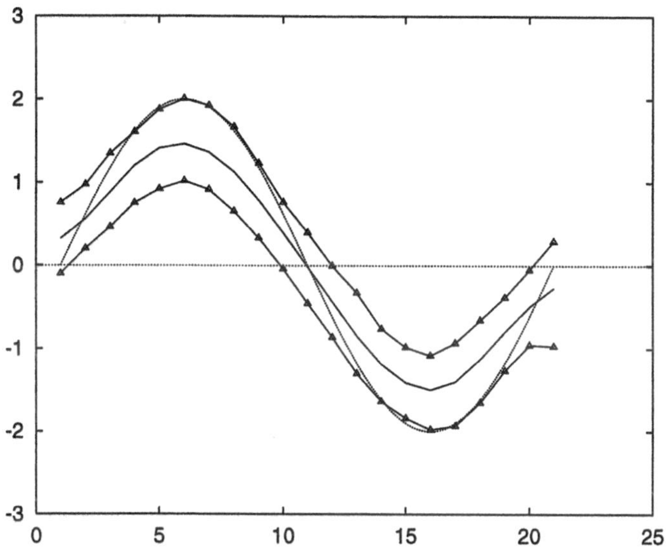

Fig. 5.1. Uncorrected weighted least squares estimate with underlying curve (dashed line) and empirical 0.95 confidence intervals.

For comparison Figure 5.3 shows the local maximum likelihood estimate with bias correction. Although the smoothing parameter is chosen with respect to the local likelihood estimate the lwls estimate with bias correction yields an qualitatively comparable result with even smaller confidence intervals.

5.2 An application to ordinal responses

In the analysis of duration of unemployment we consider three response categories, short term unemployment (≤ 6 months), medium time unemployment (between 7 and 12 months) and long time unemployment (≥ 13 months). The data have been collected over several years in the socio-economic panel in Germany (Hanefeld, 1987). We consider a varying coefficient model which is based on the cumulative logistic model (McCullagh, 1980). The model has the form

$$P(Y \leq r) = F(\theta_r(Age) + x_N \beta(Age))$$

where x_N is a dummy variable for nationality ($x_N = 1$ for Germans, $x_N = 0$ for foreigners) and the coefficients are allowed to vary across age. The coefficients $\theta_1(Age)$, $\theta_2(Age)$ may be interpreted as thresholds (see McCullagh, 1980) which show the dependence of $P(Y = 1)$ and $P(Y \leq 2)$ on age (apart from nationality). The coefficient $\beta(Age)$ shows how the effect of nationality varies across age.

Figure 5.4 shows the lwls estimates based on bias correction (4.2).

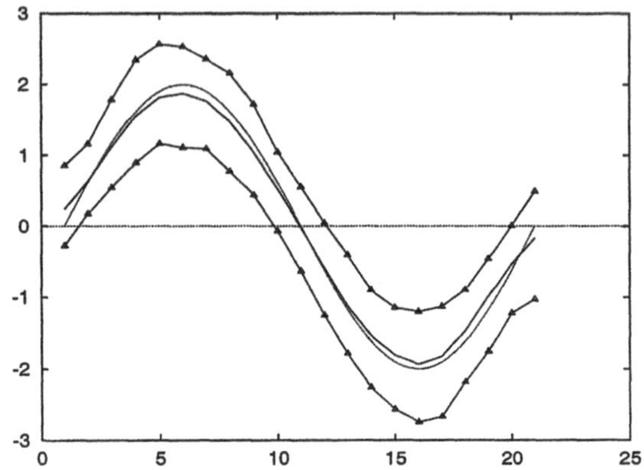

Fig. 5.2. Bias corrected estimate based on (4.1) with underlying curve (dashed line) and empirical 0.95 confidence intervals.

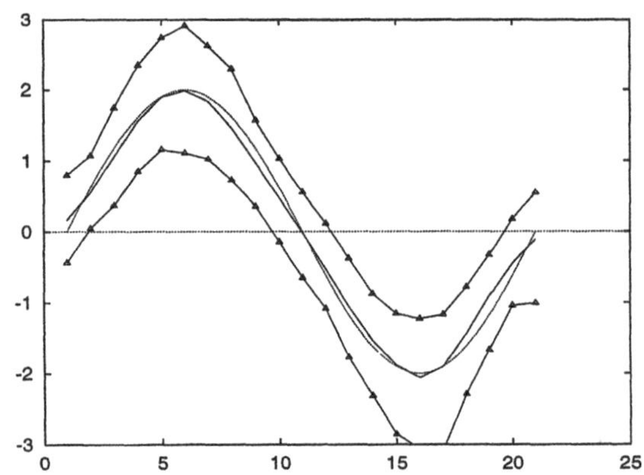

Fig. 5.3. Bias corrected ML estimate with underlying curve (dashed line) and empirical 0.95 confidence intervals.

It is seen that the threshold $\theta_1(Age)$ remains rather constant whereas the threshold $\theta_2(Age)$ is strongly decreasing. For the effect of nationality on almost linear decrease is seen. It is rather strong for younger unemployed persons, but for unemployed persons who are older than 50 years there is hardly an effect of nationality.

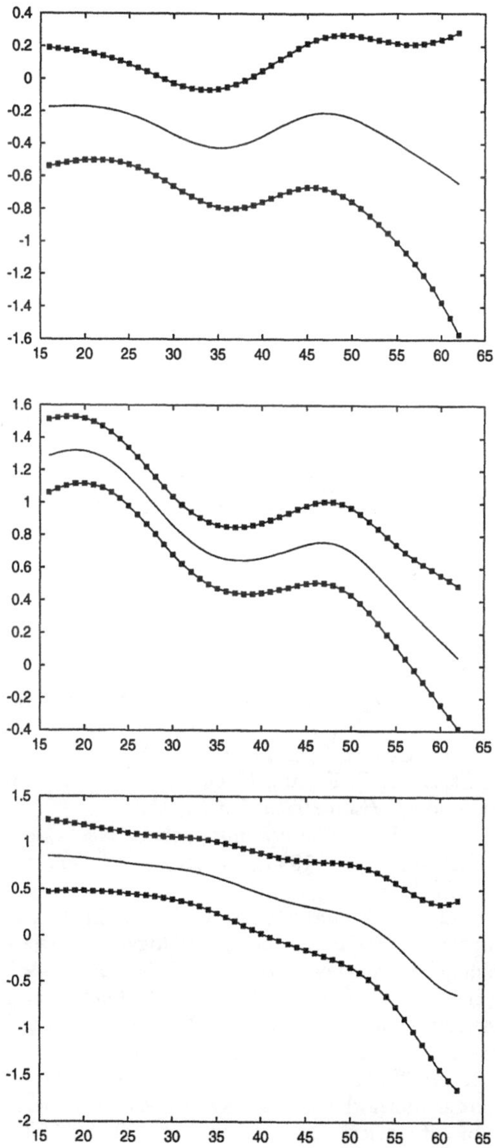

Fig. 5.4. Estimated coefficients for the cumulative model varying across age (thresholds θ_1, θ_2 and effect of nationality).

6. Concluding remarks

Asymptotic properties and simple versions of bias correction have been given. It should be noted that the asymptotic distribution is the same as for local likelihood estimates (see e.g. Tutz & Kauermann, 1997)but the computing time is much lower. Ml estimation is an iterative procedure which in the case of weighted ml estimates is sometimes numerically unstable because the inverse of the Fisher matrix has to be computed in each iteration step. Even if no problems arise the computing time of the weighted least squares estimate is only a fraction (1/5 - 1/4) of the time that is needed for the ml estimate. Moreover, the lwls estimate is more stable if cross validation is used to choose the smoothing parameter. A detailed comparison of local likelihood and lwls estimates with derivative procedures of bias correction is in work.

Acknowledgements

This research has been supported by Deutsche Forschungsgemeinschaft (DFG project VARKOFF). We thank Silke Edlich for her computational work.

References

1. Agresti, A. (1990). *Categorical Data Analysis.* Wiley, New York.
2. Fahrmeir, L. and Tutz, G. (1994). *Multivariate Statistical Modelling Based on Generalized Linear Models.* Springer Verlag, New York.
3. Grizzle, J. E., Starmer, C. F., and Koch, G. G. (1969). Analysis of categorical data by linear models. *Biometrika,* 28:137–156.
4. Hanefeld, U. (1987). *Das sozio-oekonomische Panel.* Campus, Frankfurt.
5. Hastie, T. and Tibshirani, R. (1993). Varying-coefficient models. *J. Roy. Statist. Soc.,* B 55:757–796.
6. Imrey, P. B., Koch, G. G., and Stokes, M. E. (1981). Categorical data analysis: Some reflections on the log linear model and logistic regression. Part I: Historical and methodolocgical overview. *Internat. Statist. Rev.,* 49:265–283.
7. Kauermann, G. and Tutz, G. (1995). Local likelihood estimation and bias reduction in varying coefficient models. Technical report, Technical University of Berlin, Institute of Quantitative methods. 95-9.
8. Koch, G. G., Landis, J. R., Freeman, J. L., Freeman, D. H., and Lehnen, R. G. (1977). A general methodology for the analysis of experiments with repeated measurement of categorical data. *Biometrics,* 33:133–158.
9. McCullagh, P. (1980). Regression model for ordinal data (with discussion). *J. Roy. Statist. Soc.,* B 42:109–127.
10. McCullagh, P. and Nelder, J. A. (1989). *Generalized Linear Models.* Chapman and Hall, New York, 2nd edition.
11. Tutz, G. and Kauermann, G. (1997). Local estimators in multivariate generalized linear models with varying coefficients. *Computational Statistics,* 12:193–208.

Using First Differences as a Device against Multicollinearity

Helge Toutenburg[1] and Götz Trenkler[2*]

[1] Department of Statistics, Ludwig-Maximilians-Universität München, Germany
[2] Department of Statistics, Universität Dortmund, Germany

1. Introduction

In his textbook, Hans Schneeweiß (1971) warned that taking first differences in econometric models involving data with a common trend does not offer a solution to the multicollinearity problem. In the following we will confirm his point of view by giving an alternative proof that the generalized method of least squares (GLS), applied to the model with first differences, will not produce other estimates than the ordinary least squares (OLS) method in the original model. Moreover, we shall demonstrate that related estimation procedures also cannot be expected to provide a substantial improvement over the OLS-method. For this analysis the tools from the theory of oblique and orthogonal projectors will turn out to be extremely helpful.

2. OLS- and GLS-estimation in the difference model

Consider the linear regression model

$$y = \beta_0 \mathbb{1}_n + X\beta + u, \quad \mathsf{E}(u) = 0, \quad \mathsf{Cov}(u) = \sigma^2 W, \tag{2.1}$$

where y is an $n \times 1$ observation vector on the dependent variable, $\mathbb{1}_n = (1, \ldots, 1)'$ is the $n \times 1$ vector of ones, X is an $n \times p$ nonstochastic matrix of observations on the explanatory variables (regressor matrix), β_0 is a scalar and β is a vector of type $p \times 1$, both unknown. We assume that the matrix $(\mathbb{1}_n, X)$ is of full column rank. The matrix W occurring in the covariance matrix $\sigma^2 W$ of the $n \times 1$ disturbance vector is supposed to be of the form

$$W = \rho \mathbb{1}_n \mathbb{1}_n' + (1 - \rho) I_n, \tag{2.2}$$

where the parameters ρ as well as $\sigma^2 > 0$ are unknown.

It is easy to see (cf. Pollock 1979, p.115) that the least squares estimator of β is

$$\hat{\beta} = (X'QX)^{-1} X'Qy, \tag{2.3}$$

* Support by Deutsche Forschungsgemeinschaft Grant Tr 253/2-3 is gratefully acknowledged

where $Q = I_n - \frac{1}{n}\mathbb{1}_n\mathbb{1}_n'$ is the orthogonal projector on $\mathcal{N}(\mathbb{1}_n')$, the null space of $\mathbb{1}_n'$. Due to a result by McElroy (1967), the special covariance structure (2.2) implies that GLS-estimator and OLS-estimator for β coincide.

Suppose we take first differences in model (2.1) as a means against multicollinearity. Then we obtain the transformed model

$$\Delta y = \Delta X\beta + \Delta u\,, \tag{2.4}$$

where the $(n-1)\times n$ matrix

$$\Delta = \begin{pmatrix} -1 & 1 & 0 & \cdots & 0 & 0 \\ 0 & -1 & 1 & \cdots & 0 & 0 \\ \vdots & \vdots & \vdots & \ddots & \vdots & \vdots \\ 0 & 0 & 0 & \cdots & -1 & 1 \end{pmatrix} \tag{2.5}$$

has full row rank. Clearly, in model (2.4) we have

$$\mathsf{E}(\Delta u) = 0\,, \quad \mathsf{Cov}(\Delta u) = \sigma^2 \Delta W \Delta'\,. \tag{2.6}$$

However, since $\Delta\mathbb{1}_n = 0$ we obtain

$$\mathsf{Cov}(\Delta u) = \sigma^2(1-\rho)\Delta\Delta'\,, \tag{2.7}$$

and the GLS-estimator for β becomes

$$\tilde{\beta}_\Delta = (X'P_{\Delta'}X)^{-1}X'P_{\Delta'}y\,, \tag{2.8}$$

where $P_{\Delta'} = \Delta'(\Delta\Delta')^{-1}\Delta$ is the orthogonal projector on the row space of Δ. Observe that $X'P_{\Delta'}X$ is nonsingular. For, if $X'P_{\Delta'}Xz = 0$ for some $z \neq 0$, then $z'X'P_{\Delta'}Xz = 0$ which implies $P_{\Delta'}Xz = 0$, i.e. $Xz \in \mathcal{N}(P_{\Delta'}) = \mathcal{N}(\Delta)$. Now since $\Delta\mathbb{1}_n = 0$ and Δ is of full row rank we have $Xz = \lambda\mathbb{1}_n$ for some $\lambda \neq 0$ ($\lambda = 0$ can be ruled out since $z \neq 0$). Hence $\mathbb{1}_n \in \mathcal{R}(X)$ which is a contradiction to the model setup (2.1).

For the case $\rho = 0$ it was shown by Friedmann (1977) that OLS $\hat{\beta}$ and GLS $\tilde{\beta}_\Delta$ coincide. On the other hand, he proved this identity in the more general framework where Δ is replaced by an $(n-1)\times n$ matrix of full row rank satisfying $D\mathbb{1}_n = 0$. We will now regain his result where, however, our proof is more direct and shorter.

Theorem 2.1. *Let D be an $(n-1)\times n$ matrix of full row rank satisfying $D\mathbb{1}_n = 0$. Then the estimators $\hat{\beta} = (X'QX)^{-1}X'Qy$ and $\tilde{\beta}_D = (X'P_{D'}X)^{-1}X'P_{D'}y$ are identical.*

Proof. By the same reasoning as in the lines after (2.8) we see that $X'P_{D'}X$ is nonsingular. Since D satisfies $D\mathbb{1}_n = 0$ it can be written as $D = ZQ$ for some matrix Z (cf. Ben–Israel and Greville 1974, p.39) which implies $\mathcal{R}(D') \subset \mathcal{R}(Q)$, where $\mathcal{R}(\cdot)$ denotes the column space of a matrix. As D is of full row rank we have $\dim\mathcal{R}(D') = n-1 = \dim\mathcal{R}(Q)$ such that $\mathcal{R}(D') = \mathcal{R}(Q)$. Since orthogonal projectors are uniquely determined by their column spaces we finally conclude $Q = P_{D'}$. □

3. Coincidence of OLS- and GLS-estimator in the general difference model

Consider now the general difference model

$$Dy = DX\beta + Du\,, \tag{3.1}$$

where D is an $(n-1) \times n$ matrix of full row rank such that $D\mathbb{1}_n = 0$. Then the OLS-estimator in (3.1) of β is

$$\hat{\beta_D} = (X'D'DX)^{-1}X'D'Dy\,, \tag{3.2}$$

whereas the GLS-estimator becomes

$$\tilde{\beta_D} = (X'P_{D'}X)^{-1}X'P_{D'}y\,, \tag{3.3}$$

which by Theorem 2.1 can be written as

$$\hat{\beta} = (X'QX)^{-1}X'Qy\,. \tag{3.4}$$

Note that $\mathrm{rk}(DX) = \mathrm{rk}(X) - \dim(\mathcal{R}(X) \cap \mathcal{N}(D)) = \mathrm{rk}(X)$, since $\mathcal{N}(D) = \{\lambda\mathbb{1}_n \mid \lambda \in I\!R\}$ and $\mathbb{1}_n \notin \mathcal{R}(X)$ (cf. Theorem 3.4.17 in Rao and Bhimasankaram 1992). Thus $X'D'DX$ is nonsingular.

It is clear that the GLS estimator $\hat{\beta_D}$ outperforms the OLS estimator $\hat{\beta}_{OLS}$ in model (3.1) in terms of their covariances. Nevertheless there might be situations where both estimators produce the same values.

Theorem 3.1. *The OLSE $\hat{\beta}_{OLS}$ and the GLS $\tilde{\beta}_D$ coincide for all y if and only if*

$$P_{DX}DD' = DD'P_{DX}\,, \tag{3.5}$$

where $P_{DX} = DX(X'D'DX)^{-1}X'D'$ is the orthogonal projector on $\mathcal{R}(DX)$.

Proof. By a well-known result (cf. Puntanen and Styan 1989) OLS-estimator and GLS-estimator are equal for all y if and only if $P_{DX}\mathsf{Cov}(Du) = \mathsf{Cov}(Du)P_{DX}$. However, as $\mathsf{Cov}(Du) = \sigma^2 DWD' = \sigma^2(1-\rho)DD'$, condition (3.5) is shown. □

Observe that condition (3.5) can be eqivalently written as

$$\mathcal{R}(DD'DX) \subset \mathcal{R}(DX)\,. \tag{3.6}$$

This follows from the already mentioned article by Puntanen and Styan (1989).

4. Choice of a generalized difference matrix

Suppose we are given two competing OLS estimators $\hat{\beta}_D$ and $\hat{\beta}_E$, where $D\mathbb{1}_n = 0 = E\mathbb{1}_n$. Then the question might arise which one should be preferred under model (2.1). For this purpose we compare their covariance matrices.

$$\mathsf{Cov}(\hat{\beta}_D) - \mathsf{Cov}(\hat{\beta}_E) = S[I - RR']S' , \tag{4.1}$$

where

$$S = X(X'D'DX)^{-1}X'D'D \tag{4.2}$$

and

$$R = X(X'E'EX)^{-1}X'E'E . \tag{4.3}$$

Since R is an oblique projector it can be written in the form

$$R = U \begin{pmatrix} I_r & K \\ 0 & 0 \end{pmatrix} U' , \tag{4.4}$$

where U is an orthogonal matrix, K is an $r \times (n-r)$ matrix and $r = \mathrm{rk}(R)$ (cf. Trenkler 1994). Then

$$I - RR' = U \begin{pmatrix} -KK' & 0 \\ 0 & I_{n-r} \end{pmatrix} U' , \tag{4.5}$$

and from this representation it can be seen that the covariance matrix difference in (4.1) can be expected to be indefinite. For instance, assume that $\mathcal{R}(I - RR') \cap \mathcal{N}(S) = \{0\}$. Then $I - RR'$ and $S[I - RR']S'$ have the same number of positive, negative and zero eigenvalues, respectively i.e. they have identical inertia (cf. Baksalary, Nordström and Styan 1990, Lemma 1). Since R is not symmetric, $K \neq 0$ and hence $I - RR'$ has negative and positive eigenvalues. Thus, in this case $\mathsf{Cov}(\hat{\beta}_D) - \mathsf{Cov}(\hat{\beta}_E)$ is indefinite. By the same argument $\mathsf{Cov}(\hat{\beta}_E) - \mathsf{Cov}(\hat{\beta}_D)$ will not be n.n.d. in general.

References

1. Baksalary, J.K.; Nordström, K. and Styan, G.P.H. (1990). Löwner-ordering and Antitonicity of Generalized Inverses of Hermitian Matrices, *Linear Algebra and its Applications* 127, 171–182
2. Ben–Israel,A. and Greville,T.N.E. (1974). *Generalized Inverses: Theory and methods.*, Wiley, New York
3. Friedmann,R. (1977). Trendbereinigung mit ersten Differenzen – eine Klarstellung, *Statistische Hefte* 18, 203–208
4. McElroy, F.W. (1967). A Necessary and Sufficient Condition that Ordinary Least Squares Estimators be Best Linear Unbiased, *Journal of the American Statistical Association* 62, 1302–1304
5. Pollock, D.S.G. (1979). *The Algebra of Econometrics*, Wiley, New York

6. Puntanen,S. and Styan, G.P.H. (1989). The Equality of the Ordinary Least Squares Estimator and the Best Linear Unbiased Estimator, *The American Statistician* 43, 153–164
7. Rao, A.R. and Bhimasankaram, P. (1992). *Linear Algebra*, McGraw–Hill, New Delhi
8. Schneeweiß, H. (1971). *Ökonometrie*, Physica, Würzburg
9. Trenkler, G. (1994). Characterization of Oblique and Orthogonal Projectors, *Proceedings of the International Conference of Linear Statistical Inference LINSTAT '93, Eds: T. Calinski, R. Kala*, Kluwer AcademicPublishers, Dordrecht, 255–270

Asymptotic Equivalence of Ordinary Least Squares and Generalized Least Squares with Trending Regressors and Stationary Autoregressive Disturbances

Walter Krämer

Department of Statistics, Universität Dortmund, Germany

Summary. This note generalizes previous results on the asymptotic equivalence of Ordinary and Generalized Least Squares estimates in Linear Regression models with trending data.

1. Introduction and Summary

This note considers the relative efficiency of OLS versus GLS in the linear regression model

$$y_t = x_t'\beta + u_t \quad (t = 1, 2, \ldots), \tag{1.1}$$

where x_t and β are $K \times 1$ and where the unobservable disturbances u_t are autocorrelated but independent of the regressors $x_t = (x_{t1}, \ldots, x_{tK})'$. It is well known that, given the regressors, OLS is in general no longer BLUE when disturbances are correlated, but as GLS (the BLUE) is often only of academic interest due to lack of knowledge of the disturbance correlation structure, there has been an enormous interest in statistics and econometrics in the relative efficiency of OLS (Watson 1968, Krämer 1980, Krämer and Donninger 1986, Busse et al. 1994 among many others).

One strand of this literature, originating with Grenander (1954), is concerned with conditions on regressors and disturbances which guarantee that OLS is at least *asymptotically* efficient (Rosenblatt 1956, Chipman 1979, Krämer 1982, 1985, Phillips and Park 1988, Krämer and Hassler 1997). One sufficient condition for the asymptotic efficiency of OLS that emerges in this literature is that the regressors are in some sense "trending" (for a precise definition see below). In conjunction with stationarity, in particular stationary autoregressive disturbances, this is then shown to imply that the respective limiting distributions of OLS and GLS are identical.

The present note extends and unifies this literature by suggesting a generic form of "trend", and by showing that it is this generic property of trending data which implies the asymptotic equivalence of OLS and GLS.

2. Notation and Assumptions

In what follows the disturbances u_t from (1.1) are assumed stationary $AR(p)$,

$$u_t + \rho_1 u_{t-1} + \ldots + \rho_p u_{t-p} = \varepsilon_t, \tag{2.1}$$

where the ε_t's are i.i.d. $(0, \sigma^2)$, and where stationarity implies that all roots of the polynomial $1 + \rho_1 z + \ldots + \rho_p z^p$ are outside the unit circle.

Ignoring observations $1, \ldots, p$, which are asymptotically irrelevant, the GLS–estimator $\tilde{\beta}$ for β is obtained by applying OLS to

$$\begin{aligned} \tilde{y}_t &= \tilde{x}_t'\beta + \varepsilon_t, \quad \text{where} && (2.2)\\ \tilde{x}_t &= x_t + \rho_1 x_{t-1} + \ldots + \rho_p x_{t-p} \quad \text{and} && (2.3)\\ \tilde{y}_t &= y_t + \rho_1 y_{t-1} + \ldots + \rho_p y_{t-p} \quad (t > p) && (2.4) \end{aligned}$$

i.e. $\hat{\beta} = (\sum \tilde{x}_t \tilde{x}_t')^{-1} \sum \tilde{x} \hat{y}_t$ and

$$\tilde{\beta} - \beta = \left(\sum_{t=p+1}^{T} \tilde{x}_t \tilde{x}_t' \right)^{-1} \sum_{t=p+1}^{T} \tilde{x}_t \varepsilon_t. \tag{2.5}$$

This compares with

$$\hat{\beta} - \beta = \left(\sum_{t=1}^{T} x_t x_t' \right)^{-1} \sum_{t=1}^{T} x_t u_t \tag{2.6}$$

for the OLS–estimator $\hat{\beta}$.

The regressors x_{ti} are assumed to be "trending", by which I mean that they satisfy an invariance principle

$$\frac{1}{g_i(T)} x_{[Tr],i} \xrightarrow{d} B_i(r) \quad \text{as} \quad T \to \infty, \tag{2.7}$$

where $\xrightarrow{d}$ denotes convergence in distribution, $[Tr]$ is the integer part of Tr, $g_i(T) \to \infty$ and $B_i(r)$ is some non–zero random element in $D[0,1]$ (which might be degenerate; $D[0,1]$ is the set of all real valued functions on the unit interval, endowed with the Skorohod topology, see Billingsley 1968, chapter 3). This definition includes the well known cases of stochastic $I(1)$–regressors, where $g_i(T) = \sqrt{T}$ and where (under suitable regularity conditions) $B_i(r)$ is Brownian Motion. It also includes the case of nonstochastic polynomial regressors, e.g. $x_{it} = t^i$, where $g_i(T) = T^i$ and where $B_i(r)$ is the function $f_i(r) = r^i$. And it also includes the case of nonstationary fractionally integrated regressors, where

$$(1 - L)^d x_{ti} = \varepsilon_{ti} \tag{2.8}$$

with $d > \frac{1}{2}$ and stationary ARMA ε's, and where $g_i(T) = \sqrt{T^{2d-1}}$ and $B_i(r)$ is fractional Brownian Motion (Sowell 1990, Chung 1995). However, the definition does not allow for exponential trends, as it is easily seen that invariance principles like (2.7) do then no longer hold.

3. The Main Theorem

The main theorem is concerned with the case where *all* regressors in the model (1.1) are trending (extensions to the case where there are also nontrending regressors, in particular an intercept, are discussed in section 4). To that purpose, let $g(T) := diag\,(g_1(T), \ldots, g_K(T))$ and assume in addition to (2.7) that

$$[g(T)]^{-1}x_{[Tr]} \xrightarrow{d} B(r), \tag{3.1}$$

where $B(r)$ is a random element in $D[0,1]^K$ (with components $B_i(r)$ defined in (2.7)) and that $\int_0^1 B(r)B(r)'dr$ is invertible with probability 1. Since u_t and x_ρ are independent for all t and s, this implies that

$$\begin{pmatrix} [g(T)]^{-1} & x_{[Tr]} \\ T^{-\frac{1}{2}} & \sum_{s=1}^{[Tr]} u_s \end{pmatrix} \xrightarrow{d} \begin{pmatrix} B(r) \\ W(r) \end{pmatrix}, \tag{3.2}$$

where $W(r)$ is Brownian Motion, independent of $B(r)$, with variance

$$\bar{\sigma}^2 = \frac{\sigma^2}{(1+\rho_1+\ldots+\rho_p)^2}. \tag{3.3}$$

Theorem: *Under the assumptions made above, we have*

$$\sqrt{T}g(T)(\hat{\beta}-\beta) \xrightarrow{d} \left[\int_0^1 B(r)B(r)'dr\right]^{-1}\left[\int_0^1 B(r)dW(r)\right] \tag{3.4}$$

and the same applies to GLS.

Corrollary: Since $g(T) \to \infty$, we have

$$\hat{\beta}-\beta = o_p\frac{1}{\sqrt{T}}, \tag{3.5}$$

i.e. the OLS-estimator converges to the true parameter vector faster than in the standard case with no trend in the regressors.

Proof of the Theorem: The relationship (3.4) follows immediately from

$$\frac{1}{T}[g(T)]^{-1}\sum_{t=1}^{T} x_t x_t'[g(T)]^{-1} \xrightarrow{d} \int_0^1 B(r)B(r)'dr \tag{3.6}$$

and

$$\frac{1}{\sqrt{T}}[g(T)]^{-1}\sum_{t=1}^{T} x_t u_t \xrightarrow{d} \int_0^1 B(r)dW(r), \tag{3.7}$$

where the first relationship follows from (3.1) and the continuous mapping theorem (Billingsley 1968, p. 30), and where the latter convergence follows from the independence of $W(r)$ and $B(r)$ and a general theorem on the convergence to stochastic integrals in Hansen (1992, p. 491).

The analogue for GLS follows along similar lines. Emulating the proof of theorem 2.2 in Phillips and Park (1988, p. 114), one verifies, using

$$g(T)^{-1}\tilde{x}_{[Tr]} = g(T)^{-1}(1+\rho_1+\ldots+\rho_p)x_{[Tr]} + o_p(1) \tag{3.8}$$

and

$$T^{-\frac{1}{2}}\sum_{s=1}^{[T_r]}\varepsilon_s = T^{-\frac{1}{2}}(1+\rho_1+\ldots+\rho_p)\sum_{s=1}^{[T_r]}u_t + o_p(1) \tag{3.9}$$

that the regressors $\tilde{x}_t$ and the disturbances ε_t in (2.2) satisfy the invariance principle

$$\begin{pmatrix} g(T)^{-1}\tilde{x}_{[Tr]} \\ T^{-\frac{1}{2}}\sum_{s=1}^{[T_r]}\varepsilon_s \end{pmatrix} \xrightarrow{d} \begin{pmatrix} \tilde{B}(r) \\ \tilde{W}(r) \end{pmatrix} \tag{3.10}$$

where

$$\begin{aligned} \tilde{B}(r) &= (1+\rho_1+\ldots+\rho_p)B(r) \\ \tilde{W}(r) &= (1+\rho_1+\ldots+\rho_p)W(r) \end{aligned} \tag{3.11}$$

and where $\tilde{W}(r)$ is independent of $\tilde{B}(r)$. In conjunction with

$$\frac{1}{T}[g(T)]^{-1}\sum_{t=1}^{T}\tilde{x}_t\tilde{x}_t'[g(T)]^{-1} \xrightarrow{d} \int_0^1 \tilde{B}(r)\tilde{B}(r)'dr, \tag{3.12}$$

and

$$\frac{1}{\sqrt{T}}[g(T)]^{-1}\sum_{t=1}^{[Tr]}\tilde{x}_t\varepsilon_t \xrightarrow{d} \tilde{B}(r)d\tilde{W}(r), \tag{3.13}$$

this implies (as the term $\sum_{i=1}^{p}\rho_i$ cancels out) that

$$\begin{aligned} \sqrt{T}g(T)(\tilde{\beta}-\beta) &\xrightarrow{d} \left[\int_0^1 \tilde{B}(r)\tilde{B}(r)'dr\right]^{-1}\left[\int_0^1 \tilde{B}(r)d\tilde{W}(r)\right] \\ &= \left[\int_0^1 B(r)B(r)'dr\right]^{-1}\left[\int_0^1 B(r)dW(r)\right], \end{aligned} \tag{3.14}$$

proving the theorem.

4. Discussion

A central requirement for the theorem above is that *all* regressors are trending, and that the limiting matrix $\int_0^1 B(r)B(r)'dr$ is invertible with probability 1. Both conditions are often violated in empirical applications.

Consider for instance the case of a singular limiting matrix $\int_0^1 B(r)B(r)'dr$, for example $K = 2$, $x_{t1} = t$, $x_{t2} = t + (-1)^t$. Here we have $g_i(T) = T$,

$$\sum_{t=n}^{T} x_t x_t' = \begin{bmatrix} \sum_{t=1}^T t^2 & \sum_{t=1}^T t^2 + (-1)^t \\ \sum_{t=1}^T t^2 + (-1)^t & \sum_{t=1}^T t^2 + 2(-1)^t + T \end{bmatrix} \tag{4.1}$$

and

$$\frac{1}{T^3} \sum_{t=1}^{T} x_t x_t' \to \int_0^1 B(r)B(r)'dr = \frac{1}{3}\begin{bmatrix} 1 & 1 \\ 1 & 1 \end{bmatrix}. \tag{4.2}$$

The limiting matrix $\int_0^1 B(r)B(r)'dr$ is therefore noninvertible with probability 1, and the right–hand side of (3.4) does not exist.

The limiting distribution of both OLS and GLS is in such cases best derived by a reparametrization of the model:

$$\begin{aligned} y_t &= \beta_1 t + \beta_2(t + (-1)^t) + u_t \\ &= (\beta_1 + \beta_2)t + \beta_2(-1)^t + u_t \\ &= \alpha_1 t + \alpha_2(-1)^t + u_t \end{aligned} \tag{4.3}$$

Now we have one regressor with trend and one without, and, from a general result in Rosenblatt (1956), we know that the limiting distribution of $\sqrt{T}(\hat{\alpha}_2 - \alpha_2)$ has a larger variance than the limiting distribution of $\sqrt{T}(\tilde{\alpha}_2 - \alpha_2)$. As the limiting distribution of both $\hat{\beta}_1 = (\hat{\alpha}_1 + \hat{\alpha}_2)$ and $\tilde{\beta}_1 = (\tilde{\alpha}_1 + \tilde{\alpha}_2)$ is dominated by $\hat{\alpha}_1$ and $\tilde{\alpha}_1$, respectively, this implies that the existence of a second trend destroys both the superconsistency and the asymptotic efficiency of OLS.

However, there is still hope that in a model with nontrending regressors, OLS retains both superconsistency and efficiency at least for the coefficients of the trending regressors. Consider the model:

$$y_t = x_t'\beta + z_t'\alpha + u_t, \tag{4.4}$$

where the components of x_t are trending and the components of z_t are not. In view of the Frisch–Waugh–Theorem (see Fiebig et al. 1996), the OLS–estimate for β in (4.4) is numerically identical to the OLS–estimate for β in

$$y_t^* = x_t^*\beta + u_t, \tag{4.5}$$

where y_t^* and x_t^* are the residuals from a regression on z_t. Therefore, if the x_t^* satisfy the invariance principle (3.1), the OLS estimate for β in (4.5) is asymptotically as efficient as the GLS–estimate in (4.5).

Unfortunately, the GLS–estimate for β in (4.5) need not be numerically identical to the GLS–estimate for β in (4.4). Fiebig et al. (1996) give conditions for this be the case, from which it is seen that at least for the most important case of a regression with an intercept, i.e. $z_t = 1$ and $x_t^* = x_t - \bar{x}$, the superconsistency and limiting efficiency of OLS prevails.

References

1. Billingsley, P. (1968). *Convergence of probability measures*, Chicago.
2. Busse, R., Jeske, R. and Krämer, W. (1994). "Efficiency of least– squares estimation of polynomial trend when residuals are autocorrelated", *Economics Letters* 45, 267–271.
3. Chipman, J.S. (1979). "Efficiency of least–squares estimation of linear trend when residuals are autocorrelated." *Econometrica* 47, 115 – 127.
4. Chung, Ch.-F. (1995). " Sample variance, sample covariances, and linear regression of stationary multivariate long memory processes." Mimeo, Michigan State University.
5. Fiebig, D. G., Bartels, R. and Krämer, W. (1996). "The Frish–Waugh–Theorem and Generalized Least Squares", *Econometric Reviews* 15, 431–443.
6. Grenander, U. (1954). "On the estimation of regression coefficients in the case of an autocorrelated disturbance." *Annals of Mathematical Statistics* 25, 252 – 272.
7. Hansen, B.E. (1992). "Convergence to stochastic integrals for dependent heterogeneous processes." *Econometric Theory* 8, 489 – 500.
8. Krämer, W. (1980). "Finite sample efficiency of Ordinary Least Squares in the Linear Regression Model with autocorrelated Errors." *Journal of the American Statistical Association* 75, 1005 – 1009.
9. Krämer, W. (1982). "Note on estimating linear trend when residuals are autocorrelated." *Econometrica* 50, 1065 – 1067.
10. Krämer, W. (1985). "Least squares regression when the independent variable follows an ARIMA–process." *Journal of the American Statistical Association* 81, 150 – 154.
11. Krämer, W. and Donninger, C. (1986). "Spatial autocorrelation among errors and the relative efficiency of OLS in the Linear Regression Model." *Journal of the American Statistical Association* 82, 577 – 579.
12. Krämer, W. and Hassler, U. (1997). "Limiting efficiency of OLS vs. GLS when regressors are fractionally integrated." Technical Report No. 1, SFB 475, Fachbereich Statistik, Universität Dortmund.
13. Phillips, P.C.B. and Park, J.Y. (1988). "Asymptotic Equivalence of OLS and GLS in Regressions with Integrated Regressors." *Journal of the American Statistical Association* 83, 111 – 115.
14. Rosenblatt, H.M. (1956). "Some regression problems in time series analysis." *Proceedings of the Third Berkeley Symposium on Mathematical Statistics and Probability*, 165 – 186.
15. Sowell, F. (1990). "The fractional unit root distribution." *Econometrica* 58, 495 – 505.
16. Watson, G. (1968). "Linear Least Squares regression." *Annals of Mathematical Statistics* 38, 1679 – 1698.

The Analysis of Growth and Learning Curves with Mean- and Covariance Structure Models

Gerhard Arminger

Department of Economics, Bergische Universität Wuppertal, Germany

Acknowledgement

The author is grateful for the support of the Deutsche Forschungsgemeinschaft (DFG) given to the project B2 (Multivariate Prognosesysteme in der Warenwirtschafts- und Produktionssteuerung) within the SFB 475 (Komplexitätsreduktion in multivariaten Datenstrukturen) at the University of Dortmund.

1. Introduction

Growth curves are ubiquitous phenomena occuring in psychology, medical statistics, epidemiology, economics and business administration. Typical examples are data from learning experiments, speech and behavior development, clinical trials, spread of a disease, job search behavior and product sales in the take off phase. In growth curve analysis, one considers a random variable y_{it} which varies over elements $i = 1, \ldots, n$ and time points $t = 1, \ldots, T$. Usually, there is a large number n of independent elements which are observed at a small number T of occasions. The aim is to describe the behavior of y_{it} over time, where it is assumed that the repeated measurements follow smooth and fairly similar developments over timè for each element but there are variations in initial status, final status and rate of change between elements. First models for the analysis of growth data have been provided by Rao (1958) and Tucker (1958). Important recent contributions to this area have been made by McArdle (1988), Meredith and Tisak (1990), Browne and Du Toit (1991) and Browne (1993).

In section 2 of the paper, basic models for the analysis of univariate growth data are considered. The first basic model is a random trend model with trend parameters varying across elements. The second basic model allows to condition the random trend parameters on predictor variables. In the third basic model, a stationary time series structure is imposed on the error terms. These three basic models can be combined and can be embedded in the more general mean and covariance structure models. This property allows the use of the powerful programs for mean- and covariance structure analysis for the computation of growth curve models. In section 3, extensions of the basic models are introduced. The first extension is the use of indicator variables for the growth variable of interest facilitating the analysis of growth curves in latent traits. The second extension puts the growth curve models in the context of latent variable models for non-metric, that is dichotomous, ordered categorical or censored variables. With these tools, growth curves which are only measured at non-metric measurement levels may be analyzed. In section 4, problems and issues of estimation and numerical analysis are sketched. Since all of these models may be thought of as mean- and covariance structure models with special restrictions, a brief outline suffices.

2. Basic models for univariate growth data

2.1 Random trend models

A simple model to describe the development of an element $i, i = 1, \dots, n$ in a variable y over time points $t = 1, \dots, T$ is the random trend model

$$y_{it} = \alpha_i + \beta_i t + \epsilon_{it} \tag{2.1}$$

where each element has a specific intercept α_i and a specific slope parameter β_i. ϵ_{it} is an error term with $\mathrm{E}(\epsilon_{it}) = 0$ and $\mathrm{E}(\epsilon_{it}|t) = 0$. The data are then descibed by a set of trends as shown in figure 1.

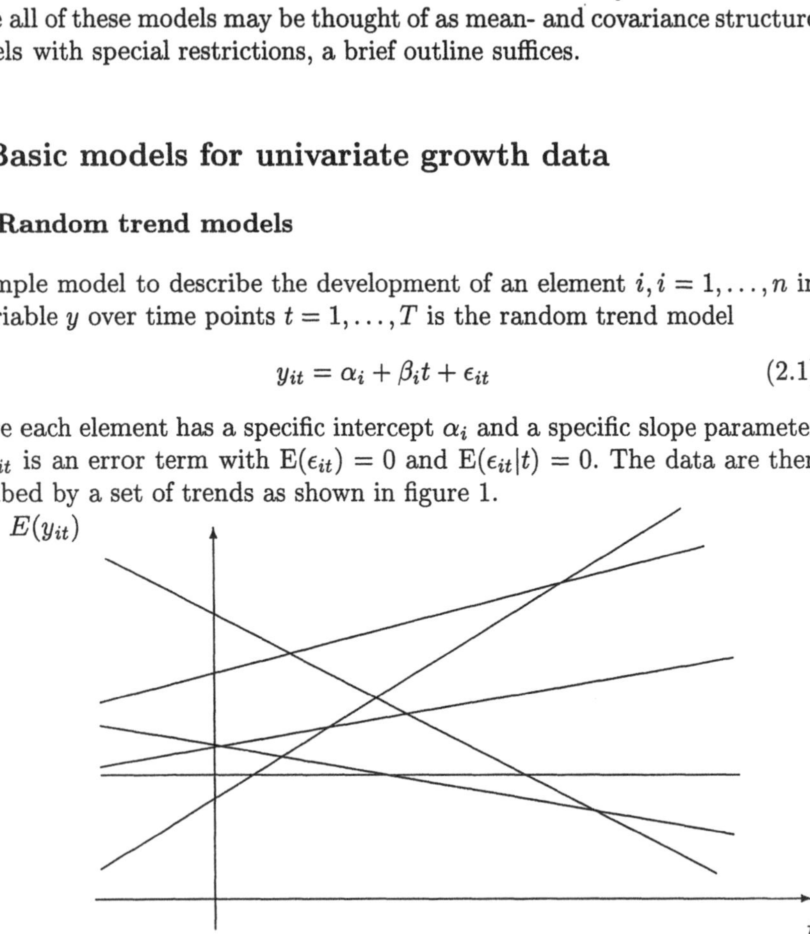

Figure 1: Random trend lines

The parameter values $\boldsymbol{\eta}_i = (\alpha_i, \beta_i)'$ are assumed to be random variables with expected values $\boldsymbol{\eta}_0$ and covariance matrix $\boldsymbol{\Phi}$:

$$\mathrm{E}(\boldsymbol{\eta}_i) = \boldsymbol{\eta}_0 = \begin{pmatrix} \alpha_0 \\ \beta_0 \end{pmatrix}, \quad \mathrm{V}(\boldsymbol{\eta}_i) = \boldsymbol{\Phi} = \begin{pmatrix} \Phi_{11} & \Phi_{12} \\ \Phi_{21} & \Phi_{22} \end{pmatrix} \tag{2.2}$$

If the data y_{it} are collected in the vector $\boldsymbol{y}_i = (y_{i1}, \ldots, y_{iT})'$ and the errors in $\boldsymbol{\epsilon}_i = (\epsilon_{i1}, \ldots, \epsilon_{iT})'$, then the model of equation (2.1) may be written as

$$\boldsymbol{y}_i = \boldsymbol{\Lambda}\boldsymbol{\eta}_i + \boldsymbol{\epsilon}_i \tag{2.3}$$

where $\boldsymbol{\Lambda}$ is the $T \times 2$ matrix of fixed regressors:

$$\boldsymbol{\Lambda} = \begin{pmatrix} 1 & 1 \\ 1 & 2 \\ \vdots & \vdots \\ 1 & T \end{pmatrix} \tag{2.4}$$

If we assume that $\mathrm{V}(\boldsymbol{\epsilon}_i) = \boldsymbol{\Theta}_\epsilon$ is a diagonal matrix, that is the errors are serially uncorrelated, the mean vector and the covariance matrix of $\boldsymbol{y}_i$

$$\mathrm{E}(\boldsymbol{y}_i) = \boldsymbol{\Lambda}\boldsymbol{\eta}_0 = \boldsymbol{\gamma} \tag{2.5}$$

$$\mathrm{V}(\boldsymbol{y}_i) = \boldsymbol{\Lambda}\boldsymbol{\Phi}\boldsymbol{\Lambda}' + \boldsymbol{\Theta}_\epsilon = \boldsymbol{\Sigma} \tag{2.6}$$

are specified in the same way as a classifical factor analytic model with a fixed matrix $\boldsymbol{\Lambda}$. The parameters in $\boldsymbol{\eta}_0$, $\boldsymbol{\Phi}$ and $\boldsymbol{\Theta}_\epsilon$ may be collected in a parameter vector $\boldsymbol{\vartheta}$, parameterizing the mean $\boldsymbol{\gamma}$ and the covariance matrix $\boldsymbol{\Sigma}$ as $\boldsymbol{\gamma}(\boldsymbol{\vartheta})$ and $\boldsymbol{\Sigma}(\boldsymbol{\vartheta})$. Under nomality assumptions, the parameters can be estimated in a straightforward manner using a program such as LISREL (Jöreskog and Sörbom 1993) which allows restrictions on $\boldsymbol{\Lambda}$.

The parameters in $\boldsymbol{\eta}_0 = (\alpha_0, \beta_0)'$ may be interpreted as average intercept and regression slope. The diagonal values of $\boldsymbol{\Phi}$ are the variances of the intercepts and slopes, the off diagonal value Φ_{21} is the covariance between intercepts and slopes. The errors ϵ_{it} may have different variances over time but are not serially correlated. The individual intercepts and slopes $\boldsymbol{\eta}_i = (\alpha_i, \beta_i)$ may be estimated as factor scores. Under the assumption of normality, that is $\boldsymbol{\eta}_i \sim \mathcal{N}(\boldsymbol{\eta}_0, \boldsymbol{\Phi})$ and $\boldsymbol{\epsilon}_i \sim \mathcal{N}(\boldsymbol{0}, \boldsymbol{\Theta}_\epsilon)$, the $\boldsymbol{\eta}_i$ are estimated as posterior means $\mathrm{E}(\boldsymbol{\eta}_i | \boldsymbol{y}_i, \hat{\boldsymbol{\vartheta}})$ where $\hat{\boldsymbol{\vartheta}}$ is the ML estimate of $\boldsymbol{\vartheta}$ (cf. Bartholomew 1981).

The random trend model of equation (2.1) is easily extended to a model that combines basic trend curves or basic functions as derived by Meredith and Tisak (1990). If the time points are denoted as $t_1, \ldots, t_T$ and there are functions $g_2(t_j), \ldots g_S(t_j)$, $S \leq T$ that are known for the time points in question, y_{it} may be written as a linear combination of basic time curves with random weights $\boldsymbol{\eta}_i = (\eta_{i1}, \ldots, \eta_{iS})'$

$$y_{it_j} = \eta_{i1} + \eta_{i2} g_2(t_j) + \eta_{i3} g_3(t_j) \ldots + \eta_{iS} g_S(t_j) + \epsilon_{it_j},\ j = 1, \ldots, T\,. \tag{2.7}$$

If the values of $g_s(t_j)$ are collected in the $T \times S$ matrix $\boldsymbol{\Lambda}$, that is

$$\boldsymbol{\Lambda} = \begin{pmatrix} 1 & g_2(t_1) & \ldots & g_S(t_1) \\ 1 & g_2(t_2) & \ldots & g_S(t_2) \\ \vdots & \vdots & & \vdots \\ 1 & g_2(t_T) & \ldots & g_S(t_T) \end{pmatrix} \tag{2.8}$$

then the model may again be written as

$$\boldsymbol{y}_i = \boldsymbol{\Lambda}\boldsymbol{\eta}_i + \boldsymbol{\epsilon} \tag{2.9}$$

The mean and covariance structure is the same as in equations (2.5) and (2.6). The parameter vector $\boldsymbol{\vartheta}$ containing $\boldsymbol{\eta}_0$, $\boldsymbol{\Phi}$ and $\boldsymbol{\Theta}_\epsilon$ is again estimated using programs for mean and covariance structure analysis.

It should be noted that the basic curves $g_s(t_j)$, $s = 2, \ldots S$ need not be explicitly specified and their function values λ_{js}, $j = 1, \ldots T$, $s = 2, \ldots S$ may be estimated independently as in the applications of McArdle (1989) and Meredith and Tisak (1990). However, identification restrictions must be introduced otherwise rotational indeterminacy as in classical factor analysis occurs if S is greater than 1. Restrictions for identification or for substantive reasons are usually introduced by parameterizing $\boldsymbol{\gamma} = \boldsymbol{\Lambda}\boldsymbol{\eta}_0$ and $\boldsymbol{\Sigma} = \boldsymbol{\Lambda}\boldsymbol{\Phi}\boldsymbol{\Lambda}' + \boldsymbol{\Theta}_\epsilon$ as differentiable functions of a parameter vector $\boldsymbol{\vartheta}$ fullfilling first and second order identifiability, that is, if for any two values $\boldsymbol{\vartheta}_1$ and $\boldsymbol{\vartheta}_2$ the equality $\boldsymbol{\gamma}(\boldsymbol{\vartheta}_1) = \boldsymbol{\gamma}(\boldsymbol{\vartheta}_2)$ and $\boldsymbol{\Sigma}(\boldsymbol{\vartheta}_1) = \boldsymbol{\Sigma}(\boldsymbol{\vartheta}_2)$ holds, then $\boldsymbol{\vartheta}_1 = \boldsymbol{\vartheta}_2$ almost surely. Systematic methods for structuring latent curves by considering $\boldsymbol{\Lambda}$ as a matrix of first derivatives of a target function with respect to the parameters in $\boldsymbol{\vartheta}$ are found in Browne (1993).

2.2 Conditioning on predictor variables

Dependence of the growth or learning curves on predictor variables $\boldsymbol{x}_i = (x_{i1}, x_{i2}, \ldots, x_{ip})'$ may be introduced in many ways. Here, only two generally applicable examples are given. The first is an example of Browne and Du Toit (1992) who consider the five point intelligence curve of children with low, medium and high amounts of television viewing. It is assumed that the learning curve $\boldsymbol{y}_i = (y_{i1}, \ldots, y_{iT})'$ is described by a logistic trend curve and an error term. The amount of television is captured in the predictive variable vector $\boldsymbol{x}_i = (x_{i1}, x_{i2}, x_{i3})'$ with $\boldsymbol{x}_i = (1,0,0)'$ for a low, $\boldsymbol{x}_i = (0,1,0)'$ for a medium and $\boldsymbol{x}_i = (0,0,1)'$ for a high amount of television exposure. The model is then written as

$$\boldsymbol{y}_i = \boldsymbol{\Lambda}\boldsymbol{x}_i + \boldsymbol{\epsilon}_i \tag{2.10}$$

with $\mathrm{E}(\boldsymbol{\epsilon}_i) = \boldsymbol{0}$ and $\mathrm{V}(\boldsymbol{\epsilon}_i) = \boldsymbol{\Theta}_\epsilon$ which is assumed to be a diagonal matrix. The logistic trend curve for the mean of $\boldsymbol{y}_i$ is modelled by the following parameterization of λ_{ts}, $t = 1, \ldots 5$, $s = 1, \ldots 3$.

$$\lambda_{ts} = \frac{\vartheta_{1s}}{(1 + \vartheta_{2s}\vartheta_{3s}^t)} \tag{2.11}$$

where $\vartheta_{1s} \geq 0, \vartheta_{2s} \geq 0$ and $0 \leq \vartheta_{3s} \leq 1$. In this model ϑ_{1s} is the asymptote, ϑ_{2s} governs the amount of change and ϑ_{3s} governs the rate of change. It should be noted that this model is non-linear in the parameters for $\boldsymbol{\Lambda}$, hence it cannot be estimated with standard programs as LISREL (Jöreskog and Sörbom 1993). Instead, general programs for the analysis of mean- and covariance structures such as RAMONA (Browne, Mels and Coward 1994) or MECOSA 3 (Arminger, Wittenberg and Schepers 1996) must be applied.

A systematic way of introducing predictive variables $\boldsymbol{x}_i$ into a growth curve model is given by using weights $\boldsymbol{\eta}_i$ that are conditioned on $\boldsymbol{x}_i$. Such a model may be written as

$$\boldsymbol{\eta}_i = \boldsymbol{\nu}_\eta + \boldsymbol{\Gamma}\boldsymbol{x}_i + \boldsymbol{\zeta}_i \quad \text{with} \quad \mathrm{E}(\boldsymbol{\zeta}_i) = \boldsymbol{0}, \ \mathrm{V}(\boldsymbol{\zeta}_i) = \boldsymbol{\Psi}. \tag{2.12}$$

Then the conditional expected value is given by

$$\mathrm{E}(\boldsymbol{\eta}_i|\boldsymbol{x}_i) = \boldsymbol{\nu}_\eta + \boldsymbol{\Gamma}\boldsymbol{x}_i \tag{2.13}$$

The conditional covariance matrix is given by

$$\mathrm{V}(\boldsymbol{\eta}|\boldsymbol{x}_i) = \boldsymbol{\Psi} \tag{2.14}$$

Using the notation of section 2.1, the conditional growth curve model may be written as

$$\boldsymbol{y}_i = \boldsymbol{\Lambda}\boldsymbol{\eta}_i + \boldsymbol{\epsilon} \tag{2.15}$$

with conditional expected value

$$\mathrm{E}(\boldsymbol{y}_i|\boldsymbol{x}_i) = \boldsymbol{\Lambda}\boldsymbol{\nu}_\eta + \boldsymbol{\Lambda}\boldsymbol{\Gamma}\mathrm{x}_i = \boldsymbol{\gamma} + \boldsymbol{\Pi}\boldsymbol{x}_i \tag{2.16}$$

and conditional covariance matrix

$$\mathrm{V}(\boldsymbol{y}_i|\boldsymbol{x}_i) = \boldsymbol{\Lambda}\boldsymbol{\Psi}\boldsymbol{\Lambda}' + \boldsymbol{\Theta}_\epsilon = \boldsymbol{\Sigma} \tag{2.17}$$

This formulation implies that conditional growth curve models can be written as conditional mean- and covariance structure models with specific parameterization of $\boldsymbol{\gamma}$, $\boldsymbol{\Pi}$ and $\boldsymbol{\Sigma}$ as $\boldsymbol{\gamma}(\boldsymbol{\vartheta})$, $\boldsymbol{\Pi}(\boldsymbol{\vartheta})$ and $\boldsymbol{\Sigma}(\boldsymbol{\vartheta})$ (cf. Browne and Arminger 1995).

2.3 Time series deviations

Until now no special structures for the covariance matrix $\boldsymbol{\Theta}_\epsilon$ of the error term have been considered. However, in applications it may be useful to take into account a serial structure for $\boldsymbol{\epsilon}_i$. Following Browne and Arminger (1995), the growth curve model

$$\boldsymbol{y} = \boldsymbol{\nu}_y + \boldsymbol{\epsilon} \quad \text{with } \mathrm{E}(\boldsymbol{\epsilon}) = \boldsymbol{0} \tag{2.18}$$

is considered (the index i is eliminated here for simplicity). It is assumed that ϵ_t, $t = 1, \ldots, T$ follows an ARMA (p, q) process

$$\epsilon_t = \alpha_1\epsilon_{t-1} + \alpha_2\epsilon_{t-2} + \ldots + \alpha_p\epsilon_{t-p} + \delta_t - \beta_1\delta_{t-1} - \ldots - \beta_q\delta_{t-q} \tag{2.19}$$

where δ_t, $t = 1, \ldots, T$ follows a white noise process with $\mathrm{E}(\boldsymbol{\delta}) = \boldsymbol{0}$ and $\mathrm{V}(\boldsymbol{\delta}_t) = \boldsymbol{\Theta}_\delta$ as a diagonal covariance matrix. Furthermore it is assumed that $\boldsymbol{\epsilon}$ may be written as

$$\epsilon = \mathbf{A}\epsilon + \mathbf{M}\delta + \mathbf{J}\omega \tag{2.20}$$

where $\mathbf{A}$ contains the coefficients $\alpha_1, \ldots, \alpha_p$ for the AR(p) process, $\mathbf{M}$ contains the coefficients for the MA(q) process, $\omega \sim r \times 1$ is a vector of random errors that is uncorrelated with δ and generates the r initial states of ϵ, that is $\epsilon_1, \ldots, \epsilon_r$ where $r = \max(p, q)$. $\mathbf{J}$ is a $T \times r$ selection matrix where the r columns are equal to the first r columns of a $T \times T$ identity matrix.

As an example, we consider $T = 6$ and an ARMA (2,2) process. In this case we find that

$$\begin{bmatrix} \epsilon_1 \\ \epsilon_2 \\ \epsilon_3 \\ \epsilon_4 \\ \epsilon_5 \\ \epsilon_6 \end{bmatrix} = \begin{bmatrix} 0 & 0 & 0 & 0 & 0 & 0 \\ \alpha_1 & 0 & 0 & 0 & 0 & 0 \\ \alpha_2 & \alpha_1 & 0 & 0 & 0 & 0 \\ 0 & \alpha_2 & \alpha_1 & 0 & 0 & 0 \\ 0 & 0 & \alpha_2 & \alpha_1 & 0 & 0 \\ 0 & 0 & 0 & \alpha_2 & \alpha_1 & 0 \end{bmatrix} \begin{bmatrix} \epsilon_1 \\ \epsilon_2 \\ \epsilon_3 \\ \epsilon_4 \\ \epsilon_5 \\ \epsilon_6 \end{bmatrix} +$$

$$\begin{bmatrix} 1 & 0 & 0 & 0 & 0 & 0 \\ -\beta_1 & 1 & 0 & 0 & 0 & 0 \\ -\beta_2 & -\beta_1 & 1 & 0 & 0 & 0 \\ 0 & -\beta_2 & -\beta_1 & 1 & 0 & 0 \\ 0 & 0 & -\beta_2 & -\beta_1 & 1 & 0 \\ 0 & 0 & 0 & -\beta_2 & -\beta_1 & 1 \end{bmatrix} \begin{bmatrix} \delta_1 \\ \delta_2 \\ \delta_3 \\ \delta_4 \\ \delta_5 \\ \delta_6 \end{bmatrix} + \begin{bmatrix} 1 & 0 \\ 0 & 1 \\ 0 & 0 \\ 0 & 0 \\ 0 & 0 \\ 0 & 0 \end{bmatrix} \begin{bmatrix} \omega_1 \\ \omega_2 \end{bmatrix} \tag{2.21}$$

The expected value of ω is zero. The covariance matrix of the initial states is denoted by $\mathrm{V}(\omega) = \boldsymbol{\Omega} \sim r \times r$.

Equation (2.21) may be transformed to

$$(\mathbf{I} - \mathbf{A})\epsilon = \mathbf{M}\delta + \mathbf{J}\omega \tag{2.22}$$

Therefore the covariance matrix $\boldsymbol{\Theta}_\epsilon$ of ϵ is given by

$$\mathrm{V}(\epsilon) = \boldsymbol{\Theta}_\epsilon = (\mathbf{I} - \mathbf{A})^{-1}(\mathbf{M}\boldsymbol{\Theta}_\delta\mathbf{M}' + \mathbf{J}\boldsymbol{\Omega}\mathbf{J}')(\mathbf{I} - \mathbf{A})^{-1'} \tag{2.23}$$

It is easily seen that complex models for growth and learning curves may be built from the basic models considered in subsection 2.1-2.3 by combining the models for random trend with fixed or estimated coefficients of $\boldsymbol{\Lambda}$, models with predictive variables for the random weights η_i and time series models for the error term ϵ_i.

3. Extensions to latent and non-metric variables

3.1 Latent growth curves

In this subsection, the basic models of section 2 are extended to analyse the growth curve of a latent variable that cannot be observed directly. It is now assumed that the variable y_{it} of interest is latent and is measured by a vector $\boldsymbol{z}_{it}$ of indicator variables. The measurement relation is given by a factor analytic model. Let $\boldsymbol{z}_i$ be the vector of indicators for $\boldsymbol{y}_i$, that is $z_{i,1}\ z_{i,2} \dots z_{i,L_1}$ are indicators for y_{i1}, $z_{i,L_1+1} \dots z_{i,L_1+L_2}$ are indicators for y_{i2}, $z_{i,L_{T-1}+1} \dots z_{i,L_{T-1}+L_T}$ are indicators for y_{iT}. Then the factor analytic model is given by

$$\boldsymbol{z}_i = \boldsymbol{\nu}_z + \boldsymbol{\Lambda}_z \boldsymbol{y}_i + \boldsymbol{v}_i$$

where $\boldsymbol{\nu}_z$ is the vector of intercepts, $\boldsymbol{\Lambda}_z$ is the matrix of factor loadings and $\boldsymbol{v}_i$ is the vector of measurement errors with $\mathrm{E}(\boldsymbol{v}_i) = \mathbf{0}$, $\mathrm{V}(\boldsymbol{v}_i) = \boldsymbol{\Theta}_v$ and $\mathrm{E}(\boldsymbol{v}_i \boldsymbol{y}_i') = \mathbf{0}$.

If one introduces now the random trend model with conditional weights $\boldsymbol{\eta}_i$ of equation (2.16) and (2.17), the following mean and covariance structure for $\boldsymbol{z}_i$ given $\boldsymbol{x}_i$ is found

$$\begin{aligned} \mathrm{E}(\boldsymbol{z}_i|\boldsymbol{x}_i) &= \boldsymbol{\nu}_z + \boldsymbol{\Lambda}_z \mathrm{E}(\boldsymbol{y}_i|\boldsymbol{x}_i) \\ &= \boldsymbol{\nu}_z + \boldsymbol{\Lambda}_z \boldsymbol{\Lambda} \boldsymbol{\nu}_\eta + \boldsymbol{\Lambda}_z \boldsymbol{\Lambda} \boldsymbol{\Gamma} \mathbf{x}_i \\ &= \boldsymbol{\gamma}_z + \boldsymbol{\Pi}_z \boldsymbol{x}_i \ , \end{aligned} \tag{3.1}$$

where $\boldsymbol{\gamma}_z = \boldsymbol{\nu}_z + \boldsymbol{\Lambda}_z \boldsymbol{\Lambda} \boldsymbol{\nu}_\eta$ and $\boldsymbol{\Pi}_z = \boldsymbol{\Lambda}_z \boldsymbol{\Lambda} \boldsymbol{\Gamma}$.

$$\begin{aligned} \mathrm{V}(\boldsymbol{z}_i|\boldsymbol{x}_i) &= \boldsymbol{\Lambda}_z \mathrm{V}(\boldsymbol{y}_i|\boldsymbol{x}_i) \boldsymbol{\Lambda}_z' + \boldsymbol{\Theta}_v \\ &= \boldsymbol{\Lambda}_z (\boldsymbol{\Lambda} \boldsymbol{\Psi} \boldsymbol{\Lambda}' + \boldsymbol{\Theta}_\epsilon) \boldsymbol{\Lambda}_z' + \boldsymbol{\Theta}_v = \boldsymbol{\Sigma}_z \end{aligned} \tag{3.2}$$

This model is similar to a conditional second order factor model and allows the estimation of the parameters of a growth curve model for a latent variable with indicators $\boldsymbol{z}_i$. It should be noted that additional identification restrictions for $\boldsymbol{\nu}_z$ and $\boldsymbol{\nu}_\eta$ must be introduced. Usually, $\boldsymbol{\nu}_\eta$ is set to $\mathbf{0}$. While $\boldsymbol{\Theta}_v$ is a diagonal matrix in factor analytic tradition (local independence) it may be useful to assume nondiagonality for $\boldsymbol{\Theta}_v$ if the same indicators are used for i at each time point. In this case a typical model for two time points and $L_1 = L_2 = 3$ is given by the factor loading matrix $\boldsymbol{\Lambda}_z$ and covariance matrix $\boldsymbol{\Theta}_v$:

$$\boldsymbol{\Lambda}_z = \begin{bmatrix} 1 & 0 \\ \lambda_2 & 0 \\ \lambda_3 & 0 \\ 0 & 1 \\ 0 & \lambda_2 \\ 0 & \lambda_3 \end{bmatrix} , \quad \boldsymbol{\Theta}_v = \begin{bmatrix} \theta_{11} & & & & & \\ 0 & \theta_{22} & & & & \\ 0 & 0 & \theta_{33} & & & \\ \theta_{41} & 0 & 0 & \theta_{44} & & \\ 0 & \theta_{52} & 0 & 0 & \theta_{55} & \\ 0 & 0 & \theta_{63} & 0 & 0 & \theta_{66} \end{bmatrix} \tag{3.3}$$

In the factor loading matrix $\boldsymbol{\Lambda}_z$, the factor loadings are set equal for the two time points to ensure that the latent variable is measured in the same way at the two time points. The form of the covariance matrix implies that the measurement errors are not correlated across items but there may be a serial correlation.

3.2 Inclusion of threshold models for non-metric growth variables

In this subsection, the analysis of univariate growth curves for metric variables is extended to non-metric variables, that may be metrically classified, one or double sided censored, dichotomous or ordered categorical. It is assumed that a growth model of the form

$$\boldsymbol{y}_i^* = \boldsymbol{\gamma}(\boldsymbol{\vartheta}) + \boldsymbol{\Pi}(\boldsymbol{\vartheta})\boldsymbol{x}_i + \boldsymbol{\epsilon}_i^* \tag{3.4}$$

with $\boldsymbol{\epsilon}_i^* \sim \mathcal{N}(\boldsymbol{0}, \boldsymbol{\Sigma}(\boldsymbol{\vartheta}))$ is to be estimated for a continuous variable $\boldsymbol{y}_i^*$. The growth model may for instance be parameterized as $\boldsymbol{\gamma}(\boldsymbol{\vartheta}) = \boldsymbol{\Lambda}\boldsymbol{\nu}_\eta$, $\boldsymbol{\Pi}(\boldsymbol{\vartheta}) = \boldsymbol{\Lambda}\boldsymbol{\Gamma}$ and $\boldsymbol{\Sigma}(\boldsymbol{\vartheta}) = \boldsymbol{\Lambda}\boldsymbol{\Psi}\boldsymbol{\Lambda}' + \boldsymbol{\Theta}_\epsilon$ as in equation (2.16) and (2.17). Following Muthén (1984) and Browne and Arminger (1995) the continuous variable cannot be observed but is connected to an observable variable on a possibly lower measurement scale through a probit threshold model based on the assumption of normally distributed errors $\boldsymbol{\epsilon}_i^*$.

Each element $y_{it}, i = 1, \ldots, n$ of the observed endogenous vector $\boldsymbol{y}_i$ is connected with an element $y_{it}^\star$ of the vector $\boldsymbol{y}_i^\star$ through one of the following threshold models. The vector of the threshold values of an endogenous variable y_{it} is denoted by $\boldsymbol{\tau} = (\tau_1, \ldots, \tau_{K+1})'$. The vector $\boldsymbol{\tau}$ is a function of the structural parameter vector $\boldsymbol{\vartheta}$. Each observed variable is a function $y_{it} = c_{it}(y_{it}^\star, \boldsymbol{\tau})$ of the corresponding latent variable and the thresholds $\boldsymbol{\tau}$.

- *metrically* scaled variable y_{it}:

$$y_{it} = y_{it}^\star \tag{3.5}$$

  that is, the observed variable is identical with the latent variable.
- *metrically classified* observed variable y_{it} with class boundaries $\tau_1 < \tau_2 < \ldots < \tau_K$ known a priori and categories $y_{it} = 1, \ldots, K+1$:

$$y_{it} = k \Longleftrightarrow y_{it}^\star \in [\tau_{k-1}, \tau_k) \tag{3.6}$$

  with $[\tau_0, \tau_1) = (-\infty, \tau_1)$ and $\tau_{K+1} = +\infty$.
- *one sided censored* variable y_{it} with threshold value τ_1 (Tobit-relation) known a priori:

$$y_{it} = \begin{cases} y_{it}^\star & \text{if } y_{it}^\star > \tau_1 \\ \tau_1 & \text{if } y_{it}^\star \leq \tau_1 \end{cases} \tag{3.7}$$

- *double sided censored* variable y_{it} with two threshold values $\tau_1 < \tau_2$ (Two-Limit-Probitrelation) known a priori:

$$y_{it} = \begin{cases} \tau_1 & \text{if } y_{it}^\star \leq \tau_1 \\ y_{it}^\star & \text{if } \tau_1 < y_{it}^\star < \tau_2 \\ \tau_2 & \text{if } y_{it}^\star \geq \tau_2 \end{cases} \tag{3.8}$$

- *ordered categorical* variable y_{it} with unknown threshold values $\tau_1 < \tau_2 < \ldots < \tau_K$ which have to be estimated in contrast to metrically classified variables, and with the ordered categories $y_{it} = 1, \ldots, K+1$ (Ordinal Probit):

$$y_{it} = k \iff y^*_{it} \in [\tau_{k-1}, \tau_k) \tag{3.9}$$

with $[\tau_0, \tau_1) = (-\infty, \tau_1)$ and $\tau_{K+1} = +\infty$.

The parameter vectors $\boldsymbol{\gamma}$, $\boldsymbol{\Pi}$ and the variances of the reduced form (3.4) for an ordered categorical variable y_{it} cannot be identified without further restrictions because the threshold values $\boldsymbol{\tau}$ are unknown and the variance of an ordered categorical variable is not defined. Therefore a scale restriction for the variance of ordered categorical endogenous variables is imposed with $\sigma_t^2 = 1$. Hence, γ and $\boldsymbol{\Pi}$ are identified only up to a scale factor. Additionally, only the difference between the thresholds and the regression constant γ_t is identified. Either the parameter γ_t or the first threshold τ_1 of an ordered categorical variable is therefore set to 0. Technical details for restricting the threshold parameters $\boldsymbol{\tau}$ to be equal for the variables y_{it} at all time points are found in Arminger (1994).

4. Estimation

As noted in the previous subsections, each model introduced in this paper may be written as a specific conditional mean and covariance structure model. Although many of these models do not belong to the standard class of mean and covariance structure models as defined by programs like LISREL, they can nevertheless be handled with programs such as RAMONA and MECOSA 3 that allow the specification of non-standard models. The general theory for the estimation of parameters of mean and covariance structure models is outlined below.

4.1 ML- and PML estimation for metrical dependent variables

For maximum-likelihood and pseudo-maximum-likelihood estimation the general mean- and covariance structure model must be formulated as a pure covariance structure model. The endogenous and exogenous variables are collected in a vector $\boldsymbol{y}^* = (\boldsymbol{y}', \boldsymbol{x}')$ with expected value $\mathrm{E}(\boldsymbol{y}^*) = \mathbf{0}$ and variance $\mathrm{V}(\boldsymbol{y}^*) = \boldsymbol{\Sigma}$. The parameter $\boldsymbol{\Sigma}$ of the covariance structure is specified as a function of the structural parameter $\boldsymbol{\vartheta}$:

$$\boldsymbol{\Sigma} = \boldsymbol{\Sigma}(\boldsymbol{\vartheta}) \tag{4.1}$$

Under the assumption of normality, the individual loglikelihood function is given by

$$\begin{aligned} l_i(\boldsymbol{\vartheta}) &= -\frac{1}{2}\left(\ln|\boldsymbol{\Sigma}(\boldsymbol{\vartheta})| + \boldsymbol{y}_i'\boldsymbol{\Sigma}^{-1}(\boldsymbol{\vartheta})\boldsymbol{y}_i\right) \\ &= -\frac{1}{2}\left(\ln|\boldsymbol{\Sigma}(\boldsymbol{\vartheta})| + \mathrm{tr}(\boldsymbol{S}_i\boldsymbol{\Sigma}^{-1}(\boldsymbol{\vartheta}))\right) \end{aligned} \tag{4.2}$$

(cf. Browne 1977), where $\boldsymbol{S}_i = \boldsymbol{y}_i\boldsymbol{y}_i'$ is the individual contribution to the empirical covariance matrix

$$\boldsymbol{S} = \frac{1}{n}\sum_{t=1}^{n}\boldsymbol{y}_i^{\star}\boldsymbol{y}_i^{\star\prime} \tag{4.3}$$

The loglikelihood function of the sample divided by n is given by

$$l(\boldsymbol{\vartheta}) = \frac{1}{n}\sum_{t=1}^{n} l_i(\boldsymbol{\vartheta}) = -\frac{1}{2}\left(\ln|\boldsymbol{\Sigma}(\boldsymbol{\vartheta})| + \mathrm{tr}(\boldsymbol{S}\boldsymbol{\Sigma}^{-1}(\boldsymbol{\vartheta}))\right) \tag{4.4}$$

The first and second partial derivatives of $l(\boldsymbol{\vartheta})$ with respect to ϑ_l, $l = 1, \ldots q$ and ϑ_k, $k = 1, \ldots, q$ are given by Browne (1977).

$$\frac{\partial l(\boldsymbol{\vartheta})}{\partial \vartheta_l} = \frac{1}{2}\,\mathrm{tr}\left(\boldsymbol{\Sigma}^{-1}(\boldsymbol{S} - \boldsymbol{\Sigma})\boldsymbol{\Sigma}^{-1}\frac{\partial \boldsymbol{\Sigma}}{\partial \vartheta_l}\right) \tag{4.5}$$

$$\begin{aligned} \frac{\partial^2 l(\boldsymbol{\vartheta})}{\partial \vartheta_l \partial \vartheta_k} &= -\frac{1}{2}\,\mathrm{tr}\left(\boldsymbol{\Sigma}^{-1}(2\boldsymbol{S} - \boldsymbol{\Sigma})\boldsymbol{\Sigma}^{-1}\frac{\partial \boldsymbol{\Sigma}}{\partial \vartheta_l}\boldsymbol{\Sigma}^{-1}\frac{\partial \boldsymbol{\Sigma}}{\partial \vartheta_k}\right. \\ &\qquad \left. -\boldsymbol{\Sigma}^{-1}(\boldsymbol{S} - \boldsymbol{\Sigma})\boldsymbol{\Sigma}^{-1}\frac{\partial^2 \boldsymbol{\Sigma}}{\partial \vartheta_l \partial \vartheta_k}\right) \end{aligned} \tag{4.6}$$

The ML estimator $\hat{\boldsymbol{\vartheta}}$ is consistent and asymptotic normal. The asymptotic covariance matrix of $\hat{\boldsymbol{\vartheta}}$ is consistently estimated by the inverse of the observed Fisher information matrix which may be computed from the second derivations of the normed loglikehood function $l(\boldsymbol{\vartheta})$

$$\hat{\mathrm{V}}(\hat{\boldsymbol{\vartheta}}) = \left(-\hat{\boldsymbol{A}}(\hat{\boldsymbol{\vartheta}})\right)^{-1} \quad \text{where} \quad \hat{\boldsymbol{A}}(\hat{\boldsymbol{\vartheta}}) = n\frac{\partial^2 l(\hat{\boldsymbol{\vartheta}})}{\partial \boldsymbol{\vartheta}\partial \boldsymbol{\vartheta}'} \tag{4.7}$$

Under ML estimation, the likelihood ratio, Lagrangian multiplier and Wald statistic are asymptotically χ^2 distributed with $p-q$ degrees of freedom under the null hypothesis.

The ML estimator $\hat{\boldsymbol{\vartheta}}$ is still a consistent estimator of $\boldsymbol{\vartheta}$ if $\boldsymbol{y}^{\star}$ is not multivariate normal (Arminger and Schoenberg 1989). The asymptotic covariance matrix $\mathrm{V}(\hat{\boldsymbol{\vartheta}})$ however has to be adjusted for non-normality using the information sandwich estimator:

$$\mathrm{V}(\hat{\boldsymbol{\vartheta}}) = \left(-\hat{\boldsymbol{A}}(\hat{\boldsymbol{\vartheta}})\right)^{-1}\hat{\boldsymbol{B}}(\hat{\boldsymbol{\vartheta}})\left(-\hat{\boldsymbol{A}}(\hat{\boldsymbol{\vartheta}})\right)^{-1} \tag{4.8}$$

where $\hat{\boldsymbol{A}}(\hat{\boldsymbol{\vartheta}})$ is again the observed Fisher information matrix of the sample.

The individual elements $\hat{A}_{lk}$, $l,\ k = 1, \ldots, q$ are given by

$$\begin{aligned}\hat{A}_{lk} &= -\frac{1}{2}\Bigg(\hat{\boldsymbol{\Sigma}}^{-1}(2\boldsymbol{S} - \hat{\boldsymbol{\Sigma}})\hat{\boldsymbol{\Sigma}}^{-1}\frac{\partial\hat{\boldsymbol{\Sigma}}}{\partial\vartheta_l}\hat{\boldsymbol{\Sigma}}^{-1}\frac{\partial\hat{\boldsymbol{\Sigma}}}{\partial\vartheta_k} \\ &\quad -\hat{\boldsymbol{\Sigma}}^{-1}(\boldsymbol{S} - \hat{\boldsymbol{\Sigma}})\hat{\boldsymbol{\Sigma}}^{-1}\frac{\partial^2\hat{\boldsymbol{\Sigma}}}{\partial\vartheta_l\partial\vartheta_k}\Bigg)\end{aligned} \tag{4.9}$$

with $\hat{\boldsymbol{\Sigma}} = \boldsymbol{\Sigma}(\hat{\boldsymbol{\vartheta}})$. Note that $\hat{\boldsymbol{A}}$ depends only on $\boldsymbol{S}$ and $\hat{\boldsymbol{\Sigma}}$ and not on the individual elements $\boldsymbol{y}_i^\star$.

$\hat{\boldsymbol{B}}(\hat{\boldsymbol{\vartheta}})$ is the sum of cross products of first order derivatives $(\hat{\boldsymbol{\vartheta}})$ with the individual elements $\hat{B}_{lk}$, $l,\ k = 1, \ldots, q$ given by:

$$\begin{aligned}\hat{B}_{lk} &= \frac{1}{2}\sum_{t=1}^{n}\operatorname{tr}\left(\hat{\boldsymbol{\Sigma}}^{-1}(\boldsymbol{S}_i - \hat{\boldsymbol{\Sigma}})\hat{\boldsymbol{\Sigma}}^{-1}\frac{\partial\hat{\boldsymbol{\Sigma}}}{\partial\vartheta_l}\right)\times \\ &\quad \operatorname{tr}\left(\hat{\boldsymbol{\Sigma}}^{-1}(\boldsymbol{S}_i - \hat{\boldsymbol{\Sigma}})\hat{\boldsymbol{\Sigma}}^{-1}\frac{\partial\hat{\boldsymbol{\Sigma}}}{\partial\vartheta_k}\right)\end{aligned} \tag{4.10}$$

The summation is over the individual contributions $\boldsymbol{S}_i$ of the empirical covariance matrix. Hence, the individual observations $\boldsymbol{y}_i^\star$ and not only the summary statistic $\boldsymbol{S}$ must be available to compute $\mathrm{V}(\hat{\boldsymbol{\vartheta}})$. As shown by Arminger and Sobel (1990), only the Lagrangian multiplier and the Wald statistic follow asymptotically a χ^2 distribution wit $p - q$ degrees of freedom under the null hypothesis. The distribution of the LR statistic need not follow a χ^2 distribution if the assumption of multivariate normality of $\boldsymbol{y}^\star$ is not fulfilled.

4.2 Multistage estimation for non-metrical dependent variables

The multistage estimation strategy is based on the work of Muthén (1984). Küsters (1987) shows that the estimation method used here yields consistent and asymptotically normally distributed (CAN) estimators. Here, only a short outline of the estimation strategy is presented. A detailed description of the estimation methods, optimization methods and numerical algorithms is found in Schepers (1991).

The estimation strategy is a modified maximum-likelihood method based on the multivariate normality of $\boldsymbol{y}_i^\star$ given $\boldsymbol{x}_i$.

$$P(\boldsymbol{y}_i^\star|\boldsymbol{x}_i) = \varphi(\boldsymbol{y}_i^\star|\boldsymbol{\gamma}(\boldsymbol{\vartheta}) + \boldsymbol{\Pi}(\boldsymbol{\vartheta})\boldsymbol{x}_i, \boldsymbol{\Sigma}(\boldsymbol{\vartheta})) \tag{4.11}$$

φ is the conditional normal density of $\boldsymbol{y}_i^\star$ given $\boldsymbol{x}_i$ with expected value $\boldsymbol{\gamma}(\boldsymbol{\vartheta}) + \boldsymbol{\Pi}(\boldsymbol{\vartheta})\boldsymbol{x}_i$ and covariance matrix $\boldsymbol{\Sigma}(\boldsymbol{\vartheta})$.

The latent variables $\boldsymbol{y}^\star$ are linked to the observed variables $\boldsymbol{y}$ through the threshold measurement relations. This yields the conditional density of $\boldsymbol{y}_i$ given $\boldsymbol{x}_i$:

$$P(\boldsymbol{y}_i|\boldsymbol{x}_i) = \int\limits_{c_{i1}^{-}(y_{i1}^{\star}|\boldsymbol{\tau}_1)} \cdots \int\limits_{c_{iT}^{-}(y_{iT}^{\star}|\boldsymbol{\tau}_T)} \varphi(\boldsymbol{y}^\star|\boldsymbol{\gamma}(\boldsymbol{\vartheta}) + \boldsymbol{\Pi}(\boldsymbol{\vartheta})\boldsymbol{x}_i, \boldsymbol{\Sigma}(\boldsymbol{\vartheta}))\, \mathrm{d}\boldsymbol{y}^\star \quad (4.12)$$

The domain of integration for each component $y_{it}^\star$ is the set of all $y_{it}^\star$ which are mapped onto the observed value of $y_{it} = c_{it}(y_{it}^\star|\boldsymbol{\tau}_t)$ depending on the threshold vector $\boldsymbol{\tau}_t$. This set is denoted by $c_{it}^{-}(y_{it}^\star|\boldsymbol{\tau}_t)$.

To estimate the parameters $\boldsymbol{\gamma}$, $\boldsymbol{\Pi}$ and $\boldsymbol{\Sigma}$ with full maximum-likelihood methods on the basis of this density function, it is necessary to compute T-dimensional normal distribution integrals, which for $T > 3$ is very cumbersome. However, if we consider just one variable y_{it} given $\boldsymbol{x}_i$ the univariate marginal density $P(y_{it}|\boldsymbol{x}_i)$, depending on the measurement level of the i-th case, is either a univariate normal distribution density or a marginal probability determined by integration of a univariate normal density. With two endogenous variables y_{it} and y_{is}, the common density $P(y_{it}, y_{is}|\boldsymbol{x}_i)$ is either a bivariate normal distribution density or it is determined by integration over a bivariate normal density. Since the normal distribution is characterized completely by the means and variances of each variable $y_{it}^\star$ and the covariances of each pair of variables $y_{it}^\star$ and $y_{is}^\star$ for given $\boldsymbol{x}$, Muthén (1984) suggests an estimation strategy based solely on the computed densities and probabilities from univariate and bivariate normal distribution densities. Reduced form parameters $\boldsymbol{\tau}$, $\boldsymbol{\gamma}$, $\boldsymbol{\Pi}$ and $\boldsymbol{\Sigma}$ can thus be estimated consistently. Estimation of the structural parameters $\boldsymbol{\vartheta}$ is then based on the estimated reduced form parameters and their asymptotic covariance matrix.

4.2.1 Estimation of the reduced form. The estimation of the parameters $\{\boldsymbol{\tau}, \boldsymbol{\gamma}, \boldsymbol{\Pi}, \boldsymbol{\Sigma}\}$ of the reduced form is based on the successive use of the maximum-likelihood method in two steps.

Step 1:. In the first step, the parameters $\{\boldsymbol{\tau}_t, \gamma_t, \boldsymbol{\Pi}_{t\cdot}, \sigma_t^2\}$ for each observed variable y_{it} are estimated separately. Here, the likelihood function of the t-th variable is based on the marginal density of y_{it}, $i = 1, \ldots, n$:

$$P(y_{it}|\boldsymbol{x}_i, \boldsymbol{\delta}_t) = \int\limits_{c_{it}^{-}} \varphi_t(y_{it}^\star|\boldsymbol{x}_i)\, \mathrm{d}y_{it}^\star \quad (4.13)$$

φ_t stands for the univariate normal density with the expected value $\gamma_t + \boldsymbol{\Pi}_{t\cdot}\boldsymbol{x}_i$ and variance $\sigma_t^2 = \boldsymbol{\Sigma}_{tt}$. $c_{it}^{-} = c_{it}^{-}(y_{it}, \boldsymbol{\tau}_t)$ is the inverse measurement relation of the t-th endogenous variable. The parameters of the t-th equation are collected in the vector $\boldsymbol{\delta}_t = (\boldsymbol{\tau}_t', \gamma_t, \boldsymbol{\Pi}_{t\cdot}, \sigma_t^2)'$. For each individual endogenous variable y_{it}, the kernel of the likelihood function is:

$$L_t(\boldsymbol{\delta}_t) = L_t(\boldsymbol{\tau}_t, \gamma_t, \boldsymbol{\Pi}_{t\cdot}, \sigma_t^2) = \prod_{i=1}^{n} P(y_{it}|\boldsymbol{x}_i) \quad (4.14)$$

In the first step, the likelihood function for each variable y_{it} is maximized with respect to $\boldsymbol{\delta}_t$. We then get the marginal maximum-likelihood estimators

$\hat{\boldsymbol{\delta}}_t = (\hat{\boldsymbol{\tau}}'_t, \hat{\gamma}_t, \hat{\boldsymbol{\Pi}}_{t\cdot}, \hat{\sigma}_t^2)'$, which under suitable regularity conditions are strongly consistent for the true parameters $\boldsymbol{\delta}_t^\star = (\boldsymbol{\tau}_t^{\star\mathrm{T}}, \gamma_t^\star, \boldsymbol{\Pi}_{t\cdot}^\star, \sigma_t^{\star 2})'$. For y_{it} metric, this procedure is a simple OLS regression; for y_{it} censored, this procedure estimates a Tobit model; for y_{it} ordered categorical, this procedure estimates an ordinal probit model.

Step 2:. The second step is divided into two stages. In stage A, correlations ρ_{ts} and covariances σ_{ts} are estimated for each pair of the endogenous variables (y_{it}, y_{is}). In stage B, the asymptotic covariance matrix of all estimators of the reduced form parameters is computed.

Stage A:. Correlations ρ_{ts} and covariances σ_{ts} are estimated separately for each pair of endogenous variables (y_{it}, y_{is}). The likelihood function for each pair of variables is based on the bivariate marginal density of (y_{it}, y_{is}):

$$P(y_{it}, y_{is}|\boldsymbol{x}_i, \boldsymbol{\delta}_t, \boldsymbol{\delta}_s, \rho_{ts}) = \iint\limits_{c_{it}^- \times c_{is}^-} \varphi_{ts}(y_{it}^\star, y_{is}^\star|\boldsymbol{x}_i)\,\mathrm{d}y_{is}^\star\,\mathrm{d}y_{it}^\star \tag{4.15}$$

φ_{ts} is the density of a bivariate normal distribution with expected values $\mathrm{E}(y_{it}^\star|\boldsymbol{x}_i) = \gamma_t + \boldsymbol{\Pi}_{t\cdot}\boldsymbol{x}_i$ and $\mathrm{E}(y_{is}^\star|\boldsymbol{x}_i) = \gamma_s + \boldsymbol{\Pi}_{s\cdot}\boldsymbol{x}_i$, with variances $\mathrm{V}(y_{it}^\star) = \sigma_t^2$ and $\mathrm{V}(y_{is}^\star) = \sigma_s^2$ and covariance $\sigma_{ts} = \rho_{ts}\sigma_t\sigma_s$. The integration domain is the set $c_{it}^- \times c_{is}^- = c_{it}^-(y_{it}, \boldsymbol{\tau}_t) \times c_{is}^-(y_{is}, \boldsymbol{\tau}_s)$ defined by the inverse measurement relation of the two endogenous variables. To estimate the correlations, the strongly consistent estimators $\hat{\boldsymbol{\delta}}_t$ and $\hat{\boldsymbol{\delta}}_s$ of the t-th and s-th variable are inserted in the bivariate likelihood function:

$$\hat{L}_{ts}(\rho_{ts}) = L_{ts}(\hat{\boldsymbol{\delta}}_t, \hat{\boldsymbol{\delta}}_s, \rho_{ts}) = \prod_{t=1}^{n} P(y_{it}, y_{is}|\boldsymbol{x}_i) \tag{4.16}$$

This likelihood function contains only the correlation coefficient ρ_{ts} as free parameter. For stabilization of the estimation, the correlations are transformed with the z-transformation

$$z_{ts} = \frac{1}{2}\ln\frac{1+\rho_{ts}}{1-\rho_{ts}} \tag{4.17}$$

In stage A, the likelihood function for each pair of endogenous variables is maximized with respect to z_{ts}. As a result, one obtains after re-transformation of $\hat{z}_{ts}$ the conditional maximum-likelihood estimators $\hat{\rho}_{ts}$ which under suitable regularity conditions are strongly consistent for the true correlation coefficient $\rho_{ts}^\star$. The covariance σ_{ts} is estimated as $\hat{\sigma}_{ts} = \hat{\rho}_{ts}\hat{\sigma}_t\hat{\sigma}_s$.

Hence all reduced form parameters $\{\boldsymbol{\tau}, \boldsymbol{\gamma}, \boldsymbol{\Pi}, \boldsymbol{\Sigma}\}$ are estimated consistently by using the two-stage approach. The covariance $\hat{\sigma}_{ts}$ is the ordinary error covariance if y_{it} and y_{is} are metric. If y_{it} and y_{is} both are ordered categorical, it is the polychoric correlation coefficient. If y_{it} is metric and y_{is} is ordered categorical, it is the polyserial covariance.

Stage B:. The structural parameters $\boldsymbol{\vartheta}$ of the general model are estimated by using a minimum distance estimation method (MDE). Here, the asymptotic covariance matrix of the estimators of the reduced form is needed as weight matrix (Küsters 1987) in order to ensure efficiency of the method. Therefore, in stage B, a consistent estimator of the asymptotic covariance matrix of all estimators of the reduced form is calculated. For that, the estimators are collected in the vector $\hat{\boldsymbol{\kappa}}_n$. The estimator of the asymptotic covariance matrix of $\hat{\boldsymbol{\kappa}}_n$ is denoted by $\hat{\boldsymbol{W}}_n$. The index n marks the dependence of the estimator on the number of cases. The derivation of the asymptotic covariance matrix $\boldsymbol{W}$ of $\hat{\boldsymbol{\kappa}}_n$ and the consistent estimator $\hat{\boldsymbol{W}}_n$ are found in Küsters (1987).

Alternatively to the proposed estimation of the asymptotic covariance matrix, one can use a bootstrap estimate of $\boldsymbol{W}$. For the bootstrap, N independent replications of the estimation of the reduced form (step 1 and step 2A) are performed, taking a random resample of size n of the data. The estimates of each bootstrap estimation are collected in the vector $\hat{\boldsymbol{\kappa}}_{vn}$, $v = 1, \dots N$. The asymptotic covariance matrix $\boldsymbol{W}$ is estimated as

$$\hat{\boldsymbol{W}}_n = \frac{1}{N} \sum_{v=1}^{N} (\hat{\boldsymbol{\kappa}}_{vn} - \bar{\boldsymbol{\kappa}}_n)(\hat{\boldsymbol{\kappa}}_{vn} - \bar{\boldsymbol{\kappa}}_n)' \tag{4.18}$$

after all N bootstrap iterations have been computed, where $\bar{\boldsymbol{\kappa}}_n$ is the mean of all $\hat{\boldsymbol{\kappa}}_{vn}$. The bootstrap weight matrix should be used if the sample size n is small or when convergence problems occur in the third estimation step.

4.2.2 Minimum distance estimation of the structural parameters. The reduced form parameters are formulated as a function of $\boldsymbol{\vartheta}$ and are collected in the vector $\boldsymbol{\kappa}$ which is function of $\boldsymbol{\vartheta}$, that is $\boldsymbol{\kappa} = \boldsymbol{\kappa}(\boldsymbol{\vartheta})$. The structural parameters $\boldsymbol{\vartheta}$ are estimated by minimizing the discrepancy function

$$Q(\boldsymbol{\vartheta}) = (\hat{\boldsymbol{\kappa}}_n - \boldsymbol{\kappa}(\boldsymbol{\vartheta}))' \hat{\boldsymbol{W}}_n^{-1} (\hat{\boldsymbol{\kappa}}_n - \boldsymbol{\kappa}(\boldsymbol{\vartheta})) \tag{4.19}$$

based on the asymptotic normality of the estimators of the reduced form coefficients. The vector $\hat{\boldsymbol{\kappa}}_n$ is asymptotically normal with expected value $\boldsymbol{\kappa}(\boldsymbol{\vartheta})$ and covariance matrix $\boldsymbol{W}$ estimated by $\hat{\boldsymbol{W}}_n$.

The quadratic form $Q(\boldsymbol{\vartheta})$ at $\hat{\boldsymbol{\vartheta}}$ is centrally χ^2 distributed with $p-q$ degrees of freedom if the model is specified correctly and the sample size is sufficiently large. Here p indicates the number of elements in $\hat{\boldsymbol{\kappa}}_n$ and q the number of elements in $\boldsymbol{\vartheta}$. Therefore Q can be used as a goodness-of-fit measure for the fit of the chosen parameterization of the reduced form parameters.

Since $\hat{\boldsymbol{W}}_n$ is a strongly consistent estimate of $\boldsymbol{W}$, the minimum distance estimator $\hat{\boldsymbol{\vartheta}}$ of $\boldsymbol{\vartheta}$ is asymptotically normal with

$$\hat{\boldsymbol{\vartheta}} \sim \mathcal{N}\left(\boldsymbol{\vartheta}, \left(\frac{\partial \boldsymbol{\kappa}}{\partial \boldsymbol{\vartheta}} \hat{\boldsymbol{W}}_n^{-1} \frac{\partial \boldsymbol{\kappa}'}{\partial \boldsymbol{\vartheta}}\right)^{-1}\right) \tag{4.20}$$

The first derivatives of $\boldsymbol{\kappa}$ with respect to $\boldsymbol{\vartheta}$ are evaluated at $\hat{\boldsymbol{\vartheta}}$. The asymptotic normality of $\hat{\boldsymbol{\vartheta}}$ is the basis for computing likelihood ratio, Lagrange multipier and Wald statistics to test specific hypotheses about $\boldsymbol{\vartheta}$.

References

1. Arminger, G. (1994). Probit models for the analysis of non-metric panel data, *Allgemeines Statistisches Archiv*, 78, 125-140.
2. Arminger, G., and Schoenberg, R. J. (1989). Pseudo maximum likelihood estimation and a test for misspecification in mean and covariance structure models, *Psychometrika*, 54, 409-425.
3. Arminger, G. and Sobel, M.E. (1990). Pseudo maximum likelihood estimation of mean and covariance structures with missing data, *Journal of the American Statistical Association* 85, 195 - 203.
4. Arminger, G., Wittenberg, J., and Schepers, A. (1996). *MECOSA 3: A Program System for the Analysis of General Mean- and Covariance Structures with Metric and Non-Metric Dependent Variables and Mixtures of Conditional Multivariate Normal Distributed Variables*, Additive GmbH, Max Planck Str. 9, D-61381 Friedrichsdorf/Ts., Germany.
5. Bartholomew, D.J. (1981). Posterior analysis of the factor model, *British Journal of Mathematical and Statistical Psychology* 34, 93-99.
6. Browne, M.W. (1977). Generalized least squares estimators in the analysis of covariance structures, in D. J. Aigner and A. S. Goldberger (eds.). *Latent Variables in Socio-Economic Models*, Amsterdam: North Holland, 205-226.
7. Browne, M.W. (1993). Structured latent curve models, in C.M. Cuadras and C.R. Rao (eds.). *Multivariate analysis: Future Directions 2*, Amsterdam: Elsevier Science Publishers B.V., 171-197.
8. Browne, M.W. and Arminger, G. (1995). Specification and Estimation of Mean- and Covariance-Structure Models, in G. Arminger, C.C. Clogg and M.E. Sobel (eds.). *Handbook of statistical modeling for the social and behavioral science*, New York: Plenum Press, 185-249.
9. Browne, M.W., and Du Toit, S.H.C. (1991). Models for learning data, in L.M. Collins and J. Horn (eds.). *Best methods for the Analysis of Change*, Washington: American Psychological Association, 47-68.
10. Browne, M. W., and Du Toit, S.H.C. (1992). Automated Fitting of Nonstandard Models, *Multivariate Behavioral Research* 27 (2). 269-300.
11. Browne, M. W., Mels, G., and Coward, M. (1994). Path Analysis: RAMONA, *SYSTAT for DOS: Advanced Applications, Version 6*, Evanston, IL: Systat Inc., 163-224.
12. Jöreskog, K.G., and Sörbom, D. (1993). *LISREL 8: Structural Equation Modeling with the SIMPLIS Command Language*, Hillsdale, NJ: Erlbaum.
13. Küsters, U. L. (1987). *Hierarchische Mittelwert- und Kovarianzstrukturmodelle mit nicht-metrischen endogenen Variablen*, Physica Verlag: Heidelberg.
14. McArdle, J.J. (1988). Dynamic but structural equation modeling of repeated measures, in J.R. Nesselbroades and R.B. Cattell (eds.). *Handbook of Multivariate Experimental Psychologie*, Second Edition, New York: Plenum Press, 561-614.
15. Meredith, W. and Tisak, J. (1990). Latent Curve Analysis, *Psychometrika* 55, 107-122.
16. Muthén, B.O. (1984). A General Structural Equation Model with Dichotomous, Ordered Categorical, and Continuous Latent Variable Indicators, *Psychometrika* 49, 115-132.
17. Rao, C.R. (1958). Some statistical methods for comparison of growth curves, *Biometrika* 14, 1-17.

18. Schepers, A. (1991). *Numerische Verfahren und Implementation der Schätzung von Mittelwert- und Kovarianzstrukturmodellen mit nicht-metrischen Variablen*, Verlag Frank Hartmann, Ahaus.
19. Tucker, L.R. (1958). Determination of parameters of a functional relation by factor analysis, *Psychometrika* 23, 19-23.

Part III

Applied Econometrics

How Important are Real Shocks for the Real Exchange Rate?

Kai Carstensen and Gerd Hansen

Institute of Statistics and Econometrics, Christian-Albrechts-University, Kiel, Germany.

Summary. This paper analyzes long-run relations and driving stochastic trends of the real exchange rate between Germany and the United States in a structural cointegrated VAR framework. This allows the identification of common trends with permanent effects.

We find that monetary shocks are predominant especially in the long run while real disturbances with permanent effects on output fail to explain real exchange rate movements.

1. Introduction

Much research has been conducted on real and nominal exchange rates in the last two decades. Several authors, e.g. Meese and Rogoff (1988), have challenged the common hypothesis that prices are sticky and monetary shocks are predominant. The aim of this paper is to investigate the long-run relation and the type and the importance of different shocks for the real exchange rate between Germany and the United States.

The theoretical background of this paper is discussed in section 2. The empirical analysis is conducted in a structural cointegrated VAR framework that allows the identification of permanent and transitory shocks as proposed by King, Plosser, Stock and Watson (1991) and Warne (1993). Consequently, hypotheses about long-run relations *and* driving stochastic trends can be imposed. The econometric methods are presented in section 3 while section 4 clarifies the identification scheme and section 5 contains the empirical part. Section 6 gives a summary.

2. Theoretical Framework

Following Meese and Rogoff (1988) or Baxter (1994) the logarithm of the real exchange rate q_t should be a function of the one period real interest rate differential $r^d_{t,t+1}$ and its long-run equilibrium value $\bar{q}_t$

$$q_t = \alpha\, r^d_{t,t+1} + \bar{q}_t \tag{2.1}$$

where $q_t \equiv e_t - p^d_t$ is defined as the difference between the logarithm of the nominal exchange rate e_t (domestic currency per foreign currency unit) and the logarithm of the price differential p_t^d. Moreover, they show that $\alpha < -1$ should hold.

This result depends crucially on three assumptions which are common to some monetary exchange rate models like those proposed by Dornbusch (1976) or Hooper and Morton (1982):

(i) the uncovered interest rate parity for the one period nominal interest rate differential $i_{t,t+1}^d$

$$E_t[e_{t+1}] - e_t = i_{t,t+1}^d, \tag{2.2}$$

(ii) a monotonic adjustment of the real exchange rate to its equilibrium value due to sluggish prices

$$E_t[q_{t+1} - \bar{q}_{t+1}] = \theta(q_t - \bar{q}_t),\ 0 < \theta < 1, \tag{2.3}$$

and (iii) *ex ante* purchasing power parity in the absence of further shocks

$$E_t[\bar{q}_{t+1}] = \bar{q}_t. \tag{2.4}$$

Substituting the identity

$$r_{t,t+1}^d \equiv i_{t,t+1}^d - (E_t[p_{t+1}^d] - p_t^d)$$

which relates real and nominal interest rate differentials, into (2.2) yields the uncovered interest rate parity condition for real variables

$$E_t[q_{t+1}] - q_t = r_{t,t+1}^d. \tag{2.5}$$

Substituting (2.4) into (2.3) one obtains

$$E_t[q_{t+1}] - q_t = (\theta - 1)(q_t - \bar{q}_t). \tag{2.6}$$

Setting (2.5) equal to (2.6) and solving for q_t yields the above result (2.1) with $\alpha = 1/(\theta - 1) < -1$.

It is reasonable to assume that the long run value of the real exchange rate is determined by domestic and foreign goods markets equilibrium which can be represented by a reduced form IS-curve for both countries

$$y_t = \beta_0 - \beta_1 r_{t,t+1} + \beta_2 g_t + \beta_3 q_t$$

with the logarithm of output y_t and the logarithm of government expenditures g_t. Assuming symmetric countries with identical elasticities the difference between the domestic and foreign IS-curve can be solved for the equilibrium real exchange rate (an upper ^{d} indicates a difference between home and foreign country)

$$\bar{q}_t = \frac{1}{\beta_3} y_t^d + \frac{\beta_1}{\beta_3} r_{t,t+1}^d - \frac{\beta_2}{\beta_3} g_t^d. \tag{2.7}$$

Substituting (2.7) into (2.1) one finally obtains

$$\begin{aligned} q_t &= \frac{1}{\beta_3} y_t^d + (\alpha + \frac{\beta_1}{\beta_3})\, r_{t,t+1}^d - \frac{\beta_2}{\beta_3} g_t^d \\ q_t &= \gamma_1\, y_t^d + \gamma_2\, r_{t,t+1}^d - \gamma_3\, g_t^d \end{aligned} \tag{2.8}$$

where γ_1 and γ_3 should be positive. This result gives rise to the hypothesis of one cointegration relation within the set of variables $x_t = \left(y_t^d, g_t^d, q_t, r_{t,t+1}^d\right)$ and it shows that real exchange rate movements may be induced by real and nominal shocks.

3. Common Trends in a Structural VAR Model

Starting from an unconstrained, stationary, n-dimensional vector autoregressive model (VAR) with lag order p

$$A(L)x_t = \mu + \varepsilon_t \tag{3.1}$$

structural VAR modelers in the line of Blanchard (1989), Sims (1986) or Giannini (1992) try to orthogonalize the covariance matrix Σ_ε of the error term ε_t by means of economic restrictions in order to obtain uncorrelated innovations e_t that allow for *structural* economic interpretation. This is most easily done by assuming a linear relationship

$$e_t = K\varepsilon_t.$$

After inverting the VAR to its vector moving average (VMA) representation

$$x_t = \nu + C(L)K^{-1}K\varepsilon_t = \nu + R(L)e_t$$

inference is drawn from impulse responses and variance decompositions of the *structural* VMA polynomial $R(z) = C(z)K^{-1}$.

In a cointegration framework the characteristic polynomial contains k unit roots and r roots outside the unit disk so that in the long run the VAR is driven by k common trends whereas the remaining r shocks have only transitory influence. Reparameterizing the VAR as a vector error correction model (VECM)

$$\Delta x_t = \alpha\beta' x_{t-1} + \sum_{i=1}^{p-1} \Gamma_i \Delta x_{t-i} + \varepsilon_t \tag{3.2}$$

makes the r stationary long-run relations $z_{t-1} = \beta' x_{t-1}$ explicit. Engle and Granger (1987) and Johansen (1995) show how the cointegrated VAR can be inverted to

$$x_t = C(1)\sum_{i=1}^{t} (\mu + \varepsilon_i) + C^*(L)\varepsilon_t + x_0. \tag{3.3}$$

Since the long-run impact matrix $C(1) = \beta_\perp \left(\alpha'_\perp \Gamma \beta_\perp\right)^{-1} \alpha'_\perp$ with $\alpha_\perp$ and $\beta_\perp$ as the orthogonal complements to α and β respectively and $\Gamma = I - \sum_{i=1}^{p-1} \Gamma_i$, has reduced rank k only k independent shocks with permanent effects can be identified. If no further shocks occur the stationary part $C^*(L)\varepsilon_t$ dies out as t tends to infinity.

King et al. (1991) and Warne (1993) have introduced the distinction between permanent and transitory shocks to identify a structural VAR. They make two assumptions:

$$\Sigma_e = E\left[e_t e_t'\right] = K\Sigma_\varepsilon K' = I_n \tag{3.4}$$

$$R(1) = C(1)K^{-1} = \left[\begin{array}{cc} F_{n\times k} & 0_{n\times r} \end{array}\right]. \tag{3.5}$$

The first assumption defines independent structural shocks and is standard for any orthogonalization approach. Of course, neither K nor K' is identified at this stage. The second assumption needs some further comments. It implies that only the **first** k structural shocks have permanent effects whereas the **last** r shocks do not. Partitioning K into the first k and the last r rows

$$e_t = K\varepsilon_t = \left[\begin{array}{c} K_k\varepsilon_t \\ K_r\varepsilon_t \end{array}\right] = \left[\begin{array}{c} \phi_t \\ \psi_t \end{array}\right] \tag{3.6}$$

Warne (1993) shows how the cointegration restrictions and the uncorrelatedness between permanent shocks ϕ_t and transitory shocks ψ_t can be used to obtain the matrices F, K_k and K_r. Rewriting (3.3) in structural form clarifies his ideas:

$$x_t = R(1)K\sum_{i=1}^{t}(\mu+\varepsilon_i) + C^*(L)K^{-1}e_t + x_0 \tag{3.7}$$

$$= \left[\begin{array}{cc} F & 0_{n\times r} \end{array}\right]\left[\begin{array}{c} K_k \\ K_r \end{array}\right]\sum_{i=1}^{t}(\mu+\varepsilon_i) + R^*(L)e_t + x_0 \tag{3.8}$$

$$= F\sum_{i=1}^{t}(K_k\mu+\phi_i) + R^*(L)e_t + x_0. \tag{3.9}$$

For $\beta' x_t$ to be stationary $\beta' F = 0$ must hold in order to cancel out the nonstationary term $FK_k\sum_{i=1}^{t}(\mu+\varepsilon_i)$ in (3.9), i.e. F lies in the null space of β:

$$F = \beta_\perp \kappa_k \tag{3.10}$$

where κ_k is an arbitrary regular $(k\times k)$-dimensional matrix that will be used to identify F.

Comparing (3.3) with (3.9) makes clear that $C(1)\varepsilon_t = F\phi_t$ must hold for every t and therefore $\phi_t = (F'F)^{-1}F'C(1)\varepsilon_t$. Making use of (3.6) and (3.10) one obtains

$$\begin{aligned}
\phi_t &= K_k\varepsilon_t = \left(F'F\right)^{-1}F'C(1)\varepsilon_t \\
&= \kappa_k^{-1}\left(\beta_\perp'\beta_\perp\right)^{-1}\left(\kappa_k'\right)^{-1}\kappa_k'\beta_\perp'\beta_\perp\left(\alpha_\perp'\Gamma\beta_\perp\right)^{-1}\alpha_\perp'\varepsilon_t \\
&= \kappa_k^{-1}\left(\alpha_\perp'\Gamma\beta_\perp\right)^{-1}\alpha_\perp'\varepsilon_t
\end{aligned}$$

and thus

$$K_k = \kappa_k^{-1} \left(\alpha'_\perp \Gamma \beta_\perp\right)^{-1} \alpha'_\perp. \tag{3.11}$$

In a last step K_r is chosen as

$$K_r = \kappa_r^{-1} \alpha' \Sigma_\varepsilon^{-1}, \tag{3.12}$$

in order to get uncorrelated permanent and transitory shocks, see appendix 1. Again, κ_r is an arbitrary regular $(r \times r)$-dimensional matrix that will be used to identify K_r.

Substituting these results, (3.10), (3.11) and (3.12) into (3.3) yields

$$\begin{aligned} x_t &= (\beta_\perp \kappa_k) \left((\alpha'_\perp \Gamma \beta_\perp \kappa_k)^{-1} \alpha'_\perp \right) \sum_{i=1}^{t} (\mu + \varepsilon_i) + R^*(L) e_t + x_0 \\ &= F \tau_t + R^*(L) e_t + x_0 \end{aligned}$$

with the k-dimensional *structural random walk* or *common trend*

$$\tau_t = \tau_{t-1} + K_k \mu + \phi_t.$$

Since $\alpha_\perp$ and $\beta_\perp$ span only the orthogonal spaces to α and β respectively, F, K_k and K_r are defined only up to nonsingular transformations which are represented by the nonsingular quadratic matrices κ_k and κ_r. In order to obtain structural shocks these matrices have at least in parts to be determined by economic restrictions. On the other hand they have to make sure that both permanent and transitory shocks are uncorrelated among themselves. But this condition offers only $k(k+1)/2$ and $r(r+1)/2$ restrictions, respectively, for the k^2 and r^2 elements in κ_k and κ_r. A pragmatic way to solve this problem is to split κ_k and κ_r into two nonsingular matrices

$$\kappa_k = \delta_k \gamma_k$$

and

$$\kappa_r = \left(\delta'_r\right)^{-1} \gamma_r$$

with δ_k and δ_r absorbing $k(k-1)/2$ and $r(r-1)/2$ economic restrictions respectively, and γ_k and γ_r being determined by a Choleski decomposition. Although this factorization is not unique it can be understood as a compromise between a pure Choleski decomposition and a fully structural approach.

With the help of zero restrictions in δ_k one can assure that in the long run some variables in x_t are not loaded by specific permanent shocks. This may be a strong source of identifying restrictions even if the remaining Choleski decomposition implies a recursiveness within the sets of permanent and transitory shocks.

4. Economic Hypotheses and Identification

The economic model in section 2 can be used to formulate hypotheses within the four-dimensional system consisting of the variables $x_t = \left(y_t^d, g_t^d, q_t, r_t^d\right)$:

(H_1) There exists $r = 1$ cointegration relation giving rise to $k = n - r = 3$ common trends:

$$\tau_t = \begin{pmatrix} \tau_{1,t} \\ \tau_{2,t} \\ \tau_{3,t} \end{pmatrix}.$$

(H_2) The cointegration vector can be normalized on the real exchange rate

$$\beta' = \begin{bmatrix} \beta_1 & \beta_2 & 1 & \beta_3 \end{bmatrix}$$

with $\beta_1 > 0$ and $\beta_2 < 0$.

Additionally, it is required that there be $k(k-1)/2 = 3$ economic restrictions to identify the permanent shocks because the $(n \times k)$-dimensional matrix F contains $nk = 12$ parameters but the condition $\beta' F = 0$ defines only $rk = 3$ equations and leaves $nk - rk = k^2 = 9$ parameters undetermined:

$$F = \beta_\perp \kappa_k = \begin{bmatrix} 1 & 0 & 0 \\ 0 & 1 & 0 \\ -\beta_1 & -\beta_2 & -\beta_3 \\ 0 & 0 & 1 \end{bmatrix} \begin{bmatrix} \kappa_{11} & \kappa_{12} & \kappa_{13} \\ \kappa_{21} & \kappa_{22} & \kappa_{23} \\ \kappa_{31} & \kappa_{32} & \kappa_{33} \end{bmatrix}. \tag{4.1}$$

Exactly $k(k+1)/2 = 6$ elements of κ_k can be obtained by a Choleski decomposition so that there remain $k(k-1)/2 = 3$ restrictions to be set by economic theory. Since these restrictions cannot be subject to a test they should not only fit into the specific economic model but also be generally accepted. In order to identify the first common trend as a real supply shock, the second one as a real demand shock and the third one as a monetary shock the following restrictions are used:

(R_1) A monetary shock does not have a long-run impact on output: $F_{13} = \kappa_{13} = 0$.
(R_2) A monetary shock does not have a long-run impact on government expenditures: $F_{23} = \kappa_{23} = 0$.
(R_3) A real demand shock does not have a long-run impact on output: $F_{12} = \kappa_{12} = 0$.

The first two restrictions imply a dichotomy between real and monetary sectors while the third one assumes in the long run a neoclassical production function that is independent of demand shocks. A suitable factorization of κ_k into a matrix of economic restrictions δ_k and a lower triangular Choleski matrix γ_k is

$$\kappa_k = \delta_k \gamma_k =$$

$$\begin{bmatrix} 1 & \frac{\kappa_{12}\kappa_{33}-\kappa_{13}\kappa_{32}}{\kappa_{22}\kappa_{33}-\kappa_{23}\kappa_{32}} & \frac{\kappa_{13}}{\kappa_{33}} \\ 0 & 1 & \frac{\kappa_{23}}{\kappa_{33}} \\ 0 & 0 & 1 \end{bmatrix} \begin{bmatrix} \frac{\det(\kappa_k)}{\kappa_{22}\kappa_{33}-\kappa_{23}\kappa_{32}} & 0 & 0 \\ \frac{\kappa_{21}\kappa_{33}-\kappa_{23}\kappa_{31}}{\kappa_{33}} & \frac{\kappa_{22}\kappa_{33}-\kappa_{23}\kappa_{32}}{\kappa_{33}} & 0 \\ \kappa_{31} & \kappa_{32} & \kappa_{33} \end{bmatrix}.$$

For $\kappa_{12} = \kappa_{13} = \kappa_{23} = 0$, one obtains

$$\kappa_k = \delta_k \gamma_k =$$

$$\begin{bmatrix} 1 & 0 & 0 \\ 0 & 1 & 0 \\ 0 & 0 & 1 \end{bmatrix} \begin{bmatrix} \gamma_{11} & 0 & 0 \\ \gamma_{21} & \gamma_{22} & 0 \\ \gamma_{31} & \gamma_{32} & \gamma_{33} \end{bmatrix}.$$

The recursive structure is obvious from

$$F\tau_t = F_0 \gamma_k \tau_t = F_0 \begin{bmatrix} \gamma_{11}\tau_{1,t} \\ \gamma_{21}\tau_{1,t} + \gamma_{22}\tau_{2,t} \\ \gamma_{31}\tau_{1,t} + \gamma_{32}\tau_{2,t} + \gamma_{33}\tau_{3,t} \end{bmatrix}.$$

The transitory shock does not have to be identified. It can probably be interpreted as a shock from international financial markets but of course it is made up of all transitory components in the four variables system.

5. Real Exchange Rate and Common Trends

The empirical analysis is organized as follows: Section 5.1 gives a description of the data and in section 5.2 the VAR is specified. In section 5.3 the cointegration properties of the four-dimensional VAR will be studied by means of the RATS program CATS. Finally, in section 5.4 a restricted VAR is estimated and identified as proposed by Warne (1993) so that structural inference can be drawn from impulse response functions and forecast error variance decompositions.

5.1 The Data

Nominal 3-month interest rates and the DM/US$ exchange rate are taken from the database of the German Bundesbank, the West German GNP, its implicit price deflator and West German government expenditures from the DIW database. The US GDP, the price deflator and US government expenditures are taken from the OECD database. The quarterly data cover the period from 1973:2 to 1993:4, are seasonally adjusted and taken in logarithms (all but the interest rates). The variables y_t^d and g_t^d are constructed by subtraction of the US from the German series, the real exchange rate as $q_t = e_{t,DM/US\$} + p_{t,US} - p_{t,Ger}$ and the real interest rate differential as $r_t^d = i_{t,Ger} - \Delta p_{t,Ger} - (i_{t,US} - \Delta p_{t,US})$.

5.2 The Specification of the VAR

Univariate ADF-Tests of the four variables $(y_t^d, g_t^d, q_t, r_t^d)$ are specified by means of the RATS procedure STEPWISE and include only significant lags of the differenced variable in each regression. The results (see table 4 in appendix 2) indicate that they all are integrated of order one.

In a next step lag order and deterministic components of the VAR (3.1) are specified in order to arrive at a statistical model that sufficiently describes the data. As a deterministic component an unrestricted constant has been taken into the VAR but not a linear trend because its exclusion is accepted at various lag lengths.

The lag order can be determined by means of the Hannan-Quinn (HQ) and the Schwarz (SC) criteria in connection with some diagnostic tests: We used two LM-Tests for autocorrelation of first and fourth order and a test for normality of the residuals (see table 5 in appendix 2).

Both the SC- and the HQ-criteria indicate that a lag length of one is optimal but because they tend to underestimate the true lag length in small samples (see Reimers, 1991) we should choose a lag order of at least two or three. Additionally, the hypothesis of nonautocorrelation should be accepted with high confidence what can be achieved by including a fourth lag. Hence we choose a lag order of $p = 4$.

5.3 The Cointegration Analysis

Statistical analysis of the cointegration properties of the VAR is conducted by means of the well-known FIML method introduced by Johansen (1988). The results are reported in table 1.

Tab. 1: Tests of the cointegration rank

	estimated values			critical values (95%)	
r	Eigenv.	λ-max	Trace	λ-max	Trace
0	0.398	40.10	66.45	28.93	47.21
1	0.167	14.46	26.36	18.28	29.78
2	0.122	10.28	11.89	11.50	15.34
3	0.020	1.62	1.62	3.84	3.84

Both the λ-max and the trace test indicate that there is one significant eigenvalue at the 95% level. Hence, we choose a cointegration rank of $r = 1$. The corresponding normalized cointegration vector β is in line with our long-run equation (2.8):

$$\hat{\beta}' = \begin{bmatrix} -9.914 & 6.525 & 1.000 & 0.170 \end{bmatrix}.$$

Moreover, the vector of adjustment parameters α contains only negative elements which are significantly different from zero:

$$\hat{\alpha}' = \begin{bmatrix} -0.012 & -0.024 & -0.058 & -2.329 \end{bmatrix}$$
$$t_{\hat{\alpha}'} = \begin{bmatrix} -2.131 & -4.467 & -2.099 & -4.139 \end{bmatrix}.$$

This means that all four variables adjust to a disequilibrium and none of them is weakly exogenous. Thus, only a common trend analysis of the kind introduced above can reveal some evidence about the driving shocks in this VAR system.

5.4 The Analysis of Permanent and Transitory Shocks

Estimation of the restricted VAR and identification as shown above yield the matrices $\hat{F}$ of the long-run impact of the common trends and $\hat{R}_0$ of the immediate impact of all shocks on the variables, see table 2.

Tab. 2: Long- and short-run impact matrices

	$\hat{F}$			$\hat{R}_0$			
	Shock			Shock			
Variable	real supply	real demand	monetary	real supply	real demand	monetary	transitory
y^d	.0147*	0	0	.0085*	.0003	-.0008	.0027*
g^d	.0004	.0108*	0	-.0015	.0048*	.0024	.0063*
q	.0242	-.0123	.0658*	-.0042	-.0218*	.0364*	.0055
r^d	.7016*	-.3411*	-.3873*	-.0020	-.4592*	-.5698*	.4907*

Parameters indicated by a * are significantly different from zero with a probability of 90%. Confidence intervals have been computed by bootstrapping with 5000 iterations since some small Monte Carlo experiments showed that asymptotic bounds tend to overestimate the empirical variances with the consequence that most parameters would be insignificant. Impulse responses and variance decompositions of different shocks can be found in the appendix. With their help the dynamic effects of supply and demand shocks will be discussed.

A real supply shock has positive effects on output both in the short and in the long run which is in line with economic propositions and follows from our identification scheme. Unfortunately, there is not any significant reaction of the real exchange rate although the real interest differential shows a substantial uprise in the medium and long run. A possible interpretation of this phenomenon is that positive trade balance effects and negative real interest rate effects on the real exchange rate cancel out.

By assumption, a real demand shock does not have a long-run impact on output. Government expenditures rise while the real exchange rate and the real interest rate differential fall. The real exchange rate shows a kind of overshooting with an initial depreciation that is twice as big in the short run than in the long run (see table 2). Moreover, the real exchange rate needs more than twelve quarters to adjust to its long-run level. This surely matches the empirical facts of the DM/US$ exchange rate.

A monetary shock does not have any significant effect on output or government expenditures even in the short run. But again the real exchange rate shows a significant reaction and an overshooting behaviour. The same holds for the real interest rate differential.

The remaining transitory shock has not been identified economically.

The importance of the different shocks at various time horizons can be analyzed by means of structural forecast error variance decompositions (FEVD). Unfortunately, the confidence intervals are very big so that only point estimates of the long-run FEVDs are reported in table 3 and in the graphics in the appendix.

Tab. 3: Long-run FEVD

	Shock		
Variable	supply	demand	monetary
y^d	1.00	0.00	0.00
g^d	0.01	0.99	0.00
q	0.12	0.03	0.85
r^d	0.65	0.15	0.20

One can see that real supply shocks are not as important for real exchange rate movements as one probably would expect. At any time horizon they explain a share of less than 12% of the forecast error variance of the real exchange rate. By contrast, real demand shocks account for 26% of the variance in the first quarter, 16% in the fifth quarter, but only 3% in the long run. Most important are the monetary shocks with some 70% in the first quarter, 80% in the fifth quarter and 85% in the long run. Therefore this shock could perhaps also be called an exchange rate shock. Since it does not have any long-run impact on output (and government expenditures) it is surely not the real shock Meese and Rogoff (1988) thought of when they argued that "real disturbances (such as productivity shocks) may be a major source of exchange rate volatility". The monetary shock does neither have any significant impact on output and government expenditures nor can it explain the forecast error variance of these two variables. The opposite is true for the real exchange rate and the real interest rate differential. Consequently, it seems to be a pure monetary shock even in the short run that mainly drives the real exchange rate. This result is of course in sharp contrast to models that deny the influence of monetary variables on the real exchange rate in the long run. Note however that according to our results real shocks have *some* importance in the short and even in the long run.

6. Conclusion

In this paper the real exchange rate between Germany and the United States has been analyzed both theoretically and empirically. The use of structural VAR methods in a cointegration framework made it possible to identify long-run relations and common stochastic trends that drive the economic variables. The real exchange rate turned out to be pushed forward mainly by monetary shocks, especially in the long run. We could not find evidence in favor of the hypothesis that real disturbances are predominant.

Appendix 1

In order to fulfill assumption (A1) $K\Sigma_\varepsilon K' = I_n$ we have to assure that the structural shocks ϕ_t und ψ_t are uncorrelated. For $E(\phi_t\psi_t') = 0$ to hold K_r is chosen as $K_r = \kappa_r^{-1}\alpha'\Sigma_\varepsilon^{-1}$ so that $E(\phi_t\psi_t') = K_k E(\varepsilon_t\varepsilon_t')K_r' = \kappa_k^{-1}\left(\alpha_\perp'\Gamma\beta_\perp\right)^{-1}\alpha_\perp'\Sigma_\varepsilon\Sigma_\varepsilon^{-1}\alpha\left(\kappa_r'\right)^{-1} = 0$. Of course, κ_r is an arbitrary matrix that has to be identified.

From $E\left(\phi_t\phi_t'\right) = K_k E\left(\varepsilon_t\varepsilon_t'\right)K_k' = \left(F'F\right)^{-1}F'C\left(1\right)\Sigma_\varepsilon C\left(1\right)'F\left(F'F\right)^{-1} = I_k$ follows $\kappa_k\kappa_k' = \left(\beta_\perp'\beta_\perp\right)^{-1}\beta_\perp'C\left(1\right)\Sigma_\varepsilon C\left(1\right)'\beta_\perp\left(\beta_\perp'\beta_\perp\right)^{-1}$ which defines only $k\left(k+1\right)/2$ restrictions on κ_k. Equivalently, from $E\left(\psi_t\psi_t'\right) = K_r E\left(\varepsilon_t\varepsilon_t'\right)K_r' = \kappa_r^{-1}\alpha'\Sigma_\varepsilon^{-1}\Sigma_\varepsilon\Sigma_\varepsilon^{-1}\alpha\left(\kappa_r'\right)^{-1} = I_r$ one obtains $\kappa_r\kappa_r' = \alpha'\Sigma_\varepsilon^{-1}\alpha$ which defines $r\left(r+1\right)/2$ restrictions on κ_r.

Appendix 2

Tab. 4: ADF-Tests for Integration

Variable	Test for I(1) vs. I(0)		Test for I(2) vs. I(1)	
	Constant, no trend	Constant, trend	Constant, no trend	Constant, trend
y^d	-2.04	-2.22	-4.41	-6.00
g^d	-1.30	-2.55	-5.44	-7.06
q	-2.78	-2.76	-4.98	-6.27
r^d	-1.66	-2.60	-9.10	-9.32
95% crit. value	-2.89	-3.45	-2.89	-3.45

Tab. 5: Specification of the VAR

Lag	Order criteria		Diagnostic tests (p-values)		
	SC	HQ	LM(1)	LM(4)	Normality
1	-23.31	-23.66	0.18	0.74	0.47
2	-22.85	-23.49	0.02	0.89	0.57
3	-22.44	-23.37	0.05	0.74	0.19
4	-21.92	-23.14	0.24	0.39	0.11
5	-21.33	-22.85	0.66	0.12	0.22

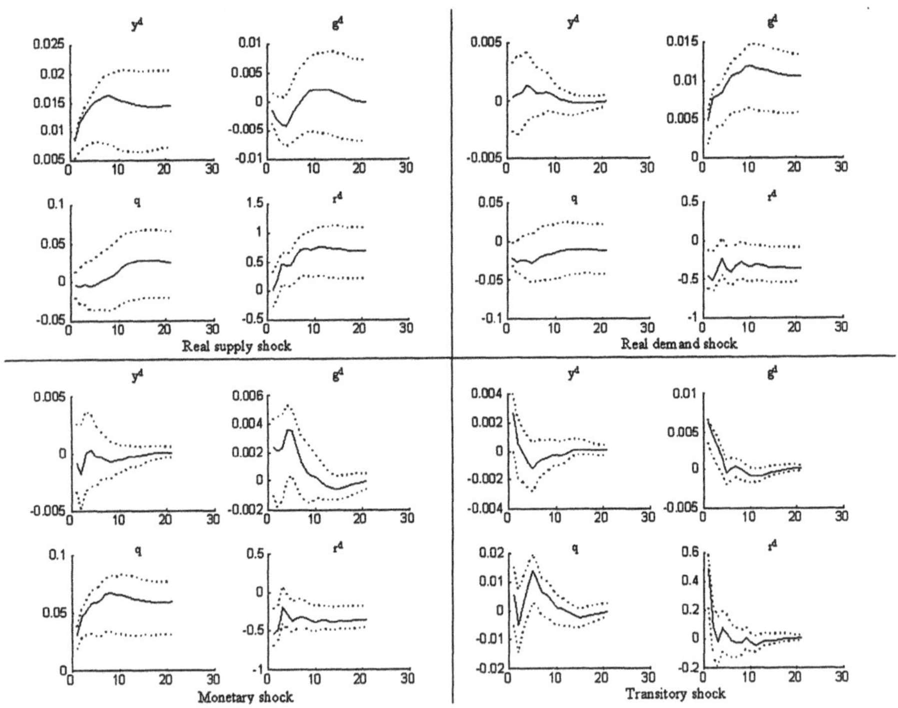

Fig. 1: Impulse Response Functions

[1] Of course, the contributions of the four shocks to the forecast error variance of each variable add up to one. In the graphs the difference between two succesive lines is the proportion of forecast error variance that is accounted for by a single shock.

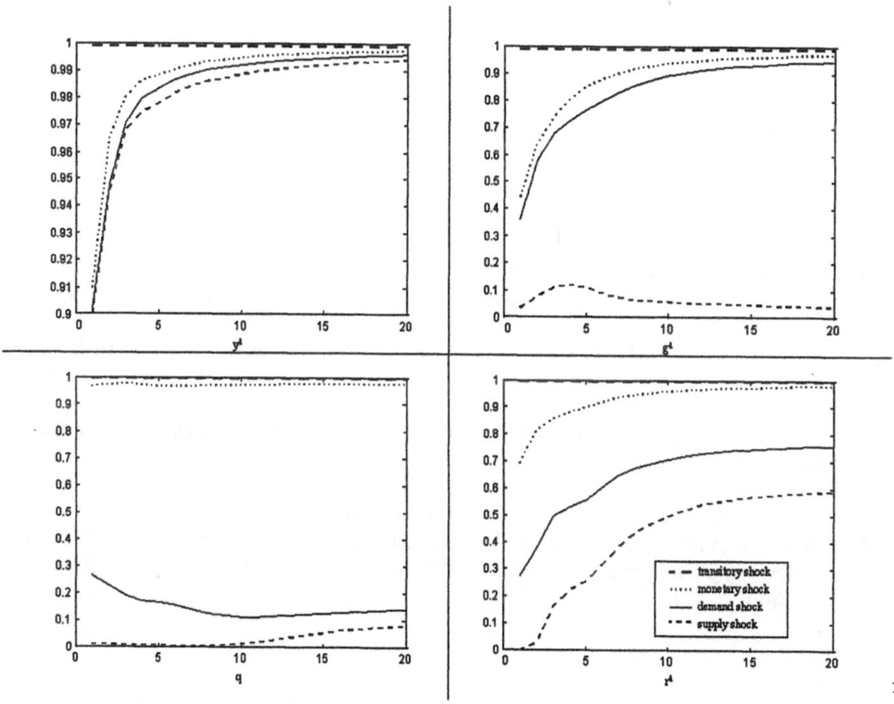

Fig. 2: Forecast Error Variance Decompositions[1]

References

1. Baxter, M. (1994). Real exchange rates and real interest differentials. Have we missed the business-cycle relationship?, *Journal of Monetary Economics*, Vol. 33, p.5-37.
2. Blanchard, O. J. (1989). A Traditional Interpretation of Macroeconomic Fluctuations, *The American Economic Review*, Vol. 79, No. 5, p.1146-1164.
3. Dornbusch, R. (1976). Expectations and Exchange Rate Dynamics, *Journal of Political Economy*, Vol.84, No.6, p.1161-1176.
4. Engle, R. F.; Granger, C. W. J. (1987). Co-integration and Error correction: Representation, Estimation, and Testing, *Econometrica*, Vol.55, No.2, p.251-276.
5. Giannini, C. (1992). Topics in Structural VAR Econometrics, Springer-Verlag, Berlin.
6. Hooper, P. and Morton, J. (1982). Fluctuations in the Dollar: A Model of Nominal and Real Exchange Rate Determination, *Journal of International Money and Finance*, Vol.1, No.1, p.39-56.
7. Johansen, S. (1988). Statistical Analysis of Cointegration Vectors, *Journal of Economic Dynamics and Control*, Vol.12, p.231-254.
8. Johansen, S. (1995). Likelihood-based Inference in Cointegrated Vector Autoregressive Models, Oxford University Press, Oxford.
9. King, R. G.; Plosser, C. I.; Stock, J. H.; Watson, M. W. (1991). Stochastic Trends and Economic Fluctuations, *The American Economic Review*, Vol.81, No.4, p.819-840.
10. Meese, R.; Rogoff, K. (1988). Was it Real? The Exchange Rate-Interest Rate Differential Relation over the Modern Floating-Rate Period, *The Journal of Finance*, Vol. 43, No. 4, p.933-948.
11. Reimers, H.-E. (1991). Analyse kointegierter Variablen mittels vektorautoregressiver Modelle, Physica-Verlag, Heidelberg.
12. Sims, C. A. (1986). Are Forecasting Models Usable for Policy Analysis?, *Federal Reserve Bank of Minneapolis Quarterly Review*, Vol. 10, No. 1, p. 2-16.
13. Warne, A. (1993). A Common Trends Model: Identification, Estimation and Inference, Institute for International Economic Studies, Seminar Paper No.555, Stockholm.

Trading Strategies of a Financially Strong Investor in Futures and Stocks

Is Profitable Manipulation Possible?

Günter Bamberg, Gregor Dorfleitner, and Klaus Röder

University of Augsburg, Germany

Summary. We consider a financially strong investor whose orders have an impact on share prices. We address the question whether trading strategies in the spot market and the corresponding market for index futures can be profitable. A criterion for profitability is derived and, given this criterion is satisfied, the manipulator's optimal order volume is calculated explicitly. It seems that under realistic conditions the profit does not exceed transaction costs.

1. Introduction

On days where trading activity is weak shares with a value of 3 to 4 billion DM are traded on the German stock market, whereas on days with large trading activity the volume is about three times as high. About 80 percent of trading in German stocks is covered by DAX stocks.[1] Especially on days with weak trading activity, it seems realistic that placing few hundred million DM on one market side will cause a price move in a desired direction. For fonds managers, wealthy private persons or investor groups such amounts seem to be achievable. Price manipulating investors are analyzed by e.g. Lindenberg (1979) and Rudolph (1982), where the resulting modifications of the CAPM are of primary interest. In this paper we concentrate on a different aspect, namely the decision problem of a possible manipulator. The term manipulation is used in a variety of contexts. In literature at least three different interpretations can be found: monopoly based manipulation[2], manipulation by insider knowledge[3], and by trading large volumes. The latter is the one of interest in our context.

The ability to move prices in a desired direction does not automatically imply profitability of manipulation. A manipulation will for example not be profitable if only the spot market is available for strategic money allocation and manipulation induced positive and negative price changes are totally symmetric. The simultaneous existence of a spot and a futures market however increases the chance of a profitable manipulation.[4]

[1] An introduction to this topic is given by Loistl (1992), Spremann (1991) or Steiner/Bruns (1995).

[2] See Easterbrook (1986).

[3] See e.g. Benabou/Laroque (1992).

[4] Cf. Jarrow (1994).

Since commodity futures markets do have a longer tradition than spot futures markets, simultaneous manipulations on spot and futures markets were first analyzed in commodity markets, e.g. Newbery (1985) and Kyle (1985). In these papers assumptions about production decisions and market structures are necessary. Here we do not want to deal with commodities, but with stock indexes. Futures markets for stock indexes were first established in 1982 in the USA. The DAX futures market in Germany started in November 1990.

The intention of this paper is to develop a simple model of a potential manipulator's decision problem based on his[5] own market assessment. The manipulation strategy considered here, which will from now on also be addressed as roundtrip, is supposed to take place at the DAX futures and the DAX stocks market within one trading day. Yet it can easily be transferred to other futures markets and their underlying market. We calculate the mean and variance of the possible profit and illustrate the consequences for profitability by considering different numerical examples. The applied modelling method can without much effort be adapted to different strategies.

Papers dealing with manipulations in the context of stocks and futures are e.g. Kumar/Seppi (1992) und Jarrow (1994). Jarrow develops an equilibrium model, stresses the timing aspect and derives a criterion for profitability of manipulation. Here we deliberately do not extend the partial model to an equilibrium model for this would lead to a variety of additional assumptions (e.g. explicit modelling of both market sides, endogenous explanation of money flows), and the danger of misspecification would be enlarged. Due to the counter-example nature of this paper misspecification should be avoided in any case.

2. Roundtrip of a financially strong manipulator

If a manipulator is able to increase prices on the spot market by purchasing stocks, he will naturally purchase futures contracts before, i.e. go long. Since arbitrageurs tie futures prices to spot prices relatively tightly, an early unwinding of the futures contracts after buying stocks can lead to a profit. When selling stocks, the manipulator has to go short in futures before.

To be more concrete, we consider DAX portfolios on the spot market in the following. A DAX portfolio is supposed to consist of the 30 DAX stocks in appropriate proportions with a value of the DAX times 100 DM.[6] The multiplier 100 corresponds to the fact that a DAX future refers to the 100-fold of the DAX. We denote the DAX value at time instant t with S_t, the

[5] The manipulator does, of course, not need to be male or a natural person at all. For convenience of the reader, however, we will in the following refer to the manipulator as if this were given.

[6] See also Janssen/Rudolph (1992).

(unique) number of shares of the ith DAX company at time t with $n_{i,t}$ and the ith shares price with $p_{i,t}$. The price of a DAX portfolio is given by:

$$\text{Price of DAX portfolio at time } t = 100 \cdot \mathrm{S}_t = \sum_{i=1}^{30} n_{i,t} \cdot p_{i,t} \quad . \tag{2.1}$$

The numbers $n_{i,t}$ in (2.1) are not generally integral. The importance of this problem decreases with the number of DAX portfolios, though.

We now divide the roundtrip in five steps. Symbols and necessary assumptions are discussed in the next section. The manipulator conducts the following 5 steps within as little time as possible on one single day.

Step 1: Go long in DAX futures (buy DAX futures).
Step 2: Buy DAX portfolios.
Step 3: Go short in DAX futures (sell DAX futures): unwind the step 1 position and open a new short position.
Step 4: Sell the DAX portfolios of step 2.
Step 5: Go long in DAX futures (buy DAX futures): unwind the remaining short positions of step 3.

Obviously all positions entered are closed after step 5. This is also important in Jarrow (1994) for transforming paper wealth into real wealth.

3. The model

When should the roundtrip be entered? How should the length of the time intervals between two steps be chosen? Timing questions like that shall not be addressed explicitly. In our model the roundtrip can be started at any instant of time t.[7] Every step requires a little amount of time τ in the range of minutes or hours.

Step 1:

The purchase of $f \in \mathbb{N}_0$ DAX futures will influence the spot and the futures market. The DAX value before step 1 is denoted by S_t. At the end of step 1 this value tends to be higher. The greater f is, the stronger this tendency will be. As motivated in the following, we assume an increase proportional to f. After step 1 the index $S_{t+\tau}$ hence is

$$S_{t+\tau} = S_t + f \cdot \Delta^+, \tag{3.1}$$

where Δ^+ describes the reaction[8] of the spot market on going long in futures. In the following we denote the effect of a step on the spot market with the symbol $\rightsquigarrow$, i.e.

[7] This does not mean, however, that the profitability of the roundtrip does not depend on time.

[8] A recent work on the effect of DAX futures sales and purchases on the DAX futures prices is Kempf/Korn (1997), which suggests that the relation is nonlinear.

$$S_t \rightsquigarrow S_{t+\tau} = S_t + f \cdot \Delta^+.$$

The temporal allocation of the order volume on the trading interval can be treated as a separate problem. If the reaction of the market on a time varying stream of orders were known, one could optimize this stream by variation or control theoretic methods. Since there are no realistic assumptions about such a detailed market reaction, however, we simplify the situation to a constant order stream, which leads to an average purchase price of

$$F_t + \lambda_F^+ \cdot (F_{t+\tau} - F_t) \quad , \tag{3.2}$$

where λ_F^+ is about 0.5, but can be a little greater or smaller. A value smaller than 0.5 represents the manipulator's capability to buy below the average price, a value equal or even greater than 0.5 his inability to do so. The first may be caused by herd effects[9] or positive feedback trading[10], which make the price still rise, when the manipulator has already stopped his transactions. The latter may origin from the fact, that the manipulator always has to buy at the (higher) ask price. Analogously we define a price averaging multiplier λ_F^- for futures selling, one for stock purchasing (λ_S^+) and one for stock selling (λ_S^-).

Arbitrageurs are responsible for the effect of futures purchasing on the spot market. When they sell futures to the manipulator, they have to buy DAX portfolios at the same time. However, the transmission from the futures market to the spot market is not perfect for two reasons:[11] Firstly arbitrageurs can not react without a time delay. Secondly on the futures market we do not only have arbitrageurs, but also other groups, e.g. hedgers, speculators and tax savers (reasons for the presence of the latter group are given in Bamberg/Trost (1995)). We regard Δ^+ and all the other proportionality constants defined in the next steps as independent random variables, whereas the price averaging multipliers are assumed to be deterministic.

According to the pure or modified cost-of-carry model the futures price F_t at the beginning of step 1 is:

$$F_t = R \cdot S_t, \tag{3.3}$$

where the multiplier $R > 1$ essentially depends on the maturity of the DAX futures. We do not intend to discuss the cost-of-carry model here. Empirical evidence shows, that large arbitrage profits resulting from violations of equation (3.3) can not be made.[12] Thus we assume the approximate validity of

---

9 See e.g. Gastineau/Jarrow (1991).

10 See DeLong/Shleifer/Summers/Waldmann (1990).

11 This is also indicated by certain lead-lag relationships between DAX and DAX future: cf. Kempf/Kähler (1993), Grünbichler/Longstaff/Schwartz (1994) and Kempf/Korn (1995).

12 See e.g. Prigge/Schlag (1992), Bühler/Kempf (1993, 1995), Bamberg/Röder (1993, 1994).

(3.3). Possible deviations of F_t from the theoretical value given by (3.3) will be representedi by an error variable.

The futures price at the end of step 1 (without error term) results from (3.3) and (3.1) as:

$$F_{t+\tau} = R \cdot (S_t + f \cdot \Delta^+) \quad . \tag{3.4}$$

Averaging price (3.3) and (3.4) with respect to (3.2) i and adding an error variable ε_1 (which represents i mispricing due to imperfect arbitrage) yields an average purchase price of

$$R \cdot (S_t + \lambda_F^+ \cdot f \cdot \Delta^+) + \varepsilon_1 \, .$$

Due to the fact that the roundtrip is supposed to take place within a few hours we will in the following not denote the time dependence of futures prices F and spot prices S by a subscript anymore. For the same reason R will be treated as a time independent constant. The average purchase price for step 1 thus is:

$$F = R(S + \lambda_F^+ f \Delta^+) + \varepsilon_1 . \tag{3.5}$$

After this relatively detailed discussion of step 1 we can shorten the description of the remaining steps.

Step 2: Purchase of $k \in \mathsf{R}_0^+$ DAX portfolios on the spot market, with d^+ denoting the reaction of the spot market to purchases of DAX portfolios.
Effect on the DAX: $S + f\Delta^+ \rightsquigarrow S + f\Delta^+ + kd^+$
Average purchase price: $S + f\Delta^+ + \lambda_S^+ kd^+$

Step 3: Sale of $f + g$ DAX futures (unwinding of the f positions of step 1 and opening of $g \in \mathsf{N}_0$ new short positions) with Δ^- denoting the reaction of the spot market to DAX portfolio sales.
Effect on the DAX: $S + f\Delta^+ + kd^+ \rightsquigarrow S + f\Delta^+ + kd^+ - (f+g)\Delta^-$
Average selling price: $R(S + f\Delta^+ + kd^+ - \lambda_F^-(f+g)\Delta^-) + \varepsilon_3$

Step 4: Sale of k DAX portfolios with d^- denoting the reaction of the spot market to DAX portfolio sales.
Effect on the DAX: $S + f\Delta^+ + kd^+ - (f+g)\Delta^- \rightsquigarrow S + f\Delta^+ + kd^+ - (f+g)\Delta^- - kd^-$
Average selling price: $S + f\Delta^+ + kd^+ - (f+g)\Delta^- - k\lambda_S^- d^-$

Step 5: Purchase of g DAX futures
Effect on the DAX: $S + f\Delta^+ + kd^+ - (f+g)\Delta^- - kd^- \rightsquigarrow S + f\Delta^+ + kd^+ - (f+g)\Delta^- - kd^- + g\Delta^+$
Average purchase price:
$R(S + f\Delta^+ + kd^+ - (f+g)\Delta^- - kd^- + \lambda_F^+ g\Delta^+) + \varepsilon_5$

The effects on the spot market caused by purchases or sales on the spot market are denoted by d^+ and d^- and that ones caused by purchases or sales on the futures market by Δ^+ and Δ^-. To get a feeling for the dimensions of these (random) variables we assume that a purchase of 500 DAX portfolios (with a value of 200 million DM at a DAX value of 4000) can be expected to increase the DAX by 10 points. This implies

$$\mathrm{E}(500 \cdot d^{+}) = 10 \quad \Leftrightarrow \quad \mathrm{E}(d^{+}) = \frac{10}{500} = 0.02 \quad .$$

Now it is time to calculate the profit (or loss) of the roundtrip. The settlement profit (or loss) on the futures market is

$$\begin{aligned} &(f+g)R\left[S + f\Delta^{+} + kd^{+} - (f+g)\lambda_F^{-}\Delta^{-}\right] + (f+g)\varepsilon_3 \\ &-fR(S + f\lambda_F^{+}\Delta^{+}) - f\varepsilon_1 \\ &-gR\left[S + f\Delta^{+} + kd^{+} - (f+g)\Delta^{-} - kd^{-} + g\lambda_F^{+}\Delta^{+}\right] - g\varepsilon_5\,, \end{aligned} \tag{3.6}$$

whereas the profit (or loss) on the spot market is:

$$k\left[S + f\Delta^{+} + kd^{+} - (f+g)\Delta^{-} - k\lambda_S^{-}d^{-}\right] - k(S + f\Delta^{+} + k\lambda_S^{+}d^{+})\,. \tag{3.7}$$

Hence we get the profit (or loss) of the complete roundtrip as:

$$\begin{aligned} G &= f^2 R\left[(1-\lambda_F^{+})\Delta^{+} - \lambda_F^{-}\Delta^{-}\right] + k^2\left[(1-\lambda_S^{+})d^{+} - \lambda_S^{-}d^{-}\right] \\ &+ g^2 R\left[(1-\lambda_F^{-})\Delta^{-} - \lambda_F^{+}\Delta^{+}\right] + fk\left[Rd^{+} - \Delta^{-}\right] \\ &+ gk\left[Rd^{-} - \Delta^{-}\right] + gfR\left(1 - 2\lambda_F^{-}\right)\Delta^{-} + f\left[\varepsilon_3 - \varepsilon_1\right] + g[\varepsilon_3 - \varepsilon_5] \end{aligned} \tag{3.8}$$

At this point a few remarks regarding result (3.8) should be made.

Remark 1: Since all transactions are executed within one single day, there are no open positions at the end of the trading time. Thus our analysis does not need to consider interest payments.

Remark 2: It should be clear that the manipulator has to act in secret. If his plans were known to the public, this would lead to a counter-reaction of the other market participants.

Remark 3: An optimal starting time can be derived from the fact that the distributions of Δ^{+}, Δ^{-}, d^{+}, d^{-}, $\sigma^2_{\varepsilon_1}$, $\sigma^2_{\varepsilon_3}$ and $\sigma^2_{\varepsilon_5}$ vary from day to day (even from one hour to another): A manipulator will only enter the roundtrip at a time, where parameters indicate profitability. Remarkably the profit does not depend on the DAX value at the starting time.

Remark 4: The mean of the error variables ε_i is rather negative, for arbitrageurs will (due to restrictions on short selling and shares borrowing) find it harder to realize reverse cash and carry arbitrage than cash and carry arbitrage. This underpricing is useful for the futures purchases of the manipulator. However, the advantage is fully compensated by the manipulator's futures sales. Therefore we can assume that the following holds:

$$\mathrm{E}(\varepsilon_3 - \varepsilon_1) = \mathrm{E}(\varepsilon_3 - \varepsilon_5) = 0 \quad . \tag{3.9}$$

Remark 5: The profit is measured in 100 DM units throughout the whole paper. Only in section 5 the profit will be presented as an absolute DM sum.

Remark 6: We have not considered transaction costs so far. This will be done at the end of section 4.

4. Mean and variance of the profit and some optimization problems

Let us now have a look upon the expected profit. Defining $\mu_{\Delta^+} := \mathrm{E}(\Delta^+)$, $\mu_{\Delta^-} := \mathrm{E}(\Delta^-)$, $\mu_{d^+} := \mathrm{E}(d^+)$ and $\mu_{d^-} := \mathrm{E}(d^-)$ and using (3.9) we can derive the mean of G from (3.8) as:

$$\begin{aligned}\mu_G := \mathrm{E}(G) = f^2 R\left[(1-\lambda_F^+)\mu_{\Delta^+} - \lambda_F^-\mu_{\Delta^-}\right] + k^2\left[(1-\lambda_S^+)\mu_{d^+} - \lambda_S^-\mu_{d^-}\right] \\ + \quad g^2 R\left[(1-\lambda_F^-)\mu_{\Delta^-} - \lambda_F^+\mu_{\Delta^+}\right] + fk\left[R\mu_{d^+} - \mu_{\Delta^-}\right] \\ + \quad gk\left[R\mu_{d^-} - \mu_{\Delta^-}\right] + gf\,R\left(1-2\lambda_F^-\right)\mu_{\Delta^-} \quad .\end{aligned}$$

This is a quadratic function in (f,g,k) and can therefore be written as:

$$\mathrm{E}(G) = (f,g,k)\,\mathbf{A}\,(f,g,k)^T \quad , \tag{4.1}$$

where $\mathbf{A}$ denotes the matrix

$$\mathbf{A} := \begin{pmatrix} R\left[(1-\lambda_F^+)\mu_{\Delta^+} - \lambda_F^-\mu_{\Delta^-}\right] & R\frac{1-2\lambda_F^-}{2}\mu_{\Delta^-} & \frac{R\mu_{d^+}-\mu_{\Delta^-}}{2} \\ R\frac{1-2\lambda_F^-}{2}\mu_{\Delta^-} & R\left[(1-\lambda_F^-)\mu_{\Delta^-} - \lambda_F^+\mu_{\Delta^+}\right] & \frac{R\mu_{d^-}-\mu_{\Delta^-}}{2} \\ \frac{R\mu_{d^+}-\mu_{\Delta^-}}{2} & \frac{R\mu_{d^-}-\mu_{\Delta^-}}{2} & (1-\lambda_S^+)\mu_{d^+} - \lambda_S^-\mu_{d^-} \end{pmatrix} .$$

From expression (4.1) we can derive a simple criterion for profitability of manipulation (before transaction costs). There is a volume allocation (f,g,k)[13], where a positive profit can be expected, if and only if the matrix is not negative semidefinite, i.e. if and only if a positive eigenvalue exists.[14]

A risk neutral manipulator would hence start a roundtrip if this criterion is fulfilled. To consider the risk aversion case we have to calculate the variance of G. Since all random variables are assumed to be independent, we get:

$$\begin{aligned}\sigma_G^2 := \mathrm{Var}(G) = f^4 R^2\left[\left(\lambda_F^-\right)^2\sigma_{\Delta^-}^2 + \left(1-\lambda_F^+\right)^2\sigma_{\Delta^+}^2\right] \\ -2f^3 g\,R^2\lambda_F^-\left(1-2\lambda_F^-\right)\sigma_{\Delta^-}^2 + 2f^3k\,R\lambda_F^-\sigma_{\Delta^-}^2 \\ +f^2g^2R^2\left[\left(6\lambda_F^-\left(\lambda_F^- - 1\right)+1\right)\sigma_{\Delta^-}^2 - 2\lambda_F^+\left(1-\lambda_F^+\right)\sigma_{\Delta^+}^2\right] \\ +f^2k^2\left[\sigma_{\Delta^-}^2 + R^2\sigma_{d^+}^2\right] + 2f^2gk\,R\left(3\lambda_F^- - 1\right)\sigma_{\Delta^-}^2 \\ +2fg^3R^2\left(1-\lambda_F^-\right)\left(1-2\lambda_F^-\right)\sigma_{\Delta^-}^2 + 2fg^2k\,R\left(3\lambda_F^- - 2\right)\sigma_{\Delta^-}^2 \\ +2fgk^2\sigma_{\Delta^-}^2 + 2fk^3R\left(1-\lambda_S^+\right)\sigma_{d^+}^2 + f^2\left(\sigma_{\varepsilon_3}^2 + \sigma_{\varepsilon_1}^2\right) + 2fg\,\sigma_{\varepsilon_3}^2\end{aligned}$$

[13] The values of f and g are as a matter of fact supposed to be integral. Rounding of f and g to the next integer does usually not make much difference, though.

[14] See Opitz (1997).

$$+g^4 R^2 \left[(\lambda_F^+)^2 \sigma_{\Delta+}^2 + (1-\lambda_F^-)^2 \sigma_{\Delta-}^2 \right] - 2g^3 k R (1-\lambda_F^-) \sigma_{\Delta-}^2$$
$$+g^2 k^2 \left[\sigma_{\Delta-}^2 + R^2 \sigma_{d-}^2 + 2R (\lambda_F^+ - \lambda_F^-)(1-\lambda_S^+) \mu_{\Delta+} \mu_{d+} \right]$$
$$+g^2 (\sigma_{\varepsilon_3}^2 + \sigma_{\varepsilon_5}^2) - 2gk^3 R \lambda_S^- \sigma_{d-}^2 + k^4 \left[(1-\lambda_S^+)^2 \sigma_{d+}^2 + (\lambda_S^-)^2 \sigma_{d-}^2 \right],$$

where $\sigma_{\Delta+}^2$, $\sigma_{\Delta-}^2$, σ_{d+}^2, σ_{d-}^2, $\sigma_{\varepsilon_1}^2$, $\sigma_{\varepsilon_3}^2$ and $\sigma_{\varepsilon_5}^2$ denote the variances of Δ^+, Δ^-, d^+, d^-, ε_1, ε_3 and ε_5, respectively. Knowing mean and variance of G one can analyze the profitability of the strategy more detailed and from different perspectives.

Without any further information about the distribution of G still at least three things can be done for more detailed risk analysis.

- Given an upper bound α for the probability that G is below a loss of $-c$ with $c \geq 0$, maximize μ_G under this restriction using the Chebyshev or the Visochanskiĭ-Petunin inequality[15]. The optimization problem is

$$\max_{f,g,k}\{\mu_G\} \qquad \text{s.t.} \quad \frac{\sigma_G^2}{(\mu_G+c)^2} \leq \alpha \quad \text{and} \quad \mu_G > -c \tag{4.2}$$

without further assumptions, respectively

$$\max_{f,g,k}\{\mu_G\} \qquad \text{s.t.} \quad \frac{4\sigma_G^2}{9(\mu_G+c)^2} \leq \alpha \quad \text{and} \quad \mu_G > -c \tag{4.3}$$

if the density of G is unimodal and $\alpha \leq \frac{1}{6}$. If the optimization restrictions hold, then

$$\mathrm{P}(G < -c) \leq \mathrm{P}(|G-\mu_G| \geq \mu_G + c) \leq \frac{\sigma_G^2}{(\mu_G+c)^2} \leq \alpha \quad ,$$

respectively

$$\mathrm{P}(G < -c) \leq \mathrm{P}(|G-\mu_G| \geq \mu_G + c) \leq \frac{4\sigma_G^2}{9(\mu_G+c)^2} \leq \alpha$$

is valid. Since the Visochanskiĭ-Petunin inequality is stronger than the Chebyshev inequality, solving problem (4.3) surely is to be preferred, unless the distribution of G is multimodal.
- Approximate the certainty equivalent $\mathrm{CEQ}_\gamma(G)$ of an investor with constant risk aversion γ by $\mu_G - \frac{\gamma}{2}\sigma_G^2$ and maximize this term dependent on f, g and k.
- Find (μ_G, σ_G^2)-efficient volume allocations.[16]

[15] Cf. Pukelsheim (1994).
[16] Cf. Schneeweiß (1967, p. 52ff).

Here we just want to consider the first two approaches.

If additionally something is known about the distribution of G, then the certainty equivalent can (by numerical integration) be calculated exactly. Under the assumption that the distribution of G is normal $\text{CEQ}_\gamma(G) = \mu_G - \frac{\gamma}{2}\sigma_G^2$ is not a proxy anymore, but the real value.[17] The optimization problem is

$$\max_{f,g,k}\{\text{CEQ}_\gamma(G)\} \quad . \tag{4.4}$$

A last extension now shall be considering transaction costs explicitly. To do this we assume a DAX value of about 4000 and assume stock transaction costs for a large trader of 0.1% one way, and future transaction costs of 50 DM one way. Therefore a proxy for total transaction costs of the roundtrip is

$$TC = 2 \cdot (0.5(f+g) + k \cdot S \cdot 0.001) = f + g + 8k \quad [100 \text{ DM}] \quad .$$

Now our optimization problem is

$$\max_{f,g,k}\{\text{CEQ}_\gamma(G) - TC\} \quad , \tag{4.5}$$

respectively for $\gamma = 0$

$$\max_{f,g,k}\{\mu_G - TC\} \quad . \tag{4.6}$$

5. Numerical examples

The potential success or failure of the roundtrip shall now be illustrated by a few examples with realistic parameter values. All optimization problems were solved with a relatively primitive, but successful method: by complete enumeration of all possibilities. This was only feasible by two additonal assumptions: Setting an upper bound of 3000 for f, g and k and choosing $k \in \mathbb{N}_0$. The first should be fairly realistic, the latter is harmless due to the flat dependence of G on k.

Example 1:

According to his personal assessment of the market a manipulator characterizes the present situation by the mean parameters

$$\mu_{d^+} = \mu_{d^-} = \mu_{\Delta^+} = \mu_{\Delta^-} = 0.02 \, .$$

Additionally the manipulator regards a 3σ interval of $[0,01; 0,03]$ as realistic. This yields:

$$\sigma_{d^+}^2 = \sigma_{d^-}^2 = \sigma_{\Delta^+}^2 = \sigma_{\Delta^-}^2 = \frac{1}{90000} \, .$$

[17] Cf. Schneeweiß (1967, p. 149).

Let the variance of the error terms ε_1, ε_3 and ε_5 be

$$\sigma^2_{\varepsilon_1} = \sigma^2_{\varepsilon_3} = \sigma^2_{\varepsilon_5} = \frac{1}{6} \quad .$$

Let the constant factors have the values

$$\lambda^+_F = \lambda^-_F = \lambda^+_S = \lambda^-_S = 0.5$$

and $R = 1.01$. The latter corresponds to a contract maturity of 3 months at a riskless interest rate of 4% or to a contract maturity of 4 months at an interest rate of 3%.

The matrix $\mathbf{A}$ here is

$$\mathbf{A} = \frac{1}{10000} \begin{pmatrix} 0 & 0 & 1 \\ 0 & 0 & 1 \\ 1 & 1 & 0 \end{pmatrix}$$

with eigenvalues 0, $-\frac{\sqrt{2}}{10000}$ and $\frac{\sqrt{2}}{10000}$. Since the third one is positive, there is a volume allocation—namely the corresponding eigenvector $(1, 1, \sqrt{2})$ and all its multiples—with a positive expected profit. The manipulator would thus just need to increase f, g and k (keeping the proportion $1 : 1 : \sqrt{2}$) to lift the expected profit to infinity. With increasing values of f, g and k, however, also the variance of G rises. This will keep a risk averse investor from choosing the volumes too high.

In our example we first solve the problems (4.2) and (4.3) with $c = 100$ and $\alpha = 0.1$. The optimal solution is to choose $(f, g, k) = (1, 44, 94)$ with an expected profit of $\mu_G = 0.846$, respectively $(f, g, k) = (0, 62, 123)$ with $\mu_G = 1.525$. Under realistic transaction costs both solutions surely are not profitable.

Assuming that the distribution of G is normal (which is for example the case if all random variables involved are normally distributed) we have to solve problem (4.4). Doing this yields the optimal volume allocation $(f, g, k) = (0, 1313, 1341)$. It is interesting that the first futures parameter equals zero, for this implies leaving out step 1. The certainty equivalent of the profit at the optimal allocation is 17500 DM, which seems too small to compensate transaction costs. Solution of the problem (4.6) comes up with the optimal allocation $(f, g, k) = (0, 0, 0)$. Thus also problem (4.5) with $\gamma > 0$ has this solution.

In other words, although the parameter constellation seems promising for the manipulator at first sight, a profit can not be realized.

Example 2:

We keep the parameter constellation of example 1, but the manipulator is assumed to have the market against him, i.e. $\lambda^+_F = \lambda^-_F = \lambda^+_S = \lambda^-_S =$

0.51. Now the matrix **A** has three negative eigenvalues and no profitable manipulation is possible.

Changing the averaging parameters for the spot market to $\lambda_S^+ = \lambda_S^- = 0.5$[18] leads to a positive eigenvalue. The solution of the problem (4.6), however, still is not to take action at all.

Even if the averaging multipiers are changed to the fairly optimistic values $\lambda_S^+ = \lambda_S^- = 0.49$ and $\lambda_F^+ = \lambda_F^- = 0.5$, where there also is a positive eigenvalue, solving (4.6) leads to the recommendation that no actions should be taken.

In summary no profitable manipulation can be made.

Example 3:

Now we change the parameter constellation of example 1 slightly by choosing $\mu_{\Delta^-} = 0.205$ and all the other values unchanged. With all averaging multipliers equaling 0.5, the matrix **A** has two positive eigenvalues. Again we first solve problem (4.6), which has got the solution $(f, g, k) = (0, 0, 0)$.

With the bearish market parameter scenario $\lambda_S^- = 0.49$, $\lambda_F^- = 0.485$ and $\mu_{d^-} = 0.0205$ this changes: Taking transaction costs into consideration positive profits can be made, even for a risk averse investor. The optimal solution (for (4.6) and (4.5) with $\gamma = 0.00001$) is to choose f and g as high as possible and k equal to zero. This means that only futures and no stocks should be traded. If we increase the risk aversion of the investor the optimal solution switches to $(f, g, k) = (0, 0, 0)$. A finite optimal solution[19] can not be realized, even if no distribution assumptions are made and the Chebyshev inequality is employed.

Example 4:

Let in the last example the parameter values be completely different. Be

$$\mu_{d^+} = \mu_{d^-} = \mu_{\Delta^+} = \mu_{\Delta^-} = 0.01$$

and

$$\sigma_{d^+}^2 = \sigma_{d^-}^2 = \sigma_{\Delta^+}^2 = \sigma_{\Delta^-}^2 = \frac{1}{36000}$$

and

$$\sigma_{\varepsilon_1}^2 = \sigma_{\varepsilon_3}^2 = \sigma_{\varepsilon_5}^2 = \frac{1}{3} \quad .$$

Let the constant factors have the values

$$\lambda_F^+ = \lambda_F^- = \lambda_S^+ = \lambda_S^- = 0.5$$

and $R = 1.001$.

Again the matrix **A** has a positive eigenvalue, but with respect to transaction costs no profits can be made, even if one changes the averaging multipliers to

$$\lambda_F^+ = \lambda_F^- = 0.49 \quad \text{and} \quad \lambda_S^+ = \lambda_S^- = 0.48 \quad .$$

[18] On the spot market it might be easier for the manipulator to hide his actions.

[19] In our context this means one with $f, g < 3000$.

6. Concluding comments

In this paper we have analyzed the profitability of a financially strong investor's roundtrip on the DAX futures and the DAX spot market. Under realistic parameter constellations a profit seems to be not achievable, which is mainly due to transaction costs.

In extreme cases, e.g. a very bearish market where prices are more likely to fall than to rise, a manipulation strategy may be profitable, but not in form of the roundtrip considered here. It seems that combined trading on both markets does (due to transaction costs on the spot market) not really increase the chances for profitable manipulations.

References

1. Bamberg, G.; Röder, K. (1993). Arbitrage am DAX–Futures–Markt unter Berücksichtigung von Einkommensteuern, Kredit und Kapital 26, 575–607.
2. Bamberg, G.; Röder, K. (1994). Arbitrage institutioneller Anleger am DAX–Futures–Markt unter Berücksichtigung von Körperschaftssteuern und Dividenden, Zeitschrift für Betriebswirtschaft 64, 1533–1566.
3. Bamberg, G.; Spremann, K. (1981). Implications of Constant Risk Aversion, Zeitschrift für Operations Research 25, 205–224.
4. Bamberg, G.; Trost, R. (1995). Können Privatanleger mit DAX–Futures Steuern sparen?, Zeitschrift für betriebswirtschaftliche Forschung 47, 265–274.
5. Benabou, R.; Laroque, G. (1992). Using Privileged Information to Manipulated Markets: Insiders, Gurus and Credibility, Quarterly Journal of Economics 107, 921–958.
6. Bühler, W.; Kempf, A. (1993). Der DAX–Future: Kursverhalten und Arbitragemöglichkeiten, Kredit und Kapital 26, 533–574.
7. Bühler, W.; Kempf, A. (1995). DAX–Index Futures: Mispricing and Arbitrage in German Markets, The Journal of Futures Markets 15, 833–859.
8. Easterbrook, F.H. (1986). Monopoly, Manipulation and the Regulation of Futures Markets, Journal of Business 59, 103–127.
9. De Long, J.B.; Shleifer, A.; Summers, L.H.; Waldmann, R.J. (1990). Positive Feedback Investment Strategies and Destabilizing Rational Speculation, Journal of Finance 45, 379–395.
10. Gastineau, G.; Jarrow, R.A. (1991). Large Trader Impact and Market Regulation, Financial Analysts Journal 47, 40–72.
11. Grünbichler, A.; Longstaff, F.A.; Schwartz, E.S. (1994). Electronic Screen Trading and the Transmission of Information: An Empirical Examination, Journal of Financial Intermediation 3, 166–187.
12. Janssen, B.; Rudolph, B. (1992). Der Deutsche Aktienindex DAX, Frankfurt/Main.
13. Jarrow, R.A. (1994). Derivative Security Markets, Market Manipulation, and Option Pricing Theory, Journal of Financial and Quantitative Analysis 29, 241–261.
14. Lindenberg, E.B. (1979). Capital Market Equilibrium with Price Affecting Institutional Investors, in: Elton, E.J., Gruber, M.J. (Eds.). Portfolio Theory, 25 Years After, 109–124, Amsterdam - New York - Oxford.

15. Kempf, A.; Kähler, J. (1995). Informationsverarbeitung auf Kassa– und Terminmarkt: DAX versus DAX–Future, ZEW–Wirtschaftsanalysen 1, 359–380.
16. Kempf, A.; Korn, O. (1995). Der Einflu von Arbitrageuren auf die Preisführerschaft von Finanzmärkten, ZEW Disc. Paper, 95–02.
17. Kempf, A.; Korn, O. (1997). Market Depth and Order Size, Working Paper of the Chair of Finance 97-05, University Mannheim.
18. Kumar, P.; Seppi, D. (1992). Futures Manipulation with "Cash Settlement", The Journal of Finance 68, 1485–1502.
19. Kyle, A.S. (1985). A Theory of Futures Market Manipulation, S. 141–173 in: Anderson, R.W. (Hrsg.). The Industrial Organization of Futures Markets, Lexington - Toronto.
20. Loistl, O. (1992). Computergestütztes Wertpapiermanagement, 4. Aufl., München.
21. Newbery, D.M.G. (1985). The Manipulation of Futures Markets by a Dominant Producer, S. 35–62 in: Anderson, R.W. (Hrsg.): The Industrial Organization of Futures Markets, Lexington - Toronto.
22. Opitz, O. (1997). Mathematik – Lehrbuch für Ökonomen, 6. Aufl., München.
23. Prigge, J.; Schlag, C. (1992). Die Bewertung des DAX–Future Kontrakts an der Deutschen Terminbörse, Zeitschrift für Bankrecht und Bankwirtschaft 4, 299–307.
24. Pukelsheim, F. (1994). The Three Sigma Rule, The American Statistician 48, 88–91.
25. Rudolph, B. (1982). Portefeuille– und Aktienkursbildung bei monopolistischem Anlegerwettbewerb, Zeitschrift für Betriebswirtschaft 52, 471–490.
26. Schneeweiss, H. (1967). Entscheidungskriterien bei Risiko, Berlin.
27. Spremann, K. (1991). Wirtschaft, Investition und Finanzierung, 5. Aufl., München.
28. Steiner, M.; Bruns, C. (1995). Wertpapiermanagement, 4. Aufl., Stuttgart.

Estimation of the Stochastic Volatility by Markov Chain Monte Carlo

Hans Boscher[1], Eva–Maria Fronk[2], and Iris Pigeot[2]

[1] Deutsche Morgan Grenfell, Frankfurt, Germany
[2] Department of Statistics, Ludwig-Maximilians-Universität München, Germany

Summary. In this paper, we consider the stochastic volatility which is used to measure the fluctuation of financial assets. Based on the stochastic volatility model introduced by Taylor (1986) a Bayesian point of view is taken to estimate the stochastic volatility by MCMC methods. The performance of these methods is evaluated in a simulation study. In addition, they are applied to a real dataset for estimating the volatility of swap rates.

1. Introduction

In financial markets, the pricing of options is an essential task which calls for an adequate quantity to measure the risk of fluctuating prices. Such a measure is given by the volatility. In the literature and also in practice, different types of volatility such as for instance the historical volatility are discussed and used. ARCH and GARCH models assume a deterministic, but time–dependent volatility (Engle, 1982; Bollerslev, 1986). Such proposals do not take into account that there are many and often also unknown factors that influence the volatility, which is therefore difficult to model in an adequate way. Taylor (1986) introduced the stochastic volatility (SV) model, which is based on a stochastic component representing all unknown influences. It is possible to consider the distribution of this latent parameter such that the volatility can be estimated, although the single factors are still unknown.
Since the SV model implies hierarchical dependencies it seems appropriate to use Markov chain Monte Carlo (MCMC) methods for estimating the model parameters. Such methods allow to generate complex and not or hardly accessible distributions. MCMC are very computer–intensive simulation techniques which are used in a Bayesian framework. Their application requires the derivation of an adequate algorithm. The use of MCMC has rapidly increased during the last few years and is a main topic in actual research.

The outline of this paper is as follows. In Section 2, we introduce the original SV model and give a modification by modelling a t–distributed instead of a normally distributed noise term. A brief description of MCMC methods is followed by presenting respective MCMC algorithms for both versions of the SV model. Section 3 describes the design of a simulation study and the results obtained from the original and the modified version of the SV model, both using MCMC. The results are briefly compared to posterior modus estimates calculated by Spanier (1997). In Section 4, the swap rates of Deutsch Mark (DEM), Japanese Yen (JPY), and US Dollar (USD) are analyzed. The volatility estimated from the original SV model is compared to the historical volatility which is a common way to ascertain the volatility in practice as mentioned above. Furthermore, the modified and the original SV model are compared. The gained results are summarized in the discussion. Some open research questions are pointed out.

2. Theoretical background and algorithms

2.1 Original SV model

The SV model proposed by Taylor (1986) is given as

$$y_t = \epsilon_t \exp(h_t/2), \qquad h_{t+1} = \gamma_0 + \gamma_1 h_t + \eta_t, \qquad \eta_t \sim N(0, \sigma_\eta^2), \tag{2.1}$$

where $\epsilon_t \sim N(0,1)$ and $t = 1, 2, \ldots, n$. The processes ϵ_t and η_t are both independent and identically distributed (iid). Here, y_t denotes the log–return of an asset r_t between time t and $t+1$, which is defined as $y_t = \log(r_{t+1}/r_t)$. Note that (2.1) implicitly assumes that $E(y_t) = 0$. The random variable h_t measures the effect of the random and unknown factors which influence the volatility (Shephard, 1996). If we assume in addition that h_t is stationary, i.e. $E(h_t)$ and $Var(h_t)$ do not depend on time t, it follows that $E(h_t) = \mu = \frac{\gamma_0}{1-\gamma_1}$. After solving this equation with respect to γ_0 and renaming γ_1 as ϕ with $|\phi| < 1$, (2.1) can be rewritten as

$$\begin{aligned} y_t &= \beta \epsilon_t \exp(h_t/2), \quad \epsilon_t \sim N(0,1), \\ h_{t+1} - \mu &= \phi(h_t - \mu) + \eta_t, \quad \eta_t \sim N(0, \sigma_\eta^2), \end{aligned} \tag{2.2}$$

for $t = 1, \ldots, n$. An advantage of Model (2.2) is that the involved parameters are easier to interpret. To ensure identifiability either β has to be set to one or μ to zero. This results in two versions of the Model (2.2). If β is set to one, μ can be calculated from the corresponding version. This value can then be used to calculate β as $\beta = \exp(\mu/2)$ in the other version.

Following Kim, Shephard, and Chib (1996), we focus on Model (2.2). Here, it is of interest to estimate the parameters σ_η^2, ϕ, μ, and the stochastic volatility given by $\exp(h_t/2)$ for $t = 1, \ldots, n$. The estimation is carried out in a Bayesian framework. That is, we assume priors with certain hyperparameters for the distributions of σ_η^2, ϕ, and μ. The full conditionals are then derived. In the next step, MCMC methods are used to simulate the posterior distribution by sampling from the full conditionals. The parameters are finally estimated from the simulated posterior distribution. The full conditionals and the according algorithm are stated in detail in Section 2.4, where the algorithm we use is mainly based on the proposals by Kim, Shephard, and Chib (1996). Thus, we also assume the stationary process h_t to begin with the initial condition $h_1 \sim N(\mu, \sigma_\eta^2/(1-\phi^2))$.

2.2 Modified SV model

The noise term η_t of the original SV model follows a normal distribution, such that we expect approximately 95 % of the realizations to lie in the interval $[-2\sigma_\eta; 2\sigma_\eta]$. In financial markets, however, it is often observed that periods of small market movements are followed by shorter periods of large changes. This behaviour is better described by a t–distribution which has fatter tails than the normal distribution. Letting η_t, $t = 1, \ldots, n-1$, follow a $t(d)$–distribution the SV model is given as

$$\begin{aligned} y_t &= \beta\epsilon_t \exp(h_t/2), \quad \epsilon_t \sim N(0,1), \\ h_{t+1} - \mu &= \phi(h_t - \mu) + \eta_t, \quad \eta_t \sim t(d). \end{aligned} \tag{2.3}$$

Thus, given the two independent random variables x_t and z_t with $x_t \sim N(0,1)$ and $z_t \sim \chi^2(d)$, η_t can be written as $\eta_t = \sqrt{\frac{d}{z_t}} \cdot x_t$, $t = 1, \ldots, n-1$, and

$$\eta_t \mid z_t \sim N(0, \sigma_t^2), \quad \sigma_t^2 = \frac{d}{z_t}.$$

That is, η_t given z_t is also a normally distributed variable, but unlike in the original model the conditional variance of η_t varies over t. On the analogy of the original SV model let the initial condition be $h_1 \mid z_0 \sim N(\mu, \frac{\sigma_0^2}{1-\phi^2})$, $\sigma_0^2 = \frac{d}{z_0}$. Let denote $\boldsymbol{\sigma^2}$ the vector of σ_t^2, $t = 0, 1, \ldots, n-1$, i.e. $\boldsymbol{\sigma^2} = (\sigma_0^2, \sigma_1^2, \ldots, \sigma_{n-1}^2)$.

The parameters of Model (2.3) are estimated using the same approach as for the original SV model. The appropriate full conditionals and the algorithm are described in Section 2.5.

2.3 MCMC methods

Markov chain Monte Carlo methods are algorithms which are based on the Markov and the Bayesian theory. For a discussion of the Markov theory we refer to Tierney (1994). A short introduction to Bayesian techniques in the context of MCMC is given by Gilks, Richardson, and Spiegelhalter (1996, p. 1–17). The Hastings algorithm typically used in MCMC was developed by Metropolis, Rosenbluth, Rosenbluth, Teller, and Teller (1953) and later generalized by Hastings (1970). A detailed introduction to the Hastings algorithm is given by Chib and Greenberg (1995) and many topics in the context of MCMC are discussed in Gilks, Richardson, and Spiegelhalter (1996).

In the following, only a brief description of the Hastings algorithm is given. Suppose $\mathbf{x} = (x_1, x_2, \ldots, x_m)$ is a m–dimensional random vector and the joint density $f(\mathbf{x})$ is only known up to an proportionality factor c, i.e. $f(\mathbf{x}) = c \cdot g(\mathbf{x})$ where $g(\mathbf{x})$ is known. Furthermore, let x_i denote the i-th component of $\mathbf{x}$ and $\mathbf{x}_{-i} = (x_1, \ldots, x_{i-1}, x_{i+1}, \ldots, x_m)$ the vector of all components of $\mathbf{x}$ except for x_i. The sampling scheme of the Hastings algorithm is as follows:

1. Initialize $\mathbf{x}^{(0)} = (x_1^{(0)}, x_2^{(0)}, \ldots, x_m^{(0)})$ and set $k = 0$.
2. For $i = 1, \ldots, m$
   a) A new candidate value x_i' is generated from a transition kernel $R_i(x_i \to x_i'; \mathbf{x}_{-i})$.
   b) The random variable $X_i^{(k+1)}$ is set to the value x_i' with the acceptance probability

$$A_i(x_i \to x_i'; \mathbf{x}_{-i}) = \min\left\{1; \frac{f(\mathbf{x}') \cdot R_i(x_i' \to x_i; \mathbf{x}_{-i})}{f(\mathbf{x}) \cdot R_i(x_i \to x_i'; \mathbf{x}_{-i})}\right\},$$

   otherwise the old value x_i is kept.
3. If $k < K$ set k to $k+1$ and continue with 2.

In Step 2(b) $\mathbf{x}'$ denotes the vector $\mathbf{x}$ after changing the i–th component to x_i', i.e. $\mathbf{x}' = (x_1, \ldots, x_{i-1}, x_i', x_{i+1}, \ldots, x_m)$. For K increasing to infinity the distribution of $\mathbf{x}^{(K)}$ converges under certain regularity conditions to a distribution with density $f(\mathbf{x})$, which is called the equilibrium of the produced chain $\mathbf{x}^{(1)}, \mathbf{x}^{(2)}, \ldots, \mathbf{x}^{(K)}$. The first b iterations for which the distribution of $\mathbf{x}^{(i)}$, $i \leq b$, is supposed to be not "sufficiently close" to the limit distribution are not used for estimation. The number b is called burn in time. Since the correlation between subsequent samples $\mathbf{x}^{(b+1)}, \mathbf{x}^{(b+2)}, \ldots, \mathbf{x}^{(K)}$ should be small, the chain has to be thinned out. This means that only every s-th sample is considered. The values of b and s depend on the data under consideration. The obtained chain $\mathbf{x}^{(b)}, \mathbf{x}^{(b+s)}, \mathbf{x}^{(b+2s)}, \ldots, \mathbf{x}^{(b+ns)}$, $b + ns < K$, is approximately distributed according to f and the properties of f can be estimated from the generated samples. The advantage of this method is that the density $f(\mathbf{x})$ has only to be known up to an unknown proportionality factor, because this factor cancels out in the acceptance probability A_i.
A special case of the Hastings algorithm is the so-called Gibbs sampler, where $R_i(x_i \to x_i'; \mathbf{x}_{-i})$ is chosen to be $f(x_i' \mid \mathbf{x}_{-i})$ for $i = 1, \ldots, m$. Thus, the acceptance probability $A_i(x_i \to x_i'; \mathbf{x}_{-i})$ equals one and the candidate x_i' proposed by $f(x_i' \mid \mathbf{x}_{-i})$ is always accepted. As the term $f(x_i \mid \mathbf{x}_{-i})$ contains all components of $\mathbf{x}$ it is called the full conditional of $\mathbf{x}$. Using the Gibbs sampler only the full conditionals $f(x_i \mid \mathbf{x}_{-i})$, $i = 1, \ldots, m$, have to be known, which are often much more easier to calculate than $f(\mathbf{x})$ up to proportionality. A more detailed description of the Gibbs sampler is found in Casella and George (1992).

2.4 Algorithm for the original SV model

The following algorithm is a slight modification of the Gibbs sampler which was suggested by Kim, Shephard, and Chib (1996):

1. Initialize $\mathbf{h} = (h_1, h_2, \ldots, h_n)$, σ_η^2, ϕ, β, and μ and set $k = 0$.
2. a) For $t = 1, 2, \ldots, n$ sample a new candidate value h_t from $h_t \mid \mathbf{h}_{-t}, y, \sigma_\eta^2, \phi, \beta, \mu$.

b) Sample a new candidate value σ_η^2 from $\sigma_\eta^2 \mid y, \mathbf{h}, \phi, \beta, \mu$.
c) Sample a new candidate value ϕ from $\phi \mid \mathbf{h}, \sigma_\eta^2, \beta, \mu$.
d) Sample a new candidate value β from $\beta \mid y, \mathbf{h}$ or a new candidate value μ from $\mu \mid \mathbf{h}, \phi, \sigma_\eta^2$.

3. If $k < K$ set k to $k+1$ and continue with 2.

Depending on whether we fix β to one or μ to zero, in Step 2(d) only μ or β has to be updated.

It is easily shown that the full conditionals $f(h_t \mid \mathbf{h}_{-t}, y, \sigma_\eta^2, \phi, \beta, \mu)$, $t = 1, \ldots, n$, are given by

$$\begin{aligned} & f(h_t \mid \mathbf{h}_{-t}, y, \sigma_\eta^2, \phi, \beta, \mu) \\ = \; & f(h_t \mid h_{t-1}, h_{t+1}, y, \sigma_\eta^2, \phi, \beta, \mu) \\ \propto \; & f(y_t \mid h_t, \sigma_\eta^2, \phi, \beta, \mu) \cdot f(h_t \mid h_{t-1}, h_{t+1}, \sigma_\eta^2, \phi, \beta, \mu). \end{aligned} \tag{2.4}$$

But since the proportionality factor $\frac{f(h_{t-1}, h_{t+1}, \sigma_\eta^2, \phi, \beta, \mu)}{f(y, h_{t-1}, h_{t+1}, \sigma_\eta^2, \phi, \beta, \mu)}$ is not known, it is difficult to sample directly from the full conditionals $f(h_t \mid \mathbf{h}_{-t}, y, \sigma_\eta^2, \phi, \beta, \mu)$. Unlike Kim, Shephard, and Chib, who coped with this problem by using an acceptance rejection algorithm, we apply the Hastings algorithm for sampling the full conditionals. The transition kernel $R_t(h_t \to h_t'; \mathbf{h}_{-t})$ of this algorithm is chosen as $f(h_t \mid \mathbf{h}_{-t}, \sigma_\eta^2, \phi, \beta, \mu) = f(h_t \mid h_{t-1}, h_{t+1}, \sigma_\eta^2, \phi, \beta, \mu)$. Because of (2.4) the acceptance probability $A_t(h_t \to h_t'; \mathbf{h}_{-t})$ then reduces to

$$A_t(h_t \to h_t'; \mathbf{h}_{-t}) = \min\left\{1; \frac{f(y_t \mid h_t', \sigma_\eta^2, \phi, \beta, \mu)}{f(y_t \mid h_t, \sigma_\eta^2, \phi, \beta, \mu)}\right\}.$$

Both $f(h_t \mid h_{t-1}, h_{t+1}, \sigma_\eta^2, \phi, \beta, \mu)$ and $f(y_t \mid h_t, \sigma_\eta^2, \phi, \beta, \mu)$ are known and easy to sample as they are both densities of normal distributions. It holds that $h_t \mid \mathbf{h}_{-t}, \sigma_\eta^2, \phi, \beta, \mu \sim N(h_t^*, v_t^2)$ with

$$h_t^* = \mu + \frac{\phi\{(h_{t-1} - \mu) + (h_{t+1} - \mu)\}}{(1+\phi^2)} \text{ and } v_t^2 = \frac{\sigma_\eta^2}{(1+\phi^2)} \text{ for } t = 2, \ldots, n-1. \tag{2.5}$$

Note that in Formula (2.5) the dependency of h_t^* on future values is of course due to the simulation technique. This means that for the estimation of h_t no information is needed which is not available at time t. For h_1^* and h_n^* we get

$$\begin{aligned} h_1^* &= \mu + \frac{1}{\phi}(h_2 - \mu) \quad \text{and} \quad v_t^2 = \frac{\sigma_\eta^2}{\phi^2} \\ \text{and} \quad h_n^* &= \mu + \phi(h_{n-1} - \mu) \quad \text{and} \quad v_t^2 = \sigma_\eta^2. \end{aligned} \tag{2.6}$$

Furthermore, $y_t \mid h_t, \sigma_\eta^2, \phi, \beta, \mu$ is normally distributed with mean zero and variance $\beta^2 \exp(h_t)$.

To sample the other full conditionals we follow the approach of Kim, Shephard, and Chib (1996). They assume the prior of σ_η^2 to be an inverse gamma distribution, such that $\sigma_\eta^2 \sim \mathrm{IG}(\sigma_r/2, S_\sigma/2)$. It follows that the posterior distribution $\sigma_\eta^2 \mid y, \mathbf{h}, \phi, \mu$ is an $\mathrm{IG}(a/2, b/2)$–distribution with parameters

$$\begin{aligned} a &= n + \sigma_r \\ \text{and} \quad b &= S_\sigma + (h_1 - \mu)^2(1-\phi^2) + \sum_{t=1}^{n-1}\{(h_{t+1}-\mu) - \phi(h_t - \mu)\}^2 \end{aligned} \quad (2.7)$$

The hyperparameters σ_r and S_σ are set to $\sigma_r = 5$ and $S_\sigma = 0.05$.

The prior distribution of ϕ is supposed to be given as

$$f(\phi) \propto \left(\frac{1+\phi}{2}\right)^{\phi^{(1)}-1} \cdot \left(\frac{1-\phi}{2}\right)^{\phi^{(2)}-1}, \quad \phi^{(1)}, \phi^{(2)} > 0.5. \quad (2.8)$$

The hyperparameters are set to $\phi^{(1)} = 20$ and $\phi^{(2)} = 1.5$. Kim, Shephard, and Chib (1996) used a Hastings algorithm to sample from the posterior $\phi \mid \mathbf{h}, \sigma_\eta^2, \mu$. Their proposal kernel $R(\phi \to \phi'; \mathbf{h}, \sigma_\eta^2, \mu)$ is a normal distribution $N(\phi^*, V_\phi^2)$ with

$$\begin{aligned} \phi^* &= \sum_{t=1}^{n-1}(h_{t+1}-\mu)(h_t-\mu) \Big/ \sum_{t=1}^{n-1}(h_t-\mu)^2 \\ \text{and} \quad V_\phi^2 &= \sigma_\eta^2\left(\sum_{t=1}^{n-1}(h_t-\mu)^2\right)^{-1}. \end{aligned} \quad (2.9)$$

If the sampled ϕ' happens to fall into the stationarity interval $(-1;1)$, the proposed value is then accepted with probability

$$A(\phi \to \phi'; \mathbf{h}, \sigma_\eta^2, \mu) = \min\left\{1; \frac{f(\phi')\cdot\sqrt{1-\phi'^2}\cdot\exp\left\{\frac{(h_1-\mu)^2}{2\sigma_\eta^2/(1-\phi'^2)}\right\}}{f(\phi)\cdot\sqrt{1-\phi^2}\cdot\exp\left\{\frac{(h_1-\mu)^2}{2\sigma_\eta^2/(1-\phi^2)}\right\}}\right\}. \quad (2.10)$$

If β is sampled we assume β to have an $\mathrm{IG}(S_\beta/2, \beta_r/2)$ distribution. Then the posterior distribution is a $\mathrm{IG}(a/2, b/2)$ distribution with parameters

$$a = n + \beta_r \qquad \text{and} \qquad b = S_\beta + \sum_{t=1}^{n} y_t^2 \exp(-h_t). \quad (2.11)$$

For sampling μ, a diffuse prior is assumed, such that a normal distribution $N(\mu^*, \sigma_\mu^2)$ is obtained as the posterior distribution $\mu \mid \mathbf{h}, \phi, \sigma_\eta^2$. Its parameters are

$$\begin{aligned}\mu^* &= \sigma_\mu^2 \left(\frac{(1-\phi^2)}{\sigma_\eta^2} h_1 + \frac{(1-\phi)}{\sigma_\eta^2} \sum_{t=1}^{n-1} (h_{t+1} - \phi\, h_t) \right) \\ \text{and } \sigma_\mu^2 &= \sigma_\eta^2 \{(n-1)(1-\phi)^2 + (1-\phi^2)\}^{-1}. \end{aligned} \tag{2.12}$$

As it has been pointed out by Kim, Shephard, and Chib (1996) the priors for μ and β are identical by selecting $S_\beta = 1$ and $\beta_r = 0$. Thus, it is sufficient to sample μ only and to calculate β as $\exp(\mu/2)$.

2.5 Algorithm for the modified SV model

The algorithm for the modified SV model is similar to the one of the original model. The only difference which has to be taken into account when deriving the full conditionals is that the conditional variance $\sigma_t^2 \mid z_t$ depends on η_t, $t = 0, 1, \ldots, n-1$, while the original model assumes a constant variance σ_η^2. When sampling $\boldsymbol{\sigma^2} = (\sigma_0^2, \sigma_1^2, \ldots, \sigma_{n-1}^2)$, first z_t, $t = 0, 1, \ldots, n-1$, is generated from $z_t \mid h_{t+1}, h_t, \phi, \mu$ and then $\sigma_t^2 \mid z_t$ is calculated as $\sigma_t^2 \mid z_t = \frac{d}{z_t}$, where d denotes the degrees of freedom of the χ^2–distributed z_t. The algorithm is as follows:

1. Initialize $\mathbf{h} = (h_1, h_2, \ldots, h_n)$, ϕ, β, and μ and set $k = 0$.
2. a) For $t = 0, 1, \ldots, n-1$ sample a new candidate value z_t from $z_t \mid h_{t+1}, h_t, \phi, \mu$ and calculate $\boldsymbol{\sigma^2} = (\sigma_0^2, \sigma_1^2, \ldots, \sigma_{n-1}^2)$.
   b) For $t = 1, 2, \ldots, n$ sample a new candidate value h_t from $h_t \mid \mathbf{h}_{-t}, y, \sigma_t^2, \phi, \beta, \mu$.
   c) Sample a new candidate value ϕ from $\phi \mid \mathbf{h}, \boldsymbol{\sigma^2}, \beta, \mu$.
   d) Sample a new candidate value β from $\beta \mid y$, $\mathbf{h}$ or a new μ from $\mu \mid \mathbf{h}, \phi, \boldsymbol{\sigma^2}$.
3. If $k < K$ set k to $k+1$ and continue with 2.

From $f(z_t \mid h_{t+1}, h_t, \phi, \mu) \propto f(\eta_t \mid z_t) \cdot f(z_t)$, $z_t \sim \chi^2(d)$ and $\eta_t \mid z_t \sim N(0, \sigma_t^2)$ we derive that $z_t \mid h_{t+1}, h_t, \phi, \mu \sim \Gamma(a/2, b/2)$ with

$$a = d + 1 \quad \text{and} \quad b = 1 + \frac{\{(h_{t+1} - \mu) - \phi(h_t - \mu)\}^2}{d}$$

for $t = 1, 2, \ldots, n-1$ and

$$a = d + 1 \quad \text{and} \quad b = 1 + \frac{(h_1 - \mu)^2 (1 - \phi^2)}{d}$$

for $t = 0$. From z_t, $t = 0, 1, \ldots, n-1$, σ_t^2 is calculated as $\sigma_t^2 \mid z_t = \frac{d}{z_t}$.

To sample the full conditionals of h_t, $h_t \mid \mathbf{h}_{-t}, y, \sigma_t^2, \phi, \beta, \mu$, by the introduced Hastings algorithm only the proposal kernel $h_t \mid h_{t-1}, h_{t+1}, \sigma_t^2, \phi, \beta, \mu$ has to be changed, because $y \mid h_t, \phi, \beta, \mu$ does not depend on σ_t^2. Again a normal distribution $N(h_t^*, v_t^2)$ as posterior is derived with

$$h_t^* = \mu + \frac{\sigma_t^2\phi(h_{t-1}-\mu)+\sigma_{t-1}^2\phi(h_{t+1}-\mu)}{\sigma_t^2+\phi^2\sigma_{t-1}^2} \quad \text{and} \quad v_t^2 = \left(\frac{\sigma_t^2+\phi^2\sigma_{t-1}^2}{\sigma_t^2\cdot\sigma_{t-1}^2}\right)^{-1},$$

$t = 2, \ldots, n-1$. In addition, we get for h_1 and h_n

$$\begin{aligned} h_1^* &= \mu + \frac{1}{\phi}(h_2-\mu) \quad \text{and} \quad v_1^2 = \sigma_1^2/\phi^2 \\ \text{and} \quad h_n^* &= \mu + \phi(h_{n-1}-\mu) \quad \text{and} \quad v_{n-1}^2 = \sigma_{n-1}^2. \end{aligned}$$

Like in the original SV model $\phi \mid \mathbf{h}, \mu, \beta, \boldsymbol{\sigma}^2$ is sampled by a Hastings algorithm. The proposal kernel is that of a normal distribution $N(\phi^*, V_\phi^2)$ with

$$\begin{aligned} \phi^* &= \left(\sum_{t=1}^{n-1}\frac{(h_t-\mu)^2}{\sigma_t^2}\right)^{-1} \cdot \sum_{t=1}^{n-1}\frac{(h_{t+1}-\mu)(h_t-\mu)}{\sigma_t^2} \\ \text{and} \quad V_\phi^2 &= \left(\sum_{t=1}^{n-1}\frac{(h_t-\mu)^2}{\sigma_t^2}\right)^{-1}. \end{aligned}$$

In case that ϕ' has fallen into the stationarity interval $(-1;1)$, the proposal is accepted with

$$\begin{aligned} &A(\phi \to \phi'; \mathbf{h}, \boldsymbol{\sigma}^2, \mu) \\ &= \min\left\{1; \frac{(\frac{1+\phi'}{2})^{\phi^{(1)}-1}(\frac{1-\phi'}{2})^{\phi^{(2)}-1}\exp\{-\frac{(h_1-\mu)^2(1-\phi'^2)}{2\sigma_0^2}\}\sqrt{1-\phi'^2}}{(\frac{1+\phi}{2})^{\phi^{(1)}-1}(\frac{1-\phi}{2})^{\phi^{(2)}-1}\exp\{-\frac{(h_1-\mu)^2(1-\phi^2)}{2\sigma_0^2}\}\sqrt{1-\phi^2}}\right\}. \end{aligned}$$

Finally, the full conditional of $\mu \mid \mathbf{h}, \phi, \boldsymbol{\sigma}^2$ is derived. Assuming a diffuse prior we again get a normal distribution $N(\mu^*, \sigma_\mu^2)$ with

$$\begin{aligned} \mu^* &= \sigma_\mu^2\left(\frac{(1-\phi^2)}{\sigma_0^2}h_1 + (1-\phi)\sum_{t=1}^{n-1}\frac{(h_{t+1}-\phi h_t)}{\sigma_t^2}\right) \\ \text{and} \quad \sigma_\mu^2 &= \left(\sum_{t=1}^{n-1}\frac{(1-\phi)^2}{\sigma_t^2} + \frac{(1-\phi^2)}{\sigma_0^2}\right)^{-1}. \end{aligned}$$

3. Simulation study

In our simulation study we use the same simulated data as Spanier (1997) to enable a comparison with his results obtained from means of a posterior modus estimation. A description of this method is given by Fahrmeir and Wagenpfeil (1996). The design of the study is as follows. Six datasets $y^{(i)}$, $i = 1, \ldots, 6$, are simulated, each consisting of 100 observations $y_t^{(i)}$, $t =$

$1, \ldots, 100$. These six datasets $y^{(i)}$ are iid with $y_t^{(i)} = \epsilon_t^{(i)} \cdot v_t$, $\epsilon_t^{(i)} \sim N(0,1)$ and $t = 1, \ldots, 100$. Here, v_t denotes the volatility at time t, being the same for each dataset $y^{(i)}$, $i = 1, \ldots, 6$. The dashed line in Figure 3.1 shows its course. The datasets were generated by an Intell Pentium Processor in S–Plus.

Using the original model for estimating the stochastic volatility, the hyperparameters are set to $S_\sigma = 0.05$, $\sigma_r = 5$, $S_\beta = 0$, $\beta_r = 1, \phi^{(1)} = 20$, and $\phi^{(1)} = 1.5$. We use the version of the SV model where β is set fix to one while the other parameters are sampled. Their initial values are chosen as $\sigma_\eta^2 = 0.01$, $\phi = 0.95$, and $\mu = 0$. As already mentioned the corresponding value of β of the equivalent model, where μ is set fix to zero, can be calculated from the μ of our version by $\beta = \exp(\mu/2)$. The burn in time consists of 10000 iterations, the distance between the thinned out values of the sampled chains is fixed as 50 iterations and the whole run time is set to 100000. The parameters σ_η^2, ϕ, and μ are estimated by the means of the thinned out chains, whereas β is estimated by the median, because there are a few outliers leading to an extreme overestimation of the true mean. For each dataset $y^{(i)}$, $i = 1, \ldots, 6$, Table 3.1 shows the obtained estimates of the four parameters.

Table 3.1: Estimated parameters from the original SV model.

dataset	$\hat{\sigma}_\eta^2$	$\hat{\phi}$	$\hat{\mu}$	$\hat{\beta}$
$y^{(1)}$	0.134725	0.975258	-10.5861	0.2640270
$y^{(2)}$	0.127140	0.976221	-10.5371	0.0162262
$y^{(3)}$	0.119330	0.974622	-10.8593	0.1484860
$y^{(4)}$	0.080962	0.097413	-10.8456	0.0066660
$y^{(5)}$	0.193533	0.969208	-10.7447	0.0103075
$y^{(6)}$	0.131884	0.970262	-10.9168	0.0074036

Table 3.2: Estimated parameters from the modified SV model.

dataset	$\hat{\hat{\sigma}}^2$	$\hat{\phi}$	$\hat{\mu}$	$\hat{\beta}$
$y^{(1)}$	1.22757	0.896442	-11.2354	0.00350254
$y^{(2)}$	1.35009	0.795973	-11.6975	0.00285255
$y^{(3)}$	1.22664	0.883797	-11.5636	0.00293246
$y^{(4)}$	1.22361	0.843507	-11.4215	0.00321888
$y^{(5)}$	1.23714	0.883367	-11.4490	0.00305220
$y^{(6)}$	1.33533	0.765293	-11.5965	0.00301589

The volatility at time t, $t = 1, \ldots, 100$, is estimated by $\hat{v}_t = \exp(\bar{h}_t/2)$, where $\bar{h}_t$ denotes the mean of the thinned out chain $h_t^{(1)}, h_t^{(2)}, \ldots h_t^{(l)}$, i.e. $\bar{h}_t = \frac{1}{l}\sum_{i=1}^{l} h_t^{(i)}$. In addition, we consider the average of the absolute deviations (AAD) of $\hat{v}_t$ from v_t, i.e. $AAD = \frac{1}{100}\sum_{t=1}^{100} |v_t - \hat{v}_t|$. The AADs of the

six datasets $y^{(i)}$, $i = 1, \ldots, 6$, are summarized in Table 3.3.
Working with the modified SV model the same hyperparameters and initial values are used as for the original SV model. The burn in time and the whole run time also remain unchanged. Since the observed correlations between subsequent samples are quite small, the chain is thinned out with a distance of 10 iterations. Five different values of the degrees of freedom, i.e. $d = 3, 5, 10, 100, 1000$, are chosen. For an additional choice of $d = 1, 2$ the proposal ϕ' does not always fall into the stationarity interval $(-1; 1)$. No problems occur for the other choices of d. Since the results obtained from the modified SV model are to be compared with those from the original model, an appropriate overall quantity has to be defined. For this purpose, we consider $\bar{\sigma}^2$ to denote the average value of the components of the vector $\boldsymbol{\sigma}^2$, so that $\bar{\sigma}^2 = \frac{1}{n}\sum_{t=0}^{n-1}\sigma_t^2$. From the resulting estimates of the parameters $\bar{\sigma}^2$, ϕ, β, and μ it can be seen that only $\hat{\bar{\sigma}}^2$ depends on the degrees of freedom. As d increases $\hat{\bar{\sigma}}^2$ converges to one, because the t–distribution converges to the N(0,1)–distribution for increasing degrees of freedom.
The four parameters and the volatility are estimated for all six datasets $y^{(i)}, i = 1, \ldots, 6$, with degrees of freedom of $d = 10$, which neither yields an approximation being too close to the N(0,1)–distribution nor leads to tails being too fat. The resulting estimates and the average of the absolute deviations are given in Table 3.2 and 3.3.

Table 3.3: Comparison of the *AAD*s of the volatility.

dataset	original SV model	modified SV model	posterior modus
$y^{(1)}$	0.0004894712	0.001177326	0.000514303
$y^{(2)}$	0.0006884088	0.001246486	0.000798108
$y^{(3)}$	0.0007757641	0.001086267	0.000879480
$y^{(4)}$	0.0009400328	0.001038901	0.000946417
$y^{(5)}$	0.0008583942	0.001261606	0.000996251
$y^{(6)}$	0.0005345060	0.001085041	0.000556795
mean	0.0007144295	0.001149280	0.000781892

From our simulation results we can conclude that the estimates calculated from the original model combined with MCMC are superior to estimates from the modified model. Comparing our results with those of Spanier (1997) we notice that estimates obtained from the original model are slightly better than the ones from the posterior modus estimation, but that the latter technique outperforms the estimation procedure based on the modified SV model. This is also confirmed by Figure 3.1 showing the volatility estimated by the three methods for the first dataset $y^{(1)}$, which is representative for the other five.

4. Analysis of swaps rates

In this section, the above SV models are used to estimate the volatility of swap rates. Reliable estimates of volatility of swap rates are needed to value

Figure 3.1: Estimated volatility of dataset $y^{(1)}$.

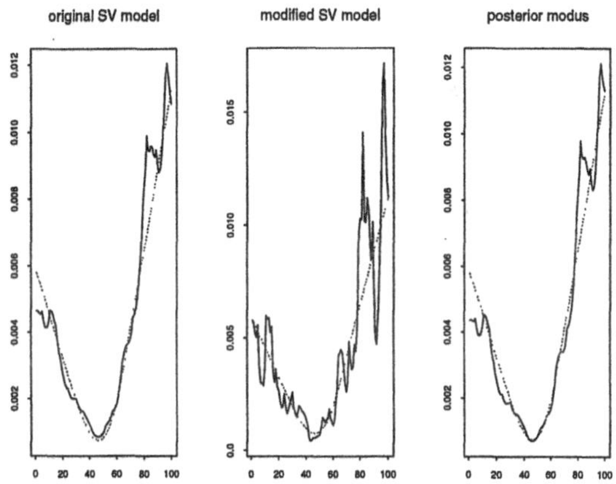

Table 4.1: Estimated parameters from the original SV model.

Currency	$\hat{\sigma}_\eta^2$	$\hat{\phi}$	$\hat{\mu}$	$\hat{\beta}$
USD	0.6962150	0.400318	-0.425631	0.8064475
DEM	0.0273681	0.948134	-0.771545	0.6806685
JPY	0.0283969	0.979199	0.3625440	1.2147800

options on swaps, so–called swaptions. More about the economic background of swaps and swaptions is found in Sender (1996) and Hull (1993). The given time series are daily swap rates of ten years swaps on the currencies Deutsch Mark (DEM), US Dollar (USD), and Japanese Yen (JPY) from 15.11.1994 to 05.11.1996. Since the assumption of a zero mean for log–returns of interest rates is rarely fulfilled in practice, we use the centered daily log–returns $y_t, t = 1, \ldots, n$,

$$y_t = 100 \cdot \{\log\,(r_{t+1}/r_t) - \frac{1}{n}\sum_{t=1}^{n} \log\,(r_{t+1}/r_t)\}.$$

For estimating the volatility and the parameters based on the original model we use the same hyperparameters and the same values for the other quantities as in the simulation study. Table 4.1 contains the estimates $\hat{\sigma}_\eta^2$, $\hat{\phi}$, $\hat{\mu}$, and $\hat{\beta}$.

It turns out that the estimate of σ_η^2 for the US Dollar is much higher (0.69622) than those for Deutsch Mark (0.02737) and Japanese Yen (0.02840). Since σ_η is the volatility of the log–volatility, the volatility of the US Dollar can be expected to fluctuate more than the volatilities of the other two currencies. The estimates of ϕ, standing for the persistence of the volatility, take values near one for Deutsch Mark (0.94813) and Japanese Yen (0.97920), but a smaller value than 0.5 for US Dollar (0.40032). There seems to be a uniform course of the volatilities of the former ones but not of the latter. The estimated β takes its greatest value for Japanese Yen (1.21478), followed by

US Dollar (0.80645) and finally for Deutsch Mark (0.68067). This behaviour can also be observed in Figure 4.1.

Figure 4.1: Estimated volatilities of the DEM–, the USD–, and the JPY–swap rates from the original SV model.

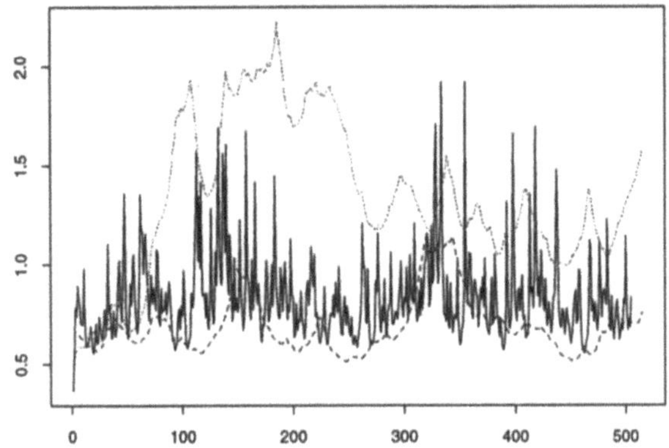

Now we focus our attention on a fraction of the DEM time series from 30.01. to 05.11.1996. The volatility of this period estimated from the original SV model is compared to the historical volatility. The historical volatility v_j at time j, taking account of the last l observations, $y_{j-l+1}, \ldots, y_j$, is given as

$$v_j = \sqrt{\frac{1}{l-1} \sum_{i=j-l+1}^{j} (y_i - \frac{1}{l} \sum_{i=j-l+1}^{j} y_i)^2}.$$

The choice of a large l leads to a smooth estimator. However, it is not able to quickly react to sudden changes. This can be achieved if a small value of l is chosen, but this has the disadvantage that single extreme observations have a huge impact on the estimate. In Figure 4.2 it can be seen that the volatility calculated from the original SV model quickly reacts to real changes and also produces a smooth estimate. Thus, estimating the stochastic volatility implies each of the advantages of the historical volatility without being forced to fix any value of l. Finally, the volatility of all three time series is estimated from the modified SV model. The estimate $\hat{\hat{\sigma}}^2$ converges to one for increasing degrees of freedom d, while the estimates of the parameters ϕ, μ, and β only change slightly. The values in Table 4.2 are obtained for degrees of freedom of $d = 10$.

Table 4.2: Estimated parameters from the modified SV model.

Currency	$\hat{\hat{\sigma}}^2$	$\hat{\phi}$	$\hat{\mu}$	$\hat{\beta}$
USD	1.24572	0.341347	-0.535356	0.766243
DEM	1.25636	0.406423	-1.016280	0.602665
JPY	1.23883	0.569048	0.2385360	1.129350

Figure 4.2: Stochastic volatility compared to the historical volatility with $l = 10$ and $l = 50$.

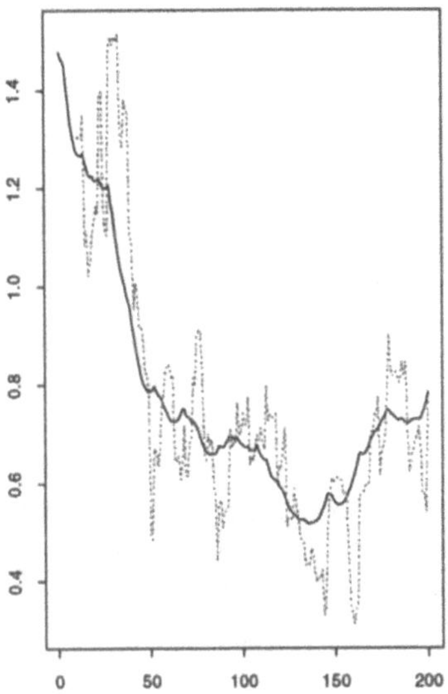

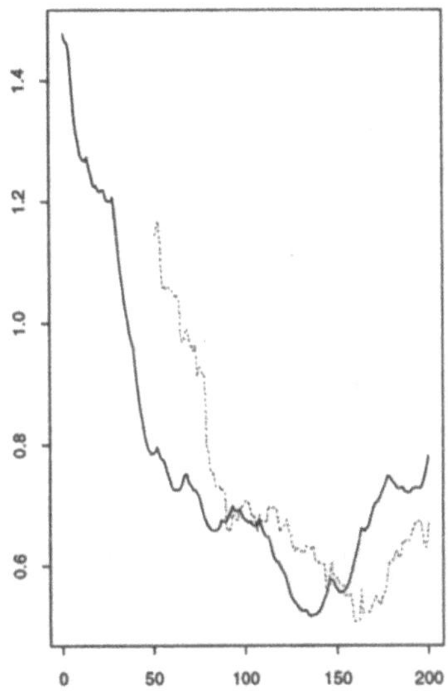

Although $\hat{\sigma}_\eta^2$ calculated from the original SV model is much higher for US Dollar than for Deutsch Mark and Japanese Yen, the corresponding quantities of the modified SV model, $\hat{\hat{\sigma}}^2$, are similar for all three currencies. Furthermore, $\hat{\hat{\sigma}}^2$ is always greater than 1.238 which causes noisy estimation of the volatility as shown in Figure 4.3. Summarizing, the modified SV model does not show the improvements it has been expected to.

Figure 4.3: Estimated volatilities of the DEM–, the USD–, and the JPY–swap rates by the modified SV model.

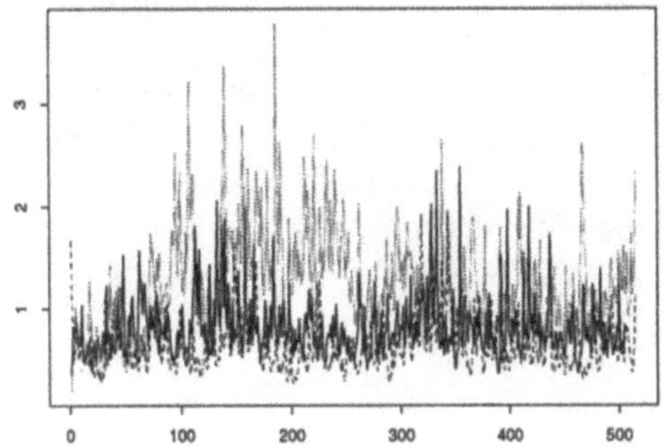

5. Discussion

Summarizing the results of our simulation study and of our analysis of the swap rates dataset we conclude that the assumption of a SV model combined with the application of MCMC methods for estimating the volatility seems to be a very promising approach. The results obtained from the MCMC techniques were especially convincing compared to the use of the historic volatility. We were, however, surprised that the proposed modification of the original SV model by introducing a t-distributed noise term did not lead to the expected improvements in our data analysis.

An additional aspect which has to be considered in our discussion concerns the assumptions on which our investigations were based because of their possible impact on the appropriateness of our results. We used for instance the same values for the hyperparameters as being suggested by Kim, Shephard and Chib (1996), who analyzed rates of exchange. We refrained from examining whether the algorithm is sensitive to the chosen values because the results we got were comprehensible from subject matter knowledge. Nevertheless, such an analysis of sensitivity may be important for judging the properties of the used algorithm.

Furthermore, we assumed the process h_t to be stationary to enable working with version (2.2) of the SV model. Although it seems reasonable to assume that the mean and the variance of this process do not depend on t, since h_t models the unknown influences, dropping this assumption may lead to additional insights into the behaviour of our investigated approach. It should, however, be noticed that this would imply a completely different algorithm derived from the SV model (2.1).

It has been shown that the volatility can be very well estimated assuming a stochastic behaviour. This assumption is in contrast to option pricing models as for instance the Black and Scholes model (Black and Scholes, 1973) as most famous representative where typically a constant volatility is supposed. Thus, further research could concern the derivation of pricing models which account for the stochastic behaviour of the volatility (cf. Hull and White, 1987).

Finally, we would like to mention that a comparison of the above results with according results obtained from ARCH or GARCH models, respectively, is under current research of the authors. In addition, MCMC methods are again investigated but now with respect to their ability to forecast.

References

1. Black, F. and Scholes, M. (1973): The pricing of options and corporate liabilities. *Journal of Political Economy*, **3**, 637-659
2. Bollerslev, T. (1986): Generalized autoregression conditional heteroscedasticity, *Journal of Econometrics*, **31**, 307-327

3. Casella, G. and George, E. I. (1992): Explaining the Gibbs sampler. *The American Statistician*, **46**, 167-174
4. Chib, S. and Greenberg, E. (1995): Explaining the Metropolis–Hastings–algorithm. *The American Statistician*, **49**, 327-335
5. Engle, R. F. (1982): Autoregressive conditional heteroscedasticity with estimates of the variance of the United Kingdom inflation. *Econometrica*, **50**, 987-1007
6. Fahrmeir, L. and Wagenpfeil, S. (1996): *Penalized likelihood estimation and iterative Kalman smoothing for non-Gaussian dynamic regression models.* Discussion Paper, **5**, Institut für Statistik, Ludwig–Maximilians–Universität, München
7. Gilks, W. R., Richardson, S., and Spiegelhalter, D. J. (1996): Introducing Markov chain Monte Carlo. In *Markov Chain Monte Carlo in Practice (Gilks, W. R., Richardson, S., and Spiegelhalter, D. J., eds.).* Chapman and Hall, London, 1-19
8. Hastings, W. K. (1970): Monte–Carlo sampling methods using Markov chains and their applications. *Biometrika*, **57**, 97-109
9. Hull, J (1993): *Options, futures and other derivative securities.* Prentice Hall International Editions, Englewood Cliffs, NJ
10. Hull, J. and White, A. (1987): The pricing of options on assets with stochastic volatility. *Journal of Finance*, **42**, 281-300
11. Kim, S., Shephard, N., and Chib, S. (1996). Stochastic volatility: Likelihood inference and comparison with ARCH models. *Technical report.* Nuffield College, Oxford
12. Metropolis, N., Rosenbluth, A.W., Rosenbluth, M. N., Teller, A. H., and Teller, E. (1953): Equations of state calculations by fast computing machines. *Journal of Chemical Physics*, **21**, 1087-1092
13. Shephard, N. (1996): Statistical aspects of ARCH and stochastic volatility. In *Time Series Models in Econometrics, Finance and Other Fields (Cox, D. R., Barndorff–Nielson, O.E., and Hinkley, D. V., eds.).* Chapman and Hall, London, 1-67
14. Sender, G. (1996): *Zinsswaps: Instrument zur Senkung der Finanzierungskosten oder zum Zinsrisikomanagement?* Schriftenreihe des Instituts für Geld und Kapitalverkehr der Universität Hamburg, **11**, Deutscher Universitäts–Verlag, Wiesbaden
15. Spanier, M. (1997): *Posteriori–Modus–Schätzung von Volatilitäten in dynamischen Modellen.* Diplomarbeit. Institut für Statistik, Ludwig–Maximilians–Universität, München
16. Taylor, St. J. (1986): *Modelling Financial Time Series.* John Wiley, Chichester
17. Tierney, L. (1994): Markov Chain for exploring posterior distributions (with discussion). *Annals of Statistics*, **21**, 1701-1762

Money and Prices in Germany

Empirical Results for 1962 to 1996.*

Imke Brüggemann and Jürgen Wolters

Department of Economics, Freie Universität Berlin, Germany

Summary. In this contribution the linkages between money growth and inflation are investigated. Two vector error correction models are estimated one with data before and the other one with data including the German monetary union (GMU), which took place on 1 July 1990. The models contain the variables money, prices, output, and interest rate. We found one cointegrating relation, which can be interpreted as a long–run money demand equation. Including the GMU this relation remains stable if the structural break is captured by dummy variables. Although the dynamic structure of the two vector error correction models is nearly not influenced by the GMU the linkages between money growth and inflation are sensitive whether international price movements are included or not.

1. Introduction

The linkage between money growth and inflation is very often explained by means of the quantity theory of money. According to this approach changes in prices and nominal income can arise either by changes in the velocity of circulation, i.e. in the real balances that people wish to hold, or by changes in the nominal balances available. Given that changes in desired balances (in the money demand) tend to proceed very slowly, the monetarist conclusion is that substantial changes in prices or nominal income are almost always the result of changes in the nominal money stock. Acceptance of the quantity theory implies that inflation can be prevented if an increase in money balances is kept in line with the growth of potential output in the economy.

The effectiveness of a policy of monetary targeting is based on the assumption that a disequilibrium in the money market results in price movements rather than in adjustments of real money demand. Moreover money supply is supposed to be exogenous, i.e. not to follow prices in an accommodating fashion. An indicator for the long–term relationship between money balances and prices is given by the p–star concept, which is based on the well known quantity equation.[1] In this context the equilibrium price level (p–star) is defined as money stock per unit of real potential output times the long–term

* Paper presented at the *Jahrestagung des Vereins für Socialpolitik*, Bern 24.–26.9.1997. Research of this paper is related to Sonderforschungsbereich 373, Teilprojekt C3, Humboldt Universität zu Berlin. Financial support by the Deutsche Forschungsgemeinschaft as well as comments by an anonymous referee are gratefully acknowledged.

[1] The p–star approach has been introduced by Hallman et al. (1991).

velocity of circulation. Theoretically, deviations of the actual price level (p) from p–star push current prices in the direction of the equilibrium price level, provided p and p–star are cointegrated.

The Deutsche Bundesbank (1992) made use of this concept to analyse the effectiveness of her monetary policy of M3 targeting up to the GMU. The results indicate a proportional relationship between money growth and inflation. Tödter and Reimers (1994) found a stable link between the price level and M3 but not for M1 and M2 using data from 1973(1) to 1992(4). Issing and Tödter (1995) also applied the p–star approach to examine the relationship between the monetary aggregate M3 and the price level including the GMU with a sample period from 1975(1) to 1993(2). In accordance with their work a long–term proportional relationship remains valid even after the unification, and hence they conclude that a policy of monetary targeting continues to be an effective strategy to control the development of prices.

Although the p–star concept seems quite attractive its application involves some problems which stem from the fact that for the construction of p–star non observable variables are used such as potential output and long–term velocity of circulation. Whereas in the original paper by Hallman et al. (1991) long–run M2 velocity for the US could be approximated by a constant, in Germany the velocities of the monetary aggregates M1, M2, and M3 exhibited a downward trend in the past.[2] Hence Tödter and Reimers (1994) and Issing and Tödter (1995) applied their (stable) money demand equation for real M3 to get estimates of the long–run velocity.[3]

Because it is difficult to get reasonable estimates of the unobservables and since the results of the p–star approach may depend on the construction of the unobserved variables the purpose of this paper is to examine the relationship between money growth and inflation considering the dynamics in the money market where only observed variables are involved.[4] In the above mentioned papers for Germany single equation approaches are used to estimate a structural error correction equation with inflation being the dependent variable. Alternatively, Weissenberger and Thomas (1983) and Schultes (1996) apply simple Granger–causality tests to analyse the channels of monetary policy in Germany. Hansen and Kim (1996) analyse the relation of money and inflation within a multivariate cointegration framework but put more emphasis on the long–run relations than on the entire dynamic relations of all the variables, as is done in this paper. Moreover they do not cover the period after GMU.

Choosing a vector error correction approach for our analysis we are in the position to have a closer look at the dynamic behaviour of the system as a whole. Thus we allow for more than one cointegrating relationship and circumvent a priori assumptions about the exogeneity or endogeneity of the

---

[2] See Deutsche Bundesbank (1992).

[3] For further approaches to model equilibrium velocity see Eitrheim (1995).

[4] See also Friedman and Kuttner (1992), Miller (1992), Rasche (1993), and Rotemberg et al. (1995) for results for the US and Hall and Milne (1994) for results for the UK.

variables and about their causal relations. Instead, this information is part of the results.

In 1975 the Deutsche Bundesbank started her policy of monetary targeting using M0 as indicator until 1988 and M3 afterwards. Here we focus on the monetary aggregate M1, for ease of international comparison. Moreover, von Hagen and Neumann (1996, p. 161) argue that for an effective monetary policy of the future European Central Bank "an intermediate target strategy based on a narrow monetary target" is necessary.

Two sample periods are considered: One runs from 1962 to 1989 while the other one running from 1962 to 1996 includes the GMU. Thus we also investigate whether the relations between money growth and inflation are influenced by the GMU or not. For the empirical analysis we choose a two–step approach where one or more cointegrating vectors are estimated in the first step. The second step involves the estimation of a vector error correction model (VECM) including regressors generated from the deviations from the long–run relations. For determining the lag structure of the VECMs Hendry's general–to–specific modeling strategy is applied to eliminate lags with insignificant parameter estimates.

The paper is organized as follows. In section 2 the stochastic properties of the variables and the number of cointegrating vectors are derived. The cointegrating relationships are estimated in section 3. In section 4 the estimated VECMs are presented and the dynamic relations between money growth and inflation are discussed. The estimated impulse responses are presented in section 5. Section 6 concludes.

2. The Data and Preliminary Analysis

According to the above mentioned approaches, in general, the relations between the following variables are investigated: money balances, income, prices, and interest rate. Here we choose as nominal money balances M1 and as interest rate the long–term interest rate (Umlaufsrendite). These variables are taken from *Monatsberichte der Deutschen Bundesbank.* As income and price variables we use real gross national product (GNP) and its implicit deflator (1991=100). These data are obtained from *Deutsches Institut für Wirtschaftsforschung, Volkswirtschaftliche Gesamtrechnung.* All data are seasonally unadjusted. After the GMU all data also include the new Bundesländer. There are remarkable breaks in the levels of M1 and GNP as well as changes in their seasonal patterns due to the unification, as one can see in Figure 2.1.[5] Figure 2.1. also presents the implicit deflator and the interest rate.

[5] Using per capita data as in Lütkepohl, Teräsvirta, and Wolters (1995) eliminates the break in M1 but not in GNP. Since we employ here a system approach with GNP also as a dependent variable we do not use per capita data here.

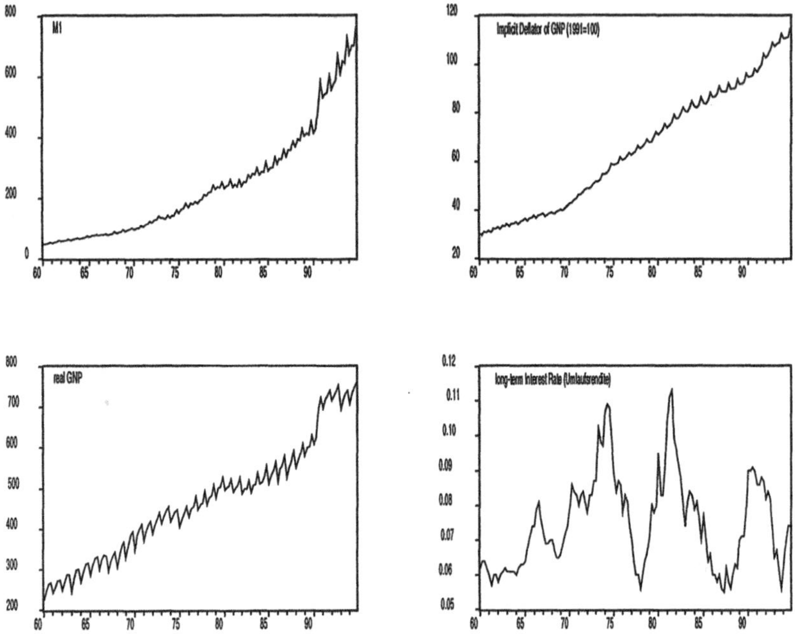

Fig. 2.1. Time series of M1, real GNP, prices, and long–term interest rate

Table 2.1. Tests for unit roots at zero and seasonal frequencies, estimation period 1962(1)–1989(4).

Variable	Auxiliary regressions[a]	$\hat{t}$ zero frequency	$\hat{t}$ biannual	$\hat{F}$ annual
m	I,SD,T (1,2)	-1.61	-3.06**	18.74***
y	I,SD,T (1)	-2.16	-3.83***	2.56
p	I,SD,T (1)	-1.59	-1.85	5.61*
r^b	I (1)	-2.35	—	—

[a] The auxiliary regressions additionally contain significant lagged values (denoted in parantheses) of the fourth (first) difference of the dependent variable.

[b] Results of the Augmented Dickey-Fuller test.
***, **, respectively * denote significance at the 1, 5, respectively 10 percent level.

In the following m_t denotes the logarithm of nominal M1, y_t denotes the logarithm of real GNP, p_t denotes the logarithm of the implicit GNP deflator and r_t the long–term interest rate in decimals. Because of the level shifts in m_t and y_t in 1990 the stationarity tests are based on time series from 1962(1) to 1989(4) only.[6] Since m_t, y_t, and p_t show strong seasonal patterns we apply the test developed by Hylleberg et al. (1990) (HEGY). The HEGY–test is a general approach to look at unit roots not only at the seasonal frequencies but also at the zero frequency. The main advantage of the HEGY–test is that one can test for stationarity individually at each frequency. That means with quarterly data we test for long–run unit roots, biannual and annual seasonal unit roots. Because r_t does not exhibit seasonal movements we apply for this variable the usual Augmented Dickey–Fuller test. Since m_t, y_t, and p_t show trending and seasonal behaviour we include in the alternative an intercept (I), seasonal dummies (SD) and a linear trend (T). The results in Table 2.1 indicate that all variables have a long–run unit root. If we apply the tests to the first differences of the variables there is no evidence for unit roots.

Thus, all variables contain a stochastic trend. With respect to the seasonal unit roots the results are mixed. Money balances contain no seasonal nonstationarities, whereas y_t exhibits a unit root at the annual and p_t at the biannual frequency. Thus, if there are seasonal nonstationarities they show up at different seasonal frequencies. Accordingly there is no basis for seasonal cointegration.

Table 2.2. Trace Test in a VAR(5), estimation period 1962(1)–1989(4).

H_0	LR	5% critical values[a]
$r = 0$	58.16	47.21
$r \leq 1$	28.15	29.68
$r \leq 2$	15.21	15.41
$r \leq 3$	6.08	3.76

[a] The critical values are taken from Osterwald-Lenum (1992).

Therefore we apply the usual Johansen procedure (see e.g. Johansen, 1995) to test for cointegration relations between the four variables m_t, y_t, p_t, and r_t. To capture the seasonal movements in the data we choose a fifth–order VAR model for the multivariate cointegration analysis.[7] Moreover, we allow for a deterministic trend in the data. The results of the Maximum

[6] All computations are performed with *EVIEWS 2.0*.

[7] The inclusion of seasonal dummies leads to the same results.

Eigenvalue–test are reported in Table 2.2. Under the null of no cointegration ($r = 0$) the value of the Likelihood Ratio statistic (LR) exceeds its corresponding critical value, thus we accept the hypothesis of one cointegrating relationship between the variables.

3. Estimating Cointegrating Relationships

A structural economic interpretation of the estimated cointegrating vector derived from the unrestricted reduced form VECM could be possible in terms of a long–run money demand equation. But as Wickens (1996) has shown, without introducing a priori information, this cointegrating vector is not always identified. Therefore, to introduce structural restrictions we estimate a long–run money demand equation using a single equation approach in the first step. Super consistent estimates for the long–run parameters could be obtained from the Engle and Granger (1987) static cointegrating regression. But as has been argued (see e.g. Wickens and Breusch (1988) and Banerjee, Dolado, Galbraith, and Hendry (1993), ch. 7) it is probable that the finite sample biases of the long–run estimates will be reduced by not omitting the short run dynamics. Therefore we use a single–equation conditional error correction model for nominal money balances including the lagged levels of the variables as regressors. Moreover, given the findings of Campos et al. (1996) in the presence of structural breaks tests based on the single equation error correction model generally are more powerful than the Engle–Granger static approach.

Starting with four lagged differences for all the variables and using seasonal dummies s_{it}, $i = 1, 2, 3$, we end up via sequential elimination of those variables with the lowest absolut t–values with the following specification for the period until the GMU (absolute t–values in parantheses):

$$
\begin{aligned}
\Delta m_t = \\
& \underset{(0.5)}{0.021} - \underset{(31.9)}{0.134}\, s_{1t} - \underset{(3.6)}{0.017}\, s_{2t} - \underset{(13.3)}{0.110}\, s_{3t} + \underset{(5.4)}{0.455}\, \Delta p_t \\
& - \underset{(5.4)}{0.296}\, \Delta y_{t-2} - \underset{(2.4)}{0.616}\, \Delta r_t - \underset{(3.1)}{0.882}\, \Delta r_{t-1} \qquad (3.1) \\
& - \underset{(3.2)}{0.115}\, (m-p)_{t-1} + \underset{(3.1)}{0.125}\, y_{t-1} - \underset{(4.3)}{0.657}\, r_{t-1} + \hat{\varepsilon}_{1t}
\end{aligned}
$$

$\bar{R}^2 = 0.95$, $JB = 4.76\ [0.10]$, $RESET(1) = 0.94\ [0.33]$,
$LM(2) = 0.06\ [0.94]$, $LM(4) = 0.24\ [0.91]$, $ARCH(2) = 0.94\ [0.39]$,
sample: 1961(4)–1989(4).

All lagged levels of the variables are significant in (3.1). Thus confirming the outcome of the Johansen test that there is (at least) one cointegrating relationship. The reported diagnostics are test statistics against non-normality (JB), residual correlation (LM), second-order ARCH-effects, and the RESET test as a general test of misspecification. None of the statistics is significant at a usual level as one can see from the corresponding p-values in brackets. Note that the levels of real money balances rather than nominal balances enter the specification. However, running the regression with nominal balances and prices as individual explanatory variables we could not reject the restriction that long-run money demand is homogeneous in prices. The corresponding F-statistic took a value of 0.15, which compared to critical values from the F-distribution with 1 and 101 degrees of freedom is not at all significant.

The long-run money demand relationship implicit in specification (3.1) is given by:[8]

$$(m-p)_t = 1.089 y_t - 5.729 r_t + ec_{1t}. \tag{3.2}$$

The expression ec_{1t} denotes the error which is to be corrected through adjustments in the money market. The derived coefficients in the long-term relationship show the expected signs, i.e. real money demand is positively related to real income, with the long-term income elasticity being slightly greater than 1, and negatively related to the interest rate. The long-run interest rate elasticity is obtained by multiplying the semi-elasticity -5.73 by the assumed interest rate level. For instance, assuming an interest rate of 6% the elasticity becomes -0.34.

For the period including GMU additional dummies are included in the regression to take account of the breaks in the levels of M1 and GNP and the changes in the seasonal pattern of the time series due to GMU. The dummy variable dv_t is assigned the value 1 from 1990(3) on and 0 before, and $ds_{it} = s_{it} \cdot dv_t,\ i = 1, 2, 3$. Starting again with four lagged differences for all variables the specification is as follows:

$$\Delta\ m_t = \tag{3.3}$$

$$- \underset{(0.3)}{0.012} - \underset{(10.3)}{0.111}\ s_{1t} - \underset{(3.4)}{0.016}\ s_{2t} - \underset{(9.0)}{0.090}\ s_{3t} - \underset{(5.2)}{0.051}\ ds_{1t}$$

$$- \underset{(5.8)}{0.051}\ ds_{2t} - \underset{(1.7)}{0.017}\ ds_{3t} + \underset{(8.5)}{0.144}\ \Delta dv_t + \underset{(5.4)}{0.480}\ \Delta p_t + \underset{(2.4)}{0.172}\ \Delta y_t$$

---

[8] From the Johansen procedure the estimated cointegrating relation under the restriction of price homogeneity is $(m-p)_t = 1.118 y_t - 6.285 r_t$. However, in view of the inflexibility of this procedure with respect to imposing zero restrictions on the coefficients of the short-run dynamics we preferred the two-step approach.

$$- \underset{(2.4)}{0.157} \Delta y_{t-2} - \underset{(1.9)}{0.493} \Delta r_t - \underset{(3.3)}{0.911} \Delta r_{t-1} - \underset{(3.4)}{0.120} (m-p)_{t-1}$$

$$+ \underset{(3.3)}{0.132} y_{t-1} - \underset{(4.1)}{0.616} r_{t-1} + \underset{(5.5)}{0.049} dv_{t-1} + \hat{\varepsilon}_{2t}$$

$\bar{R}^2 = 0.95$, JB = 4.27 [0.12], RESET(1) = 2.28 [0.13],
LM(2) = 0.21 [0.81], LM(4) = 0.12 [0.98], ARCH(2) = 0.28 [0.75],
sample 1961(4)–1996(2).

The reported test statistics for equation (3.3) suggest that the specification is as good as the one in equation (3.1). This means that the effects of GMU are completely captured by the use of additional dummies. Our interest attaches to the coefficients of the equilibrium relationship. Again, the hypothesis of long–run price homogeneity could not be rejected. The resulting equilibrium relationship is:

$$(m-p)_t = 1.105 y_t - 5.133 r_t + 0.407 dv_t + ec_{2t}. \tag{3.4}$$

Since the estimated long–term coefficients in equation (3.4) are very similar to those obtained for the shorter period there is no obvious structural break with respect to income and interest rates in long–run money demand. Again, the term ec_{2t} captures the short–run departures from the long run equilibrium. The adjustment processes of money to its long–run desired level in equations (3.1) and (3.3) are neither only in nominal terms[9] nor only in real terms as can be seen from the coefficient of Δp_t which is significantly different from 0 and 1 with a significance level less than 1 percent. Comparing to Hwang (1985) the adjustment process includes active adjustment costs, that means reallocation of nominal stocks, as well as passive adjustment costs, i.e. reallocation of assets through changes in prices.

4. Estimation of Vector Error Correction Models

Above we identified the cointegrating vectors from a conditional error correction equation for each sample. In the second step the generated deviations from equilibrium ec_{1t} and ec_{2t} (see equations (3.2) and (3.4)) will be inserted in the reduced form VECMs to examine the short–run adjustments in money, prices, output, and interest rate. With this approach we can describe the adjustment processes and the causality structure between money and prices.

The construction of VECMs involves regressing the first difference of each variable onto lagged differences of all the variables and the one period lagged value of the error correction term. As before the specifications include seasonal dummies as well as the additional dummies capturing the structural

[9] See e.g. Wolters and Lütkepohl (1997).

break. We remove lagged differences with insignificant coefficients step by step starting with specifications which contain differenced values up to the fourth lag. Irrespective of their t–values the error correction terms are included in the regressions until all insignificant lagged differences are eliminated. Being insignificant they are removed then. Since we have different explanatory variables in each equation of the system we use the method of Seemingly Unrelated Regressions for estimation.

Table 4.1 reports the estimated VECM for the preunification period and some diagnostics. To save space the constant term and seasonal dummies are not presented.

The misspecification test statistics for low–order autocorrelations indicate that the dynamics of the system are well captured with this specification. The Box–Pierce Q–statistic indicates some remaining higher order autocorrelation in the residuals of the inflation equation. The residuals in the money growth equation and in the equation for the interest rate changes show significant deviations from normality.

The error correction term is significant only in the money growth equation with the adjustment coefficient showing the expected negative sign. Hence when money balances exceed long–run money demand the money stock growth rate will decrease. Since the error correction term is not included in the other equations p_t, y_t, and r_t can be treated as weakly exogenous for m_t.[10]

The estimated system shows direct lagged influences from money growth to inflation, to output growth, and to interest rate changes, whereas lagged inflation only influences money growth in a direct way. Thus we find a feedback relation between money growth and inflation. In addition feedback relations exist between money growth and output growth and between money growth and interest rate changes, while all the other relations are unidirectional. As one can see from Table 4.2 there is no (strong) evidence for contemporaneous correlation in this specification, i.e. only weak instantaneous Granger–causal relations are present.

Estimates of the error correction model including GMU are given in Table 4.3. As before the constant term, seasonal dummies and the dummies capturing the structural break are not presented.

The reported diagnostics indicate that the properties of the residuals are more or less the same as in model (I). Starting with the full system as before we end up with a different result with respect to the error correction term. Now m_t and p_t are endogenous, whereas y_t and r_t are weakly exogenous. The adjustment coefficient of the error correction term in the equation for p_t has the expected positive sign. According to equation (3.4) this means, that in a situation where prices exceed their equilibrium level, inflation will decrease.

On the other hand, excess money balances will increase the inflation rate. We thus find a feedback relation in levels between money balances and prices

[10] For the concept of weak exogeneity see e.g. Ericsson (1992).

Table 4.1. Vector error correction model (I), estimation period 1962(1)–1989(4).

	Δm_t	Δp_t	Δy_t	Δr_t
ec_{1t-1}	-0.106 (4.5)			
Δm_{t-1}				0.083 (3.3)
Δm_{t-2}		-0.073 (2.2)		
Δm_{t-3}	0.157 (2.3)		0.315 (4.3)	
Δp_{t-1}		-0.159 (3.0)		
Δp_{t-2}		0.184 (3.1)		
Δp_{t-4}	0.460 (6.0)	0.586 (10.6)		
Δy_{t-2}	-0.284 (5.5)	0.082 (3.0)	-0.387 (5.2)	
Δy_{t-3}		0.128 (5.1)		
Δy_{t-4}			0.484 (6.5)	
Δr_{t-1}	-0.820 (3.1)	0.326 (2.8)		0.188 (2.1)
Δr_{t-3}				0.219 (2.5)
SE	0.013	0.006	0.014	0.005
$Q(16)$	18.64 [0.29]	27.86 [0.03]	15.74 [0.47]	15.78 [0.47]
JB	17.54 [0.000]	1.00 [0.61]	4.17 [0.12]	12.38 [0.002]
$LM(2)$	0.87 [0.42]	0.58 [0.56]	0.83 [0.44]	0.08 [0.93]
$LM(4)$	0.73 [0.57]	1.30 [0.27]	0.51 [0.73]	0.11 [0.98]
$ARCH(2)$	0.46 [0.63]	0.69 [0.50]	3.68 [0.03]	2.90 [0.06]

Table 4.2. Residual correlation matrix of the vector error correction model (I).

	m	p	y	r
m	1	0.23	0.09	-0.26
p		1	-0.19	-0.10
y			1	0.08
r				1

Table 4.3. Vector error correction model (II), estimation period 1962(1)–1996(2).

	Δm_t	Δp_t	Δy_t	Δr_t
ec_{2t-1}	-0.110 (6.2)	0.022 (2.9)		
Δm_{t-1}				0.036 (2.1)
Δm_{t-2}		-0.057 (2.2)	0.207 (3.2)	
Δm_{t-3}			0.113 (2.0)	
Δp_{t-1}		-0.123 (2.4)		
Δp_{t-2}		0.268 (4.8)	-0.294 (3.1)	
Δp_{t-4}	0.411 (5.4)	0.538 (10.3)		
Δy_{t-2}	-0.226 (4.8)	0.120 (4.8)	-0.440 (6.5)	
Δy_{t-3}		0.130 (6.0)		
Δy_{t-4}			0.457 (7.6)	
Δr_{t-1}	-0.966 (4.1)	0.257 (2.4)		0.194 (2.4)
SE	0.014	0.006	0.015	0.005
$Q(16)$	19.40 [0.25]	26.27 [0.05]	9.74 [0.88]	21.89 [0.15]
JB	11.11 [0.004]	0.41 [0.81]	4.45 [0.11]	4.58 [0.10]
$LM(2)$	1.02 [0.37]	0.81 [0.45]	1.24 [0.29]	0.03 [0.97]
$LM(4)$	0.73 [0.58]	1.25 [0.29]	0.65 [0.63]	0.68 [0.61]
$ARCH(2)$	0.58 [0.56]	0.99 [0.37]	0.96 [0.39]	5.18 [0.01]

for the extended sample although the adjustment coefficient is relatively small, indicating a very long adjustment period.

Table 4.4. Residual correlation matrix of the vector error correction model (II).

	m	p	y	r
m	1	0.17	0.16	-0.16
p		1	-0.13	-0.04
y			1	0.17
r				1

As far as the short–run adjustments are concerned the outcome is almost exactly the same with one substantial exception: the two quarter lagged inflation rate has now a direct influence on output growth, hence we get an additional feedback relation between inflation and output growth. Table 4.4 gives the corresponding residual correlation matrix and again contemporaneous correlations between the variables can be neglected.

To sum up, the inclusion of the data for the unified Germany does not change the causal relations of the variables very much and the point estimates for corresponding coefficients are very similar. Although the structure of the system thus is rather stable, the status of prices changed dramatically. Before GMU prices could be treated as weakly exogenous.[11] After GMU, this variable turns out to be endogenous and monetary policy has a direct influence on the price level, but with very long lags.

In Tödter and Reimers (1994) and Issing and Tödter (1995) the growth rate of import prices is included in the error correction equation for inflation as an additional variable. Considering the growth rate of import prices Δpm_t as an additional exogenous variable in the equations for prices we reestimated the VECMs in the same way as described above. As one can see from Table 4.5 we find the same specification for the equations for Δm_t, Δy_t, and Δr_t and nearly the same coefficients as in model (I). The fits for all equations are exactly the same and the residual diagnostics do not lead to different conclusions compared to model (I). In the equation for Δp_t the two period lagged growth rate of import prices, Δpm_{t-2}, is now significant at the 5% level, whereas Δm_{t-2} is no longer significant. Consequently, money growth has no direct influence on inflation if one allows for international price movements.

In model (II), again the specifications of the equations for Δm_t, Δy_t, and Δr_t and the diagnostics for all equations remain the same (see Table 4.6). In

[11] This result does not depend on choosing the two–step approach. In the unrestricted VECM we also found prices to be weakly exogenous.

Table 4.5. Vector error correction model (Ia) including import prices, estimation period 1962(1)–1989(4).

	Δm_t	Δp_t	Δy_t	Δr_t
ec_{1t-1}	-0.103 (4.3)			
Δm_{t-1}				0.084 (3.4)
Δm_{t-3}	0.160 (2.3)		0.312 (4.2)	
Δp_{t-1}		-0.178 (3.2)		
Δp_{t-2}		0.132 (2.2)		
Δp_{t-4}	0.460 (6.0)	0.588 (10.6)		
Δy_{t-2}	-0.283 (5.4)	0.069 (2.6)	-0.380 (5.1)	
Δy_{t-3}		0.129 (5.1)		
Δy_{t-4}			0.494 (6.7)	
Δr_{t-1}	-0.831 (3.1)	0.270 (2.4)		0.188 (2.1)
Δr_{t-3}				0.220 (2.6)
Δpm_{t-2}		0.058 (2.3)		
SE	0.013	0.006	0.014	0.005
$Q(16)$	18.98 [0.27]	28.16 [0.03]	15.82 [0.47]	15.80 [0.47]
JB	18.82 [0.000]	0.09 [0.95]	3.70 [0.16]	11.15 [0.004]
$LM(2)$	0.90 [0.41]	0.95 [0.39]	0.80 [0.45]	0.08 [0.92]
$LM(4)$	0.77 [0.55]	1.76 [0.14]	0.51 [0.72]	0.11 [0.98]
$ARCH(2)$	0.46 [0.63]	0.70 [0.50]	3.68 [0.03]	2.91 [0.06]

Table 4.6. Vector error correction model (IIa) including import prices, estimation period 1962(1)–1996(2).

	Δm_t	Δp_t	Δy_t	Δr_t
ec_{2t-1}	-0.115 (6.6)			
Δm_{t-1}				0.036 (2.1)
Δm_{t-2}			0.191 (3.0)	
Δm_{t-3}			0.117 (2.0)	
Δp_{t-1}		-0.133 (2.6)		
Δp_{t-2}		0.204 (3.6)	-0.284 (3.0)	
Δp_{t-4}	0.411 (5.4)	0.538 (10.0)		
Δy_{t-2}	-0.231 (4.9)	0.082 (3.7)	-0.431 (6.4)	
Δy_{t-3}		0.113 (5.3)		
Δy_{t-4}			0.457 (7.6)	
Δr_{t-1}	-0.884 (3.7)	0.240 (2.4)		0.192 (2.3)
Δpm_{t-4}		0.058 (2.4)		
SE	0.014	0.006	0.015	0.005
$Q(16)$	18.93 [0.27]	29.93 [0.02]	12.99 [0.67]	20.95 [0.18]
JB	13.99 [0.001]	0.36 [0.83]	2.16 [0.34]	5.48 [0.06]
$LM(2)$	0.61 [0.54]	1.16 [0.32]	0.98 [0.38]	0.05 [0.95]
$LM(4)$	0.64 [0.64]	1.18 [0.33]	0.51 [0.73]	0.97 [0.43]
$ARCH(2)$	0.64 [0.53]	0.06 [0.94]	2.25 [0.11]	4.29 [0.02]

this case the changes in the inflation equation are even stronger. Now Δpm_{t-4} is significant at the 5% level and ec_{2t-1} and Δm_{t-2} vanish from the equation. Thus, allowing for international price movements in the inflation equation leads to the same relations between money and prices before and after GMU. These results show the sensitivity of the linkage between monetary policy and inflation.

5. Dynamic Analysis

Impulse response functions may be used to illustrate how the system reacts to an exogenous impulse in one of the variables.[12] Suppose we want to investigate the effect of an innovation in money on the other variables of the system. This can be done by assuming that prior to time $t = 0$ all variables are zero and that only money increases by one unit in period $t = 0$. Assuming that no further shocks occur we can evaluate the reaction of the whole system during periods $t = 1, 2, 3, \ldots$. With this type of analysis it is assumed that a shock occurs in one variable at a time. This assumption may be problematic if the shocks in the different variables were not independent. But since contemporaneous correlation is very low for the VECMs presented here (see e.g. Tables 4.2 and 4.4) there is no need to orthogonalize innovations.

We calculated the impulse responses recursively after solving the estimated VECMs for their corresponding representations in the levels of the variables. Thus, not only the short–run dynamics in the variables but also the deviations from long–run equilibrium that have to be corrected are affected by the shocks. Figures 5.1.–5.4. show the computed cumulated impulse responses for the four systems estimated in Tables 4.1, 4.3, 4.5, and 4.6. Responses are shown for 24 quarters. The graphs in a given row all have the same scale. The maximum and minimum values are indicated in the very left graph in each row. The filled–in areas in the graphs in a given row provide a visual measure of the relative contributions of innovations listed in the columns to the variable listed at the left of the row. The size of a shock is one standard deviation and responses are measured in units of standard deviations of the respective variables.

Note that the persistent theoretically expected negative responses of money stock and output to positive innovations in interest rates — the second and the fourth rows of the first column of each chart — are not affected neither by GMU nor by the inclusion of import prices. The responses of prices to interest rate shocks are all initially positive, but the positive response is strong and persistent only if one does not allow for international price movements. Thus, much of the variation in prices is found to represent responses to disturbances that can be measured from knowledge of international price

[12] See e.g. Lütkepohl (1991).

movements.[13] Introducing import prices as additional exogenous variable into the price equation leads to more plausible price responses. The corresponding figures in the third row of the first column in Figures 5.3. and 5.4. show that price reactions are weaker and in the end become negative.

The responses of real income to innovations in prices are positive for the first period and only show the expected negative reaction if GMU is included, irrespective of whether import prices are included in the price equation or not. The response of money to innovations in prices is positive and persistent in every case, thus indicating that money balances follow prices to some degree in an accommodating fashion. In every case the nominal interest rate increases due to a positive price shock as expected.

Price responses to money innovations are predominantly positive with the exception of the case where import prices and GMU are not included (see Figure 5.1.). In this case price responses are negative in the beginning and become positive after one year. However, responses of prices to money innovations are absolutely small and relatively unimportant. It thus can be concluded that the linkage between money and prices is rather weak. Moreover, the effects are rather sensitive with respect to GMU when import prices are included. Income performs as expected with respect to expansionary money shocks showing positive (though weak) reactions in every case.

To complete the discussion, a positive shock in income is followed by positive reactions in all the variables.

With respect to the relative sizes of the responses innovations in the nominal interest rate and innovations in real income are the main sources of variation in the variables. Changes in prices are predominantly induced by price innovations where a large fraction of variation is probably due to international price movements. Money innovations do not generate sustained responses in any of the variables.

[13] See also Black (1997, p. 12).

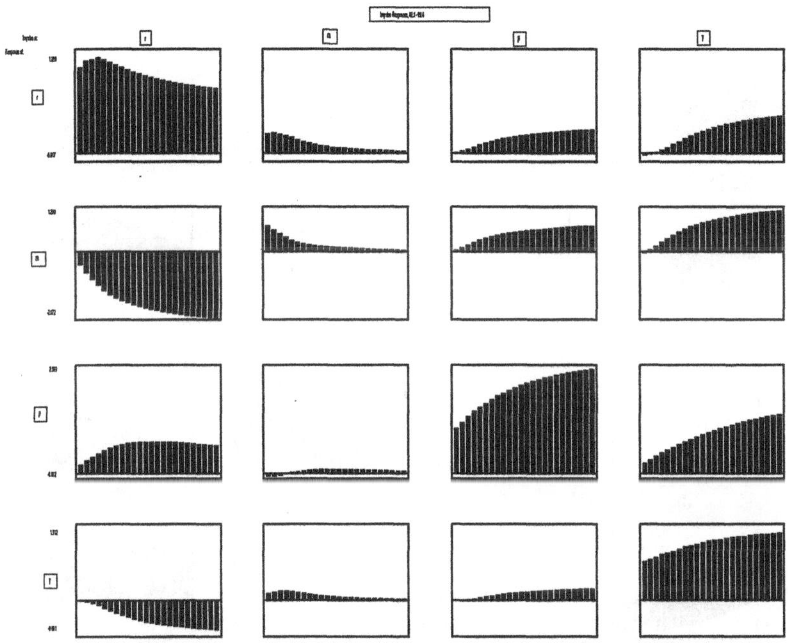

Fig. 5.1. Cumulated Impulse Responses of Model (I)

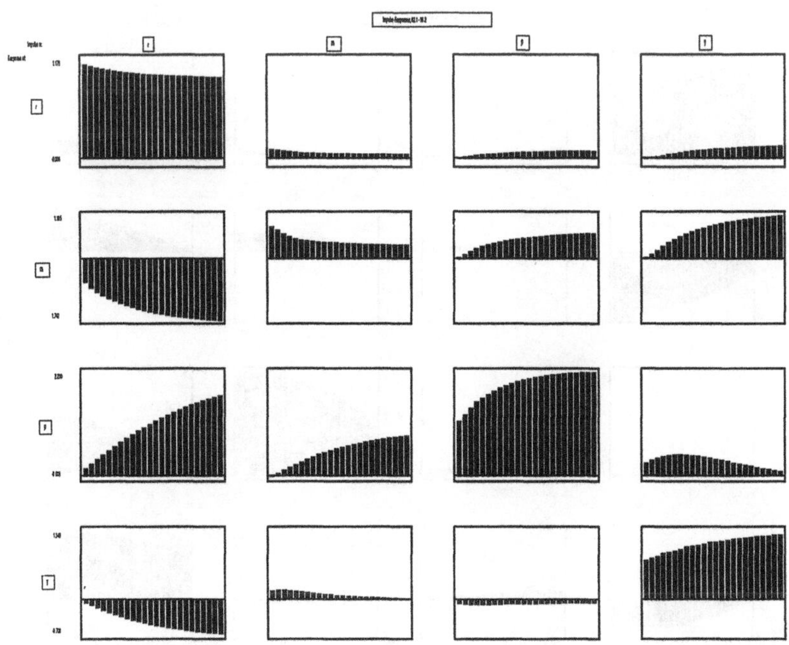

Fig. 5.2. Cumulated Impulse Responses of Model (II)

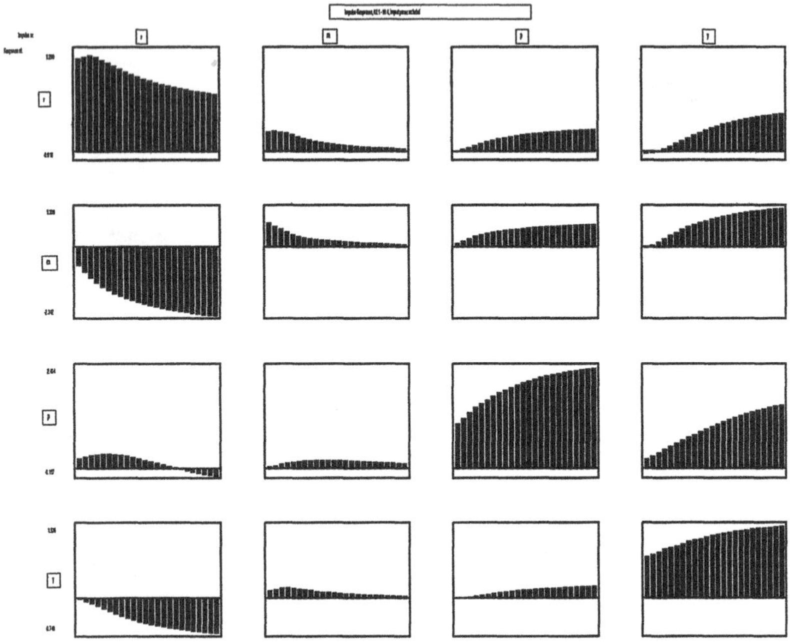

Fig. 5.3. Cumulated Impulse Responses of Model (Ia)

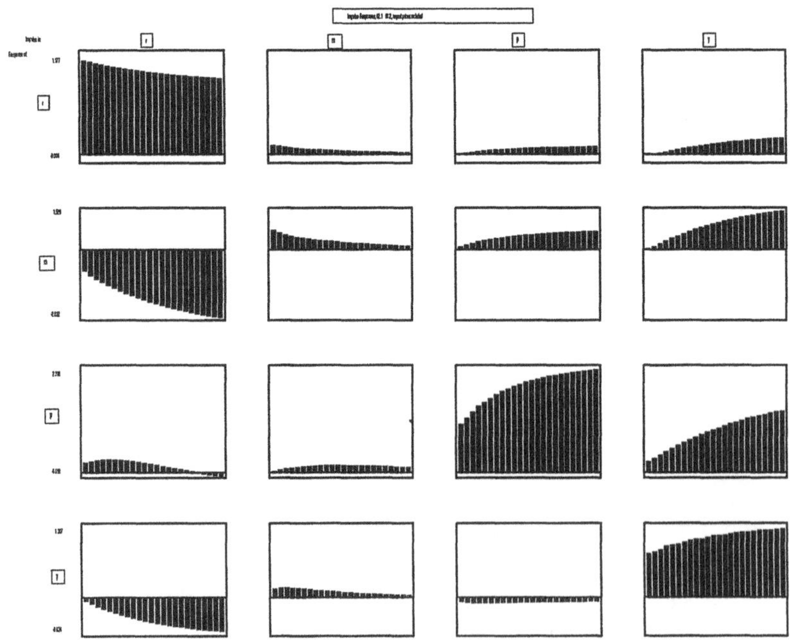

Fig. 5.4. Cumulated Impulse Responses of Model (IIa)

6. Conclusion

We analysed the linkages between money growth and inflation in a multivariate framework including money, prices, output, and a long–term interest rate as well as import prices as an additional exogenous variable. All data are seasonally unadjusted.

After the determination of the cointegration rank, which is one, the cointegrating vector is derived from a conditional error correction equation for nominal money balances. This cointegrating relation can be interpreted as a long–run money demand equation with price homogeneity, which remains stable after the GMU if one captures the shifts in the levels of the variables with a step dummy and allows for changes in the seasonal behaviour.

Applying a two step procedure we estimate vector error correction models with data before and after the GMU. Although the dynamic structures of the two error correction models not including import prices are more or less the same, there is one difference. Prices which are weakly exogenous before GMU, turn out to be endogenous after GMU. Consequently, deviations from long–run monetary equilibrium directly influence inflation. However, this does not seem to be a very stable relation, since if one includes lagged growth rates of import prices in the inflation equation, all direct influences of money growth are no longer significant. To sum up, the money demand relation seems to be stable in the long run but there is empirical evidence that the relation between money and prices is not very robust.

The following general results hold for both sample periods. We find feedback relations between money growth and all the other variables in the system if import prices are not included. In all cases the money stock is not only influenced through interest rate changes but also through changes in the inflation rate. The error correction term is always significant in the money equation. Thus, contrary to the assumptions in the *p*-star approach, we find that money in our multivariate framework is the endogenous variable. Similar results are given by Hall and Milne (1994) for the UK and Hansen and Kim (1996) with respect to German M3, whereas Issing and Tödter (1995) in their single equation analysis for M3 assume causality from money to prices. Moreover, due to the instability in the linkage between money growth and inflation the narrow monetary aggregate M1 does not seem to be very useful as intermediate target variable.

References

1. Banerjee, A., J. J. Dolado, J. W. Galbraith, and D. F. Hendry (1993). *Cointegration, Error-Correction, and the Econometric Analysis of Nonstationary Data.* Oxford: Oxford University Press.
2. Black, S. W. (1997). The Relationship of Core and Periphery in European Monetary Union. Mimeo, University of North Carolina.

3. Campos, J., N. R. Ericsson, and D. F. Hendry (1996). Cointegration Tests in the Presence of Structural Breaks. *Journal of Econometrics 70*, 221–41.
4. Deutsche Bundesbank (1992). Zum Zusammenhang zwischen Geldmengen- und Preisentwicklung in der Bundesrepublik. *Monatsberichte der Deutschen Bundesbank 44*(1), 20–29.
5. Eitrheim, Ø. (1995). The Demand for Broad Money and Tests for Neglected Monetary Effects on Inflation. Empirical Evidence for Norway 1969 to 1993. Arbeidsnotat 8, Norges Bank, Oslo.
6. Engle, R. F. and C. W. J. Granger (1987). Co-Integration and Error Correction: Representation, Estimation, and Testing. *Econometrica 55*, 251–76.
7. Ericsson, N. R. (1992). Cointegration, Exogeneity and Policy Analysis: An Overview. *Journal of Policy Modelling 14*, 251–280.
8. Friedman, B. M. and K. N. Kuttner (1992). Money, Income, Prices, and Interest Rates. *American Economic Review 82*, 472–492.
9. Hall, S. F. and A. Milne (1994). The Relevance of the p-Star Analysis to UK Monetary Policy. *The Economic Journal 104*, 597–604.
10. Hallman, J. J., R. D. Porter, and D. H. Small (1991). Is the Price Level tied to the M2 Monetary Aggregate in the long run? *The American Economic Review 81*, 841–58.
11. Hansen, G. and J.-R. Kim (1996). Money and Inflation in Germany: A Cointegration Analysis. *Empirical Economics 21*, 601–616.
12. Hwang, H. (1985). Test of Adjustment Process and Linear Homogeneity in a Stock Adjustment Model of Money Demand. *Review of Economics and Statistics 67*, 689–92.
13. Hylleberg, S., R. F. Engle, C. W. J. Granger, and B. S. Yoo (1990). Seasonal Integration and Cointegration. *Journal of Econometrics 44*, 215–38.
14. Issing, O. and K.-H. Tödter (1995). Geldmenge und Preise im vereinigten Deutschland. In D. Duwendag (ed.), *Neuere Entwicklungen in der Geldtheorie und Währungspolitik*, Duncker & Humblodt, Berlin, 97–123.
15. Johansen, S. (1995). *Likelihood-Based Inference in Cointegrated Vector Autoregressive Models.* Oxford: Oxford University Press.
16. Lütkepohl, H. (1991). *Introduction to Multiple Time Series Analysis.* Heidelberg: Springer–Verlag.
17. Lütkepohl, H., T. Teräsvirta, and J. Wolters (1995). Investigating Stability and Linearity of a German M1 Money Demand Function. Discussionpaper 57, Sonderforschungsbereich 373, Humboldt-Universität zu Berlin, Wirtschaftswissenschaftliche Fakultät.
18. Miller, S. M. (1992). Monetary Dynamics: An Application of Cointegration and Error-Correction Modeling. *Journal of Money, Credit, and Banking 23*, 139–54.
19. Osterwald-Lenum, M. (1992). A Note with Quantiles of the Asymptotic Distribution of Maximum Likelihood Cointegration Rank Test Statistics. *Oxford Bulletin of Economics and Statistics 54*, 461–72.
20. Rasche, R. H. (1993). Monetary Aggregates, Monetary Policy and Economic Activity. *Federal Reserve Bank of St. Louis Review March/April*, 1–35.
21. Rotemberg, J. J., J. C. Driscoll, and J. M. Poterba (1995). Money, Output, and Prices: Evidence from a New Monetary Aggregate. *Journal of Business and Economic Statistics 13*, 67–83.
22. Schultes, D. (1996). Geldmengenziele und diskretionäre Elemente der Politik der Bundesbank. Eine empirische Untersuchung. *Kredit und Kapital 29*, 54–89.
23. Tödter, K.-H. and H.-E. Reimers (1994). P-star as a Link between Money and Prices in Germany. *Weltwirtschaftliches Archiv 130*, 273–89.

24. von Hagen, J. and M. J. M. Neumann (1996). A Framework for Monetary Policy under EMU. In Deutsche Bundesbank (Ed.), *Monetary Policy Strategies in Europe*, pp. 141–165. München: Franz Vahlen.
25. Weissenberger, E. and J. J. Thomas (1983). The Causal Role of Money in West Germany. *Weltwirtschaftliches Archiv 119*, 64–83.
26. Wickens, M. R. (1996). Interpreting Cointegration Vectors and Common Stochastic Trends. *Journal of Econometrics 74*, 255–271.
27. Wickens, M. R. and T. S. Breusch (1988). Dynamic Specification, the Long-Run and the Estimation of Transformed Regression Models. *The Economic Journal 98*, 189–205.
28. Wolters, J. and H. Lütkepohl (1997). Die Geldnachfrage für M3: Neue Ergebnisse für das vereinigte Deutschland. *Ifo Studien 43*, 35–54.

Quasi-Minimax Estimation, Prior Information and Money Demand in Germany

Hans-Joachim Mittag[1], Dietmar Stemann[1], and Bernhard Schipp[2]

[1] Fern-Universität Hagen, Germany
[2] Technische Universität Dresden, Germany

Summary. We illustrate the application of various quasi minimax estimators in a linear regression model in which money demand in Germany is related to real GNP, inflation- and nominal interest rate. Initial interval constraints on the coefficients are transformed into ellipsoidal restrictions. The resulting quasi minimax estimators are shown to outperform ordinary least squares according to a minimax risk criterion.

1. Introduction

In recent years quite a few alternatives to the ordinary least squares estimator (OLS) in linear regression analysis have been proposed. Among those, quasi minimax estimators (Trenkler and Stahlecker 1987) offer an appropriate technique if sample information may be augmented by interval constraints on the parameters. These restrictions on the parameter space enable the computation of a maximum risk (i.e., expected quadratic loss) which, in turn, may be minimized w.r.t. an (affine) linear estimator. As definite solutions to the latter minimization problem are obtainable only in rare cases (for an overview see Toutenburg 1982 and Stahlecker 1987) upper and lower bounds of the maximum risk have been minimized instead thus leading to quasi minimax estimators (QM). The structure of the resulting statistics is comparable to that of Bayes and (generalized) Ridge estimators, i.e., quasi minimax estimators are biased but can usually be expected to be superior to OLS w.r.t the mean squared error (see Schipp, Trenkler and Stahlecker 1988). QM estimators have been proven to be most effective in situations where the matrix of regressors is affected by multicollinearity or comparatively many parameters are to be estimated on the basis of only few observations. Although unbiased, OLS is typically imprecise under these circumstances (see Schneeweiß 1978, p. 134ff.).

In the present paper we focus on illustrating the applicability of various QM estimators in the context of a linear regression model in which money demand in Germany in the period 1975-1995 is regressed on real GNP, inflation- and nominal interest rate. As the paper aims at demonstrating the usage of minimax estimators, we do not intend to model money demand by means of cointegration and error correction (see Ericsson, Hendry and Tran 1994) or by *VAR*-analysis (see Hubrich 1996).

2. Quasi minimax estimation

We consider the linear regression model

$$y = X\beta + u, \tag{2.1}$$

in which y denotes a stochastic $(T \times 1)$-vector of endogenous variables. X is a deterministic $(T \times k)$-matrix of k explanatory variables with $\operatorname{rg}(X) = k$, β is a nonstochastic $(k \times 1)$-vector of unknown regression coefficients and u denotes a $(T \times 1)$-vector of random disturbances with $E(u) = 0$ and $E(uu') = \sigma^2 I$.

Traditionally, the sum of squared deviations

$$S(\tilde{\beta}) = (y - X\tilde{\beta})'(y - X\tilde{\beta}) \tag{2.2}$$

is minimized w.r.t. $\tilde{\beta} \in \mathbb{R}^k$. Under the above assumptions, the unique solution is given by

$$\hat{\beta}_{OLS} = (X'X)^{-1}X'y, \tag{2.3}$$

and is called ordinary least squares (OLS) estimator. In order to calculate QM estimators we rely on the mean squared error, i.e., the risk of estimating β by means of a linear functional $\tilde{\beta}$, namely

$$R(\tilde{\beta}, \beta) = E(\tilde{\beta} - \beta)'(\tilde{\beta} - \beta). \tag{2.4}$$

If the class of affine linear estimators is condsidered, i.e.,

$$D = \{\tilde{\beta} \mid \tilde{\beta} = Cy + c, \quad C \in \mathbb{R}^{k \times T}, \quad c \in \mathbb{R}^k\}, \tag{2.5}$$

(2.4) may be written as

$$R(\tilde{\beta}, \beta) = \sigma^2 \operatorname{tr} C'C + B(\tilde{\beta}, \beta)' B(\tilde{\beta}, \beta), \tag{2.6}$$

where $B(\tilde{\beta}, \beta) = E(\tilde{\beta}) - \beta$ stands for the bias of the estimator $\tilde{\beta}$.

The OLS estimator assumes the information set to be given by (y, X). QM however is additionaly based on information in form of ellipsoidal restrictions

$$\beta \in B \tag{2.7}$$

where

$$B = \{\beta \mid (\beta - \beta_0)' T (\beta - \beta_0) \leq 1\}. \tag{2.8}$$

The $(k \times k)$-matrix T is required to be positive definite and known. The $(k \times 1)$-vector β_0 indicates the known center of the ellipsoid.

According to the minimax criterion we have to find the best estimator given the situation is worst, i.e., find $\hat{\beta}_M \in D$ such that for all $\tilde{\beta} \in D$ holds

$$\max_{\beta \in B} R(\hat{\beta}_M, \beta) = \min_{\tilde{\beta} \in D} \max_{\beta \in B} R(\tilde{\beta}, \beta). \tag{2.9}$$

To determine QM estimators explicitly we have to start with maximizing the risk (2.6) over the compact domain (2.8). Using the well known inequality $\gamma' A\gamma \leq \lambda_{max}\gamma'\gamma$, (e.g., Rao 1973, p. 62) we derive the upper bound

$$R(\tilde{\beta},\beta) \leq \sigma^2 \text{tr}\, C'C + \lambda_{max} Q(C) = t't \tag{2.10}$$

with $Q(C) = T^{-\frac{1}{2}}(CX - I)'(CX - I)T^{-\frac{1}{2}}$ and $t = T^{\frac{1}{2}}(\beta - \beta_0)$. If t^* is an eigenvector belonging to the maximum eigenvalue of $Q(C)$ with $t^{*\prime} t^* = 1$ we have

$$\max_{\beta \in B} R(\tilde{\beta},\beta) = \sigma^2 \text{tr}\, C'C + \lambda_{max} Q(C). \tag{2.11}$$

Much effort has been done to derive an analytical solution to the problem of minimizing the maximum risk under general specifications, but solutions were yet obtained for special cases only. The problem consists in the fact that $\lambda_{max} Q(C)$ is not differentiable w.r.t. C. The basic idea of quasi minimax estimation is thus to replace the problem of finding the minimum of a maximum eigenvalue by either minimizing an upper or lower bound for it.

Using the inequality (see Schipp 1990, p. 57)

$$k^{-1} \text{tr}\, Q(C) \leq \lambda_{max}, Q(C) \leq \text{tr}\, Q(C), \tag{2.12}$$

we are able to derive exact solutions to approximate problems, which in case $k = 1$ coincide with the original solution. Accordingly, QM estimators based on the left hand side inequality are called *lower QM* and those based on the right hand side inequality are called *upper QM*.

Both problems may be characterized by a common parameter $\alpha \in \{1/k, 1\}$. A solution to the subsidiary minimization problem, i.e.,

$$\min_{C,c} [\sigma^2 \text{tr}\, C'C + \alpha\, \text{tr}\, Q(C)], \quad \alpha \in [1/k, 1] \tag{2.13}$$

is given by (see Schipp 1990, p. 60)

$$\hat{\beta}_{QM} = C^*(y - X\beta_0) + \beta_0, \tag{2.14}$$

where

$$C^* = (X'X + \sigma^2 \alpha^{-1} T)^{-1} X'. \tag{2.15}$$

The only unknown in (2.15) is σ^2 which may be replaced by its = unbiased estimate $\hat{\sigma}^2 = \frac{1}{T-k} \sum_{t=1}^{T} \hat{u}' = \hat{u}$, leading to

$$\tilde{C}^* = (X'X + \hat{\sigma}^2 \alpha^{-1} T)^{-1} X'. \tag{2.16}$$

Simulations and theoretical results indicate that the difference between (2.15) and its operational version (2.16) is negligibly small, even in cases of less than 20 observations (see Trenkler et al. 1987 or Becker 1997, p. 77f.). Both the lower and upper QM estimator dominate OLS w.r.t. the (theoretical) mean squared error (see Hering et al. 1987).

Srivastava and Shukla (1996, p.82) have derived which may be used for efficiency comparison in empirical work. Their estimator is given by

$$\widehat{MR}(\hat{\beta},\beta) = \hat{\sigma}^2 \text{tr}\, \tilde{C}^{*\prime} \tilde{C}^* + \hat{\sigma}^4 = \lambda_{max}(\tilde{D}T\tilde{D}), \tag{2.17}$$

where $\tilde{D} = (X'X + \hat{\sigma}^2 \alpha T)^{-1}$ and $\alpha \in \{1/k, 1\}$.

3. Interval and ellipsoidal prior information

Economic theory will hardly be able to provide ellipsoidal information on relevant model parameters. Typically we find a priori ideas specified by inequalities of the form

$$a_i \leq \beta_i \leq b_i, \quad i = 1, \ldots, k, \tag{3.1}$$

which describe a k-dimensional cuboid. This cuboid may be approximated by at least two ellipsoids. An inner ellipsoid for example may be contained in the cuboid with maximum volume. An outer ellipsoid may contain the cuboid with minimum volume. Figure 3.1 displays the situation if $k = 2$. Using the outer ellipsoid weakens the prior information; the use of the inner ellipsoid corresponds to prior information that is more precise than the original cuboid. Toutenburg (1982, ch. 4) has derived an appropriate formula to calculate the outer ellipsoid with minimum volume from interval restrictions:
Given that the center β_0 of the cuboid is equal to that of the ellipsoid, i.e.,

$$\beta_0 = \frac{1}{2}\left(a_1 + b_1, \ldots, a_k + b_k\right), \tag{3.2}$$

the elements of the matrix T are obtained by

$$T_{out} = \text{diag}\left(\frac{4}{k}\left((b_1 - a_1)^{-2}, \ldots, (b_k - a_k)^{-2}\right)\right). \tag{3.3}$$

It is easy to show that the ellipsoid contained in the cuboid with maximum volume may be described by the matrix

$$T_{in} = \text{diag}\left(4((b_1 - a_1)^{-2}, \ldots, (b_k - a_k)^{-2})\right). \tag{3.4}$$

Most interestingly, the upper QM estimator corresponds to the use of the outer ellipsoid whereas the lower QM refers to the use of the inner ellipsoid. Other approximations are possible as we may, for example, construct the "'in between ellipsoid"' as the arithmetic average of outer and inner ellipsoids.

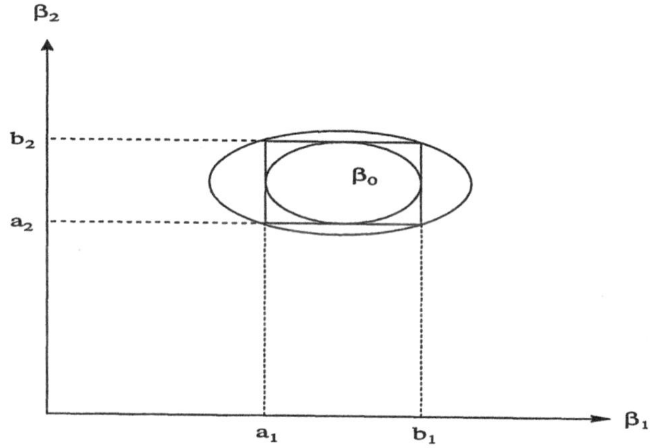

Figure 3.1: A priori rectangle und approximating ellipsoids.

4. Money demand in Germany: an empirical application of quasi minimax estimation

Efficient fiscal policy assumes a certain knowledge of the long term relationship between money demand and important macroeconomic variables, as GNP, price indices, inflation- and interest rates (see Westphal 1994).

In our setup we have used time series on german money demand M comprising (among others) real cash balances of the banking sector. Income is measured by real gross national product (GNP*), the price level will be represented by the implicit index $P = \mathrm{GNP}/\mathrm{GNP}^*$, where GNP stands for nominal gross national product. Short term interest rate Z is approximated by 30-day treasury bonds.

The corresponding econometric model of long term money demand may be written as

$$ln(M_t) = \beta_1 + \beta_2\, ln(P_t) + \beta_3 \; = ln(\mathrm{GNP}_t^*) + \beta_4\, ln(Z_t) + u_t, \quad t = 1, \cdots, T. \tag{4.1}$$

In (4.1) β_2 indicates price elasticity, β_3 income elasticity und β_4 interest elasticity w.r.t. money demand. The error term u_t is supposed to obey the assumptions of the standard linear regression model.

In what follows we examine time series from 1975-1995 on the basis of annual data. Data from 1991-1995 refer to Germany after reunification.

Using OLS yields the following results:

$$\hat{\beta}_{OLS} = 3D \begin{pmatrix} \hat{\beta}_1 \\ \hat{\beta}_2 \\ \hat{\beta}_3 \\ \hat{\beta}_4 \end{pmatrix} = \begin{pmatrix} -11.647 \\ 0.835 \\ 1.810 \\ -0.086 \end{pmatrix}. \tag{4.2}$$

There is no evidence of any violations of the standard assumptions. All parameters are significantly different from zero (t-values: -23.71, 7.93, 15.14, -4.77). The coefficient of determination is $R^2 = 3D0.997$. The value of the Durbin-Watson-statistic is $DW = 1.897$. There is no evidence of a structural change after 1990. The estimated minimax risk (i.e., scalar MSE) of OLS is $\widehat{MR}(\hat{\beta}_{OLS}, \beta) = \hat{\sigma}^2 \mathrm{tr}(X'X)^{-1} = 0.267$.

Before we estimate the model of money demand by quasi minimax estimators we have to specify a priori constraints on the parameters. On the basis of the initial OLS estimates we have used the following interval restrictions

$$-15 \leq \beta_1 \leq -10 \tag{4.3}$$
$$0.5 \leq \beta_2 \leq 1 \tag{4.4}$$
$$1.5 \leq \beta_3 \leq 2 \tag{4.5}$$
$$-0.1 \leq \beta_4 \leq 0.05. \tag{4.6}$$

The matrix T corresponding to the outer ellipsoid circumscribing the above cuboid and the vector β_0, are given by

$$T = \begin{pmatrix} 0.04 & 0 & 0 & 0 \\ 0 & 4 & 0 & 0 \\ 0 & 0 & 4 & 0 \\ 0 & 0 & 0 & 400 \end{pmatrix} \tag{4.7}$$

and

$$\beta_0 = \begin{pmatrix} -12.50 \\ 0.75 \\ 1.75 \\ -0.075 \end{pmatrix}. \tag{4.8}$$

Upper and lower quasi minimax estimates are given by

$$\hat{\beta}_{UQM} = \begin{pmatrix} -11.65 \\ 0.83 \\ 1.81 \\ -0.09 \end{pmatrix} \quad \text{and} \quad \hat{\beta}_{LQM} = \begin{pmatrix} -11.69 \\ 0.83 \\ 1.81 \\ -0.08 \end{pmatrix}. \tag{4.9}$$

The corresponding estimates for the minimax risk are given by 0.243 for $\hat{\beta}_{UQM}$ and 0.157 for $\hat{\beta}_{LQM}$. MR has thus been reduced by approximately 8.9% and 41.2% whereas the coefficient of determination and the Durbin-Watson statistic remained almost unchanged ($R^2 \approx 0.997$, $DW \approx 1.759$) in both situations.

Results for $\hat{\beta}_{UQM}$ and $\hat{\beta}_{LQM}$ are very similar. All coefficients show the expected signs. An 1% increase of the price level leads to an increase in money demand by 0.83% ceteribus paribus. Also, there is some evidence for money illusion. An 1% increase of real gross national product (GNP*) leads to an increase in money demand by approx. 1.8%. An increase in nominal gross national product by 1% leads to an increase in money demand by $1.81 \cdot 0.83 = 1.5\%$. This result may be interpreted as a partial support of the theory of luxury goods, where an increase in income leads to an increase in cash money. An increase of the interest rate by 1% leads to a decrease in money demand by 0.084% ceteris paribus.

References

1. Becker, L. (1997). Minimax-Schätz- und Testverfahren im linearen Regressionsmodell bei Vorinformation. Dissertation, eingereicht am Fachbereich Statistik, Universität Dortmund.
2. Ericsson, N.R.; Hendy, D.F.; Tran, H.A. (1994). Cointegration, Seasonality, Encompassing and the demand for money in the United Kingdom; in: Nonstationary time series analysis and cointegration (C. Hargreaves ed.) Oxford University Press, Oxford.
3. Hering, F.; Trenkler, G.; Stahlecker, P. (1987). Partial Minimax Estimation in Regression Analysis. *Statistica Neerlandica* 41, 111-128.
4. Hubrich, K. (1996). Estimation of a German money demand system - a long run analysis. Paper presented at ESEM96, Istanbul.
5. Rao, C.R. (1973). Linear statistical inference and its applications. Wiley, New York.
6. Schipp, B. (1990). Minimax-Schätzer im simultanen Gleichungsmodell bei vollständiger und partieller Vorinformation. Verlag Anton Hain, Frankfurt am Main.
7. Schipp, B.; Trenkler, G.; Stahlecker, P. (1988). Minimax estimation with additional linaer restrictions. *Communications in Statistics* 17, 393-406.
8. Schneeweiß, H. (1978). Ökonometrie. Physica, Würzburg.
9. Srivastava, K.; Shukla, P. (1996). Minimax estimation in linear regression model. *Journal of Statistical Planning and Inference* 50, 77-89.
10. Stahlecker, P. (1987). A priori Information und Minimax-Schätzung im linearen Regressionsmodell. Athenäum, Frankfurt am Main.
11. Trenkler, G.; Stahlecker, P. (1987). Quasi minimax estimation in the linear regression model. *Statistics* 18, 219-226.
12. Trenkler, G.; Stahlecker, P.; Schipp, B.; Hering F. (1987). Iterative improvements of a partial minimax estimator. *Proceedings of the Second International Tampere Conference in Statistics*, 679-690.
13. Toutenburg, H. (1982). Prior information in linear models. Wiley, New York.
14. Westphal, U. (1994). Makroökonomik. Springer Verlag, Berlin.

Bayesian Forecasting of Turning Points in Economic Cycles

Walter Naggl

Ludwig-Maximilians-Universität München, Germany

Summary. Bayesian methods are applied to the ifo business climate to predict the state of the German economy at the beginning of 1996. The models predict a cyclical downturn. However, 1996 is not registered as a recession year in Germany. It is argued that Germany was in fact in a recession and that business cycle timing is in a poor state. Official GDP data for 1996 is implausibly high.

1. Introduction

Prediction of economic turning points is a function of decision rules, which, when applied to a leading indicator, produce a forecast about the future state of economy. While checking the accuracy of the American composite leading indicator (CLI), Hymans (1973) developed a decision rule, which essentially consists of a forecast of the beginning of a downward trend, after two successive drops of the CLI within an upturn period. This decision rule led to highly unsatisfactory results even if allowance is made for Hymans' somewhat restrictive definition of false and missed turning points: 49 percent of the forecasts for upper turning points where false, 33 percent of the upper turning points and 24 percent of the lower turning points which actually happened where not recognized.

In order to reduce the error rate Vaccara and Zarnowitz (1977) suggested to predict a turning point of the economic trend out of three successive changes of the CLI against the current trend. This rule results in a distinct reduction of turning point errors[1], compared to the decision rule which requires only two successive moves against the current trend. Actually, this is currently the common rule of thumb of prediction, using the CLI. Zarnowitz and Moore (1982) refined this approach with additional requirements for the composite index of coincident indicators.

The disadvantage of all these decision rules is that they are *ad-hoc* methods, without recourse to a statistical model. An assessment of the future accuracy of these rules is therefore impossible. Probabilistic models are, on the other hand, not only theoretically superior, but also an improvement in practical forecasting. Among them are Anderson's (1966) discriminance analysis, Chaffin and Talley's (1974) hypothesis test and Bayes' theorem.

[1] Stekler (1991), p. 171

While the former two only take into account the latest changes in the leading indicator series, Bayes' theorem uses the complete history of the leading indicator within the economic phase. In the following, because of this obvious advantage, we will use the Bayes-prediction. Using the ifo business climate as a leading indicator we calculate the probability of a recession during the economic slowdown of 1995/96.

2. Qualitative Signal

Initially we apply the Bayesian method to qualitative signals, the decrease, respectively increase, of the leading indicator compared to the preceding period. Thereafter the procedure is used for a quantitative signal, namely the percent change of the leading indicator, compared to the preceding period.

We define two states of economic cycle: *upturn* and *downturn*. The downturn is also called a recession. In the following we assume to be initially in an upturn phase. Using the signals of the indicator, we predict one out of the two states: ongoing upturn and beginning of a downward trend. Hence the prediction is alternatively:

- an ongoing upturn, respectively no turn (NT) in the economic trend;
- a turn (T) in the economic trend, this means an upturn gives way to a recession.

The essential characteristic of Bayes'–model is the following reverse conclusion, known as Bayes' theorem: the frequency, with which recessions in the past led to a drop in the leading indicator determines the probability of a recession, when a decline of the indicator is observed. The other element of Bayes' theorem is the frequency of false signals in the past. This means declines of the indicator which were not followed by a recession. In the extreme case of a zero-frequency, respectively a zero-probability, of wrong signals, Bayes' theorem becomes intuitively clear: if declines of the indicator happened only during recession periods, then the probability of a recession equals 1, once a drop of the indicator has been observed. If allowance for false signals is made, there have to be more than one decline of an indicator, before the probability of a starting recession comes close to 1.

With the above notation, Bayes' theorem may be written as:

$$P(T \mid S) = \frac{P(S \mid T)P(T)}{P(S \mid T)P(T) + P(S \mid NT)P(NT)}.$$

$P(S \mid T)$ is the probability of a signal during a downward trend. $P(S \mid T)P(T)$ is the probability of a correct signal, namely the probability of a downturn signal when the economy in fact enters a recession. $P(S \mid NT)P(NT)$ is the probability of a wrong signal, namely the probability of a downturn signal when the economic upturn carries on. A good leading indicator should have a small probability for a signal during an upturn, and a large one, in case of a recession. In the extreme case of a zero probability for false signals there are just correct signals. When a recession signal is observed the probability for a recession then becomes 1.

In order to use Bayes' theorem, we determine the two model-probabilities $P(S \mid NT)$ and $P(S \mid T)$. Using the quarterly data, of the ifo-business climate, between 1969 : $Q2$ and 1994 : $Q4$ as an indicator variable, one gets 14 declines of the indicator variable, within the 65 quarters which are assigned to upturns. From this the model-probability is calculated as $P(S \mid NT) = 14/65 = 0.215$. In the 38 quarters, which belong to the downturns, the indicator variable is declining 33 times. Hence is $P(S \mid T) = 33/38 = 0.868$.

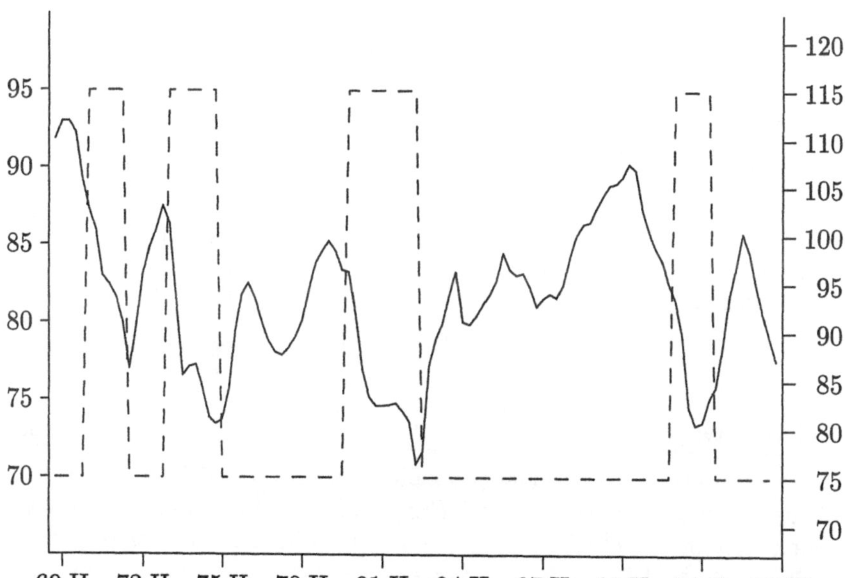

Fig. 2.1. ifo Overall Business Climate and Recessions

Bayes' theorem requires an initial value for the prior probability $P(T)$, which is the unconditional probability of a forthcoming recession during an upswing. Since turning points are quite rare, an appropriate prior choice is 0.05 . This probability roughly equals the percentage of recessions in relative to the whole number of observation periods.

In all four quarters of 1995 the indicator variable decreased. Using 0.05 as an initial value for the prior probability of recession, the posterior probability, after the first drop, is: $P(T \mid S) = 0.175$. The posterior probabilities up to the first quarter of 1996 are given in the following table.

probabilities for the beginning of a recession					
prior	posterior				
	$Q1$ 1995	$Q2$ 1995	$Q3$ 1995	$Q4$ 1995	$Q1$ 1996
0.05	0.175	0.46	0.775	0.933	0.983

On the 95% confidence level, the method forecast a downturn at the beginning of 1996.

3. Using Bayes-Theorem for Quantitative Signals

The use of qualitative signals is not fully satisfactory, because changes in the indicator variable are not taken into account. In the following the signal consists of the percentage change X of the indicator variable between two quarters, instead of qualitative information.

Deduction of probabilities out of frequencies

% change	upturn freq.	upturn prob.	downturn freq.	downturn prob.	prior prob.	total prob.	posterior prob.
x	$n(x)$	$P(S\|NT)$	$n(x)$	$P(S\|T)$	$P(T)$	$P(S)$	$P(T\|S)$
$(-10;-8]$	0	0.00	2	0.05	0.05	0.00	1.00
$(-8;-6]$	0	0.00	1	0.03	0.05	0.00	1.00
$(-6;-4]$	1	0.02	6	0.16	0.05	0.02	0.35
$(-4;-2]$	5	0.08	11	0.29	0.05	0.09	0.17
$(-2;0]$	8	0.12	13	0.34	0.05	0.13	0.13
$(0;2]$	30	0.46	5	0.13	0.05	0.45	0.01
$(2;4]$	14	0.22	0	0.00	0.05	0.20	0.00
$(4;6]$	5	0.08	0	0.00	0.05	0.07	0.00
$(6;8]$	1	0.02	0	0.00	0.05	0.01	0.00
$(8;10]$	0	0.00	0	0.00	0.05	0.00	
$(10;12]$	1	0.02	0	0.00	0.05	0.01	0.00

Instead of the conditional probability of an observed decline of the indicator during an upturn period $P(S \mid NT)$, we have now the conditional probability of a decline by a specific amount. The declines of the indicator variable of 2.0, 3.4, 2.9 and 2.8 percent in 1995 and 2.5 percent in the first quarter of 1996 led to the following probabilities of a recession:

probabilities of a recession					
prior	posterior				
	$Q1$ 1995	$Q2$ 1995	$Q3$ 1995	$Q4$ 1995	$Q1$ 1996
0.05	0.17	0.44	0.75	0.92	0.97

Since the indicator variable fell by similar amounts during the observation period, the resulting probabilities are almost like the ones calculated by using qualitative signals. This must not always be so, however. The conclusion is again a prediction of a downturn in early 1996.

Using methods of sequential analysis, Neftci (1982) developed a modified Bayes' theorem for predicting the beginning of a recession. Neftci makes the probability for a switch in the economic regime an increasing function of the time distance, from the preceding turning point. This reflects the expected duration of an economic recovery period. His approach is in stark contrast with the work of McCulloch (1975), or Diebold and Rudebusch (1991), which found that the future duration of an ongoing expansion is uncorrelated with past duration. This method is therefore not appropriate for the prediction of turning points in economic trends.

4. Outcome Versus Prediction

Real GDP during the third and fourth quarter of 1995 and the first quarter of 1996 was slightly down in Germany. According to the common rule of thumb which defines a recession by two successive quarterly declines of GDP, Germany was in fact in a recession then. The official US criterion for a recession, namely a downturn of a multitude of economic indicators was also met. New orders in manufacturing and construction had turned down, industrial production fell, employment had been declining since early 1995 and the number of unemployed was rising. Nevertheless 1995 is not considered a recession-year in Germany. Only some speak of a mini-recession. This is due to the fact that unlike the US, there exists in Germany no official agency for the timing of recession. For a while this function was carried out by the Bundesbank. In its monthly reports of seasonally adjusted data, it used to indicate recession phases where industrial production fell below trend growth. At the end of 1995 and beginning of 1996 production did fall below trend growth. However this period was not indicated as a recession. Since July of 1997 the indicator of recession has been eliminated completely from the monthly Bundesbank reports[2].

The economic setback of 1995/96 would certainly be considered a recession if GDP had fallen considerably. Production was in fact down significantly in the industrial sector, where the ifo business climate is derived from. Since GDP was up strongly in the services sector at the same time, overall GDP was only slightly down. However, an important reservation is in place here. GDP figures in the services sector can be calculated from hard data only with a time lag of three years. So currently, for 1995 and 1996 the service sector GDP is mostly based on estimates, such as assumptions about productivity in the services sector. The presumption, that the extreme divergence between industrial and services sector production is partly due to an overestimate in the latter sector cannot wholly be dismissed. An overestimate of the services sector GDP would lead to very high inventory investment figures, since inventory investment is the difference between GDP calculated as the sum of net production on the one hand and the sum of all demand components ex inventory investment on the other hand. The function of inventory investment

[2] Compare Monatsberichte der Bundesbank, Saisonbereinigte Wirtschaftszahlen, before July of 1997 and after.

in the calculation of GDP is precisely to make GDP calculated as the sum of net production and GDP calculated as the sum of all demand components the same.

Inventory investment typically rises and falls with GDP. Seasonally adjusted inventory investment as calculated by the Bundesbank was DM 22 bn in 1995 and DM 20 bn in 1996. This was exceeded only once in the history of West Germany. In the middle of the eighties, when GDP growth was on average as weak as between 1995 and 1997, annual inventory investment was close to zero. The near-record inventory investment in 1995 and 1996 is hard to explain given just in time production. This suggests that service sector and therefore total GDP in 1995 and 1996 is overestimated by official data. This supports the above arguments that Germany was in fact in a recession in 1995/96 and that the Bayesian predictions were correct.

References

1. Anderson, L.C. (1966). A Method of Using Diffusion Indexes to Indicate the Direction of National Economic Activity.*Proceedings of the American Statistical Association*, 424–34.
2. Chaffin, W. W. and Talley, W. K. (1974). Diffusion Indexes and Indifference Bands. *Proceedings of the American Statistical Association*, 408–11.
3. Diebold, F. X. and Rudebusch, G. D. (1991). Turning point prediction with the composite leading index: An ex ante analysis. in Lahiri K. and Moore G.(Eds.), *Leading Economic Indicators*, Cambridge University Press.
4. Hymans, S. H. (1973). On the Use of Leading Indicators to Predict Cyclical Turning Points.*Brookings Papers on Economic Activity.* **2**, 339–84.
5. McCulloch, J. H. (1975). The Monte Carlo-Cycle in Business Activity. *Economic Inquiry.* **13**, 303–21.
6. Neftci, S. N. (1982) Optimal Prediction of Cyclical Downturns.*Journal of Economic Dynamics and Control.* **4**, 225–41.
7. Stekler, H. O. (1991). Turning Point Predictions, errors, and forecasting Procedures, in Lahiri und Moore (eds.), *Leading Economic Indicators*, Cambridge University Press.
8. Vaccara, B. N. and Zarnowitz, V. (1977). How Good Are the Leading Indicators? *Proceedings of the Business and Economic Statistics Section, American Statistical Association*, 41-50.
9. Zarnowitz, V. and Moore, G. (1982). Sequential Signals of Recession and Recovery., *Journal of Business.* **55**, 57–85.

Regression Approaches to Rental Guides

Ludwig Fahrmeir, Christian Gieger, and Artur Klinger

Department of Statistics, Ludwig-Maximilians-Universität München, Germany

Summary. Rental guides have to provide information about "usual" rents that are paid for flats comparable in type, size, equipment, quality and location. At least in larger cities, traditional cross–classification tables have serious drawbacks. Model–based techniques of regression analysis with rent as the dependent variable are obvious alternatives in this situation. The statistician has to build a regression model that is simple, robust and easily interpretable, but also complex enough to reflect reality. In this paper, we first discuss some parametric regression approaches, including a model that has been used for the Munich'94 rental guide. We then proceed to semiparametric alternatives that are useful at least for exploratory data analysis and for the selection of adequate parametric models.

1. Introduction: Rental guides

According to the German rental law "Gesetz zur Regelung der Miethöhe (MHG)", owners of apartments or flats can base an increase in the amount that they charge for rent on the "usual rents" ("übliche Entgelte") for flats comparable in type, size, equipment, quality and location in a community. In principle, these usual rents may be justified from the rents of at least three comparable flats selected by the owner. Commonly however, they are either estimated by an official expert opinion or calculated from an official rental guide ("Mietspiegel"). Most major cities and many larger communities regularly conduct surveys of rental amounts paid by flat tenants and publish rental guides that are used in consulting and - typically, but not always - in civil court cases. These rental guides usually contain tables of "average" rents, depending on floor space, age, location and some indicators for equipment and quality. Here, the term "average" usually stands for "arithmetic mean" or "median".

Classical rental tables ("Tabellenmietspiegel") are standard cross-classification tables containing average rents cross–classified by appropriately categorized floor space and age as well as a few indicators of location and equipment. An apparent disadvantage of such classical rental tables is the following: At least for communities with a relatively differentiated, inhomogeneous market for rented flats, it will be reasonable to incorporate more covariates characterizing the flat and explaining part of the variation of rents. However, even for a moderate number of additional covariates this will result in many cells with only few or no observations.

Therefore, more recently, regression analysis has been applied to develop rental guides ("Regressionsmietspiegel") that allow to incorporate a larger number of covariates as predictors of rents. However, this advantage does not come free: For each choice of a specific regression model, e.g. linear, additive, nonparametrical etc., more or less stringent assumptions have to be made and need to be checked in each application.

It is now generally accepted that naive application of standard linear regression is not appropriate. This does not imply, however, that classical rental tables are the only and better alternative. On the contrary, analysis of rent data offers interesting and challenging opportunities for applied econometricians and statisticians to explore and further develop more advanced, non-standard regression models. Although we do not want to continue the seemingly endless discussion on cross-classification tables versus regression analysis, we would like to remark that the former can be seen as a very simple, yet not the best tool of nonparametric regression: in Tukey's terminology they are regressograms.

In this paper, we first describe parametric approaches, including a multiplicative-additive regression model that has been chosen for the Munich rental guide'94 (see Fahrmeir, Gieger, Mathes and Schneeweiß, 1994). It is a slight modification of the original model proposed by Aigner, Oberhofer and Schmidt (1993). In the next sections, we outline some semiparametric alternatives that are useful to check models and to explore other possibilities of parsimoniously parametrized nonlinear models. All empirical analysis are based on a subsample of the original data set from the Munich rental survey and on a subset of covariates selected from the official Munich rental guide'94. Therefore, our empirical results should be interpreted merely as illustrations of modelling aspects, not as a serious and realistic alternative to the official guide.

2. The Munich rental guide '94: data and regression models

2.1 Data

For the survey, conducted in April 1993 by Infratest Sozialforschung, a random sample from flats in Munich was drawn. It included single rooms, small apartments, flats and two–family houses with new tenancy agreements or raising of rents within the last four years. One–family houses, special types such as penthouses, and price–controlled rents were excluded. Interviewed tenants were asked questions on almost 200 basic variables like

- monthly rent paid by the tenant,
- utility costs, such as water and sewage, heating, garbage collection, elevator, cable hook–up,
- floor space of the flat,
- age of the building = year of construction,

- indicators of the quality of the building, such as washing machine, dryer, party room, sauna, swimming pool, play ground,
- indicators of equipment, such as central heating system, bathroom with shower, two washbasins and walls tiled, kitchen with sink only or with gas or electric oven, microwave, refrigerator, airvent.

Although exact addresses were removed from the files, additional information about the location in the city, including next public traffic access, larger parks, arterial roads, traffic conditions, was available.

Details about the survey, the questionnaire and also about calculation of utility costs can be found in Alles and Guder (1994).

This basic information was used to calculate and derive variables that were used for regression modelling. As response variable of interest we chose

R the monthly **net** rent in DM, that is the monthly rent minus calculated or estimated utility costs.

Another choice for the response variable would have been the monthly net rent per square meter. It turned out, however that regression models for R are easier to handle.

The most influential predictors are

F floor space in square meters, and
A age, that is year of construction.

Many other predictors were derived from basic variables in the questionnaire, including for example

S^+ 0/1 indicator of location ("site") above average,
S^- 0/1 indicator of location ("site") below average,
T 0/1 indicator for top location,
H 0/1 no central heating indicator,
B 0/1 no bathroom indicator,
L 0/1 indicator of bathroom equipment above average,
K 0/1 indicator of kitchen equipment above average,
G 0/1 indicator of floor plan above average,
R 0/1 indicator of fundamental renovation.

Together with some interaction variables, 24 covariates were used in the final analysis. For more details about predictors we refer to Fahrmeir, Gieger, Mathes and Schneeweiß (1994) and to the official rental guide, available from the Sozialreferat of the City of Munich.

2.2 Parametric regression models

For a concrete but simplified presentation, we consider only a smaller subset of covariates, namely the two metrical covariates floor space F, age A and the binary factors S^+, S^-, H, B and L.

A naive standard linear regression model $R = \eta + \varepsilon$ with additive predictor

$$\eta = \beta_0 + \beta_1 F + \beta_2 A + \beta_3 S^+ + \beta_4 S^- + \beta_5 H + \beta_6 B + \beta_7 L \quad (2.1)$$

will not be appropriate for several reasons. Most important is the specification of the predictor η, that is the mean of R given the covariates: First, modelling the influence of the metrical covariates floor space F and age A as simple linear functions is rather questionable. Instead, some nonlinear function $\beta_0(F)$ resp. $\beta_2(A)$, such as a low–order (piecewise) polynomial, will be reasonable. Secondly, if we consider $\beta_0 + \beta_1 F$ or some function $\beta_0(F)$ as the basic rent, then the remaining factors will cause the same global reduction or surcharge on this basic rent, regardless of floor space. For example, a positive effect β_3 of S^+ will imply the same surcharge of DM β_3 on the basic rent for a small apartment and for a big flat. This is obviously unrealistic. Instead, a predictor incorporating interactions with floor space, such as $F \cdot S^+$, might be more plausible. Specifying a predictor with interactions of the form

$$\eta = \beta_0(F) + F\beta_2(A) + \beta_3 FS^+ + \beta_4 FS^- + \beta_5 FH + \beta_6 FB + \beta_7 FL, \quad (2.2)$$

a positive effect of β_3 will now be the surcharge for good location on the rent **per square meter**. This is seen immediately by dividing (2.2) through F. Although model (2.2) seems more adequate it remains unclear whether the simple linear form of multiplicative interactions with floor space F is adequate for all effects. Also, it may be reasonable to include additional main effects as in model (2.1) that have an influence on rent R, independent of floor space F. We will explore and discuss this with a semiparametric approach in Section 3.

A second basic property of the standard model is the assumption of homogeneous error variances. A look at the scatterplot in Figure 2.1 shows that variances clearly increase with floor space. Obviously, this problem has to be addressed to, for example by some kind of weighted least squares or modelling variances as a function of floor space.

Another issue is the distribution of the net rent R, given the covariates. It has nonnegative support and is skewed, thus implying nonnormality. Exploratory data analysis shows that skewness is moderate. Since the sample size is large, one may therefore rely on asymptotic distributions of test statistics if mean and variance are specified correctly. If the distribution of R is of interest in its own, for example to calculate quantiles for prediction ("2/3–Spannen"), then this modelling aspect can also be important. We come back to this issue in Section 3.

For the Munich rental guide, we chose a parametrical model that addresses the first two issues in a parsimonious way and has been successfully applied in slightly modified form for rental guides in other cities ("Regensburger Modell"; Aigner, Oberhofer and Schmidt, 1993). With the covariates selected here for illustrative purposes it has multiplicative–additive form:

$$R = \beta_0(F)(1 + \beta_2(A) + \beta_3 S^+ + \beta_4 S^- + \beta_5 H + \beta_6 B + \beta_7 L + \varepsilon). \quad (2.3)$$

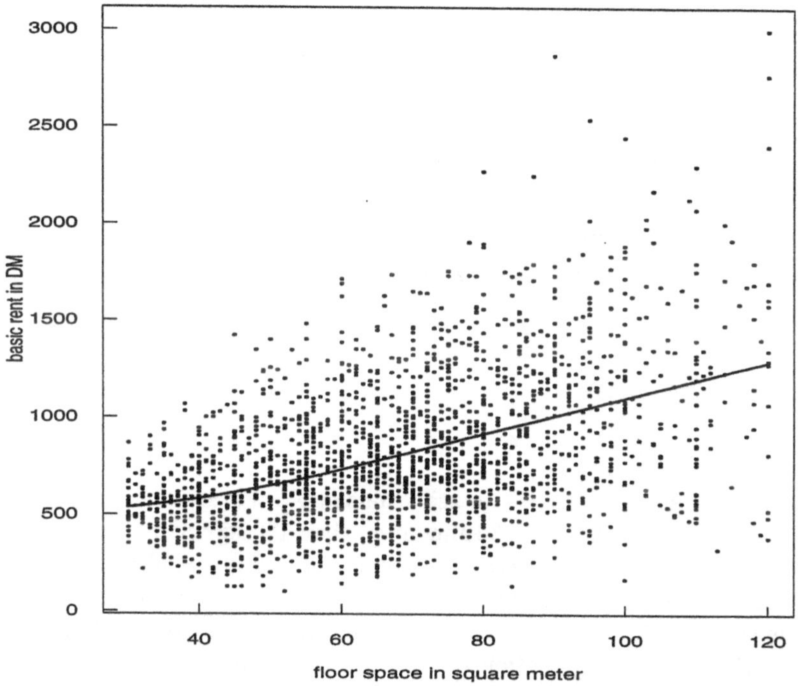

Fig. 2.1. Scatterplot of basic rent versus floor space, together with weighted least squares fit of the quadratic–linear model for $\beta_0(F)$.

The first factor $\beta_0(F)$, the "basic rent", is a - generally nonlinear - function of floor space F. A low order regression spline with a small number of knots is a flexible yet parsimonious choice. For the Munich rental guide a quadratic–linear form

$$\beta_0(F) = \alpha_0 + \alpha_1 F + \alpha_2 (c - F)_+^2, \tag{2.4}$$

with one knot or cutpoint $c = 60$ m^2 turned out to be adequate. The second factor is additive and implies percental reductions or surcharge. For example, an indicator $S^+ = 1$ of good location implies a surcharge of $\beta_3 \cdot 100\%$ on rent.

Estimation is carried out by a two step weighted least squares procedure, without assuming a specific model for the distribution of R.

Step 1 estimates the basic rent $\beta_0(F)$ by applying a two–phase weighted least squares procedure (Carroll and Ruppert, 1988, ch.2) to the heteroscedastic regression model

$$R = \alpha_0 + \alpha_1 F + \alpha_2 (c - F)_+^2 + r.$$

Phase I calculates residuals $\hat{r}$ from an unweighted least squares fit and then determines least squares estimates $\hat{\gamma}_0$, $\hat{\gamma}_1$ for the regression

$$|\hat{r}| = \gamma_0 + \gamma_1 F + \delta$$

of absolute residuals on floor space.

In phase II, the basic rent is fitted by

$$\hat{\beta}_0(F) = \hat{\alpha}_0 + \hat{\alpha}_1 F + \hat{\alpha}_2 (c - F)^2_+,$$

where $\hat{\alpha}_0$, $\hat{\alpha}_1$, $\hat{\alpha}_2$ are weighted least squares estimates for model (2.4), with weights

$$w_i = (\hat{\gamma}_0 + \hat{\gamma}_1 F_i)^{-2}, \qquad i = 1, \ldots, n.$$

Step 2 fits the second factor in (2.3) by applying unweighted least squares to

$$R/\hat{\beta}_0(F) = 1 + \beta_2(A) + \beta_3 S^+ + \beta_4 S^- + \beta_5 H + \beta_6 B + \beta_7 L + \varepsilon.$$

The estimated predictor for average rents is then

$$\hat{R} = \hat{\beta}_0(F)(1 + \hat{\beta}_2(A) + \hat{\beta}_3 S^+ + \hat{\beta}_4 S^- + \hat{\beta}_5 H + \hat{\beta}_6 B + \hat{\beta}_7 L).$$

For an illustrative reanalysis we use a subsample of size 1969, excluding flats with floor space smaller than 30 and larger than 120 square meters and year of construction before 1890 and after 1989. Results of the empirical analysis for the full data and covariate set are described in Fahrmeir, Gieger, Mathes and Schneeweiß (1994). As in that work, we specify the function $\beta_2(A)$ by $\beta_2 \tilde{A}$, where $\tilde{A}$ is a smooth function of A. For the multiplicative–additive model (2.3) with the quadratic–linear specification (2.4) for the function $\beta_0(F)$ we obtain the following estimates:

Basic Rent				
	Value	Std. Error	t–value	p–value
Intercept	174.8542	37.1806	4.7028	0.0000
F	9.2704	0.5361	17.2923	0.0000
$(c-F)^2_+$	0.0925	0.0361	2.5619	0.0105
Percental Reduction or Surcharge				
	Value	Std. Error	t–value	p–value
Intercept	1.0000	0.0117	85.4586	0.0000
$\tilde{A}$	0.7512	0.0662	11.3408	0.0000
S^+	0.0768	0.0182	4.2313	0.0000
S^-	-0.1709	0.0286	-5.9715	0.0000
B	-0.1994	0.0553	-3.6046	0.0003
H	-0.2093	0.0215	-9.7166	0.0000
L	0.1428	0.0291	4.9029	0.0000

Results and interpretations are as expected. The estimated effect of basic rent, plotted in Figure 2.1, is quite close to the corresponding estimate in the official rental guide. Reductions and surcharges have the same sign as in the rental guide. However, their absolute values are greater because a number of influential variables have been omitted in the present analysis.

3. Semiparametric regression models

Semiparametric approaches to regression analysis replace one or more of the parametric components by some nonparametric alternative. They allow to relax underlying assumptions, to check existing models and to explore possibilities for modified but still parsimonious and comparably simple parametric models. The focus in Section 3.1 is on modelling and fitting certain semiparametric forms of the predictor, still regarding the rent as the dependent variable. Section 3.2 deals with the aspect of transformation, that is how to transform the original dependent variable in order to obtain symmetrization and variance stabilization.

3.1 Varying coefficient models

Multiplying out model (2.3) and omitting interaction terms involving $\alpha_2(c-F)_+^2$, that are negligible compared to the remaining effects, we obtain a predictor of the form

$$\begin{aligned}\eta = \beta_0(F) + \alpha_0\beta_2(A) + \alpha_1 F\beta_2(A) + \alpha_0\beta_3 S^+ + \alpha_1 F\beta_3 S^+ \\ +\alpha_0\beta_4 S^- + \alpha_1 F\beta_4 S^- + \alpha_0\beta_5 H + \alpha_1 F\beta_5 H \\ +\alpha_0\beta_6 B + \alpha_1 F\beta_6 B + \alpha_0\beta_7 L + \alpha_1 F\beta_7 L. \end{aligned} \quad (3.1)$$

It incorporates main effects and interactions with floor space, but with a very specific parametrization. For example, the **same** function $\beta_2(A)$ is used to model the main effect of age A and its interaction with floor space. Although there are some economic arguments leading to the multiplicative-additive model, we want to explore the adequacy of a specific parametrization such as in (3.1). To this end, the predictor (3.1) is generalized to the semiparametric predictor

$$\begin{aligned}\eta &= \beta_0(F) + \beta_1(A) + F\beta_2(A) + \beta_3(F)S^+ + \beta_4(F)S^- \\ &\quad +\beta_5(F)H + \beta_6(F)B + \beta_7(F)L.\end{aligned}$$

In this "varying coefficient model" (Hastie and Tibshirani, 1993), the unknown functions $\beta_0(F)$, $\beta_1(A)$, $\beta_2(A)$ etc. are modeled and estimated nonparametrically. No specific parametric form, only some kind of smoothness has to be assumed. In Fahrmeir, Gieger and Klinger (1995), the functions were estimated by cubic smoothing splines, based on a weighted penalized least squares criterion that accounts for the problem of heteroscedasticity.

The following semiparametric analysis differs from this work with respect to two aspects. First, to account for skewness, we assume a Gamma distribution for R in the model $R = \eta + \varepsilon$. By the properties of the Gamma distribution, this implies Var $\varepsilon = v^2\eta^2$ with v as the coefficient of variation. Thus, the Gamma model simultaneously takes into account skewness and heteroscedasticity. The assumption of a Gamma distribution is also supported by the transformation analysis in Section 3.2. Secondly, modelling and estimation of the unknown functions in (3.2) is different.

The semiparametric approach is based on Klinger (1997). There, an adaptively selected low rank approximation to spline smoothing called "generalized soft–thresholding" is introduced. One advantage of this basis function approach over more conventional smoothing techniques is that each varying coefficient can explicitly be separated into linear and nonlinear parts. This separation is particularly useful to ensure identifiability for varying coefficient models. For the predictor (3.2) we restrict the coefficients $\beta_1(A)$ and $\beta_2(A)$ to have sample mean zero by dropping constant terms from the set of basis functions used. Due to the economical description of the results in terms of basis functions, further characteristics, like the correlation between nonlinear parts of the estimates can be studied. To account for the prediction of the net rent as the actual target of analysis, the degree of smoothness was determined by 50–fold cross validation of the Kullback–Leibler distance. This means, that the data was randomly divided into 50 partitions of equal size. Then, the net rent for each flat in one particular partition was predicted using information from the flats in the remaining 49 partitions. Results are plotted in Figure 3.1. The figures include 95% pointwise confidence intervals, which are drawn around a bias corrected estimate of the varying effects. See Klinger (1997) for details.

For comparison, we also consider a parametric model, where the functions $\beta_0(F)$, $\beta_1(A)$ and $\beta_2(A)$ are quadratic–linear regression splines as in (2.4), with cutpoints at $F = 60$ and $A = 1950$ respectively, and the remaining effects $\beta_3(F)$ to $\beta_7(F)$ are linear functions of F. Compared to (3.1), this model does not put additional restrictions on the coefficients.

The model is fitted by unweighted and weighted least squares, as described in Section (2.2), as well as by maximum likelihood, assuming a Gamma distribution for R. The latter approach corresponds to fitting a generalized linear model with Gamma distribution and identity link. The estimated functions are plotted in Figure 3.2.

In Figure 3.1, the effect $\beta_0(F)$ of basic rent and the interaction effects $\beta_3(F)$ resp. $\beta_7(F)$ with S^+ and L are almost linear. Corresponding plots in Figure 3.2 are in good agreement within confidence bands and all three parametric fits are quite near to each other. Also, interpretation is as expected. Things are not so clear with the remaining effects. The main effect $\beta_1(A)$ of age in Figure 3.1 indicates a rent reduction for flats constructed in the post–war era followed by a steep ascent afterwards. A similar pattern appears in Figure 3.2. The unweighted least squares estimate and the maximum likelihood estimate for the Gamma model are quite close to each other and in good agreement with the nonparametric estimate in Figure 3.1, while the weighted least squares estimate shows less curvature. For the interaction effect $\beta_2(A)$ with floor space F, the nonparametric and parametric estimates

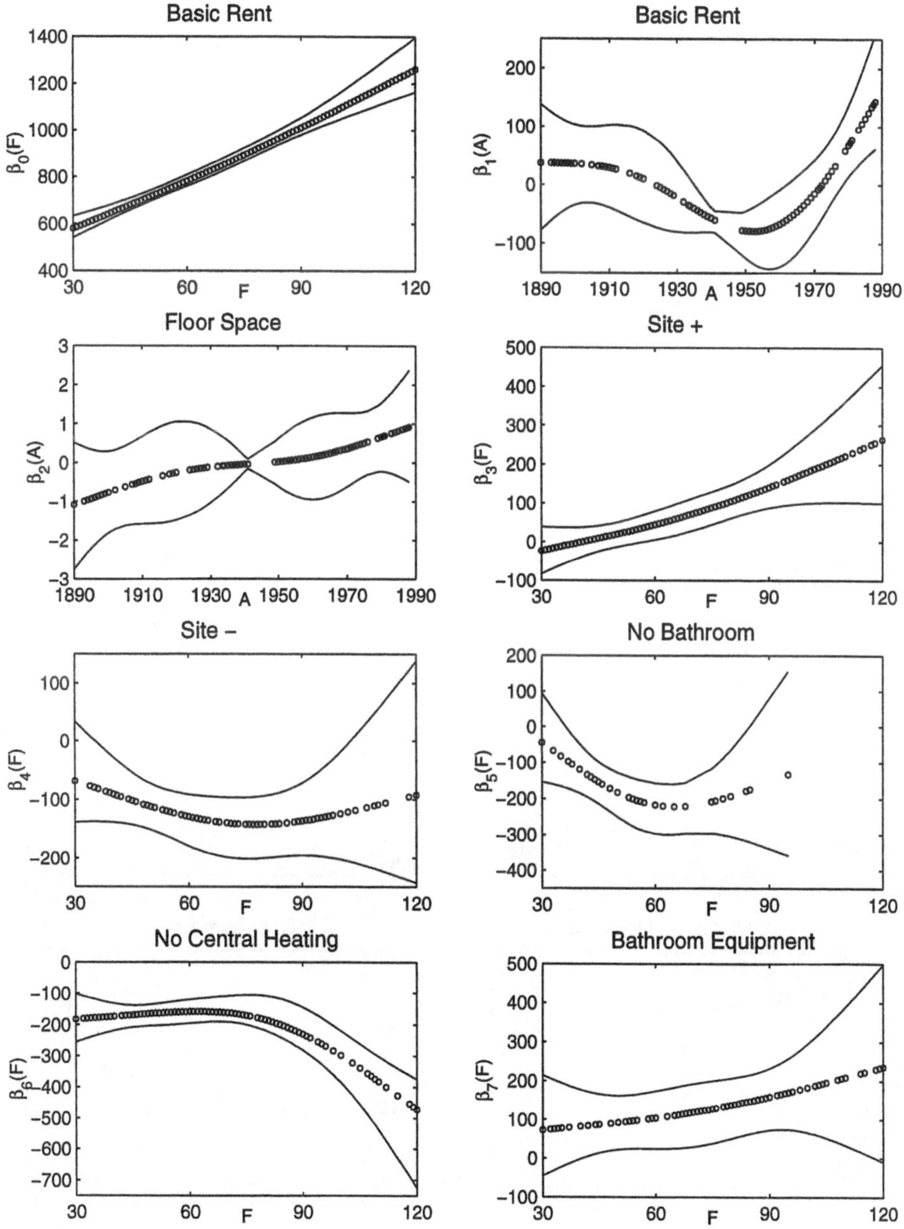

Fig. 3.1. Estimated varying coefficients for the Gamma model, together with bias corrected pointwise 95 % confidence bands

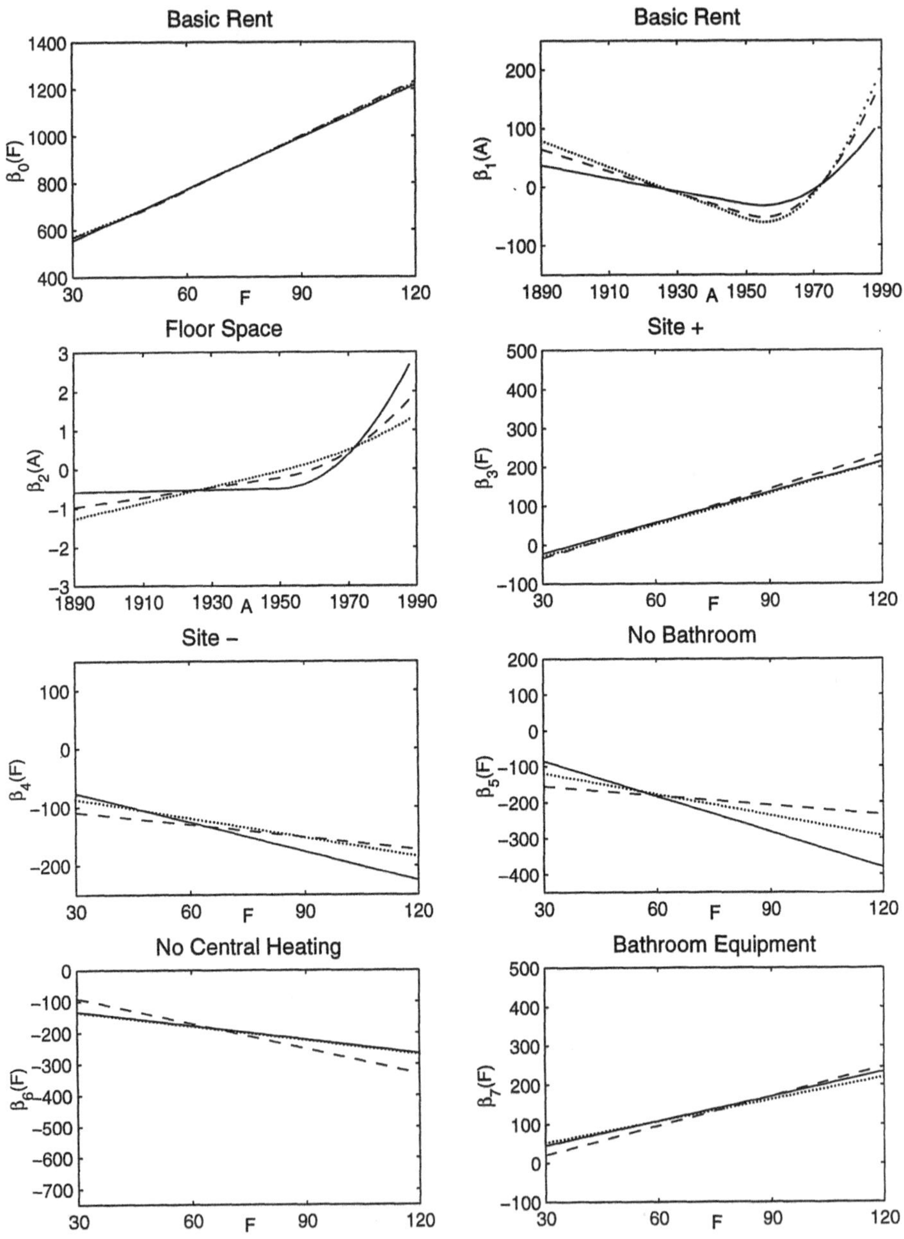

Fig. 3.2. Estimated coefficients from the parametrical model. Results are based on unweighted least squares (- - -) and weighted least squares (—) estimation and on a linear Gamma model (···)

for the Gamma model are in reasonable agreement. However, the weighted least squares estimate now shows more curvature. Further experiments with varying smoothness parameters or knot selections showed that the effects of age are quite sensitive to model specification. One possible explanation is high correlation between main and interaction effects. Obviously, specification of the influence of age is critical and deserves careful consideration. Another reason might be the different form of the variance function. For the weighted least squares estimate, the variance function is of the form $(\gamma_0 + \gamma_1 F)^2$, while the variance function η^2 of the Gamma model also includes the effect of age as well as other covariates. It appears that modelling of heteroscedasticity is an important aspect and that additional work is needed here. The effects of site below average (S^-) and no bathroom (B) in Figure 3.1 look reasonable up to floor spaces of about 70 m^2. Within this range, the corresponding linear approximations in Figure 3.2 are not overwhelming but still reasonable. The increase in Figure 3.1 for higher floor space seems to be counterintuitive. A look at the confidence bands tells that one should be cautious here. For example, the increase of $\beta_5(F)$ is mainly caused by one big flat without bathroom. Maybe this was simply a coding error! It is also remarkable that differences between various parametric estimates in Figure 3.2 become bigger here.

The absence of central heating has an interesting nonlinear effect in Figure 3.1 that cannot be uncovered be the linear counterpart in Figure 3.2: It seems that a less efficient heating system is considered as more disadvantages in bigger flats than in small ones. This plausible result would presumably not have been discovered with simple parametric approaches.

3.2 Transformation models

A conceptual different approach to deal with skewness and heteroscedasticity is to transform the dependent variable R by some function g and to base analysis on the model $g(R) = \eta + \varepsilon$. The aim is to find a transformation g that symmetrizes the distribution of the error ε and stabilizes its variance. In semiparametric transformation models, the function g as well as the unknown functions in the predictor are estimated nonparametrically. A well-known method is the ACE algorithm. Here, we use an extension of AVAS (additivity and variance stabilization; Tibshirani, 1988) to varying coefficient models. The transformation g is assumed to be smooth and strictly increasing and, for identifiability reasons, $g(R)$ is standardized, i.e. E $g(R) = 0$ and Var $g(R) = 1$. The basic idea of AVAS is that provided R has a mean u and a variance function $v(u)$ then

$$g(r) = \int^{r} 1/\sqrt{v(u)}du \tag{3.2}$$

is the asymptotic variance–stabilizing transform for R.

The main steps of the AVAS procedure are as follows:

1. Estimate the variance function $\hat{v}(u)$ by smoothing the logarithm of the absolute residuals $\log\{|\hat{g}(R_i) - \eta_i|\}$ versus R.
2. Compute the variance stabilizing transform $\hat{g}(r)$ from (3.2) based on $\hat{v}(u)$ by using numerical integration.
3. Standardize $\hat{g}(R)$ to have sample mean zero and sample variance one.
4. Fit the varying coefficient model (3.2) on this standardized transformation.

These steps iterate until convergence in $\hat{g}(R)$ and $\hat{\beta}$ is obtained. More details on the algorithm, including results on convergence are given in Tibshirani (1988).

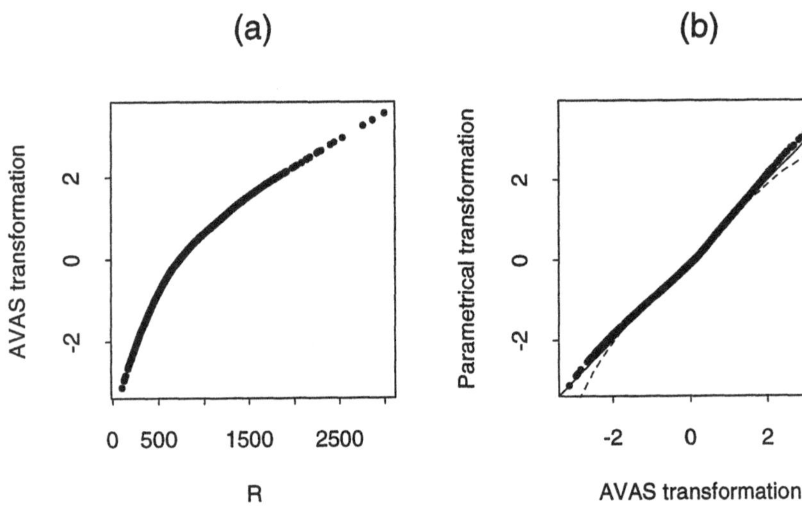

Fig. 3.3. The AVAS transform of rent is shown in (a). In (b), $\log(R)$ (- - -) and the cube–root (···) transform are drawn versus the AVAS transformation.

In Figure 3.3 (a), the resulting AVAS transformation for a varying coefficient model (3.2) is shown as a function of R. As expected, the slope of $\hat{g}(R)$ decreases monotonically with R and thus, the transformed response variable $\hat{g}(R)$ has reduced variance for higher R. Furthermore, we compared the AVAS transformation with the cube–root transform

$$g(R) = 3\{(R/\mathrm{E}(R))^{\frac{1}{3}} - 1\} \tag{3.3}$$

and with $\log(R)$ as conventional alternatives. In Figure 3.3 (b) the parametric transforms are plotted, after appropriate standardization, versus $\hat{g}(R)$. One can see, that the AVAS transform is very close to the cube–root transform, which is the accurate normalizing transformation for a Gamma–distributed random variable R. Also, the shape of the simultaneously estimated varying–coefficients from the model (3.2) are quite similar to those shown in Figure 3.1.

Transformation models target on a transformed predictor variable and therefore, they are not particularly suited for our prediction problem. Nevertheless the AVAS procedure helps to find an appropriate regression model for R. Results in Figure 3.3 strongly support the assumption of a Gamma model.

4. Conclusions

In this paper we focussed on the question: How can we build an adequate regression model? We believe that recent semiparametric techniques within the generalized linear model setting provide useful explanatory tools that can give guidance to arrive at the ultimate goal: construction of regression–based rental guides that are easy to understand, give plausible results and reflect the real market. However, we did not touch upon important problems concerning the data base: How can we draw a reliable random sample from registers with reasonable costs? How do we characterize complex variables like type, equipment, location etc. by basic indicators? How to handle non–responses and missing values? Good answers to these questions are an undispensable requirement for good data analysis and construction of rental guides.

Acknowledgement

We would like to thank Hans Schneeweiß for his guidance and experienced advice during our joint work for the Munich'94 rental guide.

References

1. Aigner, K., Oberhofer, W. and Schmidt B. (1993). Eine neue Methode zur Erstellung eines Mietspiegels am Beispiel der Stadt Regensburg. *Wohnwirtschaft und Mietrecht*, 1/2/1993, 16–20.
2. Alles, R. and Guder, R. (1994). Gutachten zur Erstellung des Mietspiegels für München 1994, Teil A: Erhebung und Berechnung der Nettomieten. Hrsg: Landeshauptstadt München, Sozialreferat - Amt für Wohnungswesen.
3. Carroll, R.J. and Ruppert, D. (1988). *Transformation and weighting in regression*. Chapman and Hall, New York.
4. Fahrmeir, L., Gieger, C. and Klinger, A. (1995). Additive, dynamic and multiplicative regression. In *Applied statistics - recent developments*. Frohn, J., Gather, U., Stute, W. and Thöni, H. (eds.). Vandenhoeck and Ruprecht, Göttingen.
5. Fahrmeir, L., Gieger, C., Mathes, H. and Schneeweiß, H. (1994). Gutachten zur Erstellung des Mietspiegels für München 1994, Teil B: Statistische Analyse der Nettomieten. Hrsg: Landeshauptstadt München, Sozialreferat - Amt für Wohnungswesen.

6. Hastie, T. and Tibshirani, R. (1993). Varying–coefficient Models. *Journal of the Royal Statistical Society*, B 55, 757–796.
7. Klinger, A. (1997). Generalized soft–thresholding and varying coefficient models. Discussion paper 59, SFB 386, München.
8. Tibshirani, R. (1988). Estimating transformations for regression via additivity and variance stabilization. *Journal of the American Statistical Association*, 83, 394–405.

An Econometric Model for the Transition Process of China's Economy

Chen Pu and Joachim Frohn

[1] China Europe International Business School (CEIBS), Shanghai, P.R. China
[2] University of Bielefeld, Germany

Summary. The Chinese economy has experienced the most striking changes in the last two decades, with a structural transition from a centrally planned economy to a market oriented economy with a growth of GNP. The economic reform was the basis for a new industrialization mechanism that is responsible for a fast growth of production, mainly outside the planned segment.

This paper presents an econometric model that can be used for an analysis of the quantitative expansion of the non-planned activities and the qualitative changes of the state-owned enterprises.

1. Introduction

The transition from a centrally planned economy to a market economy in China has attracted increasingly more attention in the world for its success, especially if one compares it with the transition crises in Eastern European countries. Many economists studied the Chinese transition process and have explained the specific features during the transition from different aspects: Perkins [18] has given a compact overview of the Chinese economic reform; Kueh [14] analysed the impact of rural reform; Byrd [3], Wu and Zhao [22] and Fang Gang [7] analysed the consequences of the two-tiers/dual system policy in the economic reform; Byrd et al. [4] discussed the development of TVEs (township village enterprises) and their impact on the whole economy; Kwok et al. [15] analysed the economic reform and its consequence on industrialization and urbanization.

All of these studies are to a very large extent qualitative descriptions and/or concentrate on a partial analysis of impacts of different policies on the economy. This study approaches the transition process quantitatively: Using empirical observations, we are analyzing the specific features of the Chinese transition process within the framework of an econometric model.

In the following section the empirical and theoretical framework for the econometric model is given. In section 3. we present this model and the results of the estimation of the parameters.

2. Theoretical Considerations

2.1 Introduction

The main features of the Chinese reform and of the development in the last 20 years are described in detail in Chen [5]. Here we can indicate only the most important points.

There are a number of main reforms that have strongly influenced the transition process of the Chinese economy:

- the rural reform composed of the decollectivization (household responsibility system) and the release of the market for agricultural products;
- the price reform that started with the introduction of a dual price system and was followed by an almost total abandonment of the price control;
- the reform of the financial system through transformation of the profit-transfer into taxation;
- the replacement of subsidies through bank loans;
- the reform of state-owned enterprises aiming at the transformation of the management mechanism.

Contrary to other countries where the government tried to change the economic system by the implementation of many drastic measures at one point of time, the economic reform in China followed a strategy of small steps. A complete elimination of the planned economy was not the ultimate goal. By contrast, the government tried to introduce market activities into the economy and promoted them, while keeping the planned economy functioning as before. It was a gradual process rather than an implementation of a complete blue print.

In order to depict this gradual development of a market section in the Chinese economy, while the planned section - at least in part - stayed in existence, the production part of the model has to be partitioned into a market and a planned segment (with the SOEs (state-owned-enterprises)). As there are considerable differences between the economic situation in rural and urban areas these two areas also had to be distinguished. Finally, the main political measures of the Chinese government, which had been undertaken to foster the reform, had to be implemented in the model.

2.2 The Basic Structure of the Model

2.2.1 The Supply-Side. As in many econometric models, the gross national product is the starting point for the specification of the model. GDP (X_t) consists of the industrial production in both the planned segment (X_{IPt}) and the market segment (X_{IMt}), and the agricultural production (X_{AMt}). Hence, we have[1]:

[1] Since the rural reform was organised on family-basis, we assume that the agricultural production is carried out only in the market segment. A list of variables and their definitions is given in the appendix.

$$X_t = X_{IPt} + X_{IMt} + X_{AMt}.$$

The subindex P denotes the planned segment, M the market segment, I the industrial sector and A the agricultural sector. The final demand of GNP can be divided into personal consumption (C_t), investment (I_t) , the public consumption (G_t), and the net export ($Ex_t - Im_t$):

$$X_t = C_t + I_t + G_t + Ex_t - Im_t$$

Production. We assume CES production functions (with L: labour, K: capital) for both segments:

$$X_{IPt} = F(L_{IPt}, K_{IPt-1}) = e^{\gamma P}\left(\delta_P K_{IPt-1}^{-\rho P} + (1-\delta_P) L_{IPt}^{-\rho P}\right)^{-\frac{\nu_P}{\rho_P}}$$

and

$$X_{IMt} = F(L_{IMt}, K_{IMt-1}) = e^{\gamma M}\left(\delta_M K_{IMt-1}^{-\rho M} + (1-\delta_M) L_{IMt}^{-\rho M}\right)^{-\frac{\nu_M}{\rho_M}}.$$

The technological and institutional differences between the two segments can then be expressed by different values of the parameters in these functions. Due to the flexibility and higher efficiency in the market segment, the elasticity of substitution, the returns to scale and technical progress are expected to be larger in the market segment than in the planned segment.

Because there are no reliable data for the labour input and capital input, we use the indirect form for the agricultural production, in which the factor inputs are themselves functions of the relative prices:

$$X_{AMt} = F\left(L_{AMt}\left(\frac{w_{AMt}}{p_{AMt}}\right), K_{AMt}\left(\frac{P_t}{p_{AMt}}\right)\right)$$

Factor Demand. Considering the special situation during the transition period in China, where labour surplus prevailed, we assume that the available capital is always completely utilized. The labour input in the industrial production in the market segment is determined through the marginal value of production. Therefore, we can derive the following labour demand functions:

$$L_{IMt} = L(K_{IMt}, w_{IMt}/p_{IMt})$$

The employment policy in the centrally planned segment (expressed directly by the labour demand of SOEs) seems to differ from the one in the market economy: It is supposed to pursue, at least in principle, full employment. However, there is strong evidence that in China the costs of labour have played an important role in the determination of labour demand in SOEs, too. Therefore, we use the same form of the labour demand function for the planned segment:

$$L_{IPt} = L(K_{IPt}, w_{IPt}/p_{IPt})$$

Incomes. The total income from production is divided into: labour income (LI) and capital income (CI). Labour income is equal to the product of wage rate (w) times labour input (L):

$$\begin{aligned} p_{IPt}X_{IPt} &= CI_{IPt} + LI_{IPt} \quad \text{with:} \quad LI_{IPt} = w_{IPt}L_{IPt}, \\ p_{IMt}X_{IMt} &= CI_{IMt} + LI_{IMt} \quad \text{with:} \quad LI_{IMt} = w_{IMt}L_{IMt}. \end{aligned}$$

Capital income (CI) is used for tax (T), interest payment (RI), dividend (DIV) which is redistributed to share holders, and business income (BI) which is kept in the companies:

$$\begin{aligned} CI_{IPt} &= T_{IPt} + RI_{IPt} + BI_{IPt}, \\ CI_{IMt} &= T_{IMt} + RI_{IMt} + DIV_{IMt} + BI_{IMt}. \end{aligned}$$

DIV_{IPt} is equal to zero, because in the planned segment the property right belongs to the state.

In the agricultural area we do not distinguish between labour income and capital income, as the production is mainly based on farmer households in which these two kinds of incomes cannot be identified. So farmer income (FI) is given by:

$$p_{AMt}X_{AMt} = FI_t + T_{AMt}.$$

Personal income (PI) is the sum of labour income, interest earnings and dividend plus farmer income (FI):

$$PI_t = LI_{IMt} + LI_{IPt} + RI_{IMt} + RI_{IPt} + DIV_{IMt} + FI_t.$$

Thus the total income from production consists of personal income, tax, and business income:

$$P_tX_t = PI_t + BI_t + T_t.$$

2.2.2 The Demand-Side

Investment. Investment-funds ($INVS$) in the two segments had to be treated separately, in order to identify the transition process explicitly. We assume that the availability of financial sources will restrict investment demand in the two segments. In official Chinese statistics, the sources of investment funds are divided into four groups: fund raising (FDR), government appropriation ($INVG$), domestic loans ($BKLOAN$) and foreign investment ($INVF$):

$$\begin{aligned} INVS_{IPt} &= FDR_{IPt} + INVG_{IPt} + BKLOAN_{IPt} + INVF_{IPt}, \\ INVS_{IMt} &= FDR_{IMt} + INVG_{IMt} + BKLOAN_{IMt} + INVF_{IMt}. \end{aligned}$$

The Financial sector. The reform of the financial sector is still in an early stage of development, as the state-owned banks still have a monopoly position through institutional regulations. The banks collect savings from households and enterprises and offer them to producers as bank loans. The determinants of the volume of bank loans are therefore personal savings, the interest rate, and the issuance of money. We model the volume of bank loans as a linear function of changes in personal savings (ΔS) and the supply of money ($\Delta M1$):

$$BKLOAN_t = F(\Delta S_t, \Delta M1_t).$$

As there is no competition, the market force does not play a significant role in the distribution of bank loans. By contrast, bank loans have become a main political instrument of the government to support SOEs. Thus the distribution of bank loans between the producers in the planned segment and the market segment has to be regarded as a matter of political intention and of economic interest. We try to approximate this through:

$$BKLOAN_{IPt} = F(BKLOAN_t, \tilde{\rho}_t)$$

with $\tilde{\rho}_t$ the production share of the planned segment. The coefficient of $\tilde{\rho}_t$ t will then indicate the political preference of the government for the SOEs as far as financial support is concerned. Fund raising is endogenized through a linear function with business income as explanatory variable:

$$FDR_t = F(BI_t).$$

For the growth of production, only the productive investment (investment in equipment and non-residential structure) *NIPRD* is relevant. We use a linear function to fit the relation between total investment and productive investment. Real productive investment can be calculated through deflating nominal investment:

$$I_{IPt} = \frac{NIPRD_{IPt}}{P_t^I} \qquad \text{and} \quad I_{IMt} = \frac{NIPRD_{IMt}}{P_t^I}.$$

Capital accumulation in both segments can be calculated as the sum of the level in the previous period minus depreciation (D) plus real investment:

$$K_{IPt} = K_{IPt-1} + I_{IPt} - D_{IPt-1}$$

and

$$K_{IMt} = K_{IMt-1} + I_{IMt} - D_{IMt-1}.$$

Consumption. Following classical assumptions about consumption behaviour, we model the demand for personal consumption as a function of real personal income and the price of consumption:

$$C_t = C_t(PI_t/P_t^C, P_t^C).$$

We treat consumption in rural areas and urban areas separately to account for the difference between rural and urban income. As the price of agricultural products influences the income and the consumption of farmer households to a great extend in the same way, we model the consumption in rural areas in nominal terms, which is assumed to depend on the personal income in rural areas (PI_{Rt}):

$$\begin{aligned} C_t &= C_{Rt} + C_{Ut}, \\ NC_{Rt} &= NC_{Rt}(PI_{Rt}). \end{aligned}$$

2.2.3 Prices

Commodity Prices. There are five implicit price deflators in the model: for industrial products in the market segment and planned segment; for agricultural products; for investment goods and consumer goods. The market price in the market segment adjusts supply and demand and keeps them in equilibrium. Because the supply in this segment depends on the production, and demand comes from both the planned and the market segment, the equilibrium price is expected to be dependent on the ratio of shares of the two segments in the economy. Furthermore, the issuance of money will strongly influence the level of the inflation. Hence, we have:

$$p_{IMt} = F\left(\rho_t, \frac{M1_t}{X_t}\right).$$

On one side, the price for the industrial products in the planned segment can be considered as an instrument of the central planners and therefore has to be treated as an exogenous variable. On the other hand, the price reform policy has continuously reduced the range of price control and increased the remaining planned prices to reduce its difference to the market price. Thus we use an adaptive adjustment process as approximation:

$$p_{IPt} = \lambda p_{IPt-1} + (1-\lambda) p_{IMt-1}.$$

The average price of industrial products is given by:

$$p_{It} = \frac{p_{IMt} X_{IMt} + p_{IPt} X_{IPt}}{X_{IMt} + X_{IPt}}.$$

The price of the agricultural product is modelled as a function of the average wage rate:

$$p_{AMt} = F(w_t).$$

The price of consumer products can be approximated by a linear combination of the price for agricultural products and of the average price for industrial products:

$$P_t^C = \alpha p_{It} + \beta p_{AMt}.$$

For the price of investment products we assume that it depends on the average price of industrial products and the changes in inventory stocks:

$$P_t^I = F(P_{It}, \Delta STOCKS_t).$$

Wage determination. The determination of the wage rate in the planned segment originally was a matter of government control. However, the enterprises gained more flexibility through increases of bonuses. From 1978 to 1994 the share of bonus was increased from 14.5% to 50%. So, actually central planning did not play a very decisive role in the wage determination.

Thus we treat the wage rate as an endogenous variable that is determined by the decision-makers of SOEs. According to empirical observation, we assume that the decision on the wage rate is done in favour of the workers of SOEs, i.e. the real wage can grow at a positive rate even if the business income will decrease:

$$\ln\left(w_{IPt}/P_t^C\right) = a + \beta t.$$

The wage in the market segment differs from that in the planned segment. The determinant of the market wage rate followed market principles. Following neo-classic theory, in an economy with labour surplus the wage rate will be fixed at a minimum level until the labour surplus is exhausted. However, if we consider that the workers of non-state-owned-enterprises (NSOEs) come mainly from rural families, this minimum level must be above the opportunity income level (income of farmers), otherwise farmers would not be willing to work for NSOEs. Given the growth of farmers' income the wage rate in the market segment has to grow at least at the same rate as farmers' income. We assume that real wage in the market segment will grow at the rate of productivity changes:

$$w_{IMt}/p_{IMt} = \alpha + \beta(X_{IMt}/L_{IMt}) \qquad \text{with:} \quad w_{IMt} > w_{AMt}.$$

2.2.4 The Government. The government is modelled by its main economic activities: Collection of tax as source of government's income, monetary policy through the issuance of currency, and public spending. Considering the taxation situation in China, where the wage income of individuals is mostly well below the taxation limit, we assume that tax is only imposed on business income. Tax is levied on three kinds of business income: enterprises in the planned segment and in the market segment, and farmers.

Public consumption and investment are not endogenously modelled but assumed as exogenous. Fiscal policy can be modelled exogenously through changing the tax rate, borrowing from domestic and foreign banks, and through changes of government expenditure. The same assumptions holds for the determination of money supply *M1*.

3. The Econometric Model and Estimation of Parameters

3.1 Introduction

On the basis of the theoretical considerations an econometric model was specified. In almost all cases the economic assumption from 2.2 were directly transformed into econometric equations without major adjustments and without adding additional explanatory variables, as it was our intention in this first analysis to concentrate on the main driving forces of the reform.

The model consists of 26 behavioural equations and 48 identities. The data we used are annual data from 1978 to 1994, mainly from the official statistical publications. Exceptions are X_{IPt}, X_{IMt} (which are calculated from the total industrial production and the shares of gross industrial production value of the planned segment and the market segment), and K_{IMt} (which is calculated as accumulated investment starting with the beginning of the economic reform).

The model is of an interdependent structure. To avoid possible misspecification effects across the equations we used single equation estimation methods. The parameters were estimated by OLS, NLLS and LIML (if autocorelation of the residuals had to be incorporated).

3.2 The Econometric Model

In this section we present all equations and the parameter estimates. R^2 indicates the coefficient of determination, DW the Durbin-Watson statistics.

Production

$$\ln X_{IPt} = \underset{(-1.41)}{-2.36} - \underset{(6.414)}{\tfrac{1.158}{4.444}} \cdot \ln\Big(\underset{(3.662)}{0.222} \underset{(2.7229)}{K_{IPt-1}^{-4.444}} + (1-0.222) L_{IPt}^{-4.444} \Big) \quad (3.1)$$

$$DW = 0.97 \qquad R^2 = 0.99$$

$$\ln X_{IMt} = \underset{(-7.443)}{-3.365} + \underset{(29.835)}{\tfrac{1.363}{0.754}} \cdot \ln\Big(\underset{(-2.571)}{0.796} K_{IMt-1}^{0.754} + \underset{(9.703)}{(1-0.796)} L_{IMt}^{0.754} \Big) \quad (3.2)$$

$$DW = 1.96 \qquad R^2 = 0.99$$

$$\ln X_{AMt} = \underset{(141.079)}{0.997} \ln X_{AMt-1} - \underset{(-1.308)}{0.016} \ln\left(\frac{w_{AMt}}{P_{AMt}}\right) \quad (3.3)$$

$$DW = 1.98 \qquad R^2 = 0.982$$

Labour demand

$$\ln(L_{IPt}) = \underset{(35.6137)}{6.888} + \underset{(11.7159)}{0.225} \cdot \ln(K_{IPt-1}) \tag{3.4}$$

$$R^2 = 0.9797 \qquad DW = 1.5358$$

$$u_{4t} = \underset{(2.979)}{0.679}\; u_{4t-1} + \varepsilon_{4t}$$

$$\ln(L_{IMt}) = \underset{(36.4263)}{6.659} + \underset{(10.9696)}{0.316} \ln(K_{IMt-1}) \tag{3.5}$$

$$+ \underset{(8.1117)}{0.411}\; DUMMY84^{2}$$

$$R^2 = 0.9860 \qquad DW = 1.4474$$

Consumption

$$C_t = \underset{(6.6306)}{821.193} + \underset{(11.3844)}{0.807} \left(\frac{PI_t}{P_t^C}\right) - \underset{(-2.1733)}{363.678}\; P_t^C \tag{3.6}$$

$$R^2 = 0.9951 \qquad DW = 2.0067$$

$$u_{6t} = \underset{(1.523)}{0.458}\; u_{6t-1} + \varepsilon_{6t}$$

$$NC_{Rt} = \underset{(2.0855)}{347.661} + \underset{(37.8129)}{0.840}\; PI_{Rt} \tag{3.7}$$

$$R^2 = 0.9991 \qquad DW = 2.2063$$

Productive investment

$$NIPRD_{IPt} = \underset{(1.4624)}{324.562} + \underset{(16.9310)}{0.533}\; INVS_{IPt} \tag{3.8}$$

$$R^2 = 0.9933 \quad DW = 1.4643$$

---

[2] In 1984 there was a new classification in the labour statistics of the nonstate-owned companies. The dummy variable is introduced to take this effect into account.

$$u_{8t} = \underset{(4.439)}{0.87} \; u_{8t-1} + \varepsilon_{8t}$$

$$NIPRD_{IMt} = \underset{(-1.3929)}{-92.435} + \underset{(30.9134)}{0.572} \; INVS_{IMt} \tag{3.9}$$

$$R^2 = 0.9940 \qquad DW = 1.7302$$

$$u_{9t} = \underset{(3.322)}{0.657} \; u_{9t-1} + \varepsilon_{9t}$$

Formation of funds for investment

$$FDR_t = \underset{(-2.6378)}{-760.515} + \underset{(20.0329)}{0.483} \; BI_t \tag{3.10}$$

$$R^2 = 0.9884 \qquad DW = 1.7463$$

$$u_{10t} = \underset{(2.552)}{0.645} \; u_{10t-1} + \varepsilon_{10t}$$

$$FDR_{IMt} = \underset{(6.3628)}{0.247} \; BI_{IMt} + \underset{(3.4530)}{0.155} \; FI_t \tag{3.11}$$

$$R^2 = 0.9754 \qquad DW = 1.8735$$

$$u_{11t} = \underset{(1.24)}{0.334} \; u_{11t-1} + \varepsilon_{11t}$$

$$BKLOAN_{IPt} = \underset{(2.1798)}{500.275} + \underset{(16.0614)}{0.575} \; BKLOAN_t \tag{3.12}$$

$$- \underset{(-1.9409)}{613} \; \tilde{p}_t$$

$$R^2 = 0.9961 \qquad DW = 1.3991$$

$$u_{12t} = \underset{(1.53)}{0.531} \; u_{12t-1} + \varepsilon_{12t}$$

$$BKLOAN_t = \underset{(1.8966)}{0.253} \; BKLOAN_{t-1} + \underset{(3.1058)}{0.221} \; \Delta S_t \tag{3.13}$$

$$+ \underset{(5.8795)}{0.909} \; \Delta M1_t$$

$$R^2 = 0.9912 \qquad DW = 1.8189$$

Wage determination

$$w_{IPt} = \underset{(-7.1994)}{-0.101} + \underset{(23.1244)}{0.162} \; P_t^c \tag{3.14}$$

$$R^2 = 0.9917 \qquad DW = 1.2574$$

$$u_{14t} = \underset{(2.989)}{0.639} \; u_{14t-1} + \varepsilon_{14t}$$

$$w_{IMt} = \underset{(6.1095)}{0.111} + \underset{(4.0345)}{0.085} \; (X_{IMt}/L_{IMT}) \tag{3.15}$$

$$R^2 = 0.9931 \qquad DW = 2.024$$

$$u_{15t} = \underset{(15.219)}{0.954} \; u_{15t-1} + \varepsilon_{15t}$$

Price determination

$$p_{IMt} = \underset{(20.424)}{8.056} \left(\frac{M1_t}{X_t}\right) + \underset{(12.105)}{1.407} \; \rho_t \tag{3.16}$$

$$R^2 = 0.9824 \qquad DW = 1.64$$

$$u_{16t} = \underset{(3.287)}{0.678} \; u_{16t} + \varepsilon_{16t}$$

$$p_{IPt} = \underset{(5.6797)}{0.436} + \underset{(7.3202)}{(1 - 0.436)} \; p_{IMt-1} \tag{3.17}$$

$$R^2 = 0.9834 \qquad DW = 1.6117$$

$$p_{AMt} = \underset{(3.8052)}{0.383} + \underset{(1.9147)}{0.277} \; p_{AMt} + \underset{(6.7928)}{5.776} \; w_t \tag{3.18}$$

$$R^2 = 0.9897 \qquad DW = 1.6087$$

$$P_t^C = \underset{(3.9792)}{0.421}\ p_{It} + \underset{(7.0729)}{0.674}\ p_{AMt} \tag{3.19}$$

$$R^2 = 0.9946 \qquad DW = 1.8727$$

$$u_{19t} = \underset{(2.9559)}{0.632}\ u_{19t-1} + \varepsilon_{19t}$$

$$P_t^I = \underset{(4.723)}{0.259} + \underset{(22.141)}{0.723}\ p_{It} - \underset{(-2.927)}{0.000028}\ \Delta STOCKS_t \tag{3.20}$$

$$R^2 = 0.9911 \qquad DW = 1.5522$$

$$u_{20t} = \underset{(1.804)}{0.460}\ u_{20t-1} + \varepsilon_{20t}$$

Tax income

$$T_{AMt} = \underset{(-1.87298)}{-10.763} + \underset{(16.32486)}{0.022}\ p_{AMt}X_{AMt} \tag{3.21}$$

$$R^2 = 0.946 \qquad DW = 1.390$$

$$T_{IMt} = \underset{(3.041)}{215.445} + \underset{(24.232)}{0.168}\ BI_{IMt-1} \tag{3.22}$$

$$R^2 = 0.994 \qquad DW = 1.435$$

$$u_{22t} = \underset{(4.865)}{0.796}\ u_{22t-1} + \varepsilon_{22t}$$

$$T_{IPt} = \underset{(2.485)}{191.066} + \underset{(22.520)}{0.417}\ BI_{IPt-1} \tag{3.23}$$

$$R^2 = 0.9731 \qquad DW = 1.8251$$

Calculation adjustment[3]

$$INV_t = \underset{(108.829)}{1.04}\ INVS_t \tag{3.24}$$

[3] There is a difference between the statistics of sources of investment funds and the use of investment funds. We use a linear regression equation to approximate the relationship between these terms.

$$R^2 = 0.999 \qquad DW = 1.612$$

$$u_{24t} = \underset{(6.372)}{0.839}\ u_{24t-1} + \varepsilon_{24t}$$

Dividends

$$DIV_t = \underset{(1.7664)}{72.481} + \underset{(49.4179)}{0.442}\ BI_{IMt} \tag{3.25}$$

$$R^2 = 0.994 \qquad DW = 1.915$$

$$DIV_{Rt} = \underset{(2.1611)}{318.657} + \underset{(5.3953)}{0.267}\ DIV_t \tag{3.26}$$

$$R^2 = 0.896 \qquad DW = 1.412$$

$$u_{26t} = \underset{(2.127)}{0.632}\ u_{26t-1} + \varepsilon_{26t}$$

Identities

$$\rho_t = \frac{X_{IPt}}{X_{IMt}} \tag{3.1}$$

$$X_t = X_{IPt} + X_{IMt} + X_{AMt} \tag{3.2}$$

$$\tilde{\rho}_t = \frac{X_{IPt}}{X_{IPt} + X_{IMt}} \tag{3.3}$$

$$P_t X_t = p_{IPt} X_{IPt} + p_{IMt} + p_{AMt} X_{AMt} \tag{3.4}$$

$$C_t = C_{Rt} + C_{Ut} \tag{3.5}$$

$$C_{Rt} = NC_{Rt}/P_t^c \tag{3.6}$$

$$INVG_t = INVG_{IPt} + INVG_{IMt} \tag{3.7}$$

$$BKLOAN_t = BKLOAN_{IPt} + BKLOAN_{IMt} \tag{3.8}$$

$$INVS_{IPt} = FDR_{IPt} + BKLOAN_{IPt} + INVG_{IPt} + INVF_{IPt} \tag{3.9}$$

$$INVS_{IMt} = FDR_{IMt} + BKLOAN_{IMt} + INVG_{IMt} + INVF_{IMt} \tag{3.10}$$

$$INVS_t = INVS_{IPt} + INVS_{IMt} \tag{3.11}$$

$$L_t = L_{IPt} + L_{IMt} + L_{AMt} \tag{3.12}$$

$$LI_{IPt} = w_{IPt} L_{IPt} \tag{3.13}$$

$$LI_{IMt} = w_{IMt} L_{IMt} \tag{3.14}$$

$$LI_t = LI_{IPt} + LI_{IMt} \tag{3.15}$$

$$CI_{IPt} = T_{IPt} + RI_{IPt} + BI_{IPt} \tag{3.16}$$

$$CI_{IMt} = T_{IMt} + RI_{IMt} + DIV_{IMt} + BI_{IMt} \tag{3.17}$$

$$BI_t = BI_{IPt} + BI_{IMt} \tag{3.18}$$

$$FI_t = p_{AMt} X_{AMt} - T_{AMt} \tag{3.19}$$

$$T_t = T_{IPt} + T_{IMt} + T_{AMt} \tag{3.20}$$

$$PI_t = LI_{IMt} + LI_{IPt} + RI_{IMt} + RI_{IPt} + DIV_{IMt} + FI_t \tag{3.21}$$

$$PI_{Rt} = RI_{Rt} + FI_t \tag{3.22}$$

$$RI_t = RI_{IMt} + RI_{IPt} \tag{3.23}$$

$$RI_t = r_{t-1} S_{t-1} \tag{3.24}$$

$$RI_{IPt} = RI_t \tag{3.25}$$

$$RI_{Rt} = r_{t-1} S_{Rt-1} \tag{3.26}$$

$$RI_{Ut} = r_{t-1} S_{Ut-1} \tag{3.27}$$

$$CI_{IPt} = p_{IPt} X_{IPt} - w_{IPt} L_{IPt} \tag{3.28}$$

$$CI_{IMt} = p_{IMt}X_{IMt} - w_{IMt}L_{IMt} \tag{3.29}$$

$$S_t = S_{Rt} + S_{Ut} \tag{3.30}$$

$$\Delta S_t = PI_t - C_t P_t^C - \Delta M_t^P \tag{3.31}$$

$$\Delta S_{Rt} = PI_{Rt} - NC_{Rt} - \Delta M_{Rt}^P \tag{3.32}$$

$$\Delta M_t^P = \Delta M_t^P (C_t P_t^C / P_t X_t) \tag{3.33}$$

$$\Delta M_{Rt}^P = \Delta M_t^P (NC_{Rt} / P_t X_t) \tag{3.34}$$

$$DEBT_t = P_t^C C_t^{Pub} + INVG_t - T_t \tag{3.35}$$

$$GDE_t = P_t X_t + ERROR_t{}^4 \tag{3.36}$$

$$X_t = I_t + C_t + C_t^{Pub} + (\Delta STOCKS_t + Ex_t - Im_t - ERROR_t)/P_t^{ST} \tag{3.37}$$

$$\Delta STOCKS_t = GDE_t - EX_t - IM_t - NC_t - NC_t^{Pub} - INV_t \tag{3.38}$$

$$K_{IPt} = 0.95 K_{IPt-1} + \frac{NIPRD_{IPt}}{P_t^I} \tag{3.39}$$

$$K_{IMt} = 0.95 K_{IMt-1} + \frac{NIPRD_{IMt}}{P_t^I} \tag{3.40}$$

$$P_{It} = \frac{p_{IMt}X_{IMt} + p_{IPt}X_{IPt}}{X_{IMt} + x_{IPt}} \tag{3.41}$$

$$rPI_t = \frac{PI_t}{P_t^C} \tag{3.42}$$

$$\Delta M1_t = M1_t - M1_{t-1} \tag{3.43}$$

$$rw_{AMt} = \frac{w_{AMt}}{p_{AMt}} \tag{3.44}$$

---

[4] There is a statistical discrepancy between domestic production and expenditure.

$$\rho Mp_t = \frac{M1_t}{X_t} \tag{3.45}$$

$$w_t = \frac{w_{IMt}L_{IMt} + w_{IPt}L_{OPt}}{L_{IMt} + L_{IPt}} \tag{3.46}$$

$$w_{AMt} = \frac{w_{IMt}L_{IMt}}{L_{IMt} + L_{AMt}} \tag{3.47}$$

$$LP_{IMt} = \frac{X_{IMt}}{L_{IMt}} \tag{3.48}$$

The estimated model fits the observations quite well. This can be seen from the following graphs for all 26 behavioural equations.

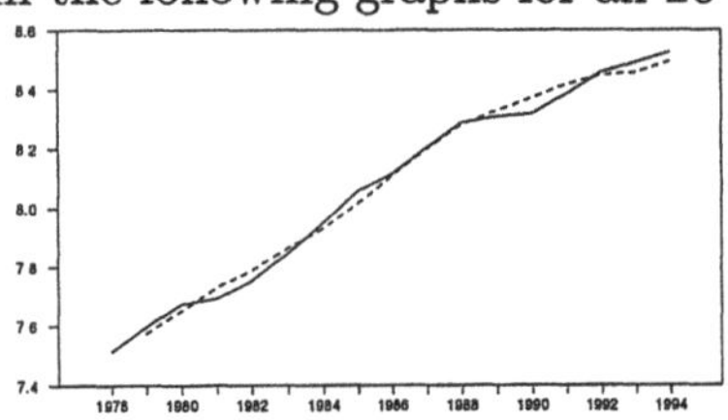

Fig. 1: Observed and estimated values of $\ln(X_{IPt})$[5]

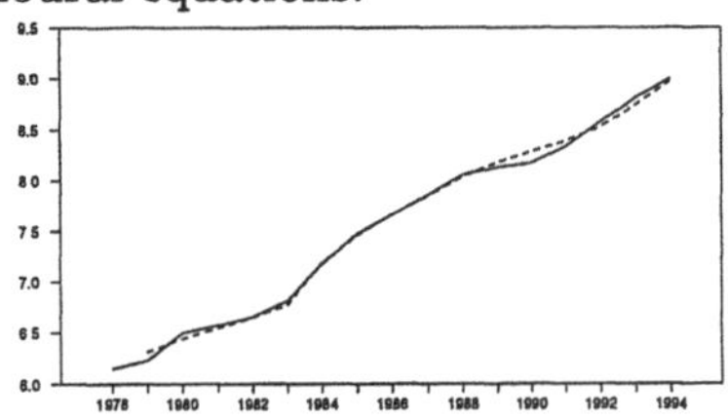

Fig. 2: Observed and estimated values of $\ln(X_{IMt})$

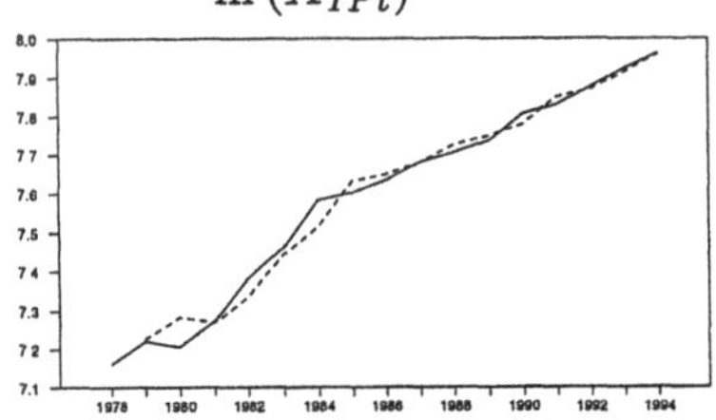

Fig. 3: Observed and estimated values of $\log(X_{AMt})$

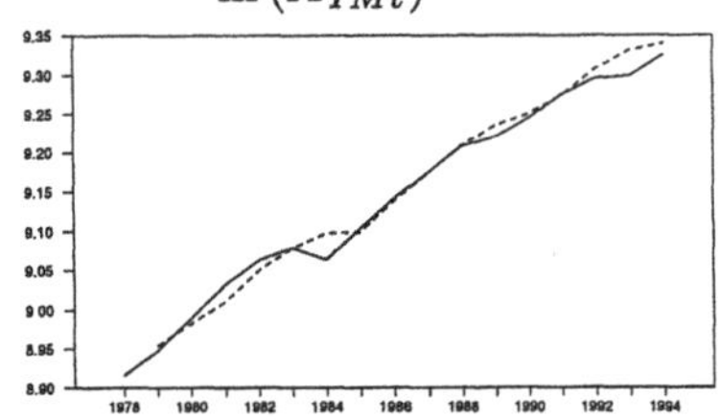

Fig. 4: Observed and estimated values of $\log(L_{IPt})$

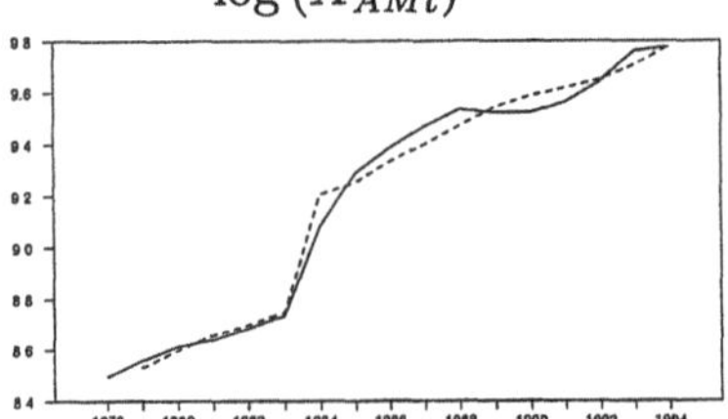

Fig. 5: Observed and estimated values of $\log(L_{IMt})$

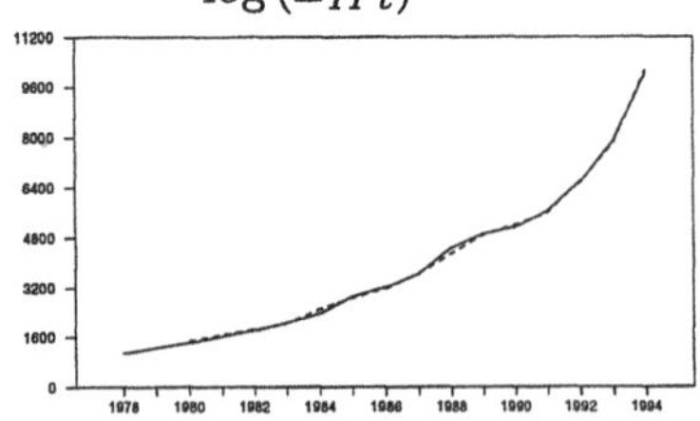

Fig. 6: Observed and estimated values of C_t

[5] The dashed line stands for the observed values, the dotted line for the estimated values.

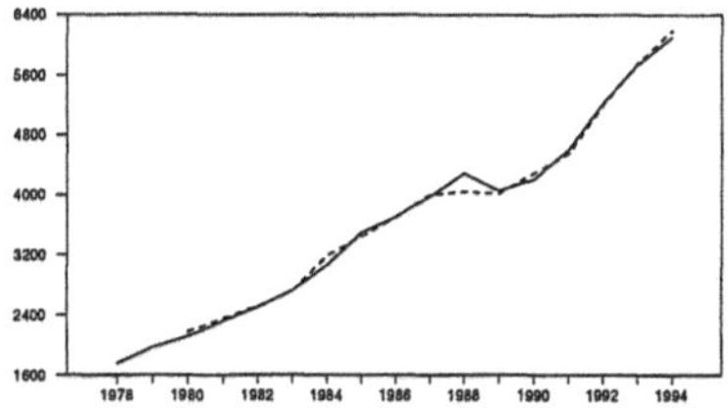

Fig. 7: Observed and estimated values of NC_{Rt}

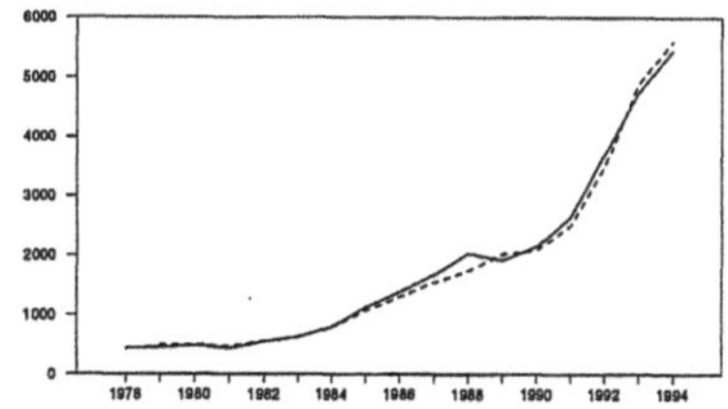

Fig. 8: Observed and estimated values of $NIPRD_{IPt}$

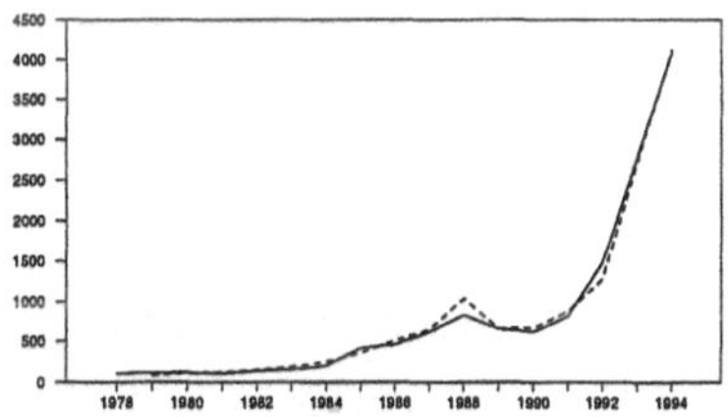

Fig. 9: Observed and estimated values of $NIPRD_{IMt}$

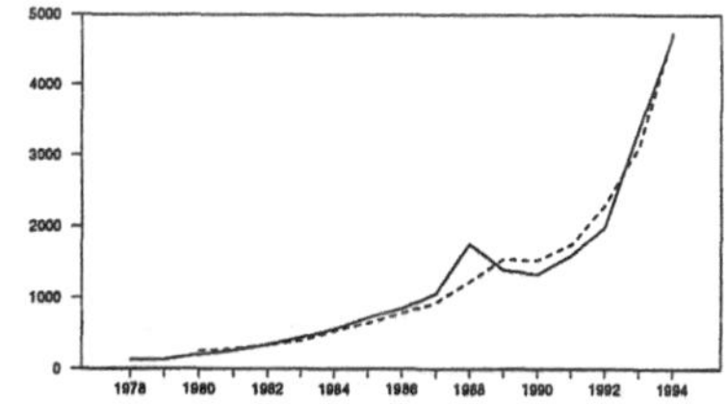

Fig. 10: Observed and estimated values of FDR_t

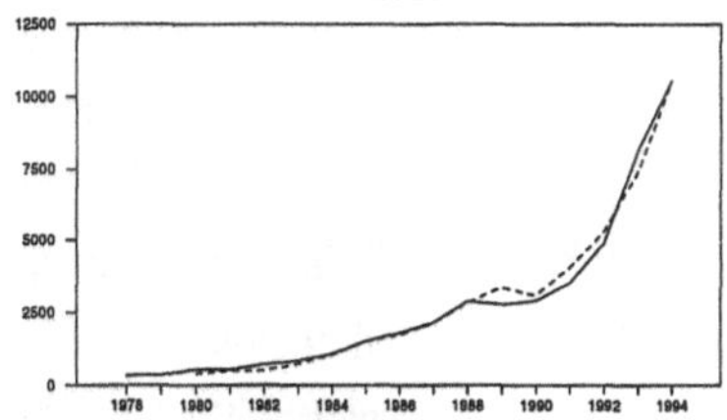

Fig. 11: Observed and estimated values of FDR_{IMt}

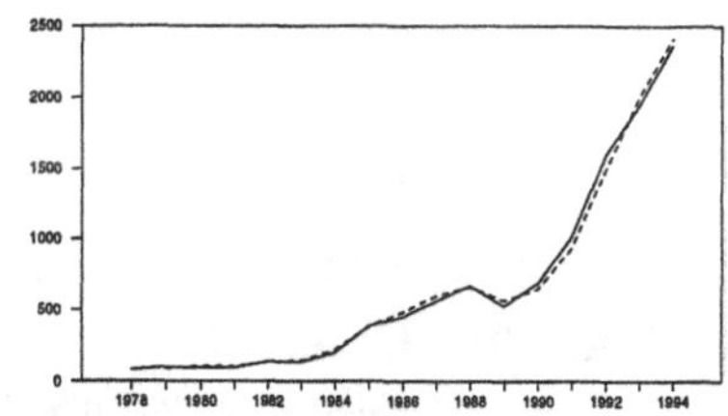

Fig. 12: Observed and estimated values of $BKLOAN_{IPt}$

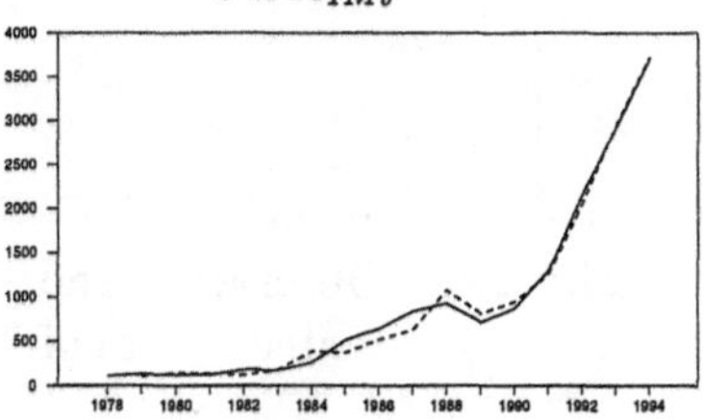

Fig. 13: Observed and estimated values of $BKLOAN_t$

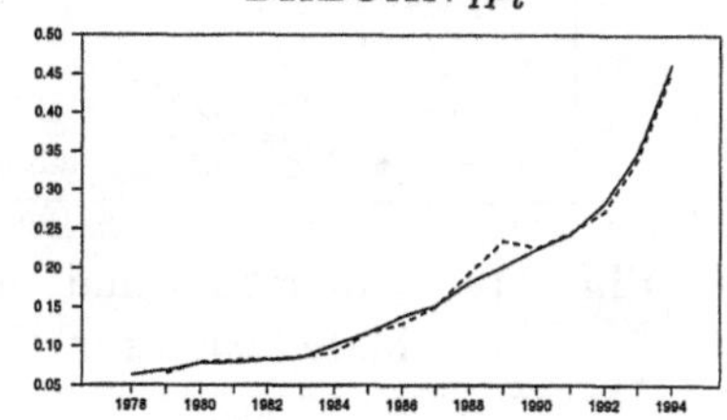

Fig. 14: Observed and estimated values of w_{IPt}

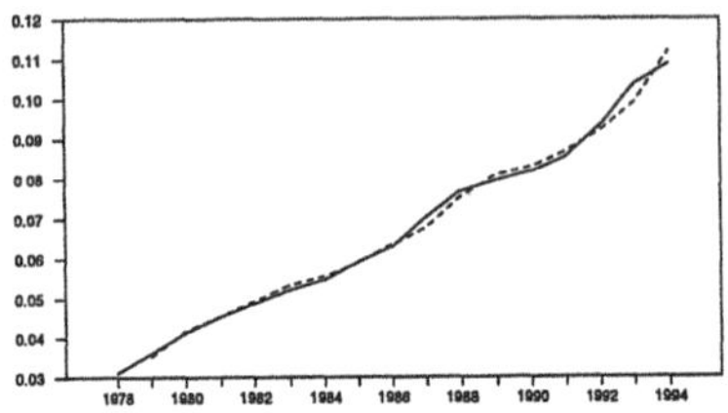

Fig. 15: Observed and estimated values of w_{IMt}

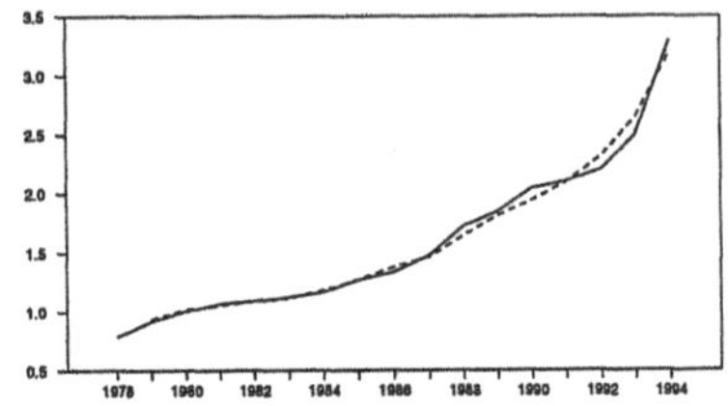

Fig. 16: Observed and estimated values of p_{IMt}

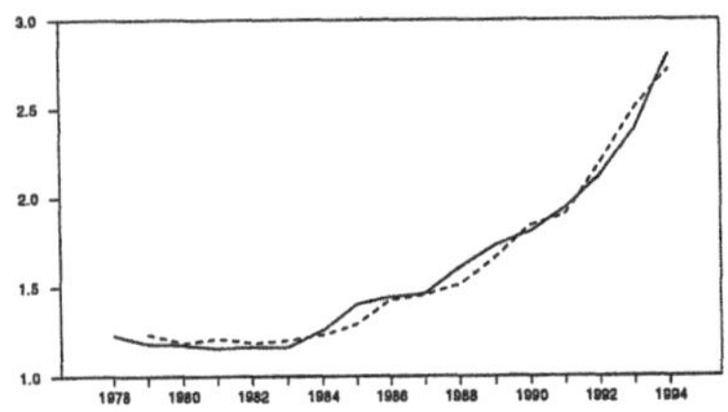

Fig. 17: Observed and estimated values of p_{IPt}

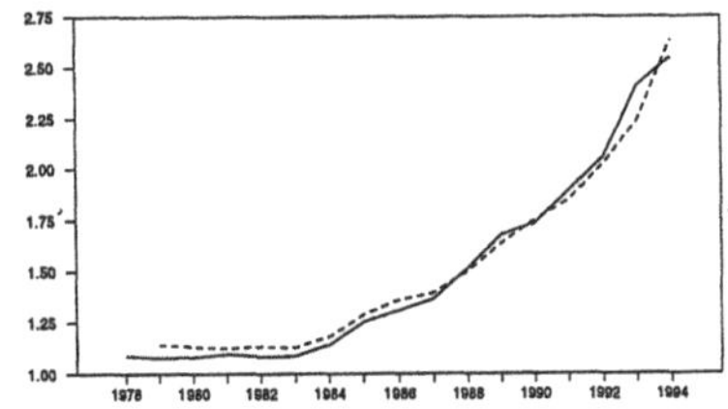

Fig. 18: Observed and estimated values of p_{AMt}

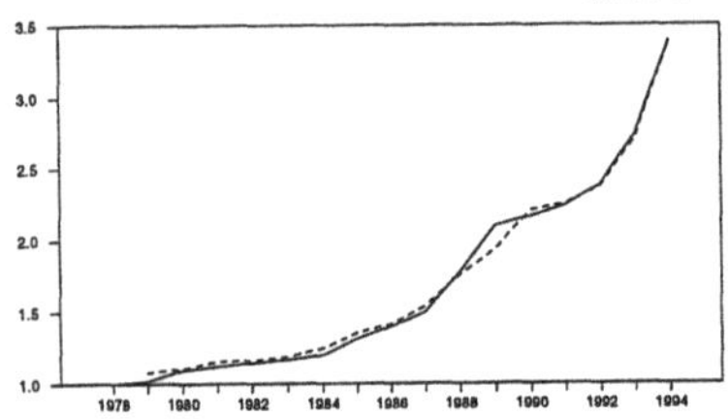

Fig. 19: Observed and estimated values of P_t^C

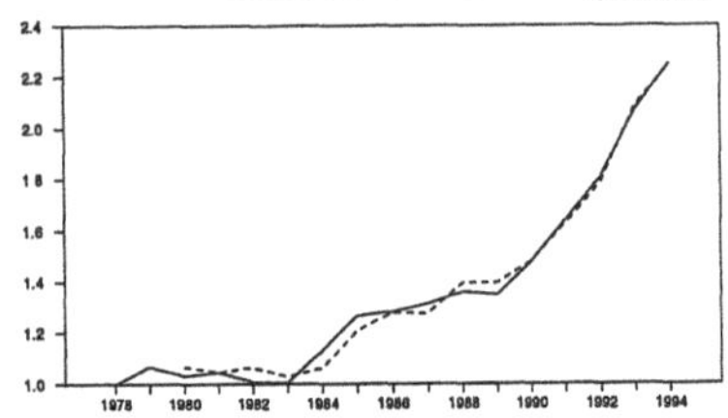

Fig. 20: Observed and estimated values of P_t^I

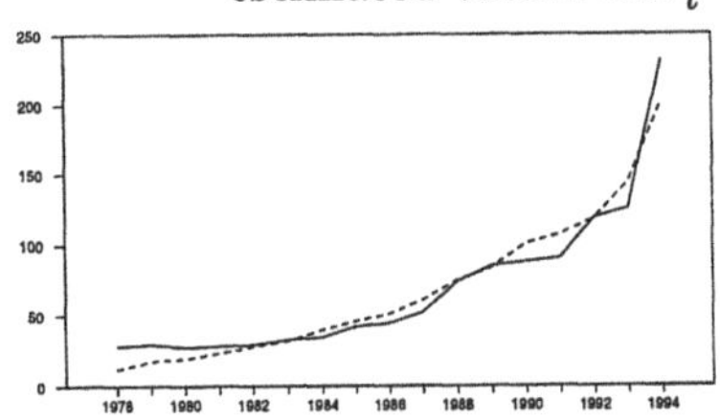

Fig. 21: Observed and estimated values of T_{AMt}

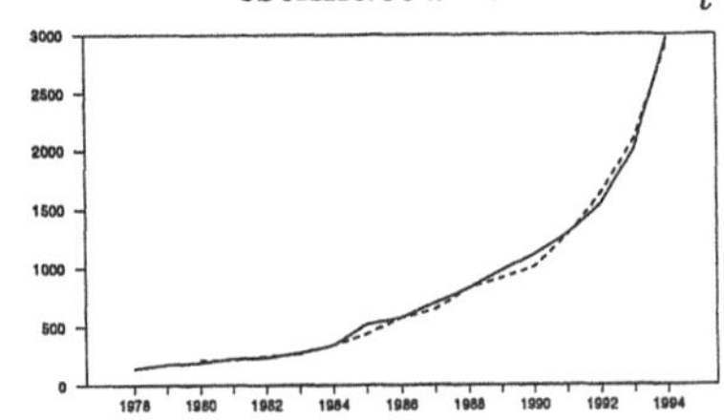

Fig. 22: Observed and estimated values of T_{IMt}

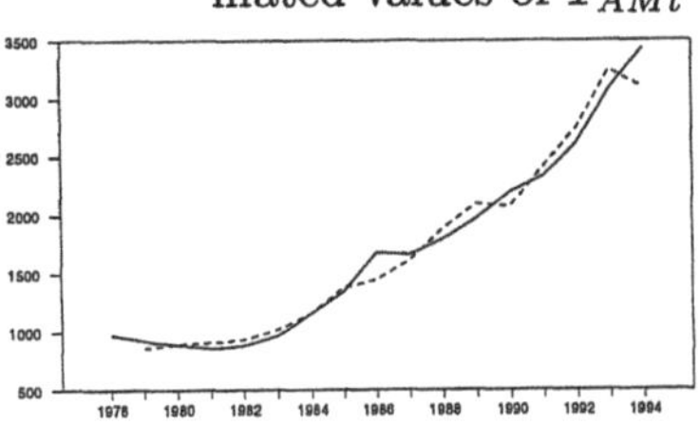

Fig. 23: Observed and estimated values of T_{IPt}

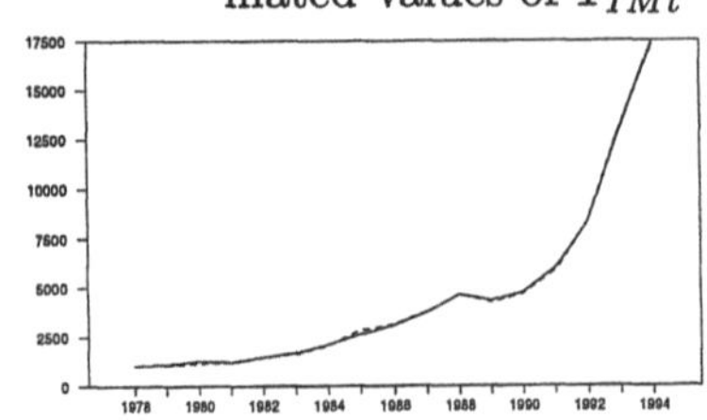

Fig. 24: Observed and estimated values of INV_t

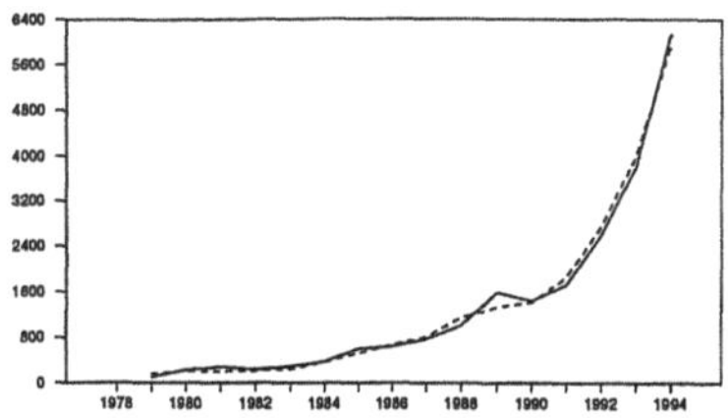

Fig. 25: Observed and estimated values of DIV_t

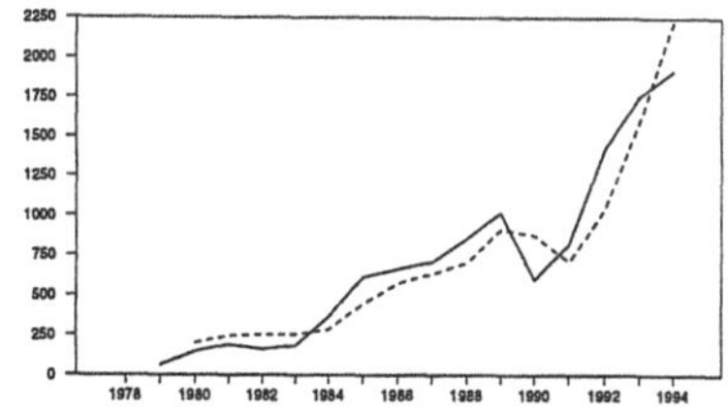

Fig. 26: Observed and estimated values of DIV_{Rt}

4. Conclusion

In the next stage the model will be tested by ex post and ex ante simulation experiments (empirical data are now available for 1995 and 1996) and will be respecified. It lateron will be used for an analysis of the effects of alternative economic policy measures and for predictions.

Appendix

List of variables

BI_{IMt}:	business income in the market segment
BI_{IPt}:	business income in the planned segment
BI_t:	total business income
$BKLOAN_{IMt}$:	domestic loans for investment in the market segment
$BKLOAN_{IPt}$:	domestic loans for the planned segment
$BKLOAN_t$:	domestic loans
CI_{IMt}:	capital income in the market segment
CI_{IPt}:	capital income in the planned segment
CR_t:	real consumption in rural areas
C_t:	real personal consumption
C_t^{Pub}:	real public consumption
C_{Ut}:	real consumption in urban areas
$DEBT_t$:	debt of the government
D_{IMt}:	depreciation in the market segment
D_{IPt}:	depreciation in the planned segment
DIV_{IMt}:	dividends paid to share holders
DIV_{Rt}:	dividends paid to rural households
DIV_t:	total dividends
$DUMMY84$:	dummy variable for 1984
$ERROR_t$:	statistical discrepancy between domestic production and expenditure
Ex_t:	export

FDR_{IMt}:	fund raising in the market segment
FDR_{IPt}:	fund raising in the planned segment
FDR_t:	total fund raising
FI_t:	farmers' income
GDE_t:	gross domestic expenditure
Im_t:	import
$INVF_{IMt}$:	government investment in the market segment
$INVF_{IPt}$:	foreign investment used in the planned segment
$INVG_{IMt}$:	government investment in the market segment
$INVG_{IPt}$:	government investment in the planned segment
$INVG_t$:	investment appropriated by the government
$INVS_{IMt}$:	sum of the funds for investment in the market segment
$INVS_{IPt}$:	sum of the funds for investment in the planned segment
$INVS_t$:	total of funds for investment
INV_t:	total nominal investment
I_t:	total investment
K_{AMt}:	capital stock in agriculture
K_{IMt}:	capital stock in the market segment
K_{IPt}:	capital stock in the planned segment
L_{AMt}:	labour used in the agriculture
LI_{IMt}:	labour income in the market segment
LI_{IPt}:	labour income in the planned segment
L_{IMt}:	labour used in the market segment
L_{IPt}:	labour used in the planned segment
LI_t:	total labour income
LP_{IMt}:	labour productivity in the market segment
L_t:	total labour force
$M1_t$:	money
NC_{Rt}:	nominal personal consumption in rural areas
NC_t:	nominal consumption
NC_t^{Pub}:	nominal public consumption
$NIPRD_{IMt}$:	nominal productive investment in the market segment
$NIPRD_{IPt}$:	nominal productive investment in the planned segment
p_{AMt}:	price deflator of agricultural products
p_{IMt}:	price deflator of industrial products in the market segment
p_{IPt}:	price deflator of industrial products in the planned segment
PI_{Rt}:	personal income in rural areas
PI_t:	personal income

PI_t:	price index for industrial products
P_t:	overall price index
P_t^c:	price index for consumption goods
P_t^I:	price index for investment goods
P_t^{ST}:	deflator of stocks
RI_{IMt}:	interest income from the market segment
RI_{IPt}:	interest income from the planned segment
RI_{Rt}:	interest income in rural areas
RI_t:	interest income
RI_{Ut}:	interest income in urban areas
rPI_t:	real personal income
r_t:	interest rate
rw_{AMt}:	real wage rate in agriculture (with respect to agricultural price)
ΔS_{Rt}:	change in personal savings in rural areas
ΔS_t:	change in personal savings
$\Delta STOCKS_t$:	inventory stocks
ΔS_{Ut}:	change in personal savings in urban areas
TAM_t:	tax from agriculture
TIM_t:	tax from the market segment
TIP_t:	tax from the planned segment
T_t:	total tax
w_{AMt}:	expected average wage rate in agriculture
w_{IMt}:	wage rate in the market segment
w_{IPt}:	wage rate in the planned segment
w_t:	average wage rate
X_{AMt}:	agricultural production of the market segment
X_{IMt}:	industrial production of the market segment
X_{IPt}:	industrial production of the planned segment
X_t:	real domestic production
$\Delta M1_t$:	change of M1
ΔM_{RT}^P:	change of M1 in farmer households
ΔM_t^P:	change of M1 in households
ρM_t^P:	Money-product-ratio
ρt:	ratio of products between the planned and the market segment
$\tilde{\rho}_t$:	production share of the planned segment in the economy

References

1. Berndt, Ernst R. P. (1990). The Practice of Econometrics: Classic and Contemporary, Eddison-Wesly, P. 277.

2. Blank, Grant and Parish, William L. (1990). Rural Industry and Nonfarm Employment: Comparative Perspectives, in Kwok R.Yin-Wang , P.109-130.
3. Byrd, William A. (1987). The two-tier plan/market system, *Journal of Comparative Economics*, **11**, P.299.
4. Byrd, William. A. (1991). "The Market Mechanism and Economic Reforms in China", M.E.Sharpe, Inc. 1991, Armonk, New York, London, P.19.
5. Chen Pu (1996). Economic Reform and the Transition from Plan to Market, Lit, Germany.
6. Cheng, Xuan (1990). Problems of urbanization, in Kwok R.Yin-Wang, P.65-77.
7. Fang Gang (1994). Dual-Track Transition in China, *Economic Policy*, December, P. 99.
8. Grosfeld, Irena (1987). Modelling planner behaviour: Poland 1956-1981, *Journal of Comparative Economics*, **11**, P.180-191.
9. Gruchy, Allen G. (1985). Comparative Economic Systems, 2nd Edition translated by Xu Jiewen, Beijing.
10. Jorgenson, D. W. (1961). The Development of a Dual Economy, *The Economic Journal*, June, **71**, P.309
11. Jefferson Gary H. and Xu, Wenyi (1991). The impact of reform on socialist enterprises in transition: structure, conduct, and performance in Chinese industry, *Journal of Comparative Economics*, **15**, P.45-64.
12. Jefferson, Gary H. and Rawski, G. Thomas.(1994). Enterprises reform in Chinese industry, *Journal of Economic Perspectives*, Spring, **8**, P.50
13. Kelley, Allen C. Williamson, Jeffrey G. and Cheetham, Russell J. (1972). Dualistic Economic Development, The University of Chicago Press, Chicago and London.
14. Kueh, Yak-Yeow (1984). China's new agricultural-policy program: major economic consequences, 1979-1983, *Journal of Comparative Economics*, **8**, P. 353.
15. Kwok R.Yin-Wang (1990). Chinese Urban Reform: What Model Now? Share, Armon, New York, London.
16. Murrell, Peter (1991). Can neoclassical economics underpin the reform of centrally planned economy?, *Journal of Economic Perspectives*, 1991, **5**, P.59-76.
17. Perkins, Dwight H. (1990), The Influence of Economic Reforms on China's Urbanization in Kwok R.Yin-Wang, P.78-106.
18. Perkins, Dwight H. (1994). Completing Chinese reform, *Journal of Economic Perspectives*, Spring, **15**, P.22-46.
19. Schmieding (1994). From plan to market: on the nature of the transition crisis, *Weltwirtschaftliches Archiv*, P.244.
20. en, Amartya (1988). Hand Book of Development Economics, Vol. 1.
21. Wing Thye Woo (1994). The Art of Reforming Centrally Planned Economies. *Journal of Comparative Economics*, **18**, P. 286.
22. Wu, Jinglian and Zhao, Renwei (1987). The dual pricing system in China's industry, *Journal of Comparative Economics*, **11**, P.309-318.
23. Chinese Statistic Year Book 1988 Chinese Bureau of Statistics China, Statistics Publishing House, Beijing.
24. Chinese Statistic Year Book 1994 Chinese Bureau of Statistics China, Statistics Publishing House, Beijing.
25. Chinese Statistic Year Book 1995 Chinese Bureau of Statistics China, Statistics Publishing House, Beijing.

Part IV

Decision Theory and Statistics

Information Value as a Metacriterion for Decision Rules Under Strict Uncertainty

Franz Ferschl

Department of Statistics, Ludwig-Maximilians-Universität München, Germany

Summary. This contribution proposes the notions of information structure and information value as a tool for judging on the rationality of decision rules in decision theory under uncertainty. Traditionally, sets of axioms which consider the ranking of alternatives or the choice set are used for this purpose. But some intuitively unfavourable criteria are not rejected decidedly enough with the help of the known axioms only, as for instance the maximax–rule. With the concept of information resistance, here newly introduced in the discussion, so called "global decision rules" can be criticized in an adequate manner.

On the other hand it is pointed out, that the concept of information value must sometimes used with caution. For instance, A. Wald's much esteemed maximin–rule, in general reacts to a intuitively "worthless" information with a positive information value.

1. Introduction

Since its beginning in the early fifties decision theory can be seen as divided into two main parts. On the one hand there is decision theory under risk with deep roots in the history of probability and of the utility concept. Hans Schneeweiß has given essential contribution to this field, see e.g. Schneeweiß (1966). On the other hand we encounter decision theory under uncertainty, often which emphasis on "strict" or "complete" uncertainty. Its origin can be located in the theory of games which uses the — in some sense — probably best known decision rule under uncertainty, namely A. Wald's decision rule of maximin return resp. minimax loss. Besides, since the very beginning of decision theory a lot of different decision rules were proposed and also very early advantages and disadvantages of such rules were discussed very early as well. These discussion quickly led to the consideration of metacriteria[1] for decision rules. Such metacriteria try to assess the rationality of a given decision rule, in implicit or even axiomatic form. Lists of such metacriteria are given, with minor modifications, in many places of literature. Let us mention here only Milnor (1954), Luce and Raiffa (1957), or French (1988) as a more recent representative. Some sets of metacriteria refer to the ranking of all alternatives resp. actions, some to the choice set, which denotes the set of optimal actions with respect to a given decision rule. As a typical example French's list will be given here:

[1] I will use here the expression "metacriterion" instead of the usual "criterion" which will be used in the definition of decision rules.

Axiom 1 Complete ranking of all possible actions.
Axiom 2 Independence of labelling of actions and states.
Axiom 3 Independence of scale, i.e. of positive linear transformation of values.
Axiom 4 Compatibility with strict domination.
Axiom 5 Independence of irrelevant alternatives.
Axiom 6 Independence of addition of a constant to a column.
Axiom 7 Independence of row permutation i.e. permutation of the values within a row.
Axiom 8 Independence of column duplication.

In parenthesis it should be noted, that Savage's "sure thing principle", which led to intense discussions in the foundation of subjective probability, is never included in such a list.

But the situation, concerning the rationality, remained rather unsatisfactory during all the time. Firstly, it can be shown, that no non trivial decision rule can satisfy the whole set of axioms above. But since the early days of decision theory the community of experts in this field seems to be accustomed to this fact. Maybe much more disturbing is another fact. Some intuitive weak decision rules, which are based on a crude "global" optimization over all values within a decision table as for instance the rule of "maximax–return" (see e.g. Bitz (1981), p. 63) get the same rating with respect to such axiom systems as much more esteemed rules as for instance Wald's maximin decision rule. The maximax–return rule fulfills exactly the same axioms as Wald's rule, namely all but axiom 6.

In short: The usual axioms do not always distinguish between decision rules of different intuitive soundness.

One way out of this dilemma may be the introduction of metacriteria which are inspired by a completely new point of view. In this contribution we propose to use the concept of information value, which is built into decision theory via the transition from a no–data problem to a data problem (see e.g. Ferschl (1975) p. 52 and Ferschl (1981), p. 53).

Therefore in the subsequent section 2 we give a short description of the terminology needed for the introduction of the decision theoretic concept of information and information value. Then, in section 3, we will show, that the maximax rule (and similar constructions) is insensitive resp. resistant to receiving any information about the states of the decision problem at all, which renders this rule clearly unsatisfactory. In section 4 we touch the more subtle point, that some decision rules follow an opposite behavior: they are too sensitive against nearly "worthless information". It will be shown, that this concept is essentially equivalent to a randomization of actions. This in turn, suggests to stick only a Bayes rules, if decision theoretic information values are constructed, or as another possible consequence, to consider only convex sets of alternatives.

2. Decision Table, Information and Information Value

A very general concept of information value in decision theory is developed in Ferschl (1981) which fully takes into account the possible nonlinearity of utility. Fortunately, this general version is not needed in the subsequent constructions and we can proceed with a much more simpler approach.

2.1 The Decision Table

The basic structure of decision theory under uncertainty is the decision table. It consists of two sets, [2] namely the set of

$$\textit{actions (alternatives)} \quad A = \{a_1, a_2, \ldots, a_m\}$$

$$\textit{states of the world} \quad \Theta = \{\theta_1, \theta_2, \ldots, \theta_m\}$$

and a mapping u, the *utility function*

$$u \, : \, A \times \Theta \to \mathbb{R}$$

which relates each pair (a_i, θ_j) to a real number

$$u_{ij} := u(a_i, \theta_j) \quad i = 1, \ldots, m \, ; \; j = 1, \ldots, n \, .$$

In this way an action can be identified with a n–dimensional row vector resp. a point in $\mathbb{R}^n$

$$a_i := (u_{i1}, u_{i2}, \ldots, u_{in}) \in \mathbb{R}^n \, . \tag{2.1}$$

2.2 The Decision Problem

Given the decision table, the focus of decision theory is to select a set of optimal alternatives, called the *choice set.* A procedure, which identifies a choice set, is called a *decision rule.* There are two types of decision rules:

a) *Decision rules of the first kind.* They are based on a comparison of the rows of entries in the decision table with respect to a real function ϕ

$$\phi(a_i) = \phi(u_{i1}, u_{i2}, \ldots u_{in})$$

where ϕ can be interpreted as a real function in n variables

$$\phi : \mathbb{R}^n \to \mathbb{R} \, .$$

Most decision rules are of this type.

---

[2] To avoid unnecessary measure theoretic complications, all basic sets are assumed finite.

b) *Decision rules of the second kind.* Here, in principle $\phi(a_i)$ can depend on all the entries u_{ij} of the decision table. For instance, the minimax–regret rule of Savage–Niehans is of this type. Clearly such rules do not fulfill axiom 5. The function ϕ is also called the *criterion* of the decision rule. An action α^* is *optimal* (belongs to the choice set), if

$$\phi(a^*) = \max_i \phi(a_i)$$

holds.

2.3 Source of Information

Information in decision theory means information concerning the true state of the world. Information is received by observing the outcome of a random variable Y. Let $\mathcal{Y} = \{y_1, y_2, \ldots, y_s\}$ be the (finite) sample space of $\mathcal{Y}$. In order to really convey information, the distribution of Y should depend on the state θ_j. We write

$$P(Y = y_k \mid \theta_j) = p_{jk} \ , \qquad \begin{array}{l} k = 1, \ldots, s \\ j = 1, \ldots, n. \end{array} \tag{2.2}$$

It is assumed, that these distributions are completely known. The conditional probabilities in (2.2) can be arranged in a table, called the *information structure*

$$\begin{array}{c|cccc} & y_1 & y_2 & \cdots & y_s \\ \hline \theta_1 & p_{11} & p_{12} & \cdots & p_{1s} \\ \theta_2 & p_{21} & p_{22} & \cdots & p_{2s} \\ \vdots & \vdots & \vdots & & \vdots \\ \theta_n & p_{n1} & p_{n2} & & p_{ns} \end{array} \tag{2.3}$$

The p_{jk} can also be interpreted as transition probabilities from the unknown states θ_j to the realization y_k of the observable Y. Concerning the information structure there are two extreme situations possible:

a) *Perfect information.* In this case every column of the matrix (2.3) contains at most one component different from zero. Every outcome belongs to an unique state.
b) *Useless information.* All rows of the information structure are equal, which means, that the distribution of Y is independent of the true state of the world. This situation is equivalent to carrying out an arbitrary random experiment without any further connection to the decision problem.

2.4 Information Processing

2.4.1 The Decision Function. Use of information in decision theory means to connect the two concepts of information structure and decision table by the tool of the *decision function*. A decision function is nothing else than a recipe which tells in advance, what to do in any circumstances, i.e. which action should be taken if any outcome y_k , $k = 1, \ldots, s$ is observed. For suitable description we simply write a decision function as a mapping

$$d = \begin{pmatrix} y_1 \ldots y_k \ldots y_s \\ a_{i_1} \ldots a_{i_k} \ldots a_{i_s} \end{pmatrix}$$

with $a_{i_i} := d(y_k)$, $k = 1, \ldots, s$. The set D of all possible decision functions has cardinality $\#D = m^s$.

2.4.2 The Data–problem. Looking at the set of decision functions we are really confronted with a new decision problem, called the *data–problem* in contrast to the original *no–data–problem*. The data–problem consists of a new decision table

$$\bar{u} : D \times \theta \to \mathbb{R}$$

whose entries are defined as expected utilities in the following way

$$\begin{aligned} \bar{u}(d, \theta_j) &= \sum_{k=1}^{s} u(d(y_k), \theta_j) P(Y = y_k \mid \theta_j) \\ &= \sum_{k=1}^{s} u(a_{k_k}, \theta_j) p_{j_k} \end{aligned} \tag{2.4}$$

2.4.3 Action Probabilities. Consider at first a given decision function d and the subset of the sample space $\mathcal{Y}$, which gives rise to the choice of action a_i via d. We can write

$$d^{-1}(a_i) = \{y_k \mid d(y_k) = a_i\} =: S_i(d) \tag{2.5}$$

and call $S_i(d)$ the *acceptance region for action* a_i. The sample space can be considered as sum of the (possibility empty) acceptance regions

$$\mathcal{Y} = S_1(d) + \ldots + S_i(d) + \ldots + S_m(d). \tag{2.6}$$

Next we consider the *action probabilities*

$$\begin{aligned} P(Y \in S_i(d) \mid \theta_j) &= \sum_{y_k \in S_i(d)} P(Y = y_k \mid \theta_j) =: \pi_{ij}(d) \ , \\ &= 1, \ldots, m \ ; \ j = 1, \ldots, n \ . \end{aligned} \tag{2.7}$$

$\pi_{ij}(d)$ is the probability of ultimately choosing the action a_i, if the decision maker has already choosen the decision function d and is looking now for the result delivered by the information structure, if θ_j is the true state.

Action probabilities actually are the weights which form the entries $\bar{u}(d, \theta_j)$ of the data–problem from the j–column of the no–data–problem

$$\bar{u}(d, \theta_j) = \sum_{i=1}^{m} \pi_{ij}(d) u_{ij} \ . \tag{2.8}$$

This can be easily seen by using the partition (2.6) and both definitions (2.4) and (2.7). Version (2.7) will be better suited for the subsequent discussion than the original definition (2.4).

Note in passing, that the acceptance regions and action probabilities introduced above are direct generalizations of the corresponding notions in the theory of hypothesis testing.

2.5 The Value of Information

Consider a decision problem together with a fixed decision rule ϕ. A rather obvious way to arrive at a sound concept of the value of a decision problem is to ask for the best possible criterion value. Therefore two notions are proposed:

value of the no–data–problem $\quad v_0 := \max(\phi(a) \mid a \in A)$
value of the data–problem $\quad v_1 := \max(\phi(d) \mid d \in D)$

Now consider an information structure J, which mediates the transition from the no–data to the data–problem. A reasonable concept of the *value of the information structure* J, or expressed more concise, *value of information* then is the difference

$$v_J := v_1 - v_0 \tag{2.9}$$

It is easily shown, that

$$v_1 - v_0 \geq 0 \quad \text{or} \quad v_J \geq 0 \tag{2.10}$$

Economically, v_J can be interpreted as an upper bound for the price the decision maker is willing to pay for the information structure J, if it is offered for sale.

In definition (2.9) we introduced the difference of two utility values. This can be criticized in view of nonlinear utility theory and be seen as a rather serious simplification. Theoretically one has a use a much more general construction; see for instance Ferschl (1981), p. 60. But as will be pointed out shortly afterwards, our subsequent discussion of information value as a metacriterion for decision rules can be carried out in a sensible way with the more simple concept given in (2.9).

3. Information Resistance of Global Decision Rules

3.1 Global Decision Rules

Consider the criterion ϕ given by $\phi(a_i) = \max_j u_{ij}$. An optimal action a^* with respect to the criterion fulfills

$$\phi(a^*) = \max_i \max_j u_{ij} =: u^*. \tag{3.1}$$

The corresponding decision rule is called the *maximax–rule.* it is a special case of a *global rule*, because it rests on simple optimization over all entries u_{ij} in the decision table.

It should be noted in passing, that the notion of a global rule must not be confused with that of a decision rule of the second kind, where the criterion itself rests on the full decision table. Other examples of global rules besides the maximax rule can be easily found, e.g. a *minimin–loss rule or a minimin–regret rule*. The latter can serve as an example of a global decision rule of the second kind.

3.2 The Information Value under Global Decision Rules

Incorporation of an information structure leads to the data–problem. Now we look at its entries. These may be calculated according to (2.8). Using this version one sees immediately, that

$$\bar{u}(d, \theta_j) = \sum_{i=1}^{m} \pi_{ij}(d) u_{ij} \leq u^* \tag{3.2}$$

for all $d \in D$ and $j = 1, \ldots, n$, because the entries $\bar{u}(d, \theta_j)$ are weighted means of the values u_{ij} of the j–th column in the original decision table. Application of the maximax–rule to the data problem considers the global optimum $\bar{u}^*$, which in turn is bounded above by u^* because of (3.2)

$$\bar{u}^* = \max_{d \in D} \max_j \bar{u}(d, \theta_j) \leq u^* \ . \tag{3.3}$$

According to the definition of the values v_0, v_1, (3.3) means $v_1 \leq v_0$. With relation (2.10), namely $v_1 - v_0 \geq 0$, we get $v_1 = v_0$ or

$$v_J = 0 \ . \tag{3.4}$$

The information value, using the maximax–rule, is always zero, irrespective of the quality of the information structure. Even perfect information does not alter this strange situation. This is a rather strong argument against the use of the maximax–rule. With considerations completely analogue to that given above, one gets similar results for other global decision rules.

3.3 Resistance against Information and the Role of Perfect Information

Information processing with global decision rules can also be seen from a somehow different angle. Let a^* be an optimal action of the no–data–problem, according to (3.1). Now consider the special decision rule

$$d^* := \begin{pmatrix} y_1 \cdots & y_k \cdots & y_s \\ a^* \ldots & a^* \ldots & a^* \end{pmatrix} \tag{3.5}$$

d^* simply means to stick to action a^* of the no–data–problem, irrespective of the outcome of the random variable Y. Whatever information, it could not alter the decision maker's behaviour. This situation is exactly what can be called "*informations resistance*". Evidently d^* guarantees the maximal criterion value $\phi(d^*) = u^*$ and therefore according to (3.3) lies in the choice set of the data–problem. This means, that information resistance is optimal in view of the maximax–rule.

Admittedly, there could be extreme cases, where the maximax decision maker can alter his curious behaviour, but this will be possible only with the help of additional rules, not belonging to the set of axioms given in sec.1. This will be the case, if perfect information is available for instance. To see this, we compare the "optimal" decision function d^* with another decision function d^{**}, which can be constructed with perfect information.

Geometrically, action a^* and decision function d^* are represented by the same row vector resp. point in $\mathbb{R}^n$. Let the maximum $u^* = \max_i \max_j u_{ij}$ be in row i_0 and column j_0 of the decision table, then we can write

$$a^* = (u_{i_0 1} \ldots u_{i_0 j_0} = u^* \ldots u_{i_0 n}) = d^* .$$

Now perfect information tells us with certainty the true state of the world. If θ_j is told us, we can choose an action which guarantees us maximum utility under θ_j,

$$u_j^* := \max_i u_{ij} .$$

But this obvious behaviour is equivalent to the choice of a decision function d^{**} with its corresponding row vector

$$d^{**} = (u_1^* \ldots u_{j0}^* \ldots u_n^*) .$$

Note, that $u_{j0}^* = \max_i u_{ij_0} = u^*$ and $u_{i_0 j} \leq u_j^*$ hold. Comparing d^* and d^{**} componentwise, we see that d^{**} dominates d^*. But because of equality in column j_0, the domination is not strong. We recognize the well known phenomenon of possible domination in the choice set. But with this remark concerning perfect information, the above criticism against the maximax rule is not invalidated. Because in any case, if domination is used as a preliminary procedure to eliminate unfavourable decision function, d^{**} is choosen as optimal, irrespective of the use of any decision rule, if it only obeys axiom 4 of compatibility with (strict) domination.

4. The Role of Intuitively Worthless Information

Considering information structure, there may be situations, where the term "worthless information" would be quite appropriate. So one would like to speak of worthless information, if nobody is willing to pay any price for it, however small its price would be. Such a situation surely is present, if the conditional distributions $P(Y = y_k \mid \theta_j)$ do not depend on the states θ_j at all, or statistically speaking, the distribution of Y is independent of the states of the world. Formally this means, that all rows of the information structure (2.3) are equal. One may ask what would happen if such a worthless information structure is applied to the transition from a no–data–problem to the corresponding data–problem. The answer is simple. The procedure will be equivalent to a randomization of actions in the no–data–problem. Consider again the general expression

$$\bar{u}(d, \theta_j) = \sum_{i=1}^{m} \pi_{ij}(d) u_{ij} \tag{4.1}$$

for the entries in the data–problem. If the distribution of Y is independent of the θ_j, then the action probabilities are as well and we can write $\pi_{ij}(d) =: \pi_i(d)$. Thus (4.1) becomes

$$\bar{u}(d, \theta_j) = \sum_{i=1}^{m} \pi_i(d) u_{ij} \tag{4.2}$$

(4.2) means nothing else but that the entries of the data–problem are determined by randomization of the actions A in the no–data–problem. Every choice of a decision function d gives rise to a randomization with probability vector $(\pi_1(d) \ldots \pi_m(d))$. The points of the data–problem are, geometrically speaking, a subset of the convex hull of A. So it is clear that no one likes to pay for the result of mere randomizations.

But now look at the value v_1 of such a data–problem as introduced in sec. 2.5. It is well known from the theory of zero–sum games, that with the use of maximin–rules randomization is in general advantageous: For player I the value of the game in the mixed extension can be higher than that one in the original matrix game. These two values in game theory however, are equivalent to the values v_1 and v_0 in our decision theoretic discussion, provided the maximin–rule is used. In turn it follows, that with the use of the maximin–rule one may have $v_1 - v_0 = v_J > 0$, in spite of the fact, that worthless information was used, or to say it more blankly, no information was transferred at all.

To make things much worse, most of the decision rules proposed in the case of uncertainty, show more or less the same behaviour. Only the class of Bayes rules is not affected by this phenomenon. Transition to the convex hull of a decision problem does not raise the Bayes value. After all the founder of the theory of information value in decision models is J. Marschak, and it is no mere accident that originally, his theory remained fully in the area of Bayesian constructs. See for instance Marschak (1963) and Marschak (1971) and as a rather elaborated model, La Valle (1968). Furthermore, as a consequence, some former attempts to extend Marschak's theory to other types of decision rules must be reconsidered critically. Of course our development in sec. 2.5 is concerned too. It seems, that an incontestable theory of information value, which wants to use general decision rules, should be based on a comparison of two randomized problems: A fully randomized no–data–problem with its corresponding fully randomized data–problem, see e.g. Ferschl (1975), p. 138 for an example.

5. Concluding Remarks

In sec. 3 we used the concept of information value and the concept of information resistance in order to recommend rejection of so–called global decision rules. In the somehow sidestepping sec. 4 we noticed an opposite behaviour. Decision rules may react *too sensitive* to information structure, as the maximin–rule in the case of worthless information. An extreme viewpoint would be, to throw into doubt one of two possibilities: The use of maximin–rules, or, if one would prefer to stick to this rules, the use of information value for non–Bayesian rules. This may cover doubt on the conclusions of sec. 3 as well. But this conclusion is not cogent. Firstly, it is information resistance, which makes no use of the notion of information value. Secondly, also with full randomization, the results with respect to the maximax–rule would be the same. Thirdly, we admit that some rules may *overestimate*, uncritically used, the value of information. But this must not weaken the argument against global rules, which rests on "*totally underestimating*" information value.

References

1. Bitz, M. (1981). *Entscheidungstheorie.* Franz Vahlen, München
2. Ferschl, F.(1975). *Nutzen– und Entscheidungstheorie.* Westdeutscher Verlag, Opladen
3. Ferschl, F.(1981). *Entscheidungstheoretische Grundlagen der Informationsökonomik.* Verhandlungen des Vereins für Sozialpolitik in Graz 1981. Duncker & Humbolt, Berlin
4. French, S.(1988). *Decision Theory.* Ellis Horwood, Chichester
5. La Valle, I.H.(1968). On Cash Equivalence and Information Evaluation in Decision Under Uncertainty I, II, III. *Journal of the American Statistical Association* **63**.
6. Luce, R.D., Raiffa, H.(1957). *Games and Decisions.* John Wiley, New York
7. Marschak, J.(1963). *The Payoff–Relevant Description of States and Acts. Econometrica* **31**.

8. Marschak, J. (1971). Economies and Information system. *Journal of the American Statistical Association* **66**.
9. Milnor, J.W.(1954). *Games against Nature in: Thrall, Coombs and Davis, Decision Processes.* John Wiley, New York
10. Schneeweiß H.(1966). *Entscheidungskriterien bei Risiko.* Springer Verlag, Berlin

Analysing Ellsberg's Paradox by Means of Interval-Probability

Kurt Weichselberger and Thomas Augustin

Department of Statistics, Ludwig-Maximilians-Universität München, Germany

Summary. The results reported by Ellsberg (1961) are often considered paradoxical. Indeed they reveal behaviour contrasting the sure-thing principle. An analysis employing modern tools produces two insights: 1) The experimental setting of Ellsberg can be adequately described only by means of interval-probability. 2) The validity of the sure-thing principle is restricted to those situations which can sufficiently be described by classical probability. — In addition Ellsberg's results indicate a typology of behaviour when knowledge is given by interval-probability.

1. Introduction

In 1961 Daniel Ellsberg published results of some experiments revealing behaviour not in accordance with the axioms of classical probability, especially contradicting the famous "sure-thing principle" given by L.J. Savage (1954). Due to the high importance of the Savage axioms in decision theory, economists and statisticians paid much attention to Ellsberg's results and tried to solve the paradox. It was understood that the "Ellsberg paradox" was meant to prove the necessity of distinguishing between two different types of uncertainty – the one measurable by classical probability, the other one not. If these results were accepted, application of the Savage axioms should have to be restricted to the first type of uncertainty, while the second type of uncertainty, called "ambiguity" by Ellsberg, should have to be treated in a different way.

An important type of answering to the Ellsberg paradox is the one given by Hans Schneeweiß (1968, 1973). He uses a game theoretic approach to explain the behaviour described by Ellsberg and as a consequence denies any violations of Savage's axioms to be seen in the Ellsberg paradox.

The object of the present study consists in demonstrating that the Ellsberg paradox remains a paradox only, if it is assumed that uncertainty always may adequately be described by classical probability. As soon as the theory of interval-probability is applied, the behaviour described by Ellsberg can be explained consistently. This theory was not available in the sixties, but is well established in the meanwhile. It can be used to provide theoretical tools for an exact modelling of the situations produced by Ellsberg's experiments.

In section 2 a very short introduction to those concepts of interval-probability is given, which are needed in the following sections. Section 3 describes some formal aspects of ordering random events, if an assessment of interval-probability is given. In section 4 it is shown, how the choice of a special ordering is related to a certain behavioural type. In section 5 the consequences of the foregoing considerations are applied to the results of Ellsberg's experiments – leading to a remarkable typology of behaviour in decision-making, but surely revealing nothing like a paradox.

2. Some essentials of the theory of interval-probability

Selected results concerning the theory of interval-probability were published in recent years (e.g. Weichselberger (1995),(1996)), a monograph is forthcoming (Weichselberger (1998)). For the present purpose it is sufficient, therefore, to quote only those axioms and consequences needed directly.

Axiomatic foundation of the theory is based on the concept of classical probability described by the axioms of KOLMOGOROV. Given a sample space Ω and a σ-field $\mathcal{A}$ of random events in Ω, a function

$$\begin{aligned} p(.):\quad & \mathcal{A} \to [0;\,1] \\ & A \mapsto p(A) \end{aligned} \tag{2.1}$$

is called *K-function*, if it obeys the axioms of KOLMOGOROV ("K.I–K.III").

Totally determinate interval-probability in

$$\mathcal{Z}_0 := \{[L;\,U] \mid 0 \le L \le U \le 1\}, \tag{2.2}$$

the concept relevant with respect to the present subject, is defined by adding three axioms.

T.IV:

$$\begin{aligned} P(.):\quad & \mathcal{A} \to \mathcal{Z}_0 \\ & A \mapsto P(A) = [L(A);\,U(A)] \end{aligned} \tag{2.3}$$

T.V: The set $\mathcal{M}$ of K-functions

$$\mathcal{M} := \{p(.) \mid L(A) \le p(A) \le U(A), \quad \forall A \in \mathcal{A}\} \tag{2.4}$$

is not empty.

$P(.)$ obeying T.IV and T.V is called *totally determinate R-probability in* $\mathcal{Z}_0$, the quadruple $\mathcal{R} = (\Omega;\,\mathcal{A};\,L(.),\,U(.))$ is called an *R-(probability) field* and $\mathcal{M}$ is called *structure* of $\mathcal{R}$. While Axiom T.V describes the minimum standard of a reasonable interval-probability assessment, a probability assessment of a higher quality is defined by the last axiom.

T.VI: Totally determinate R-probability in $\mathcal{Z}_0$ with structure $\mathcal{M}$ is called *totally determinate F-probability* in $\mathcal{Z}_0$, if the relation

$$\left.\begin{aligned} \inf_{p(.)\in\mathcal{M}} p(A) = L(A) \\ \sup_{p(.)\in\mathcal{M}} p(A) = U(A) \end{aligned}\right\} \forall A \in \mathcal{A} \tag{2.5}$$

holds.

$\mathcal{F} = (\Omega;\ \mathcal{A};\ L(.))$ then is designated as an *F-(probability) field* in $\mathcal{Z}_0$.

It is easy to show that for an F-probability field always

$$\begin{array}{lllll} L(\Omega) & = & U(\Omega) & = & 1 \\ L(\emptyset) & = & U(\emptyset) & = & 0 \end{array} \tag{2.6}$$

and

$$U(A) = 1 - L(\neg A), \quad \forall A \in \mathcal{A}, \tag{2.7}$$

must hold.

3. Complete orderings of the set of random events

For the purpose of the present study there is one very important difference between F-probability fields and classical probability fields: In the latter the probability of each event consists of a single real value. Then there is no doubt how events should be ordered with respect to their probability. Since the structure $\mathcal{M}$ of an F-probability field, however, may consist of more than one K-function, there may be more than one reasonable order.

While there exist several obvious methods of constructing *partial* orderings of the random events, for the purpose of modelling decision processes only *complete* orderings should be aimed at. A very general type of complete orderings can be described as follows.

3.1 Definition. Let $\Theta_1 = \Theta_1(L, U)$, $\Theta_2 = \Theta_2(L, U)$, $0 \leq L \leq U \leq 1$, be given so that the inverse functions $L = L(\Theta_1, \Theta_2)$, $U = U(\Theta_1, \Theta_2)$ are well defined. Furthermore $\Theta_1(\cdot,\cdot)$ as well as $\Theta_2(\cdot,\cdot)$ must obey one of the following two conditions of monotonicity:

For $i = 1, 2$ either

$$\left.\begin{array}{lll} \Theta_i(L_1;U) & > & \Theta_i(L_2;U) \quad \forall L_1 > L_2, \forall U \\ \Theta_i(L;U_1) & \geq & \Theta_i(L;U_2) \quad \forall L, \forall U_1 > U_2 \end{array}\right\} \tag{3.1}$$

or

$$\left.\begin{array}{lll} \Theta_i(L_1;U) & \geq & \Theta_i(L_2;U) \quad \forall L_1 > L_2, \forall U \\ \Theta_i(L;U_1) & > & \Theta_i(L;U_2) \quad \forall L, \forall U_1 > U_2 \end{array}\right\} \tag{3.2}$$

must hold.

Then for an F-probability field $\mathcal{F} = (\Omega;\ \mathcal{A};\ L(.))$ a relation $\prec$ on $\mathcal{A} \times \mathcal{A}$ is called a *complete ordering of the elements of $\mathcal{A}$ with respect to the (Θ_1, Θ_2)-criterion*, if for all $A, B \in \mathcal{A}$

$$\begin{array}{lll} A \prec B \iff & \Big[\Theta_1(L(A), U(A)) & < \Theta_1(L(B), U(B))\Big] \vee \\ & \vee \Big[\big[\Theta_1(L(A), U(A)) & = \Theta_1(L(B), U(B))\big] \wedge \\ & \wedge\big[\Theta_2(L(A), U(A)) & < \Theta_2(L(B), U(B)) \text{ big}\Big] \end{array} \tag{3.3}$$

comes true. □

It can easily be seen that for different $P(A) = [L(A); U(A)]$ and $P(B) = [L(B); U(B)]$ either $A \prec B$ or $B \prec A$ must hold.[1]

The influence of Θ_1 upon the resulting ordering is much greater than that of Θ_2: The effect of Θ_2 is restricted to those pairs, where Θ_1 is unable to specify an order.

Two cases of (Θ_1, Θ_2)-criteria are obvious choices: *(L, U)-criterion* and *(U, L)-criterion.* In the first case the lower interval-limit is used as decisive, in the second case the upper interval-limit. In both situations the interval-limit in the second place is of importance for those pairs only, where the first one is the same for both events.

Criteria producing complete orderings may be viewed from two sides: from the formal view-point and from the behaviouristic one. In the present section only the formal aspects are considered. Some remarks on the behavioural interpretation will follow later.

The ordering of events in a *classical* probability field by use of $p(.)$ shows two – at a first glance – convincing properties:

1. $\forall A, B \in \mathcal{A} : p(A) < p(B) \Longleftrightarrow p(\neg B) = 1 - p(B) < 1 - p(A) = p(\neg A)$
   Therefore:
   $$A \prec B \Longleftrightarrow \neg B \prec \neg A. \qquad (3.4)$$
   This may be designated as *principle of complementarity*, **(BI)**.
2. $\forall A, B, C \in \mathcal{A}, \quad A \cap B = B \cap C = \emptyset$:
   $$p(A) < p(B) \quad \Longleftrightarrow \quad p(A) + p(C) = p(A \cup C) < p(B \cup C) = p(B) + p(C).$$
   Therefore:
   $$A \prec B \Longleftrightarrow A \cup C \prec B \cup C. \qquad (3.5)$$
   This is a necessary condition for the famous *sure-thing principle*, here it is called "sure-thing principle" **(BII)**.

Using a very simple example, which has to be considered later again, it can be shown that neither (BI) nor (BII) may be taken as granted for orderings of random events in $\mathcal{A}$ via the (L, U)-criterion or the (U, L)-criterion.

3.2 Example. Let $\Omega = E_1 \cup E_2 \cup E_3$ with $E_i \cap E_j = \emptyset$, $i \neq j$, $i, j = 1, 2, 3$, $\mathcal{A} = \mathcal{P}(\Omega)$, and let $\mathcal{F} = (\Omega; \mathcal{A}; L(.))$ be given by

$$L(E_1) = \tfrac{1}{3} \qquad L(E_1 \cup E_2) = \tfrac{1}{3}$$
$$L(E_2) = 0 \qquad L(E_1 \cup E_3) = \tfrac{1}{3}$$
$$L(E_3) = 0 \qquad L(E_2 \cup E_3) = \tfrac{2}{3}.$$

[1] For $P(A) = P(B)$ either $A \sim B$ ("A is equivalent to B") is accepted or an additional criterion – not relying on $L(\cdot)$ and $U(\cdot)$ – may be employed; in this case the resulting order is described by properties of the structure. An example is given in Footnote 4.

Using equation (2.7) one arrives at

$$\begin{aligned} U(E_1) &= 1 - L(E_2 \cup E_3) = \tfrac{1}{3} & U(E_1 \cup E_2) &= 1 - L(E_3) = 1 \\ U(E_2) &= 1 - L(E_1 \cup E_3) = \tfrac{2}{3} & U(E_1 \cup E_3) &= 1 - L(E_2) = 1 \\ U(E_3) &= 1 - L(E_1 \cup E_2) = \tfrac{2}{3} & U(E_2 \cup E_3) &= 1 - L(E_1) = \tfrac{2}{3}. \end{aligned}$$

The F-probability assessment therefore may be described as:

$$\begin{aligned} P(E_1) &= \left[\tfrac{1}{3}; \tfrac{1}{3}\right] =: \left[\tfrac{1}{3}\right] & P(E_1 \cup E_2) &= \left[\tfrac{1}{3}; 1\right] \\ P(E_2) &= \left[0; \tfrac{2}{3}\right] & P(E_1 \cup E_3) &= \left[\tfrac{1}{3}; 1\right] \\ P(E_3) &= \left[0; \tfrac{2}{3}\right] & P(E_2 \cup E_3) &= \left[\tfrac{2}{3}; \tfrac{2}{3}\right] =: \left[\tfrac{2}{3}\right]. \end{aligned}$$

That this assignment indeed produces an F-field, is shown by demonstrating that all interval-limits are reached by elements of the structure:

$p_1(.) : \; p_1(E_1) = \frac{1}{3}, \; p_1(E_2) = \frac{2}{3}, \; p_1(E_3) = 0$ reaches
$L(E_1)$, $U(E_1)$, $U(E_2)$, $L(E_3)$, $U(E_1 \cup E_2)$, $L(E_1 \cup E_3)$, $L(E_2 \cup E_3)$, $U(E_2 \cup E_3)$.

$p_2(.) : \; p_2(E_1) = \frac{1}{3}, \; p_2(E_2) = 0, \; p_2(E_3) = \frac{2}{3}$ reaches in particular
$L(E_2)$, $U(E_3)$, $L(E_1 \cup E_2)$, $U(E_1 \cup E_3)$.

If the (L, U)-criterion is applied to this F-field, the following complete ordering is produced:

$$\emptyset \prec E_2 \sim E_3 \prec E_1 \prec (E_1 \cup E_2) \sim (E_1 \cup E_3) \prec (E_2 \cup E_3) \prec \Omega.$$

(BI) from relation (3.4) is violated by

$$E_2 \prec E_1, \quad \neg E_2 = (E_1 \cup E_3) \prec (E_2 \cup E_3) = \neg E_1;$$

relation (3.5), the sure-thing principle (BII), is not fullfilled because of:

$$E_2 \prec E_1, \quad (E_1 \cup E_3) \prec (E_2 \cup E_3).$$

If the (U, L)-criterion is applied, on arrives at the following complete ordering of the random events:

$$\emptyset \prec E_1 \prec E_2 \sim E_3 \prec (E_2 \cup E_3) \prec (E_1 \cup E_2) \sim (E_1 \cup E_3) \prec \Omega.$$

Although this order differs considerably from that created by the (L, U)-criterion, it also contains violations of (BI):

$$E_1 \prec E_2, \quad \neg E_1 = (E_2 \cup E_3) \prec (E_1 \cup E_3) = \neg E_2$$

and (BII): $\quad E_1 \prec E_2, \quad (E_2 \cup E_3) \prec (E_1 \cup E_3).$ □

Both (L, U)-criterion and (U, L)-criterion may be characterized as being "extreme criteria": As long as possible they rely on one interval-limit alone. Simple criteria which may be seen as "more moderate" are found by using

$$\begin{aligned} \Theta_1 &= \alpha L + (1-\alpha)U, \quad 0 \le \alpha \le 1, \\ \Theta_2 &= \beta L + (1-\beta)U, \quad 0 \le \beta \le 1, \quad \beta \ne \alpha. \end{aligned} \tag{3.6}$$

Do they all violate (BI) and (BII) as well? It can be shown that the answer is "Yes". Again the F-field of Example 3.2 is used.

3.3 Example. For the F-probability field considered, any criterion of type (3.6) provided $\alpha > \frac{1}{2}$ produces just the same ordering as the (L, U)-criterion and therefore the same violations of (BI) and (BII). In the case of $\alpha < \frac{1}{2}$ the same ordering is produced as by the (U, L)-criterion – and again (BI) and (BII) are violated.

There remains the case $\alpha = \frac{1}{2}$ which necessarily involves $\beta \ne \frac{1}{2}$. Concerning Θ_1,

$$\tfrac{1}{2}\left(L(A) + U(A)\right) = \tfrac{1}{3}$$

holds for $A = E_1,\ E_2,\ E_3$, and the relation

$$\tfrac{1}{2}\left(L(A) + U(A)\right) = \tfrac{2}{3}$$

holds for $A = (E_1 \cup E_2),\ (E_1 \cup E_3),\ (E_2 \cup E_3)$.

Therefore the order of E_1, E_2, E_3 is determined by the size of β only and so is the order of $(E_1 \cup E_2)$, $(E_1 \cup E_3)$, $(E_2 \cup E_3)$.

If $\beta > \frac{1}{2}$, the same order is produced as with the (L, U)-criterion – and, therefore, the same violations of (BI) and (BII). In case of $\beta < \frac{1}{2}$, the order of the (U, L)-criterion together with its violations of (BI) and (BII) is created. □

If the choice of criteria is restricted to the linear type described by (3.6) it is obvious that either by α or – if $\alpha = \frac{1}{2}$ – by β the dominance of one of the two interval-limits must be decided. Therefore, a distinction between *L-dominated criteria* and *U-dominated criteria* is useful – as already hinted at in discussing Example 3.3.

Only *bijective criteria* have been employed so far: They ensure that either $A \prec B$ or $B \prec A$ must hold whenever $P(A) \ne P(B)$. Now it may be asked whether different results can be achieved, if *weaker* criteria are admitted which also allow for $A \sim B$ in some cases with $P(A) \ne P(B)$.

Such a criterion is produced, if a bijective (Θ_1, Θ_2)-criterion is reduced to becoming a Θ_1-criterion, where the values of Θ_2 are not taken into account. Therefore the criterion states $A \sim B$ for all pairs with $\Theta_1(L(A), U(A)) = \Theta_1(L(B), U(B))$. To ensure monotonicity, either (3.1) or (3.2) must hold for Θ_1.

Again obvious choices for $\Theta(\cdot,\cdot) := \Theta_1(\cdot,\cdot)$ are

$$\Theta(L, U) = L$$

producing the *L-criterion*, a weakening of the (L, U)-criterion, and

$$\Theta(L, U) = U$$

producing the *U-criterion*, a weakening of the (U, L)-criterion.

More generally, using in analogy to (3.6):

$$\Theta(L, U) = \alpha L + (1 - \alpha)U, \quad 0 \leq \alpha \leq 1, \tag{3.7}$$

an L-dominated criterion results for $\alpha > \frac{1}{2}$ and an U-dominated one for $\alpha < \frac{1}{2}$.

In Example 3.3 it was shown that for the F-field described in Example 3.2 both principles, – (BI) as well as (BII) – are violated for $\alpha > \frac{1}{2}$ and for $\alpha < \frac{1}{2}$. Nevertheless there remains the case $\alpha = \frac{1}{2}$, the *m-criterion*, where $m = \frac{1}{2}(L+U)$. Using this criterion for the random events of the F-field under consideration the order

$$\emptyset \prec E_1 \sim E_2 \sim E_3 \prec (E_1 \cup E_2) \sim (E_1 \cup E_3) \sim (E_2 \cup E_3) \prec \Omega$$

is created. Evidently this is in full accordance with (BI) and (BII). Indeed it can easily be checked that due to (2.7) principle (BI) can never be violated by the m-criterion and that in order to demonstrate a violation of (BII) by this criterion at least an F-field with $\Omega = E_1 \cup E_2 \cup E_3 \cup E_4$ must be considered.

3.4 Example. Let $\Omega = E_1 \cup E_2 \cup E_3 \cup E_4$ with $E_i \cap E_j$, $i \neq j$, $i, j = 1, 2, 3, 4$, $\mathcal{A} = \mathcal{P}(\Omega)$ and $\mathcal{F} = (\Omega, \mathcal{A}; L(\cdot))$ be given by

$$\begin{aligned}
&L(E_1) = 0.25\\
&L(E_2) = L(E_3) = L(E_4) = 0.00\\
&L(E_1 \cup E_2) = L(E_1 \cup E_3) = L(E_1 \cup E_4) = 0.25\\
&L(E_2 \cup E_3) = L(E_2 \cup E_4) = L(E_3 \cup E_4) = 0.00\\
&L(E_1 \cup E_2 \cup E_3) = L(E_1 \cup E_2 \cup E_4) = L(E_1 \cup E_3 \cup E_4) = 0.25\\
&L(E_2 \cup E_3 \cup E_4) = 0.75
\end{aligned}$$

Using Equation (2.7) one arrives at

$$\begin{aligned}
&P(E_1) = [0.25] \ \ldots\ldots\ldots\ldots\ldots\ldots\ldots\ldots\ldots\ldots & m(\cdot) = 0.250\\
&P(E_2) = P(E_3) = P(E_4) = [0.00; 0.75] \ \ldots\ldots\ldots\ldots & m(\cdot) = 0.375\\
&P(E_1 \cup E_2) = P(E_1 \cup E_3) = P(E_1 \cup E_4) = [0.25; 1] \ \ldots & m(\cdot) = 0.625\\
&P(E_2 \cup E_3) = P(E_2 \cup E_4) = P(E_3 \cup E_4) = [0.00; 0.75] & m(\cdot) = 0.375\\
&P(E_1 \cup E_2 \cup E_3) = P(E_1 \cup E_2 \cup E_4) = & \\
&= P(E_1 \cup E_3 \cup E_4) = [0.25; 1] \ \ldots\ldots\ldots\ldots\ldots\ldots & m(\cdot) = 0.625\\
&P(E_2 \cup E_3 \cup E_4) = [0.75] \ \ldots\ldots\ldots\ldots\ldots\ldots\ldots & m(\cdot) = 0.750
\end{aligned}$$

The m-criterion produces therefore:

$$\begin{aligned}
\emptyset \prec \ & E_1 \prec E_2 \sim E_3 \sim E_4 \sim (E_2 \cup E_3) \sim\\
\sim \ & (E_2 \cup E_4) \sim (E_3 \cup E_4) \prec (E_1 \cup E_2) \sim (E_1 \cup E_3) \sim\\
\sim \ & (E_1 \cup E_4) \sim (E_1 \cup E_2 \cup E_3) \sim (E_1 \cup E_2 \cup E_4) \sim (E_1 \cup E_3 \cup E_4) \prec\\
\prec \ & (E_2 \cup E_3 \cup E_4) \prec \Omega,
\end{aligned}$$

violating (BII) through

$$E_1 \prec E_i \quad , \quad (E_i \cup E_j) \prec (E_1 \cup E_j), \quad \text{where } i \neq j, \quad i,j = 2,3,4,$$

as well as through

$$(E_i \cup E_j) \prec (E_1 \prec E_i) \quad , \quad (E_1 \cup E_i \cup E_l) \prec (E_2 \cup E_3 \cup E_4),$$

where $i \neq j \neq l, i \neq l, \quad i,j,l = 2,3,4.$ □

Summarizing the considerations described above one recognizes that (BII) often is violated, when a complete ordering of the random events in an F-field is used: The theory of interval-probability includes situations where the the general validity of the sure-thing principle need not to be presupposed.

4. The behaviouristic point of view

The importance of the concept of ordering random events according to their probability with respect to modelling decisions, is widely acknowledged – at least as long classical probability is applied. Prior to any considerations concerning expected utility it is accepted that a person who may choose between two events – with an exactly described consequence if the chosen event occurs – will select the event which the person feels is more likely to occur, if the consequence is felt as being favourable, – and otherwise select the event less likely.

While in case of classical probability the meaning of "more likely" and "less likely" is obvious and not exposed to interpersonal variations, this may not be expected with respect to any alternative tool, employed if classical probability is not sufficient to describe a situation. In the first line this applies to interval-probability.

If the situation is described by an F-probability field, relevant differences to the classical situation must be taken into account: Since a *unique* ordering of the events with respect to their "likelihood" does not always exist, decisions of a person may be dependent on the actual ordering the person relies on. Different persons may possess different attitudes towards orderings and the same applies to one person with respect to different purposes: Inevitably some elements of decision-theoretic strategies – other than the simple maximization of expected utility in the classical case – will influence the persons' behaviour.

If the consequence of an event A is felt to be favourable by the person, necessarily the consequence of the complementary event $\neg A$ must be felt unfavourable – at least relatively. If the person decides rationally, there must be *consistency*, whether the favourable consequence of A or the unfavourable one of $\neg A$ is considered: If $A \prec B$ holds for favourable consequences, $\neg B \prec \neg A$ must hold for unfavourable ones. Using classical probability consistency is guaranteed by (BI), the principle of complementarity.

If an F-probability field is applied, (BI) must no more be taken as granted. Therefore, consistency does not allow to maintain the *same ordering* for both types of deliberation. Equation (2.7) describes the necessary procedure: When switching from A to $\neg A$ and from a favourable consequence to an unfavourable one, the rôles of $L(.)$ and $U(.)$ have to be exchanged.

4.1 Definition. If $\Theta_i = \Theta_i(L, U)$ and $\Theta_i^* = \Theta_i(U, L)$, $i = 1, 2$, then the (Θ_1, Θ_2)-criterion and the (Θ_1^*, Θ_2^*)-criterion are called *conjugate* to each other. □

This definition immediately leads to the following result.

4.2 Corollary. For all $A, B \in \mathcal{A}$ it holds that $A \prec B$ is produced by the (Θ_1, Θ_2)-criterion if and only if $\neg B \prec \neg A$ is produced by the conjugate criterion. □

With respect to conditions for consistent decision-making one arrives at the following rules and at a typology of behaviour.

1. A person consistently using the (L, U)-criterion for comparing events with possibly favourable consequences employs the (U, L)-criterion in the comparison of events with possibly unfavourable consequences – and vice versa. The behaviour of such a person fits to suggestions given already in 1943 by Borel: If forced to bet on an event A, one will demand that the price $L(A)$ is adopted (cf. Borel (1943; Chapter 5.8)). Also it is in accordance with Walley's (1991; especially Chapter 2.3) interpretation: $L(A)$ is the "supremum buying price for a bet on the event A".
2. A person consistently using the (U, L)-criterion when comparing events which may have favourable consequences will employ the (L, U)-criterion when comparing possibly unfavourable events. The behaviour of such persons is not supported by theoretical considerations. On the contrary: Buying a bet for a higher price and selling it for a lower one is not a strategy avoiding sure loss. It must lead to a Dutch book. Such persons may be viewed as extremely optimistic: They judge a situation by its most favourable aspects.
   More generally:
3. Using consistently an L-dominated criterion in comparisons of favourable events implies the use of the U-dominated conjugate criterion for unfavourable ones. This type includes type 1 and may be characterized as "uncertainty-averse".
4. Persons consistently using an U-dominated criterion when comparing events with possibly favourable consequences and the L-dominated conjugate criterion in case of unfavourable consequences may be called "uncertainty-attracted". This type obviously includes type 2.

The importance of the foregoing considerations lies in the fact that they can be used to overcome the Ellsberg paradox.

5. Ellsberg's experiments

Ellsberg reports the results of two experiments. Since the first one is of rather introductory character, it is sufficient for the purpose of this study to discuss the second one. (cf. Ellsberg (1961; pp.653ff.))

5.1 Example. He asked persons to imagine an urn containing 30 *red* balls and 60 *black* and *yellow* balls, the latter in unknown proportion.[2] One ball is to be drawn at random from the urn.

The first question was: "You can either get the prize, if the ball drawn is *red* or you can get it, if it is *black*. Which possibility do you prefer?"

Then a second question was asked: "Either you get the prize, if the ball is *red or yellow* or you get it, if it is *black or yellow*? Which of the two possibilities do you prefer?"

Ellsberg reports: "A very frequent pattern of response is":
Question 1: *Red* is preferred to *black*.
Question 2: *Black or yellow* is preferred to *red or yellow*.
This pattern of behaviour is named type A in the following.

"Less frequent is" the next pattern of response:
Question 1: *Black* is preferred to *red*.
Question 2: *Red or yellow* is preferred to *black or yellow*.
This pattern of behaviour will be designated as type B in the following.

It seems that all other types of response have numerically not been remarkable, since Ellsberg does not mention any of them explicitly.

The interest in these results is due to the relations (5.1) and (5.2) below: Let the event "the *red* ball is drawn" be designated by E_1, the event "the *black* ball is drawn" by E_2 and the event "the *yellow* ball is drawn" by E_3. Always the event preferred will be the one, the person feels more likely to occur. Therefore the pattern of response named type A must be interpreted as

$$E_2 \prec E_1, \quad (E_1 \cup E_3) \prec (E_2 \cup E_3). \tag{5.1}$$

In the same way type B means

$$E_1 \prec E_2, \quad (E_2 \cup E_3) \prec (E_1 \cup E_3). \tag{5.2}$$

This shows that the behaviour of type A as well as that of type B violates the sure-thing principle (BII) and therefore is in contradiction with the axioms of Savage. No ordering obtained by any classical probability measure is able to describe the most frequent types of behaviour.[3] It was felt paradoxical

[2] For demonstrating the essentials of the experiment it seems preferable to use the denomination "other colours than red and black" instead of "yellow": The results remain unchanged, if more than three colours are distinguished.

[3] Since the sure-thing principle is strongly connected with the axiom of additivity (cf. the considerations leading to equation (3.5)), the criticism of the sure-thing principle applies to each of the variants of classical probability .

that Savage's theory – which aims at modelling rational behaviour – fails in describing this simple situation.

Exclusive application of classical probability demands that every behaviour contradicting the sure-thing principle is classified as irrational. — But is behaviour of type A or of type B really irrational? Indeed, most of the participants of Ellsberg's thought-experiments insisted on their opinions and refused to judge their ordering of the events as irrational.

If today the setting of this experiment is described by means of probability, automatically one is led to the use of interval probability: The F-probability field used in Example 3.2 is the exact description of the information given by Ellsberg. For convenience the assessment is cited a second time:

$$\begin{aligned} P(E_1) &= \left[\tfrac{1}{3}\right] & P(E_1 \cup E_2) &= \left[\tfrac{1}{3};\, 1\right] \\ P(E_2) &= \left[0;\, \tfrac{2}{3}\right] & P(E_1 \cup E_3) &= \left[\tfrac{1}{3};\, 1\right] \\ P(E_3) &= \left[0;\, \tfrac{2}{3}\right]. & P(E_2 \cup E_3) &= \left[\tfrac{2}{3}\right] \end{aligned}$$

Considering the responses of type A, relation (5.1) describes the information available concerning the decision-making behaviour of these persons. In Examples 3.2 und 3.3 it is demonstrated that by all L-dominated criteria, among them the (L, U)-criterion, – and only by these criteria – equation (5.1) is created for the given F-field. Therefore, it is possible to conclude from Ellsberg's results that the persons responding in this way belong to type 3. The majority may therefore be characterized as uncertainty-averse.

In the same way the members of the smaller group giving statements of type B are identified as belonging to behavioural type 4 of uncertainty-attracted persons.

It should be noted: In Ellsberg's results there is no proof at all, that patterns of type A correspond to behaviour of type 1 or that patterns of type B correspond to behaviour of type 2. Relations (5.1) and (5.2) can be produced by much "milder" criteria as well.

Somebody determined not to violate the sure-thing principle will use the m-criterion, which leads to: $E_1 \sim E_2$, $(E_1 \cup E_3) \sim (E_2 \cup E_3)$. His response would be: It makes no difference, whether *red* or *black* and in the same way *red or yellow* and *black or yellow* are equivalent. This could be called "uncertainty-neutrality." □

5.2 Example. A slight modification of Ellsberg's experiment produces further insights: Example 3.4 provides the opportunity to consider a slightly modified experiment: Imagine an urn with 120 balls in it, 30 of them are *red*, the other 90 are either *black* or *yellow* or *white* in unknown proportion. You have no further information about the urn. One ball is drawn randomly.

Three questions may be asked:

Question 1: "Do you prefer to get the prize, if the ball drawn is *red* or if it is *black*?"

Question 2: "Do you prefer to get the prize, if the ball drawn is *red or yellow* or to get the prize, if it is *black or yellow*?"

Question 3: "Do you prefer to get the prize, if the ball drawn is *red or yellow or white* or to get the prize, if it is *black or yellow or white*?"

If the draw of a *red* ball is identified with random event E_1 and that of a *black*, a *yellow* or a *white* ball is identified with E_2, E_3 and E_4 respectively, the F-field of Example 3.4 exactly describes the information given above.[4] Simple considerations produce a typology of response-patterns which contains more information than that of Ellsberg's experiment:

1. If the L-criterion is applied or a linear criterion as described in (3.7) with $\alpha > \frac{2}{3}$ is applied, the answers are : Question 1: *red*, Question 2: *red or yellow*, Question 3: *black or yellow or white.* This pattern indicates behaviour of type 3, uncertainty averse.
2. If $\alpha = \frac{2}{3}$ in (3.7), the criterion Θ produces $E_1 \sim E_2$. If a decision is wanted, whether *red* or *black* should be the response to the first question, a bijective criterion is needed.
3. If $\frac{2}{3} > \alpha > \frac{1}{3}$ in (3.7) the pattern is given as: Question 1: *black*, Question 2: *red or yellow*, Question 3: *black or yellow or white.* This pattern indicates a "moderate" type of behaviour which is either mildly uncertainty-averse or uncertainty-neutral or mildly uncertainty-attracted. For instance: To employ the m-criterion means belonging to this type.
4. In case of $\alpha = \frac{1}{3}$, by (3.7) the equivalence $(E_2 \cup E_3 \cup E_4) \sim (E_1 \cup E_3 \cup E_4)$ is produced. For a decision again a bijective criterion would be necessary.
5. If $\frac{1}{3} > \alpha$ in (3.7), the responses are: Question 1: *black*, Question 2: *red or yellow*, Question 3: *red or yellow or white.* Behaviour of type 4 is indicated: uncertainty-attracted.

Pattern 1 violates (BI) and (BII) by

$$E_2 \prec E_1 \quad , \quad (E_1 \cup E_3 \cup E_4) \prec (E_2 \cup E_3 \cup E_4)$$

and (BII) by

$$(E_2 \cup E_3) \prec (E_1 \cup E_3) \quad , \quad (E_1 \cup E_3 \cup E_4) \prec (E_2 \cup E_3 \cup E_4).$$

Pattern 3 violates (BII) by

$$E_1 \prec E_2 \quad , \quad (E_2 \cup E_3) \prec (E_1 \cup E_3)$$

and by

[4] This example may be used to demonstrate that – if one relies on criteria additionally employing properties of the structure – the relation $A \prec B$ is possible in the case $P(A) = P(B)$ (cf. Footnote 1): "Do you prefer to get the prize, if the ball drawn is *black* or if it is *black or yellow*?" Consider: $P(E_2) = P(E_2 \cup E_3) = [0.00; 0.75]$!
Does a similiar phenomenon exist in classical probability? (Compare A with $A \cup B$, for $A \cap B = \emptyset$, when $p(B) = 0$!)

$$(E_2 \cup E_3) \prec (E_1 \cup E_3) \quad , \quad (E_1 \cup E_3 \cup E_4) \prec (E_2 \cup E_3 \cup E_4).$$

Pattern 5 violates (BII) by

$$E_1 \prec E_2 \quad , \quad (E_2 \cup E_3) \prec (E_1 \cup E_3)$$

and (BI) as well as (BII) by

$$E_1 \prec E_2 \quad , \quad (E_2 \cup E_3 \cup E_4) \prec (E_1 \cup E_3 \cup E_4).$$

In this experiment somebody relying on the m-criterion could not avoid violating the sure-thing principle. This applies in the same way to persons using $\alpha = \frac{1}{3}$ and $\alpha = \frac{2}{3}$. — One kind of response in accordance with the sure-thing principle is "undecided" to all three questions. Such pattern could be founded on the argument: "In the *average* of all possible settings there is the same proportion for all four colours." Behaviour of this type could be characterized as "uncertainty-neglecting".[5] It does not employ a criterion based on the interval-limits $L(\cdot)$ and $U(\cdot)$. Because of Ellsberg's results it may be assumed that this type of behaviour can be neglected. □

6. Conclusion

The résumé must be: While violations of the principle of complementarity only show that the criterion employed is not self-conjugate, actual violations of the sure-thing principle always are a strong evidence for the insufficiency of classical probability theory in describing the type of uncertainty prevailing in the given situation. The sure-thing principle only seems to be evident, if it is tacitly assumed that all kinds of uncertainty must be described by classical probability. It is by no means forced in any theory of more expressive power. Experiments of the Ellsberg-type may provide valuable insights into behaviour under uncertainty. Up to now they have demonstrated, that there exist situations in which analysing rationality asks for a more comprehensive theory of behaviour under uncertainty than that restricted to classical probability theory. Ellsberg's comments show that he strongly felt the need for new tools to analyse types of uncertainty not covered by classical probability.[6] The

[5] In case of Ellsberg's original experiment it is not possible to distinguish between uncertainty-neutrality (i.e. application of the m-criterion) and uncertainty-neglecting behaviour (only possible in special cases of symmetry and equivalent to the principle of insufficient reason producing classical uniform distribution in the symmetric components.)

[6] "Responses from confessed violators [of the sure-thing principle, K.W. and T.A.] indicate that the difference is not to be found in terms of the two factors commonly used to determine a choice situation, the relative desirability of the possible pay-offs and the relative likelihood of the events affecting them, but in a third dimension of the problem of choice: the nature of one's information concerning the relative likelihood of events. What is at issue might be called

theory of interval-probability exactly meets these requirements. Ellsberg's experiments therefore may be understood as an additional motivation for the study and the application of the theory of interval-probability.

References

1. Borel, E. (1943). *Les Probabilitiés et la Vie.* Universitaires de France. – English translation: (1962) *Probabilities and Life.* Dover. New York
2. Ellsberg, D. (1961). Risk, ambiguity, and the Savage axioms. *Quarterly Journal of Economics.* **75**; 643-669
3. Savage, L.J.(1954). *The Foundations of Statistics.* Dover. New York
4. Schneeweiß, H. (1968). Spieltheoretische Analyse des Ellsberg-Paradoxons. *Zeitschrift für die gesamte Staatswissenschaft* **124**; 249-255
5. Schneeweiß, H. (1973). The Ellsberg paradox from the point of view of game theory. *Inference and Decision.* **1**; 65-78
6. Walley, P. (1991). *Statistical Reasoning with Imprecise Probabilities.* Chapman & Hall. London
7. Weichselberger, K. (1995). Axiomatic foundations of the theory of interval-probability. In: Mammitzsch, V.; Schneeweiß, H. (Hg.): *Proceedings of the Second Gauß Symposion, Section B.* de Gruyter. Berlin; 47-64
8. Weichselberger, K. (1996). Interval-probability on finite sample-spaces. In: H. Rieder (Hg.): *Robust Statistics, Data Analysis and Computer Intensive Methods. In Honor of Peter Huber's 60th Birthday.* Springer. New York; 391-409
9. Weichselberger, K. (1998). *Elementare Grundbegriffe einer allgemeineren Wahrscheinlichkeitsrechnung. Vol.I* forthcoming

the ambiguity of this information, a quality depending on the amount, type, reliability and 'unanimity' of information, and giving rise to one's degree of 'confidence' in an estimate of relative likelihoods." (Ellsberg (1961; p.657))

Some Robust and Adaptive Tests Versus F–Test for Several Samples

Herbert Büning

Department of Statistics and Econometrics, Freie Universität Berlin, Germany

Summary. Testing the equality of c means the application of the F–test depends on very restrictive assumptions such as normality and equal variances of the c populations. If these assumptions are not satisfied it is more appropriate to apply a robust version of the F–test. We consider the Welch test, a rank version of the Welch test, the trimmed Welch test and some nonparametric counterparts where each of them is very efficient for a special class of distributions. But usually the practising statistician has no clear idea of the underlying distribution. Therefore, an adaptive test should be applied which takes into account the given data. We compare the F–test with its robust and adaptive competitors under normality and nonnormality as well as under homoscedasticity and heteroscedasticity. The comparison is referred to level α and power β of the test and is carried out via Monte Carlo simulation. It turns out that the Welch test is the best one in the case of unequal variances, for equal variances, however, special rank tests are to prefer. It is also shown that the adaptive test behaves well over a broad class of distributions.

1. Introduction

One of the fundamental problems of statistics is the c–sample location problem. The one-way ANOVA F–test is generally applied under the assumptions of normality and equal group variances. In practice, however, unequal variances and nonnormality appear to be the rule rather than the exception, as demonstrated by two real data sets. Thus we have to look for alternatives to the F–test if the classical assumptions seem to be violated. We consider the Welch test, see Welch (1951), a rank version of the Welch test following a proposal of Conover and Iman (1981) and the trimmed Welch test, introduced by Lee and Fung (1983).

The purpose of this paper is twofold, first, to compare the F–test with its robustified counterparts under normality and nonnormality as well as under homoscedasticity and heteroscedasticity, and second, to present an adaptive distribution–free test and to compare it with the single rank tests in the adaptive scheme and with the parametric tests. The adaptive test is based on Hogg's concept, that is, to classify at first the type of the underlying distribution with respect to some measures like tailweight and skewness and then to select an appropriate rank test for the classified type of distribution. Robust and adaptive tests for the two-sample problem are studied e.g. by Büning (1994).

Monte Carlo simulations are used for the comparison of the tests with respect to level α and power β assuming short-, medium- and long-tailed distributions as well as asymmetric ones. It turns out that the Welch test is very α–robust in the case of unequal variances (except for the Cauchy distribution) but for equal variances special rank tests are to prefer. It is also shown for the case of equal variances that the proposed Welch rank test is more efficient than the Welch test for long-tailed and asymmetric distributions, but, on the whole, the adaptive test is the best one over the broad class of distributions considered.

2. The F–test and some robust competitors

Let $X_{i1},\ldots,X_{in_i}$, $i = 1,\ldots,c$, be independent and normally distributed random variables, i.e.

$$X_{ij} \sim N\left(\mu_i, \sigma_i^2\right), j = 1,\ldots,n_i \,.$$

We wish to test
$H_0 : \mu_1 = \ldots = \mu_c$ versus $H_1 : \mu_r \neq \mu_s$ for at least one pair $(r,s), r \neq s$.

1. If $\sigma_1^2 = \ldots = \sigma_c^2$ we choose the likelihood ratio F–test which is based on the statistic

$$F_c = \frac{(N-c)\sum\limits_{i=1}^{c} n_i(\bar{X}_i - \bar{X})^2}{(c-1)\sum\limits_{i=1}^{c}\sum\limits_{j=1}^{n_i}(X_{ij} - \bar{X}_i)^2}$$

where $N = \sum\limits_{i=1}^{c} n_i, \bar{X}_i = \dfrac{1}{n_i}\sum\limits_{j=1}^{n_i} X_{ij}$ and $\bar{X} = \dfrac{1}{N}\sum\limits_{i=1}^{c} n_i\bar{X}_i$.

Under H_0, the statistic F_c has an F–distribution with $c-1$ and $N-c$ degrees of freedom. If we assume nonnormal distributions with at least finite second moments it can be shown that, under H_0, F_c has asymptotically a chi-square distribution with $c-1$ degrees of freedom, see e.g. Tiku et al. (1986).

2. If $\sigma_r^2 \neq \sigma_s^2$ for at least one pair $(r,s), r \neq s$, we select the test of Welch (1951) which may be considered as a robustified version of the F–test in the case of unequal variances. The Welch statistic V_c is given by

$$V_c = \frac{\dfrac{1}{c-1}\sum\limits_{i=1}^{c} g_i(\bar{X}_i - \tilde{X})^2}{1+[2(c-2)/(c^2-1)]\sum\limits_{i=1}^{c}(1 - g_i/g)^2/(n_i - 1)} \quad \text{where}$$

$g_i = \frac{n_i}{S_i^2}$ with $S_i^2 = \frac{1}{n_i - 1}\sum_{j=1}^{n_i}(X_{ij} - \bar{X}_i)^2$, $g = \sum_{i=1}^{c} g_i$ and $\tilde{X} = \frac{1}{g}\sum_{i=1}^{c} g_i \bar{X}_i$.

Assuming normality then (even in the case of unequal variances) the null distribution of V_c can be approximated by the F–distribution with $c-1$ and $[f]$ degrees of freedom where f is determined by

$$1/f = \left[3/\left(c^2 - 1\right)\right]\sum_{i=1}^{c}(1 - g_i/g)^2/(n_i - 1), \text{see Welch (1951).}$$

The difference between the F_c–statistic and V_c–statistic is that the denominator of the F_c–statistic is based on the pooled sample variance, whereas in the denominator of the V_c–statistic the variances of the c samples are considered separately.

Now, let us consider two modifications of the Welch test, first, a rank version of V_c following a proposal of Conover and Iman (1981), in which the original observations are replaced by its ranks in the combined ordered sample. We denote the corresponding test statistic by V_{cr}. Second, we include the trimmed Welch test introduced by Lee and Fung (1983), the statistic of which is defined by

$$V_{cg} = \frac{\sum_{i=1}^{c} b_i\left(\bar{X}_{i\gamma g} - \tilde{X}_{\gamma g}\right)^2/(c-1)}{1 + [2(c-2)/(c^2-1)]\sum_{i=1}^{c}(1 - b_i/b)^2/(h_i - 1)}$$

$$\begin{aligned} \text{with } b_i &= h_i/S_{iw}^2 \,, \\ h_i &= (1-2\gamma)n_i, 0 \le \gamma \le 0.25 \,, \\ S_{iw}^2 &= SSD_{iw}/(h_i - 1) \\ b &= \sum_{i=1}^{c} b_i \text{ and} \\ \tilde{X}_{\gamma g} &= \sum_{i=1}^{c} b_i \bar{X}_{i\gamma g}/b \,, \end{aligned}$$

where $\bar{X}_{i\gamma g}$ and SSD_{iw} are the γ–trimmed mean and the γ–winsorized sum of squared deviations of the ith sample, $i = 1, \ldots, c$, respectively, see Lee and Fung (1983). Under H_0, the statistic V_{cg} is approximately distributed as an F– distribution with $c-1$ and ν degreesw of freedom where

$$\frac{1}{\nu} = \left[3/\left(c^2 - 1\right)\right]\sum_{i=1}^{c}(1 - b_i/b)^2/(h_i - 1).$$

It will be shown that the V_{cr}–test and the V_{cg}–test are more efficient than the V_c–test in the case of long-tailed distributions. There are further robustified versions of the F–test for unequal variances, see e.g. Brown and Forsythe (1974), Sen (1962) and James (1951).

3. Two real data examples

In this section we present two real data sets in order to demonstrate that the assumptions of normality or equal variances are often violated in practice. Example 3.1 is given by Leinhardt and Wasserman (1979) and example 3.2 by Heiler et al. (1993).

Example 3.1: In 1975, the New York Times published a data set in which two of the variables are life expectancy (in years) and per capita income (in 1974 U.S. dollars) for 105 nations. The nations were classified into five categories: industrialized, petroleum exporting, higher income, middle income and low income. Table 1 shows the data of life expectancy for 102 nations (the data of 3 nations are missing).

Table 1: Life expectancy in years

Industrialized		Petroleum Exporting		Higher	
Australia	71.0	Algeria	50.7	Argentina	67.1
Austria	70.4	Ecuador	52.3	Brazil	60.7
Belgium	70.6	Indonesia	47.5	Chile	63.2
Canada	72.0	Iran	50.0	Colombia	45.1
Denmark	73.3	Iraq	51.6	Costa Rica	63.3
Finland	69.8	Libya	52.1	Dominican Republic	57.9
France	72.3	Nigeria	36.9	Greece	69.1
West Germany	70.3	Saudi Arabia	42.3	Guatemala	49.0
Ireland	70.7	Venezuela	66.4	Israel	71.4
Italy	70.6			Jamaica	64.6
Japan	73.2			Malaysia	56.0
Netherlands	73.8			Mexico	61.4
New Zealand	71.1			Nicaragua	49.9
Norway	73.9			Panama	59.2
Portugal	68.1			Peru	54
South Africa	68.2			Singapore	67.5
Sweden	74.7			Spain	69.1
Switzerland	72.1			Trinidad	64.2
Britain	72.0			Tunesia	51.7
United States	71.3			Uruguay	68.5
				Yugoslavia	67.7
				Zambia	43.5

Table 1: Continuation

Middle		Lower		Lower	
Bolivia	49.7	Afghanistan	37.5	Pakistan	51.2
Cameroon	41	Burma	42.3	Rwanda	41
Congo	41	Burundi	36.7	Sierra Leone	41
Egypt	52.7	Cambodia	43.7	Somalia	38.5
El Salvador	58.5	C. African Rep.	34.5	Sri Lanka	65.8
Ghana	37.1	Chad	32	Sudan	47.6
Honduras	49	Dahomey	37.3	Tanzania	40.5
Ivory Coast	35	Ethiopia	38.5	Togo	35
Jordan	52.3	Guinea	27	Uganda	47.5
South Korea	61.9	Haiti	32.6	Upper Volta	31.6
Liberia	44.9	India	41.2	South Yemen	42.3
Morocco	50.5	Kenya	49	Yemen	42.3
Papua	46.8	Laos	47.5	Zaire	38.8
Paraguay	59.4	Madagascar	36		
Philippines	51.1	Malawi	38.5		
Syria	52.8	Mali	37.2		
Thailand	56.1	Mauritania	41		
Turkey	53.7	Nepal	40.6		
South Vietnam	50	Niger	41		

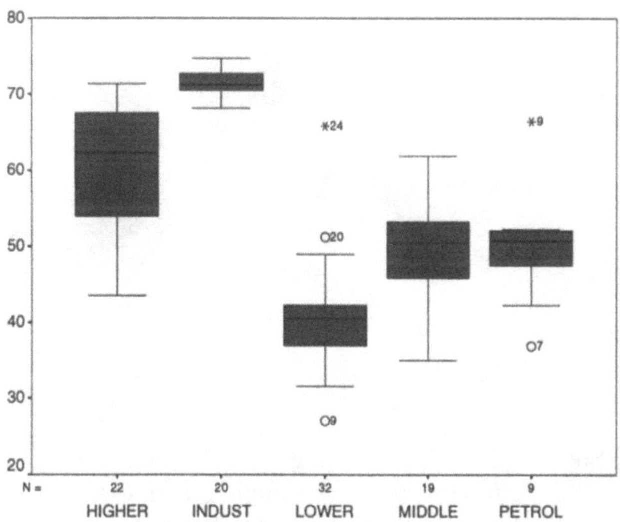

The distributions of the data in the five groups of example 3.1 seem to be asymmetric and they have different tailweight. Also, all the group variances are not equal. Thus, the assumptions of the F–test are obviously violated.

Example 3.2: The investigation deals with differences of the total number of scores of the Abitur (a German school leaving exam) between students of the first course of different departments. In 1992, the data below were collected in four different departments of the University of Konstanz. The random samples were taken out of the students list.

Table 2: Total scores

Total scores of students of the University of Konstanz arranged by department									
Physics	358	423	427	443	459	536	559	581	594
	614	616	619	629	651	662	675	685	751
	755	768	811	828					
Economics	402	440	453	486	493	500	521	538	542
	544	550	564	570	584	609	620	634	660
	674	690	776	829					
Laws	365	425	441	445	455	466	468	472	485
	501	509	522	534	548	560	583	591	607
	611	618	628	696	715				
Social Sciences	366	368	412	415	435	457	470	476	506
	512	533	533	535	556	564	631	633	634
	741	770							

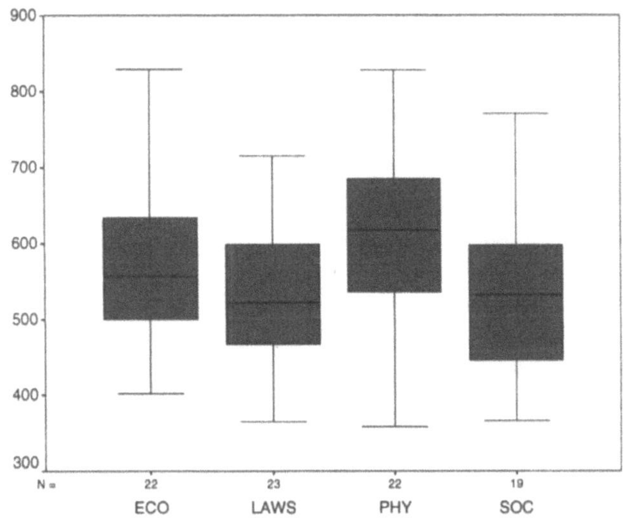

The distributions of the data in example 3.2 do not all seem to be symmetric and have different tailweight as in example 3.1. In example 3.2, however, we may assume homogeneity of the group variances.

4. Rank tests and an adaptive test

As a generalization of the model in section 2 we now consider the following location-scale model: Let $X_{i1}, \ldots, X_{in_i}, i = 1, \ldots, c$, be independent random variables with

$$X_{ij} \sim F\left(\frac{x-\Theta_i}{\tau_i}\right) \quad , \ j=1,\ldots,n_i, \Theta_i \in \mathbb{R}, \quad \tau_i \quad \in \mathbb{R}^+$$

where the distribution function F is assumed to be continuous. If we set $\tau_1 = \ldots = \tau_c \doteq \tau$ (= 1 without loss of generality) we have the pure location model $X_{ij} \sim F(x - \Theta_i)$.
Now, we wish to test

$H_0 : \Theta_1 = \ldots = \Theta_c$ against
$H_1 : \Theta_r \neq \Theta_s$ for at least one pair $(r, s), r \neq s$.

Let $X_{(1)}, \ldots, X_{(N)}$ be the combined ordered sample of

$$X_{11,\ldots,X_{1n_1},\ldots,X_{c1},\ldots,X_{cn_c}} \ , N = \sum_{i=1}^{c} n_i$$

We define indicator variables V_{ik} by

$$V_{ik} = \begin{cases} 1 & \text{if } X_{(k)} \text{belongs to the ith sample} \\ 0 & \text{otherwise.} \end{cases}$$

Furthermore, we have real valued scores $a(k), k = 1, \ldots, N$, with mean

$$\bar{a} = \frac{1}{N} \sum_{k=1}^{N} a(k).$$

Now, we define for each sample a statistic A_i in the following way

$$A_i = \frac{1}{n_i} \sum_{k=1}^{N} a(k) V_{ik}, 1 \leq i \leq c \,.$$

A_i is just the average of scores for the ith sample.

Then the linear rank statistic L_N is given by

$$L_N = \frac{(N-1) \sum_{i=1}^{c} n_i (A_i - \bar{a})^2}{\sum_{k=1}^{N} (a(k) - \bar{a})^2}.$$

Under H_0, L_N is distribution–free and has asymptotically a chi–square distribution with $c - 1$ degrees of freedom (see e.g. Puri (1972)), that means, H_0 has to be rejected in favour of H_1 if $L_N \geq \chi^2_{1-\alpha}(c-1)$.

In the following, some examples of rank tests are given; for references see e.g. Büning (1991, 1996). In the parenthesis that type of distribution is indicated for which the test has high power.

Example 4.1: Gastwirth test G (short tails)

$$a_{\mathrm{G}}(k) = \begin{cases} k - \dfrac{N+1}{4} & \text{if} \quad k \leq \dfrac{N+1}{4} \\ 0 & \text{if} \quad \dfrac{N+1}{4} < k < \dfrac{3(N+1)}{4} \\ k - \dfrac{3(N+1)}{4} & \text{if} \quad k \geq \dfrac{3(N+1)}{4} \end{cases}$$

Example 4.2: Kruskal-Wallis test KW (medium tails)

$$a_{\mathrm{KW}}(k) = k$$

Example 4.3: Test LT (long tails)

$$a_{\mathrm{LT}}(k) = \begin{cases} -\left(\left[\dfrac{N}{4}\right]+1\right) & \text{if} \quad k < \left[\dfrac{N}{4}\right]+1 \\ k - \dfrac{N+1}{2} & \text{if} \quad \left[\dfrac{N}{4}\right]+1 \leq k \leq \left[\dfrac{3(N+1)}{4}\right] \\ \left[\dfrac{N}{4}\right]+1 & \text{if} \quad k > \left[\dfrac{3(N+1)}{4}\right] \end{cases}$$

Example 4.4: Hogg-Fisher-Randles test HFR (right-skewed)

$$a_{\mathrm{HFR}}(k) = \begin{cases} k - \dfrac{N+1}{2} & \text{if} \quad k \leq \dfrac{N+1}{2} \\ 0 & \text{if} \quad k > \dfrac{N+1}{2} \end{cases}$$

For left-skewed distributions we interchange the terms $k - (N+1)/2$ and 0 in the definition of the scores $a_{\mathrm{HFR}}(k)$.

As pointed out, the choice of a suitable rank test depends on the distribution of the data. Since in most cases, however, the practising statistician has no information about the underlying distribution an adaptive test should be applied which takes into account the given data set. We apply the concept of Hogg (1974), i.e., to classify, at first, the type of the underlying distribution with respect to some measures like skewness and tailweight and then to select an appropriate rank test for the classified type of distribution. As measures of skewness and tailweight we use (see Hogg (1974))

$$\hat{Q}_1 = \frac{\bar{U}_{0.05} - \bar{M}_{0.50}}{\bar{M}_{0.50} - \bar{L}_{0.05}} \quad \text{and} \quad \hat{Q}_2 = \frac{\bar{U}_{0.05} - \bar{L}_{0.05}}{\bar{U}_{0.50} - \bar{L}_{0.50}}$$

where $\bar{U}_\gamma(\bar{M}_\gamma, \bar{L}_\gamma)$ denote the average of the largest (middle, smallest) γN order statistics in the combined sample $X_{(1)} \leq \ldots \leq X_{(N)}$; fractional items are used when γN is not an integer. Obviously, $\hat{Q}_1 \geq 0$; more detailed $\hat{Q}_1 < 1$ if the data are skewed to the left, $\hat{Q}_1 = 1$ if the data are symmetric and $\hat{Q}_1 > 1$ if the data are skewed to the right. $\hat{Q}_2 \geq 1$, the longer the tails the greater $\hat{Q}_2$.

Now, we define the following four categories which are based on the so called selector statistic $S = (\hat{Q}_1, \hat{Q}_2)$:

$$\begin{aligned} D_1 &= \left\{S \mid 0 \leq \hat{Q}_1 \leq 2 \,;\; 1 \leq \hat{Q}_2 \leq 2\right\} \\ D_2 &= \left\{S \mid 0 \leq \hat{Q}_1 \leq 2 \,;\; 2 < \hat{Q}_2 \leq 3\right\} \\ D_3 &= \left\{S \mid \hat{Q}_1 \geq 0 \,;\; \hat{Q}_2 > 3\right\} \\ D_4 &= \left\{S \mid \hat{Q}_1 > 2 \,;\; 1 \leq \hat{Q}_2 \leq 3\right\} \end{aligned}$$

This means, the distribution is classified as symmetric with short- or medium tails, if S falls in the category D_1 or D_2, respectively, as long tailed if S belongs to D_3 and as skewed to the right with short– or medium tails if S falls in D_4.

We now consider the following adaptive test A,

$$A = \begin{cases} \text{G} & \text{if} \quad S \in D_1 \\ \text{KW} & \text{if} \quad S \in D_2 \\ \text{LT} & \text{if} \quad S \in D_3 \\ \text{HFR} & \text{if} \quad S \in D_4 \,. \end{cases}$$

It can be shown that this two-staged adaptive test A is, under H_0, distribution- free over the class of all continuous distribution functions, see e.g. Büning (1991, p. 219). For the simple proof it is fundamental, that the rank statistic L_N and the selector statistic S as a function of order statistics are independent.

Now, let us carry out the adaptive test A for the data of example 3.2. We get $\hat{Q}_1 = 1.064$ and $\hat{Q}_2 = 2.438$. Thus, we have to apply the KW–test and we obtain $KW = 7.45$. Because of $\chi^2_{0.95}(3) = 7.82$ we cannot reject H_0 at level $\alpha = 0.05$.

5. Simulation study

We investigate via Monte Carlo simulation (10 000 runs) the estimated level and power of the tests presented above for normal and nonnormal data. In the study of the estimated level the case of unequal variances is included. Here the selected distributions are (with the abbreviation in the paranthesis) uniform (Uni), normal (Norm), contaminated normal $0.5N(1.4) + 0.5N(-1,1)$ (CN, skewed to the right), double exponential (Dexp) and the Cauchy (Cau), where each of them has mean or median (Cauchy) zero. We consider the cases of $c = 3$ and $c = 4$ samples with equal and unequal sample sizes. For the Cauchy distribution different scale parameters are generated by the transformation $X_i = \sigma_i X_1, \sigma_i > 0$, where $X_i, i = 2, \ldots, c$, is the random variable related to the ith sample. For all tests we use critical values as described in section 2 and 4.

In the following table 3 we present estimated levels for $c = 4, n_i = n = 20, i = 1, \ldots 4$.

Table 3: Estimated level of the tests under various distributions, $c = 4, n_i = n = 20, \alpha = 0.05$

Tests	$(\sigma_1, \sigma_2, \sigma_3, \sigma_4, \sigma_5)$	Uni	Norm	Dexp	Cau	CN
F_c	(1,1,1,1)	4.8	5.2	4.8	1.6	4.9
	(1,1.5,2,2.5)	6.5	6.2	5.9	1.8	6.3
	(1,2,3,4)	7.2	6.7	6.6	2.1	7.3
V_c	(1,1,1,1)	5	5	4.5	1.5	4.9
	(1,1.5,2,2.5)	5.4	5.2	4.3	1.3	5.5
	(1,2,3,4)	5.3	4.8	4.6	1.2	5.6
V_{cr}	(1,1,1,1)	5.0	5.1	5.0	5.4	5.1
	(1,1.5,2,2.5)	6.1	5.9	5.4	5.5	8.9
	(1,2,3,4)	7	5.9	5.8	5.6	13.5
V_{cg}	(1,1,1,1)	5.4	5.1	4.4	2.4	5.4
	(1,1.5,2,2.5)	5.9	5.3	4.5	2.2	6.7
	(1,2,3,4)	5.8	5	4.4	2.2	7.8
G	(1,1,1,1)	4.4	4.9	4.6	4.9	4.8
	(1,1.5,2,2.5)	6	5.5	5	4.8	6.9
	(1,2,3,4)	5.8	5.1	5.2	4.6	7.2
KW	(1,1,1,1)	4.5	4.9	4.8	5.1	4.7
	(1,1.5,2,2.5)	6.1	5.4	5.3	5.2	8.0
	(1,2,3,4)	6.5	5.7	5.5	5.4	10.4
LT	(1,1,1,1)	4.7	4.7	5.0	4.8	4.6
	(1,1.5,2,2.5)	6.4	5.8	5.3	5.3	8.4
	(1,2,3,4)	8.1	6.9	6.0	5.8	13.2
HFR	(1,1,1,1)	4.7	4.7	4.5	4.8	4.7
	(1,1.5,2,2.5)	24.4	16.7	12.2	9.6	34.3
	(1,2,3,4)	40.8	30.9	21.3	15.7	62.2
A	(1,1,1,1)	4.5	4.9	4.9	4.8	4.7
	(1,1.5,2,2.5)	6.1	5.4	5.3	5.3	9.7
	(1,2,3,4)	6.5	6.3	6.0	5.8	13.6

From table 3 we get the following results:

—In the case of equal variances the parametric $F-$, V_c- and V_{cr}–tests maintain the level α well for all distributions, except for the Cauchy, and the

V_{cr}–test also maintains the level for this extremely long-tailed distribution. The rank tests and the adaptive test A are distribution-free with respect to the pure location model.

—In the case of unequal variances the Welch test V_c is the best one (except for the Cauchy), whereas most of the other tests including the test A maintain the level more or less only for the symmetric distributions considered. The HFR-test exceeds the level dramatically.

Altogether, the estimated level α is obviously more (sometimes extremely more) influenced by heteroscedasticity than by nonnormality. Similar results hold for $c = 4$ and other sample sizes and in the case of $c = 3$ samples, too.

Now, let us apply an appropriate test for the data in example 3.1. Because of the supposed unequal group variances we choose the V_c–test and obtain $V_c = 174.4$ and $[f] = 32$. Since $F_{0.95}(4, 32) = 2.67$ we have to reject H_0 at level $\alpha = 0.05$.

For a power comparison of the tests we include in the study the exponential distribution as a further example of a right-skewed distribution. But now we assume the pure location model $X_{ij} \sim F_X(x - \Theta_i), i = 1, \ldots, c, j = 1, \ldots, n_i$, because most of the tests do not maintain the level in the case of unequal variances. We choose the location parameters Θ_i as a multiple of the standard deviation σ_{F_X} of the underlying distribution F_X , i.e. $\Theta_i = k_i \sigma_{F_X}, i = 1, \ldots, c$. For the Cauchy we set $\sigma_{\mathrm{Cau}} = F_{\mathrm{Cau}}^{-1}(0.8413) = 1.8373$, because $\Phi(1) = 0.8413$, where Φ is the standard normal distribution. In table 4 we present power values of the tests for $c = 4$, $n_i = n = 20$ and $\alpha = 5\%$.

From table 4 we obtain:

—The power values of the F– and V_c–test are nearly the same for each distribution considered, whereas the V_{cr}– and V_{cg}–test have higher power than the F–test and V_c–test for long-tailed distributions as it would be expected. The V_{cr}–test is also better than the F–test and V_c–test for both right-skewed distributions. It is, on the whole, the best one among the parametric competitors.

—For each of the distributions considered, except, of course, for the normal, there is a rank test which has higher power than V_{cr} or the other parametric tests, e.g., the Gastwirth test is the best one for the uniform, the LT–test for the double exponential and the Cauchy and the Hogg–Fisher–Randles test is the best one for both distributions skewed to the right. The KW–test has highest power among the rank tests for the normal distribution.

—The adaptive test A behaves very well over this broad class of distributions. It is not the best one for a special distribution but mostly second best. That is just the idea of an adaptive test, to select the "best one" for a given data set. This result might be convincing for applying an adaptive test in statistical practice.

Table 4: Estimated power of the tests under various distributions, $c = 4, n_i = n = 20, \alpha = 0.05$

Tests	(k_1, k_2, k_3, k_4)	Uni	Norm	Dexp	Cau	CN	Exp
F_c	(0,0.2,0.4,0.6)	33.8	34.5	34.6	3.7	33.6	36.9
	(0,0.3,0.6,0.9)	68.1	69.3	69.2	5.6	69	70.5
	(0,0.4,0.8,1.2)	92.2	91.9	91.4	9.7	92.1	90.9
V_c	(0,0.2,0.4,0.6)	31.3	33.3	35.3	5.9	32.8	38.3
	(0,0.3,0.6,0.9)	65	67.2	69.5	11.5	67.1	71.9
	(0,0.4,0.8,1.2)	90.6	90.8	91.3	20.9	91.1	91.9
V_{cr}	(0,0.2,0.4,0.6)	29.9	33.3	46.4	33.5	37.2	66
	(0,0.3,0.6,0.9)	61.3	66.2	81.4	62	72.5	93.8
	(0,0.4,0.8,1.2)	87.2	89.8	96.3	82.7	93.4	99.4
V_{cg}	(0,0.2,0.4,0.6)	24.9	32.7	44.8	23	32.4	43.3
	(0,0.3,0.6,0.9)	50.9	64.9	80.1	49.7	65.7	78.1
	(0,0.4,0.8,1.2)	78.3	88.9	96.2	73.4	89.5	95.1
G	(0,0.2,0.4,0.6)	50.7	28.6	25.2	12.6	31.8	71.1
	(0,0.3,0.6,0.9)	85.3	60.4	52.9	21.6	65.5	91.3
	(0,0.4,0.8,1.2)	97.7	86	80.1	35	88.8	97.7
KW	(0,0.2,0.4,0.6)	29.9	32.5	45.7	31.8	36.7	64.5
	(0,0.3,0.6,0.9)	61.7	65.9	81.2	60.9	72.1	92.3
	(0,0.4,0.8,1.2)	87.3	90	96.6	82.9	93.3	99.1
LT	(0,0.2,0.4,0.6)	18.7	28.8	49.9	40.4	32.6	52.1
	(0,0.3,0.6,0.9)	39.9	59.4	84.6	72.8	66.8	87.8
	(0,0.4,0.8,1.2)	67.5	85.5	97.3	91.6	89.7	98.4
HFR	(0,0.2,0.4,0.6)	24.8	26.1	37.3	27	42.2	85.6
	(0,0.3,0.6,0.9)	49.9	54.3	70.8	51.7	78.8	99.1
	(0,0.4,0.8,1.2)	76.4	80.9	91.5	73.6	96.2	100
A	(0,0.2,0.4,0.6)	40.2	32.3	48.2	40.4	37	74.7
	(0,0.3,0.6,0.9)	65.9	65.8	83	72.8	72.1	94.6
	(0,0.4,0.8,1.2)	87.6	89.9	96.9	91.6	93.2	99.3

6. Conclusions and comments

What do we conclude from the results on estimated level α and power β in the previous section? In the case of *unequal variances* the V_c–test is the clear candidate among all the tests considered. The classical F–test should be applied with great caution only.

In the case of *equal* variances, i.e. for a pure location model, we should prefer an adaptive test which is distribution–free and has high power for symmetric distributions with different tailweight as well as asymmetric distributions.

For further studies of several parametric and nonparametric tests in the c–sample location problem, see Büning (1997). In this paper we considered only the case of two-sided alternatives. Recently, Büning and Kössler (1996) studied the case of ordered alternatives and compared some parametric tests and so called Jonckheere-type tests with respect to level α and power β. Adaptive tests for ordered alternatives have been proposed e.g. by Büning (1995) and Beier and Büning (1997).

References

1. Beier, F. and Büning, H. (1997). An adaptive test against ordered alternatives. *Computational Statistics and Data Analysis*, **25**, 441–452.
2. Brown, M. B. and Forsythe, A. B. (1974). The small sample behaviour of some statistics which test the equality of several means. *Technometrics*, **16**, 129–132.
3. Büning, H. (1991). Robuste und adaptive Tests. Berlin, De Gruyter
4. Büning, H. (1994). Robuste and adaptive tests for the two–sample location problem, *OR Spektrum*, **16**, 33–39.
5. Büning H. (1995). Adaptive Jonckheere–type tests for ordered alternatives. Diskussionsbeiträge des Fachbereichs Wirtschaftswissenschaft der Freien Universität Berlin, Nr. 7.
6. Büning, H. (1996). Adaptive tests for the c–sample location problem — the case of two-sided alternatives. *Communications in Statistics — Theory and Methods*, **25**, 1569–1582.
7. Büning, H. (1997). Robust analysis of variance. Journal of Applied Statistics, 24, 319–332.
8. Büning, H. and Kössler, W. (1996). Robustness and efficiency of some tests for ordered alternatives in the c–sample location problem. *Journal of Statistical Computation and Simulation*, **55**, 337–352.
9. Conover, W. J. and Iman, R. L. (1981). Rank transformation as a bridge between parametric and nonparametric statistics. *The American Statistician*, **35**, 124–133.
10. Heiler, S., Michels, P. and Abberger, K. (1993). "Abiturzeugnisse und Studienwahl — Ein Beispiel zur Anwendung graphischer Verfahren in der Explorativen Datenanalyse". *Allgemeines Statistisches Archiv*, **77**, 166–182.
11. Hogg, R. V. (1974). Adaptive robust procedures. A partial review and some suggestions for future applications and theory.*Journal of the American Statistical Association*, **69**, 909–927.

12. James, G. S. (1951): Tests of linear hypotheses in univariate and multivariate analysis when the ratios of the population variances are unknown. *Biometrika*, **38**, 19–43.
13. Lee, H. and Fung, K. Y. (1983). Robust procedures for multi-sample location problems with unequal group variances. *Journal of Statistical Computation and Simulation*, **18**, 125–143.
14. Leinhardt, S. and Wasserman, S.S. (1979). Teaching Regression: An exploratory approach. *The American Statistician*, **33**, 196–203.
15. Puri, M. L. (1972). Some aspects of nonparametric inference. *International Statistical Review*, **40**, 299–327.
16. Sen, P. K. (1962). On studentized non-parametric multi-sample location tests. *Annals of Statistical Institute*, **14**, 119–131.
17. Tiku, M. L., Tan, W. Y. and Balakrishnan N. (1986): Robust Inference. New York, Marcel Dekker.
18. Welch, B. L. (1951). On the comparison of several mean values: An alternative approach. *Biometrika*, **38**, 330–336.

A Sequential Test for the Comparison of the Precision of Two Measurement Methods

Peter-Th. Wilrich

Institut für Statistik und Ökonometrie, Freie Universität Berlin, Germany

Summary. In order to compare the precision (expresed by the variance) of a new measurement method with that of a traditional measurement method the null hypothesis of equality of the two variances can be tested with a one–sided F–test. A sequential Wald test is proposed as an alternative, and its operating characteristic function is investigated by means of a simulation study. This study shows that the test can be ended with twice the sample size of the corresponding F–test without a substantial change of the operating characteristic function.

1. Introduction

Especially in the fields of material testing and chemical analysis, it is often required to substitute a measurement method by an alternative method which is cheaper, easier to perform or less time consuming – provided that the accuracy of the new method is not worse than that of the traditional method.

If a bias between the two methods exists, it can be corrected by an appropriate calibration. In order to compare their standard deviations repeated measurements have to be performed under defined conditions. In the International Standard ISO 5725, Part 6 "Accuracy (trueness and precision) of measurement methods and results; use in practice of accuracy values" the following assumptions are made:

- For both measurement methods the precision does not depend on the true value of the measurand, i.e. the standard deviation is constant over the whole measurement range,
- measurement errors are independent and normally distributed,
- the measurements are performed under repeatability conditions, i.e. conditions where independent test results are obtained with the same method on identical test items in the same laboratory by the same operator using the same equipment within short intervals of time.

Under these assumptions it is recommended to measure one and the same measurement object n times with each of the two measurement methods and to perform a one–sided F–test with the null hypothesis $H_0 : \sigma_x^2 = \sigma_y^2$ against the alternative hypothesis $H_1 : \sigma_x^2 > \sigma_y^2$ where σ_x^2 and σ_y^2 are the repeatability variances of the traditional measurement method and the new measurement method, respectively.

ISO 5725 Part 6 presents a table giving for the significance level $\alpha = 0.05$ and a probability of error of the second kind $\beta = 0.05$ the ratio σ_x/σ_y for which the probability of acceptance is equal to β, as a function of the sample size $n = n_1 = n_2$. If, for example, it is required to detect a ratio of standard deviations $\sigma_x/\sigma_y = 2$ with probability $1 - \beta = 0.95$, the sample size is $n_1 = n_2 = 30$. For measurement methods which are very expensive a sample size of 30 is much too high. On the other hand it often appears that the new method has a much smaller standard deviation than the traditional one, and this becomes intuitively event after only a few measurements.

It is therefore reasonable to look for a sequential method. Rushton [3] presents a sequential test for the case of known means μ_x and μ_y and simple hypotheses $H_0 : \sigma_x^2 = \sigma_y^2$ and $H_1 : \sigma_x^2 = \delta^2\sigma_y^2$ with fixed δ^2, and proposes a modification of the test for unknown means. The following test is based on his proposal.

2. A sequential F–test

Let X_1, X_2, K and e_1, e_2, K be independent and normally distributed random variables, i.e.

$$\begin{aligned} X_1 &\sim N(\mu_x; \sigma_x^2); \qquad i = 1, 2, \ldots \text{ and} \\ Y_1 &\sim N(\mu_y; \sigma_y^2); \qquad i = 1, 2 \ldots \end{aligned} \tag{2.1}$$

We wish to test

$$H_0 : \sigma_x/\sigma_y \leq \delta_0 \tag{2.2}$$

versus

$$H_1 : \sigma_x/\sigma_y > \delta_0 \tag{2.3}$$

so that

$$P(\text{Rejection of } H_0 \mid \sigma_x/\sigma_y = \delta) \leq \alpha, \quad \forall \delta \leq \delta_0 \tag{2.4}$$

$$P(\text{Acceptance of } H_0 \mid \sigma_x/\sigma_y = \delta) \geq \beta, \quad \forall \delta \geq \delta_1$$

for given values $\delta_0 > 0,\ \delta_1 > \delta_0,\ 0 < \beta < 1 - \alpha < 1$.
For each sample size k the random variable

$$\frac{S_{xk}^2/\sigma_x^2}{S_{yk}^2/\sigma_y^2} = \frac{\sum_{i=1}^{k}(X_i - \bar{X}_k)^2}{\sum_{i=1}^{k}(Y_i - \bar{Y}_k)^2} \cdot \frac{\sigma_y^2}{\sigma_x^2} := z_k \cdot \frac{1}{\sigma^2} \tag{2.5}$$

with

$$\bar{X}_k = \frac{1}{k}\sum_{i=1}^{k} X_i \ , \ \bar{Y}_k = \frac{1}{k}\sum_{i=1}^{k} Y_i \ , \tag{2.6}$$

$$z_i = \frac{\sum_{i=1}^{k}(X_i - \bar{X}_k)^2}{\sum_{i=1}^{k}(Y_i - \bar{Y}_k)^2} \tag{2.7}$$

and

$$\delta = \sigma_x / \sigma_y \tag{2.8}$$

follows the F–distribution with $f_1 = f = k-1$ and $f_2 = f = k-1$ degrees of freedom. The probability density function of the F–distribution is

$$g_F(x, f_1, f_2) = c(f_1, f_2) \cdot \frac{x^{(f_1-2)/2}}{(f_2 + f_1 x)^{(f_1+f_2)/2}} \tag{2.9}$$

with $c(f_1, f_2)$ as a multiplicative constant, and for the special case $f_1 = f_2 = f$ we have

$$g_F(x, f, f) = c(f, f) \cdot \frac{x^{(f-2)/2}}{f^f (1+x)^f} . \tag{2.10}$$

The probability density of z_k is

$$g_{z_k}(z_k) = g_F(x) \frac{dx}{dz_k} \tag{2.11}$$

and with $z_k = \delta^2 x$

$$g_{z_k}(z_k) = g_F\left(\frac{z_k}{\delta^2}\right) \cdot \frac{1}{\delta^2} . \tag{2.12}$$

Wald's sequential probability ratio test uses the likelihood ratio

$$L(z_k) = \frac{g_{z_k}(z_k; \delta_1)}{g_{z_k}(z_k; \delta_0)} = \frac{\frac{1}{\delta_1^2} \cdot \frac{(z_k/\delta_1^2)^{(f-2)/2}}{(1 + z_k/\delta_1^2)^f}}{\frac{1}{\delta_0^2} \cdot \frac{(z_k/\delta_0^2)^{(f-2)/2}}{(1 + z_k/\delta_0^2)^f}} = \left(\frac{\delta_0}{\delta_1}\right)^f \cdot \frac{(1 + z_k/\delta_0^2)^f}{(1 + z_k/\delta_1^2)^f} \tag{2.13}$$

as test statistic; as long as the likelihood ratio lies inside the indifference region, i.e.

$$\frac{\beta}{1-\alpha} < L(z_k) < \frac{1-\beta}{\alpha}, \tag{2.14}$$

the test continues: k is increased by one and two further measurements X_k and Y_k are obtained.

The test stops with acceptance of H_0 as soon as the likelihood ratio reaches the acceptance region, i.e.

$$L(z_k) \leq \frac{\beta}{1-\alpha} \tag{2.15}$$

and with rejection of H_0 as soon as the likelihood ratio reaches the rejection region, i.e.

$$L(z_k) \geq \frac{1-\beta}{\alpha}. \tag{2.16}$$

With Wald's approximations (2.15) and (2.16) for the stopping bounds (see [4]) the SPRT has error probabilities

$$\begin{aligned} P(\text{Rejection of } H_0 \mid \sigma_x/\sigma_y = \delta_0) &\approx \alpha \\ P(\text{Acceptance of } H_0 \mid \sigma_x/\sigma_y = \delta_1) &\approx \beta\,. \end{aligned} \tag{2.17}$$

For $z_k \to 0$ we have $L(Z_k) \to (\delta_0/\delta_1)^f$. As long as

$$\begin{aligned} L(z_k) \geq (\delta_0/\delta_1)^f &> \frac{\beta}{1-\alpha} \\ f\ln(\delta_0/\delta_1) > \ln\frac{\beta}{1-\alpha} &= -A \\ f < \frac{A}{\ln(\delta_1/\delta_0)} &= f_A\,, \end{aligned} \tag{2.18}$$

acceptance is not possible.
For $z_k \to \infty$ we have $L(z_k) \to (\delta_1/\delta_0)^f$. Therefore, as long as

$$\begin{aligned} L(z_k) \leq (\delta_1/\delta_0)^f &< \frac{1-\beta}{\alpha} \\ f\ln(\delta_1/\delta_0) &< \ln\frac{1-\beta}{\alpha} = B \\ f &< \frac{B}{\ln(\delta_1/\delta_0)} = f_B \end{aligned} \tag{2.19}$$

rejection is not possible.
The test is easier to perform if z_k instead of the likelihood ratio is used as the test statistic.
After a few computations the following test algorithm follows:

1. Take an initial sample of size $k = \min(f_A, f_B) + 1$

2. Compute the value of the test statistic

$$z_k = \frac{\sum_{i=1}^{k}(x_i - \bar{x}_k)^2}{\sum_{i=1}^{k}(y_i - \bar{y}_k)^2} = \frac{\sum_{i=1}^{k} x_k^2 - \frac{1}{k}\left(\sum_{i=1}^{k} x_i\right)^2}{\sum_{i=1}^{k} y_i^2 - \frac{1}{k}\left(\sum_{i=1}^{k} y_i\right)^2} \tag{2.20}$$

with

$$\bar{x}_k = \frac{1}{k}\sum_{i=1}^{k} x_i \ , \ \bar{y}_k = \frac{1}{k}\sum_{i=1}^{k} y_i \ . \tag{2.21}$$

The test statistic in the form of the right hand side of (2.20) can easily be updated in adding the values x_k, x_k^2, y_k, y_k^2 to the sums for the previous $k, \sum x_i, \sum x_i^2, \sum y_i, \sum y_i^2$, respectively.

3. If

$$k \geq f_A + 1 \ \text{ and } \ z_k \leq \underline{z}_k = \delta_0\delta_1 \frac{\delta_1 e^{-A/(k-1)} - \delta_0}{\delta_1 - \delta_0 e^{-A/(k-1)}} \tag{2.22}$$

with

$$A = \ln\frac{1-\alpha}{\beta} \ \text{ and } \ f_A = \frac{A}{\ln(\delta_1/\delta_0)}, \tag{2.23}$$

accept H_0: if

$$k \geq f_B + 1 \ \text{ and } \ z_k \leq \bar{z}_k = \delta_0\delta_1 \frac{\delta_1 e^{B/(k-1)} - \delta_0}{\delta_1 - \delta_0 e^{B/(k-1)}} \tag{2.24}$$

with

$$B = \ln\frac{1-\beta}{\alpha} \ \text{ and } \ f_B = \frac{B}{\ln(\delta_1/\delta_0)}, \tag{2.25}$$

reject H_0;
if $\underline{z}_k < z_k < \bar{z}_k$, proceed with the test, i.e. increase k by 1, take two further measurements x_k and y_k and go to 2.

For the example $\delta_0 = 1$, $\delta_1 = 2$, $\alpha = \beta = 0.05$ we have $A = B = \ln 19 = 2.944$ and $f_A = f_B = 6$. The boundaries $\underline{z}_k$ and $\bar{z}_k$ of the acceptance and rejection region are shown in Figure 1.

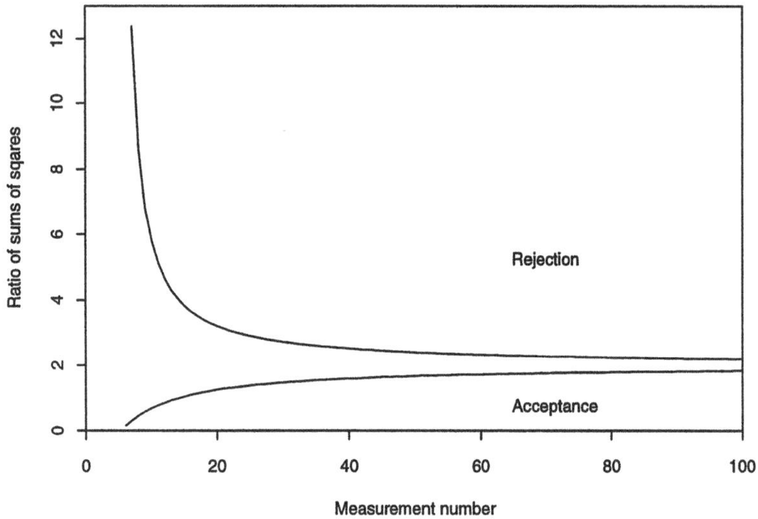

Figure 1. The boundaries of the acceptance region and the rejection region of the sequential F–test for $\delta_0 = 1,\ \delta_1 = 2,\ \alpha = \beta = 0.05$

3. The operating characteristic function and the average sample size

In order to investigate the operating characteristic function an the sample size a simulation study was performed. For the case $\alpha = 0.05,\ \beta = 0.05,\ \delta_0 = 1$ and $\delta_1 = 2$ for which the F–test needs sample sizes $n_1 = n_2 = 30$ and for each of the ratios of standard deviations $\delta = 0.5(0.1)2.5$ 1000 simulations have been performed using the $N(0;1)$–random number generator rnorm in S–Plus. Figure 2 shows the operating characteristic function together with the OC's of the procedures studied in section 4, and Figure 3 the smallest, average, 95%–quantile and largest sample size.

A expected, α and β are upper limits for the error probabilities of the first and second kind, respectively.

The average sample size is always smaller than that of the F–test. However, for $\delta = \sqrt{\delta_0\delta_1} \approx 1.4$ for which the probability of acceptance is about 50% the average sample size has its maximum 28.6 which is not much less than the sample size of the F–test. The largest sample size is more than four times the sample size of the F–test.

For other design parameters $\delta_0, \delta_1, \alpha$ and β the results are similiar.

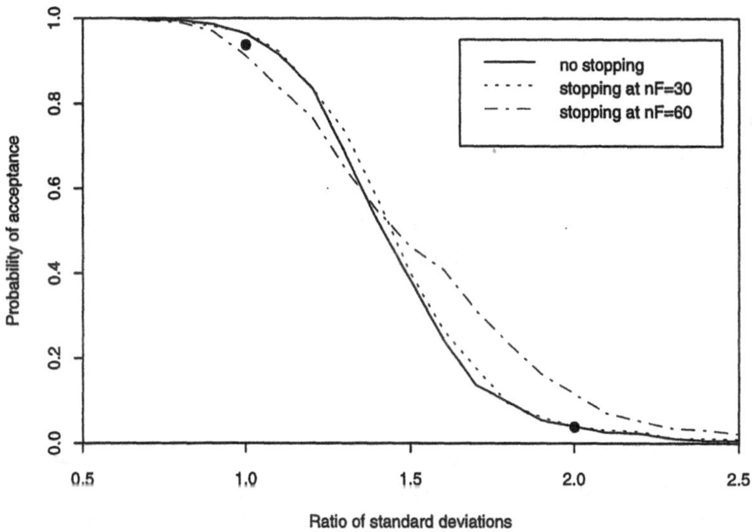

Figure 2. The operating characteristic function of the sequential F–test for $\delta_0 = 1,\ \delta_1 = 2,\ \alpha = \beta = 0.05$.

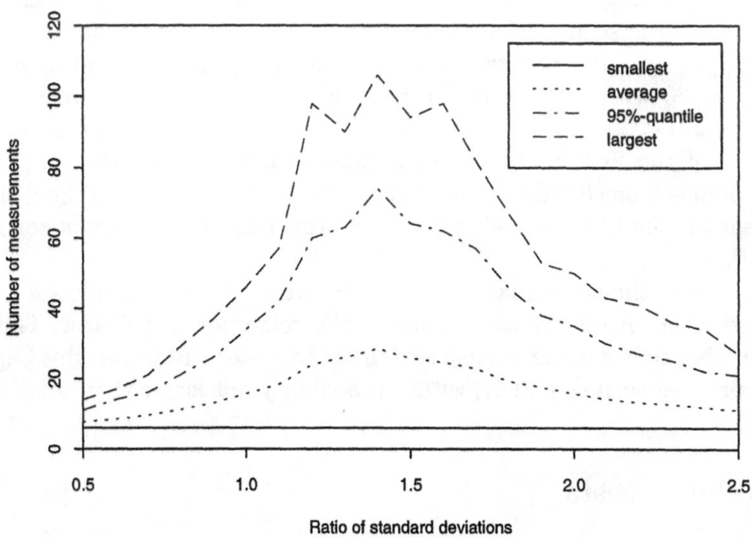

Figure 3. Sample sizes of the sequential F–test for $\delta_0 = 1,\ \delta_1 = 2,\ \alpha = \beta = 0.05$

4. A modification of the test

In a further simulation study it was investigated whether the operating characteristic function is still acceptable if the sequential test is stopped when a) the sample size of b) twice the sample size of the corresponding F–test is reached.

For given values of $\delta_0 > 0$, $\delta_1 > 0$ and $0 < 1 - \alpha < 1$ the operating characteristic function of the upper one–sided F–test for sample sizes n_1 and n_2 is

$$P(\text{acceptance of } H_0 \mid \delta) = G_{f_1 f_2}\left(\frac{F_{f,f_2};1-\alpha}{\delta^2}\right) \tag{4.1}$$

where $G_{f_1,f_2}(\cdot)$ denotes the cumulative distribution function of the F–distribution with f_1 and f_2 degrees of freedom and $F_{f_1,f_2;1-\alpha}$ the $(1-\alpha)$–quantile of this distribution. For given β the sample size is $n_F = n_1 = n_2 = f+1$, where f is the smallest integer which fulfills the equation

$$\frac{F_{f,f,1-\alpha}}{F_{f,f,\beta}} \leq (\delta_1/\delta_0)^2. \tag{4.2}$$

For the example $\delta_0 = 1, \delta_1 = 2, \alpha = \beta = 0.05$ for which the sample size of the corresponding F–test is $n_F = n_1 = n_2 = 30$, the operating characteristic functions of the sequential tests a) stopped at $n_F = 30$ with acceptance for $z_k \leq F_{n_F-1,n_F-1;1-\alpha}$ and rejection for $z_k > F_{n_F-1,n_F-1;1-\alpha}$ and b) stopped at $2_{n_F} = 60$ with acceptance for $z_k \leq F_{2n_F-1,2n_F-1;1-\alpha}$ and rejection for $z_k > F_{2n_F-1,2n_F-1;1-\alpha}$ are shown in Figure 2. Both tests have a probability of error of the first kind not larger than α, however, the test stopped at $n_F = 30$ has a much larger probability of the error of the second kind than β whereas for the test stopped at $2n_F = 60$ this error probability is not larger than β.

As a rule, the sequential F–test can be stopped if the sample size $2n_F$ is reached where n_F is the sample size of the corresponding F–test. This test eventually needs a larger sample size than the F–test. However, this happens only for δ between δ_0 and δ_1, with a probability not larger than 5%.

5. Related tests

Similar to the sequential F–test a sequential χ^2–test for the test of the null hypothesis $H_0 : \sigma_x^2 = \sigma_0^2$ against the alternative hypothesis $H_1 : \sigma_x^2 > \sigma_0^2$ can be constructed.

In some cases a two–sided sequential F–test is required. The operating characteristic function and the average sample size of this test are under investigation.

References

1. Ghosh, B.K. (1970). *Sequential Tests of Statistical Hypotheses.* Reading, MA.: Addison–Wesley.
2. Ghosh, B.K., and P.K. Sen(Editors) (1991). *Handbook of Sequential Analysis.* New York: Marcel Dekker.
3. Rushton, S. (1953). *On sequential tests of the equality of variances of two normal populations with known means.* Sankhay 12 63–78.
4. Wald, A. (1947). *Sequential Analysis.* New York: Wiley.

List of Publications of Hans Schneeweiß

Research Papers

1. Zur Theorie der Warteschlangen. *Zeitschrift für handelswissenschaftliche Forschung* 12 (1960), 471–507.
2. Monte-Carlo-Simulation eines einfachen Warteschlangenmodells. *Ablauf- und Planungsforschung* 2 (1961), 17–20.
3. Einige Experimente mit Entscheidungsspielen. *Statistische Hefte* 3 (1962), 62–78.
4. Ein allgemeines Schema des stochastischen Programmierens. *Statistische Hefte* 3 (1962), 131–157.
5. Nutzenaxiomatik und Theorie des Messens. *Statistische Hefte* 4 (1963), 178–220.
6. Eine Entscheidungsregel für den Fall partiell bekannter Wahrscheinlichkeiten. *Unternehmensforschung* 8 (1964), 86–95.
7. Lagerhaltung bei beschränkter Information. In: R. Henn (Ed.), *Operations Research-Verfahren II.* Meisenheim am Glan 1965, 41–64.
8. Konsequenzen des Bernoulli-Prinzips für die Präferenzstruktur von Normalverteilungen. *Unternehmensforschung* 9 (1965), 238–249.
9. Das Aggregationsproblem. *Statistische Hefte* 6 (1965), 1–26.
10. Minimax-Lösung eines einfachen Lagermodells, wenn nur Mittelwert und Streuung der Nachfrageverteilung bekannt sind. *Unternehmensforschung* 10 (1966), 101–117.
11. Organisatorische Regelungen beim Transport der Lagergüter vom Stapelplatz zum Anstellplatz (with K. Brock). *Unternehmensforschung* 10 (1966), 197–212.
12. Das Grundmodell der Entscheidungstheorie. *Statistische Hefte* 7 (1966), 125–137.
13. Bemerkungen zur lexikographischen Ordnung. In: R. Henn (Ed.), *Operations Research-Verfahren III.* Meisenheim am Glan, 1966, 336–352.
14. Theorie der rationalen Entscheidungskriterien bei Ungewißheit. *Industrielle Organisation* 36 (1967), 501–507.
15. Die angebliche Ausschaltung des Risikos durch das Gesetz der großen Zahlen. *Unternehmensforschung* 12 (1968), 96–105.
16. Spieltheoretische Analyse des Ellsberg-Paradoxons. *Zeitschrift für die gesamte Staatswissenschaft* 124 (1968), 249–256.
17. Die Unverträglichkeit von (μ,σ)–Prinzip und Dominanzprinzip. *Unternehmensforschung* 12 (1968), 180–184.
18. Simulationstechniken (with R. K. Bauer). *Zeitschrift für wirtschaftliche Fertigung* 63 (1968), 365–368.
19. Monte-Carlo-Simulation als Entscheidungshilfe. In: G. Menges (Ed.), *Entscheidung und Information.* Alfred Metzner Verlag, Frankfurt-Berlin, 1968, 37–51.

20. Monte-Carlo-Methoden in Statistik, Unternehmensforschung und Ökonometrie. In: R. Henn (Ed.), *Operations Research-Verfahren V*. Meisenheim am Glan, 1968, 365–380.
21. Note on Two Dominance Principles in Decision Theory. *Unternehmensforschung* 12 (1968), 213–216.
22. Fiscal and Monetary Policies Under Alternative Exchange Rate Systems: A Correction (with E. Sohmen). *The Quarterly Journal of Economics* 83 (1969), 336–340.
23. Monte-Carlo-Methoden. In: G. Menges (Ed.), *Beiträge zur Unternehmensforschung*. Physica-Verlag, Würzburg-Wien, 1969, 129–152.
24. Wartemodelle. Stichwort in: E. Kosiol (Ed.), *Handwörterbuch des Rechnungswesens*. Poeschel Verlag, Stuttgart, 1970.
25. On the Onassis Problem (with H. Laux). *Theory and Decision* 2 (1972), 353–370.
26. Entscheidungskriterien mit metrischen und ordinalen Parametern. *Operations Research Verfahren* 13 (1972), 380–386.
27. Über die Unabhängigkeit von exogenen und latenten Variablen. *Operations Research Verfahren* 14, (1972), 203–223.
28. The (μ, σ)-Decision Criterion on the Class of Normal Distributions. *Selecta Statistica Canadiana* 1 (1973), 23–30.
29. On the Consistency of Classical Decision Criteria. *Selecta Statistica Canadiana* 1 (1973), 31–44.
30. The Ellsberg Paradox from the Point of View of Game Theory. *Selecta Statistica Canadiana* 1 (1973), 65–78.
31. Probability and Utility–Dual Concepts in Decision Theory. In: G. Menges (Ed.), *Information, Inference and Decision.*. D. Reidel Publishing Company. Dodrecht, Boston, 1974, 113–144.
32. Struktur-Inferenz an drei Beispielen. *Statistische Hefte* 16 (1975), 316–325.
33. Consistent Estimation of a Regression with Errors in the Variables. *Metrika* 23 (1976), 101–115.
34. Kritische Bemerkungen zur Kritik am Wahrscheinlichkeitssubjektivismus. *Statistische Hefte* 18 (1977), 218–232.
35. Identifikation. In: *Handwörterbuch der Wirtschaftswissenschaften*. Gustav Fischer, Stuttgart-New York; J. C. B. Mohr, Tübingen; Vandenhoek & Ruprecht, Göttingen-Zürich, 1978, 73–79.
36. Different Asymptotic Variances of the Same Estimator in a Regression with Errors in the Variables. *Methods of Operations Research* 36 (1980), 249–269.
37. Modelle mit Fehlern in den Variablen. *Methods of Operations Research* 37 (1980), 41–77.
38. A Linear Combination of Estimators in an Errors-in-Variables Model–a Monte Carlo Study (with H. Witschel). In: H. Büning and P. Naeve

(Eds.), *Computational Statistics*. Walter de Gruyter, Berlin-New York, 1981, 263–280.

39. A Simple Regression Model with Trend and Error in the Exogenous Variable. In: M. Deistler, E. Fürst, G. Schwödiauer (Eds.), *Games, Economic Dynamics, and Time Series Analysis. A Symposium in Memoriam Oskar Morgenstern*. Physica-Verlag, Wien-Würzburg, 1982, 347–358.
40. Note on Creasy's Confidence Limits for the Gradient in the Linear Functional Relationship. *Journal of Multivariate Analysis* 12 (1982), 155–158.
41. An Efficient Linear Combination of Estimators in a Regression with Errors in the Variables. In: M. J. Beckmann, W. Eichhorn, W. Krelle (Eds.), *Mathematische Systeme in der Ökonomie*. Athenäum Verlag, Königstein/Ts., 1983, 479–489.
42. Estimating Linear Relations with Errors in the Variables: The Merging of two Approaches. In: H. Schneeweiß and H. Strecker (Eds.), *Contributions to Econometrics and Statistics Today*. Springer-Verlag, Berlin-Heidelberg, 1985, 207–221.
43. Statistische Behandlung von Modellen mit fehlerbehafteten Daten. *Allgemeines Statistisches Archiv* 69 (1985), 106–123.
44. An Approximate Conditional Analysis of the Linear Functional Relationship (with D. A. Sprott and R. Viveros). *Statistische Hefte* 28 (1987), 183–202.
45. Correlated Measurement Errors in Repeated Measurements. Korrelierte Meßfehler bei wiederholten Messungen. *Jahrbücher für Nationalökonomie und Statistik* 203 (1987), 600–610.
46. Small Sample Properties of Estimators in a Linear Relationship with Trend–a Monte Carlo Study (with H. Witschel). In: Opitz and Rauhut (Eds.), *Ökonomie und Mathematik*. Springer-Verlag, Berlin Heidelberg, 1987, 341–352.
47. Modelle mit latenten Variablen: LISREL versus PLS. In: G. Nakhaeizadeh and K.-H. Vollmer (Eds.), *Neuere Entwicklungen in der Angewandten Ökonometrie*. Physica-Verlag, Heidelberg, 1990, 100–125.
48. Models with Latent Variables: LISREL versus PLS. Extended Abstract. *Contemporary Mathematics* 112 (1990), 33–40.
49. Models with Latent variables: LISREL versus PLS. *Statistica Neerlandica* 45 (1991), 145–157.
50. Note on a Linear Model with Errors in the Variables and with Trend. *Statistical Papers* 32 (1991), 261–264.
51. Consistency at Large in Models with Latent Variables. In: K. Haagen, D. J. Bartholomew, M. Deistler (Eds.), *Statistical Modelling and Latent Variables*. North-Holland, Amsterdam, 1993, 299–320.
52. Canonical Correlations in a two-Blocks LISREL Model. In: W. E. Diewert, K. Spremann, F. Stehling (Eds.), *Mathematical Modelling in Eco-*

nomics. Essays in Honor of Wolfgang Eichhorn. Springer-Verlag, Berlin, 1993, 576–584.

53. The Reduced Form of Recursive Models: Asymptotic Properties. In: H. Schneeweiß and K. F. Zimmermann (Eds.), *Studies in Applied Econometrics*. Physica-Verlag, Heidelberg, 1993, 92–115.
54. The Role of Risk Aversion in the Capital Asset Pricing Model. *OR Spektrum* 16 (1994), 169–173.
55. Bias and Mean Square Error of the Slope Estimator in a Regression with not Necessarily Normal Errors in both Variables (with V. K. Srivastava). *Statistical Papers* 35 (1994), 329–335.
56. Factor Analysis and Principal Components (with H. Mathes). *Journal of Multivariate Analysis* 55 (1995), 105–124.
57. Factors and Principal Components: Their Approach to each other when the Factor Loadings are Orthogonal. In: H. Rinne, B. Rüger, H. Strecker (Eds.), *Grundlagen der Statistik und ihre Anwendungen. Festschrift für Kurt Weichselberger*. Physica-Verlag, Heidelberg, 1995, 188–198.
58. Prognosen mittels rekursiver Systeme. *Ifo Studien, Zeitschrift für empirische Wirtschaftsforschung* 41 (1995), 545–559.
59. The Reduced Form of Recursive Models: Small Sample Properties. *Linear Algebra and its Applications, Fifth Special Issue on Linear Algebra and Statistics (Special Issue Honoring Calyampudi Radhakrishna Rao)*, 1996, 277–300.
60. Eine Bemerkung zur reduzierten Form rekursiver Modelle (Note on the Reduced Form of Recursive Models). *Jahrbücher für Nationalökonomie und Statistik* 215 (1996), 586–597.
61. Note on two Estimators for the Polynomial Regression with Error in the Variables (with C. L. Cheng). *Discussion Paper 98 of SFB 386*, 1997.
62. Korrigierte Scnätzgleichungen für allgemeine Regressionsmodelle mit Fehlern in den Variablen. *Jahrbücher für Nationalökonomie und Statistik* 217 (1998), 116–122.
63. Polynomial Regression with Errors in the Variables (with C. L. Cheng). *Journal of the Royal Statistical Society B* 60 (1998), 189–199.
64. Factors and Principal Components in the near Spherical Case. *Multivariate Behavioural Research* 32 (1998), 375–401.

Monographs

- Entscheidungskriterien bei Risiko. Springer-Verlag, Berlin-Heidelberg-New York, 1967 (Ökonometrie und Unternehmensforschung, Vol. VI).
- Ökonometrie. Physica-Verlag, Würzburg-Wien, 1971, 2. Aufl. 1976, 3. Aufl. 1978, 4. Aufl. 1990.
- Lineare Modelle mit fehlerbehafteten Daten (with H.-J. Mittag). Physica-Verlag, Heidelberg-Wien, 1986.

List of Contributors

Gerhard Arminger
Fachbereich Wirtschaftswissenschaft
Bergische Universität Wuppertal
Gauss Str. 20
42097 Wuppertal
Germany

Thomas Augustin
Forschungsgruppe Intervallwahrscheinlichkeit
Institut für Statistik
Ludwig-Maximilians-Universität
Ludwigstraße 33
D-80539 München
Germany

G. Bamberg
Institut für Statistik und Mathematische Wirtschaftstheorie
Universität Augsburg
D-86135 Augsburg
Germany

David J. Bartholomew
London School of Economics and Political Science
Houghton St.
London WC2A 2AE
U.K.

Martin J. Beckmann
Department of Economics
Brown University
Providence, RI, USA

Hans Boscher
Deutsche Morgan Grenfell
GM, OTC-Derivatives
Taunusanlage 12
D-60325 Frankfurt
Germany

Imke Brüggemann
Institut für Statistik und Ökonometrie
Freie Universität Berlin
Boltzmannstr. 20
D-14195 Berlin
Germany

Herbert Büning
Institut für Statistik und Ökonometrie
Freie Universität Berlin
Bolzmannstraße 20
D-14195 Berlin
Germany

Raymond J. Carroll
Department of Statistics
Texas A&M University
College Station
TX 77843–3143
USA

Kai Carstensen
Institut für Statistik und Ökonometrie
Christian-Albrechts-Universität
Olshausenstr. 40–60
D-24118 Kiel
Germany

Chen Pu
China Europe International Business School
Shanghai
P.R. China

Chi-Lun Cheng
Institute of Statistical Science
Academia Sinica
Taipeh, Taiwan 115,
R. O. C.

G. Dorfleitner
Institut für Statistik und Mathematische Wirtschaftstheorie
Universität Augsburg
D-86135 Augsburg
Germany

Ludwig Fahrmeir
Institut für Statistik
Universität München
Ludwigstr. 33
D-80539 München
Germany

Yuanhua Feng
Fakultät für Wirtschaftswissenschaften und Statistik
Universität Konstanz
Universitätsstr. 10
D-78464 Konstanz
Germany

Franz Ferschl
Institut für Statistik
Universität München
Akademiestr. 1
D-80799 München
Germany

Joachim Frohn
Fakultät für Wirtschaftswissenschaften
Universität Bielefeld
Postfach 100131
D-33501 Bielefeld
Germany

Eva–Maria Fronk
Institut für Statistik
Ludwig-Maximilians-Universität
Öttingenstraße 67
D-80538 München
Germany

Wayne A. Fuller
Department of Statistics
Iowa State University
Ames
IA 50010, USA

Christian Gieger
Institut für Statistik
Universität München
Ludwigstr. 33
D-80539 München
Germany

Gerd Hansen
Institut für Statistik und Ökonometrie
Christian-Albrechts-Universität
Olshausenstr. 40–60
D-24118 Kiel
Germany

Siegfried Heiler
Fakultät für Wirtschaftswissenschaften und Statistik
Universität Konstanz
Universitätsstr. 10
D-78464 Konstanz
Germany

Göran Kauermann
Institut für Statistik
Universität München
Akademiestr. 1
D-80799 München
Germany

Artur Klinger
Institut für Statistik
Universität München
Ludwigstr. 33
D-80539 München
Germany

Walter Krämer
Fachbereich Statistik
Universität Dortmund
Vogelpothsweg 87
D-44221 Dortmund
Germany

Helmut Lütkepohl
Institut für Statistik und Ökonometrie
Wirtschaftswissenschaftliche Fakultät
Humboldt–Universität
Spandauer Str. 1
D-10178 Berlin
Germany

J. D. Maca
Department of Statistics
Texas A&M University
College Station
TX 77843–3143, USA

Hans–Joachim Mittag
Fachbereich Wirtschaftswissenschaften
Fern-Universität Hagen
Postfach 940
D-58084 Hagen
Germany

Walter Naggl
WIM-RES
Bayer. Hypobank
Arabellastr. 12
81925 München
Germany

John W. van Ness
Univ. of Texas at Dallas
PO Box 830688
Richardson, TX 75083
USA

Iris Pigeot
Institut für Statistik
Ludwig-Maximilians-Universität
Ludwigstraße 33
D-80539 München
Germany

Don S. Poskitt
Department of Statistics
Australian National University
GPO Box 4
Canberra ACT 2601
Australia

K. Röder
Institut für Statistik und Mathematische Wirtschaftstheorie
Universität Augsburg
D-86135 Augsburg
Germany

Gerd Ronning
Wirtschaftswissenschaftliche Fakultät
Universität Tübingen
Mohlstr. 36
D-72074 Tübingen
Germany

Bernhard Schipp
Fakultät Wirtschaftswissenschaften
Technische Universität Dresden
01069 Dresden
Germany

Gerhard Schuster
Institut für Statistik
Ludwig-Maximilians-Universität
Akademiestraße 1/I
D-80799 München
Germany

Dietmar Stemann
Fachbereich Wirtschaftswissenschaft
Fern-Universität Hagen
Postfach 940
D-58084 Hagen
Germany

Markus Thamerus
Institut für Statistik
Ludwig-Maximilians-Universität
Akademiestraße 1/I
D-80799 München
Germany

Helge Toutenburg
Institut für Statistik
Ludwig-Maximilians-Universität
Akademiestraße 1/I
D-80799 München

Götz Trenkler
Fachbereich Statistik
Universität Dortmund
D-44221 Dortmund
Germany

Gerhard Tutz
Institut für Statistik
Universität München
Akademiestr. 1
D-80799 München
Germany

S. J. Wang
Department of Statistics
Texas A&M University
College Station
TX 77843–3143
USA

Kurt Weichselberger
Forschungsgruppe Intervallwahrschein-lichkeit
Institut für Statistik
Ludwig-Maximilians-Universität
Ludwigstraße 33
D-80538 München
Germany

Peter–Theodor Wilrich
Institut für Statistik und Ökonometrie
Freie Universität Berlin
Garystraße 21
D-14195 Berlin
Germany

Jürgen Wolters
Institut für Statistik und Ökonometrie
Freie Universität Berlin
Boltzmannstr. 20
D-14195 Berlin
Germany

SPRINGER NATURE

GPSR Compliance

The European Union's (EU) General Product Safety Regulation (GPSR) is a set of rules that requires consumer products to be safe and our obligations to ensure this.

If you have any concerns about our products, you can contact us on ProductSafety@springernature.com

In case Publisher is established outside the EU, the EU authorized representative is:

Springer Nature Customer Service Center GmbH
Europaplatz 3
69115 Heidelberg, Germany

Kolibri 360 GmbH
Ferdinand-Jühlke-Straße 7
99095 Erfurt, Deutschland
produktsicherheit@kolibri360.de